The Administrator's Gu
SharePoint Portal Server 2001

The Administrator's Guide to SharePoint Portal Server 2001

Bill English

✦Addison-Wesley

**Boston • San Francisco • New York • Toronto • Montreal
London • Munich • Paris • Madrid
Capetown • Sydney • Tokyo • Singapore • Mexico City**

The publisher offers discounts on this book when ordered in quantity for special sales. For more information, please contact:

Pearson Education Corporate Sales Division
201 W. 103rd Street
Indianapolis, IN 46290
(800) 428-5331
corpsales@pearsoned.com

Visit A-W on the Web: www.awprofessional.com

Library of Congress Cataloging-in-Publication Data

English, Bill, 1961-
    The administrator's guide to SharePoint Portal Server 2001 / Bill
English.
        p.   cm.
    Includes index.
    ISBN 0-201-77574-3 (acid-free paper)
    1. Intranets (Computer networks) 2. Web servers. I. Title.
TK5105.875.16 E54 2002
004.6'8—dc21

                                    2002003777

ISBN 0-201-77574-3

Text printed on recycled paper

1 2 3 4 5 6 7 8 9 10—MA—0605040302

First printing, July 2002

To Kathy, David, and Anna—
the three most wonderful people I know

Contents

Preface

Welcome to SharePoint Portal Server!

I was introduced to SharePoint Portal Server when I attended the beta presentation of Microsoft Official Curriculum Course 2095 in February 2001. The course was taught by Goga Kukrika, one of the technical editors for this book. I remember being excited about what this product could do and how it would enjoy a wide install base. My excitement remains, and I think time will prove that this product will be widely installed and heavily used.

SharePoint Portal Server is both simple and complex. Although it has a simple front end for nontechnical users, under the hood it's complex. In this book, I hope to illustrate the ease of using SharePoint Portal Server, its depth (especially in its architecture), and the current problems that I hope will be resolved in future revisions.

When this product was first developed (over more than two years), it was written by developers who were under the larger .NET server umbrella development group. Since its release, it has been moved under the Office group's management. This means, among other things, that SharePoint Portal Server and SharePoint Team Services will meld into a single product in the coming releases.

Some observers have suggested that, over time, public folder functionality will be trimmed and then removed from Exchange 2000 Server and placed into SharePoint Portal Server. Whether this is true remains to be seen. But it is certain that SharePoint Portal Server is here to stay and will mature as a product over the next five years.

This book reflects my honest thoughts about SharePoint Portal Server. I state at times that this or that feature is a great one and, in some cases, is a compelling reason to purchase the product. In other places, however, I express my less-than-positive thoughts on parts of this product. Overall, I'm hopeful that the negatives of this product will be rectified in future releases, and I think it will enjoy wide support in the market.

This book is not about programming in SharePoint Portal Server, although you will see some code where it is appropriate. If you're an experienced developer, you'll probably find the code elementary. I have included what I think will be helpful to a nonprogramming administrator. Chapters 2–4 are the most difficult to read. And frankly, they were the most difficult to write. In them, you'll find granular information that any SPS administrator must understand in order to effectively administer SPS. I find that many administrators can better troubleshoot a problem if they have good architectural information.

Who Should Read This Book

This book is written for coordinators and those who administer a SharePoint Portal Server. Some server-level activities belong to the person in the Coordinator role, but in many environments, a fairly nontechnical person is the coordinator and the IT person ends up being responsible for the overall functionality of the SharePoint server.

Hence, I don't expect a nontechnical coordinator to be interested in reading Chapter 4 (Planning for SharePoint Portal Server 2001) or Chapter 12 (Monitoring SharePoint Portal Server 2001). However, I would expect a nontechnical coordinator to read the chapters that are more focused on the workspace and management of documents, categories, and profiles. Therefore, this book will benefit both the nontechnical coordinator and the technically oriented IT administrator.

Contacting the Author

I've decided to try something new and make available a newsgroup that will be specific to the readers of this book. Simply point your newsreader client to `snoopy.networkknowledge.com` and subscribe to the `book.share-pointportalserver` newsgroup. I will monitor this group regularly and will keep an up-to-date errata list posted that will enumerate this book's corrections.

I view the existence of such as newsgroup as doing two positive things. First, it gives us a chance to interact. Too often, authors are not available to their readers for interaction on their own book's contents, and I feel that if people are going to invest their own hard-earned money and read my book, I would like to be available to interact with them. Second, a well-developed errata list from the first edition of a book will mean that future editions will have even greater technical integrity and accuracy. It may sound crazy, but I've seen technical mistakes in one edition carried over to the next edition of a book without the authors or editors catching it. Hard to believe, but it's true.

What I will not do in the newsgroup is to try to answer situational questions about why something isn't working. In other words, I won't do "newsgroup consulting," to coin a phrase. I will, however, discuss concepts in the book and try to field questions about the material. There will probably be times that I'll need to find the answer, and thus all of us will learn and grow. If you want help with a specific problem, use the public newsgroups at news.microsoft.com. These groups exist for this purpose, and I visit the SharePoint groups regularly and try to answer some questions there.

So I hope to see you on my newsgroup. And if you'd like to learn more about me and my work, please visit my Web site at www.networknowledge.com. Remember that this is a marketing Web site. I also run a SharePoint-specific Web site at www.sharepointknowledge.com. In addition, here are some great SharePoint-focused sites from which you might get additional information:

- www.sharepointcode.com
- www.spsfaq.com
- www.sharepointserver.com
- www.sharepointtips.com (focused on SharePoint Team Services)
- www.microsoft.com/sharepoint

I'll also suggest that if you are a coordinator or administrator of a SharePoint Portal Server, you should seriously consider taking course 2095 at your local Microsoft Certified Technical Education Center, or contact me directly for a private delivery of this course. Course 2095 will give you hands-on experience in working with SharePoint Portal Server and will help you learn how to install and deploy this product. Also, if you don't know Active Directory very well, take courses 1560 (Updating Support Skills from Windows NT Server to Windows 2000 Server) and 2154 (the advanced course focused on Active Directory in Windows 2000 Server). These two courses are essential to an understanding of Active Directory.

Thank you for purchasing this book. I hope you'll enjoy it and find it to be a great reference that helps you grow in your knowledge of and expertise with SharePoint Portal Server.

Acknowledgments

I have to say that this has been a fantastic project to work on. And, as with all books, there is no way that this book would have been brought to completion without the aid of many people.

First, I'd like to thank Michael Slaughter, acquisitions editor at Addison-Wesley, who was persistent enough to grab my attention to write this book. I think I put him off twice before responding to his offer, and if he hadn't been persistent, I probably would not have written this book. Thanks, Michael! Stephane Thomas at Addison-Wesley was my project editor, and she has been one of the easiest editors I've ever worked with. This book was scheduled to be done and ready for production at about the same time that Service Pack 1 was being released. We didn't plan it this way; it's just how the schedule worked out. Well, we didn't want to go to press without incorporating Service Pack 1 into the book, so Stephane made generous time adjustments to ensure that I had time to finish the book and cover all the details. Stephane, your commitment to excellence is outstanding, and I hope that I've kept up my end of the bargain in writing an excellent book.

Also, I'd like to thank Laura Lawless, of Atlanta, for helping me understand what a quality publisher Addison-Wesley is. There's a story here: Laura is a neighbor of some close family friends that my wife, Kathy, and I visit every so often in Atlanta. Kathy and I were visiting those friends, and all our children were playing outside. Laura's daughter came over to play, and Laura came with her to help watch the growing brood. We introduced ourselves, and, much to my surprise, I found out she works in marketing technical books for Addison-Wesley. She was surprised to learn that I was considering a contract from Addison-Wesley to write this book. It's a small world. Laura, our brief conversation in Gary and Lisa's yard helped me understand what a quality publisher Addison-Wesley is. Believe it or not, that conversation helped me decide in favor of taking on this project. I'm glad we met when we did!

I'd like to thank Betsy Hardinger, who did the copy edits on my book. You took my chapters that read pretty rough and made it all flow and work together. Thanks for your hard work.

I'd like to thank Neil Salkind and the folks at StudioB for your help in securing this contract and publisher for this project. Neil, as usual, you're the best agent any author could ever want.

Even though my home training center, MindSharp Learning Center, is no longer in business, I still want to thank Dave Fletcher, training manager and all-around great guy, for allowing me three months out of the classroom to focus my energies on this book. Your willingness to give me time away from the classroom and flexibility in finding replacements for my Exchange 2000 classes were deeply appreciated. Dave, you're a great manager and friend. I hope we can work together in the future.

There were several people who also helped with this book in significant ways. First, Scott Schnoll lent a helping hand near the beginning of this project. (Some of you may know that Scott and I coauthored, along with Nick Cavalencia, an Exchange 2000 book.) Scott, your help was invaluable, and I don't know that I can fully thank you for what you did. Second, I'd like to thank Dave Braunschweig, who created the script for me that created the 1,000,000 documents I referenced (and used) in the book. Although he had never met me, Dave responded to a general request of mine on the Microsoft MCT news-groups and quickly created the script I needed for Chapter 4. Dave, I really appreciate your help and kindness. Be sure to send me some Exchange questions, and I'll see if I can repay you that way. Or better yet, I'll buy you a Coke at the next MCT convention. Third, I'd like to thank James Edelen who offered valuable tips on ideas and content for this book.

Fourth, I'd like to thank Daryl Tabor for his help with some research early on in this project. Daryl, let me know if I can come to Texas to give you some help sometime—preferably in the winter! <g> Fourth, I'd like to thank Jody Ansley for helping me understand the functionality of some of the SPS files. Similarly, I'd like to thank Stephen Cummins for helping out on some programming issues in SPS. Both of these guys jumped in and added value to this book in their own ways, even though we had only met through the public newsgroups.

At Microsoft, a *huge* thanks goes to Scott Hay for his patience with me as I attempted to understand the architecture of SharePoint Portal Server. His willingness to lend me a hand and give me excellent information on Share-Point's architecture is a tribute to the type of person he is. Scott, I can't thank you enough. Without your help, Chapter 2 would have been laughable compared with what it is in this book. I'd also like to thank Bill Rebozo at Microsoft for being willing to answer some general questions and helping me clarify my thinking in a number of areas. And I can't forget Alex Hankin, who explained to me how licensing really works, in addition to what's on the Microsoft SharePoint Web site.

I had several technical editors who really did a bang-up job. Gary Bushey, Goga Kukrika, Lu Patrick, and Russ Kauffman all offered comments and criticisms that changed the scope, focus, and content in many of the chapters. They also helped me understand parts of SPS that were, at best, fuzzy when I was writing the first draft. You all added real value to this book, and I'd really enjoy working with you all again. Thank you very much! Any mistakes in this book are mine.

Here at home, my ever-loving and patient wife, Kathy, has more to do with the book you're holding than you'll ever know. She allows me time in the office to write and think. She respects what I do as an author and doesn't constantly nag me to get out of the office right on time. Kathy, thank you for being an easy person to live with and a great mate for life. I value our friendship and love more than anything else on this earth. David and Anna, my two wonderful children, also kept reminding me of what was really important when they would come and ask me to play trains or to wrestle with them when I was deep in thought. When you two are older and read this, I hope you'll remember that I tried hard to balance time between work and play. I also hope you'll remember how very much I love you two.

Finally, I'd like to thank Jesus Christ, who gave me the talent and opportunity to write this book and without whom I would be lost forever.

Bill English
Maple Grove, Minnesota
May 10, 2002

Introduction and Architecture

SharePoint Portal Server Overview

When I graduated from college in 1983, I specifically remember the commencement speaker telling us that we were entering the "Information Age"—an era when the ability to manage knowledge would be just as important as producing a quality product. I heard the words, but I didn't really catch the message.

Flash forward to 1999. Bill Gates and Microsoft dominate the computer industry. In conjunction with Intel, Cisco, and a handful of other companies, Microsoft has participated in the creation of a new industry—one that is providing a plethora of new, high-paying jobs. And Bill Gates pens these words: "I have a simple but strong belief. The most meaningful way to differentiate your company from your competition, the best way to put distance between you and the crowd, is to do an outstanding job with information."[1]

The ability to manage information is now discussed under the umbrella of *knowledge management* (KM) and is a common topic of conversation and presentations at conferences all over the world. Many people are coming to realize that to be successful in today's business environment, not only must they produce a top quality product, but also they must know how to manage their information well.

What is knowledge management? A concise definition is difficult, but here is one that you might consider: the ability to put workers in touch with the knowledge they need to do their job at any time, from any place, using any device. Smart knowledge management ensures that the correct type and quality of knowledge is made available to workers when needed through tools that allow them to engage in rapid, accurate analysis of the content and then act on that analysis.

---

[1] Gates, Bill, *Business @ the Speed of Thought*. Warner Books, 1999. p. 3.

Therefore, for a knowledge management solution to work effectively, it must provide the following:

- Capture of information
- Storage of information
- Organization of information
- Indexing of information
- Security of the information
- Establishment of a workflow process
- Distribution of information

Most organizations have a difficult time with these areas. For instance, most really don't know how to leverage the information they might have at their disposal through an indexing, search, and retrieval system. And nearly all organizations (and individuals) face the task of filtering an increasing volume of information to retain what is important at a given point in time. Without an effective KM solution, an organization is likely to miss important information that could better inform mission-critical decisions.

For those who make efforts to maximize their information, they face the challenges of securing and dispersing it to the correct people. Those who are successful at implementing a corporate-wide KM solution will reduce their overall costs, increase worker effectiveness, streamline the decision-making process, and consequently increase their profits. Moreover, they will be in a better position to be more responsive to their customers' needs and to secure better vendor relationships.

An overall KM solution is seldom found in a single software package, given the complexity of performing each part of the KM process. For instance, the storage of information is usually a single process in and of itself, especially when you're working with both structured and unstructured information. Moreover, if there is a need (and there usually is) to relate individual bits of information with one another, the methods of information storage can become complex. Hence, an overall KM solution usually involves a suite of software products, including databases, e-mail, document management (DM), security, Web, and file services.

Document Management in a Knowledge Management Solution

An essential part of an overall KM solution is the ability to manage information. Using a broad brush here, most organizations will find that their information is held in either a database or a document. Hence, access to that information is generally through client software that is specific to either the database or the document program. Although information may continue to be held in documents and databases for the coming years, client access to this information is going to change dramatically to a browser-based *portal*: a single access point that puts workers in touch with the necessary information and applications required for their jobs.

Microsoft's SharePoint Portal Server (SPS) works at both ends. First, it offers a basic portal-out-of-the-box solution that can be customized to meet an organization's needs. Second, it offers DM capabilities that are tightly integrated with Office XP and later. As shown in Table 1–1, SharePoint Portal Server impacts each part of the KM process.

Table 1–1 Comparison of KM solutions and SPS features

KM Solution Component	SPS Feature
Capture of information	Through the use of content sources, SPS can crawl and index content that is hosted in a file server, Exchange 5.5 and Exchange 2000 public folders, Lotus Notes databases, Web sites, and other SPS workspaces.
Storage of information	Nearly any type of information can be held in an SPS workspace. This is made possible by the Web store, a similar database structure that exists in Exchange 2000 Server.
Organization of information	SPS lets you categorize documents according to any matrix of metadata you create, locate them in folder hierarchies, and associate keywords and other document metadata with each document. This metadata can then be used for search and retrieval processes.
Indexing of information	SPS upgrades the MSSearch process found in Windows 2000 to provide the most robust and extensive searching capabilities offered by Microsoft.
Securing information	SPS supports the access control lists (ACLs) of content sources and implements security in the workspace using a role-based model.
Establishment of a workflow process	Documents can be required to undergo an approval process before being published. This workflow process can be modified or overridden by the workspace coordinator.
Distribution of information	Information is securely distributed through the portal that is created using Digital Dashboard (DD) technology. In addition, through the use of subscriptions, workers can be notified of changes to documents, allowing them to stay current on information.

The Organizational Effects of Poor Document Management

In many organizations, documents are managed through the use of file servers. Users access information by browsing through lists to find documents. Most desktop support personnel in large corporate environments have probably been asked to help a user find a document that the user knows was saved but now cannot be found.

Not only is it sometimes difficult to locate a saved document, but also naming the document can be difficult, too. It's not uncommon for documents in different departments to have different naming conventions, thus making it difficult for users to find documents across departmental lines. Furthermore, when users are out of the office, others who need to access their documents can be perplexed as to the document names, forcing them to open multiple documents before they find the one they are looking for.

When information is difficult to find, users become unproductive, not to mention frustrated. And this frustration often leads to Help desk support calls, making the cost of hard-to-find information very high. Hence, poor document organization lowers a company's profits because its users (and the support personnel who are asked to assist) are less productive than they would be with an efficient DM system.

When information is held on a file server that is not indexed, several common problems arise. Let's briefly discuss these problems.

Inability to Access Documents Quickly and Easily

When documents are not well organized, users spend valuable time browsing through the file servers and directory hierarchies to find documents. Because most file servers do not have a search and retrieval method, users must know a document's location in advance in order to retrieve it quickly.

In addition, traditional file servers do not provide any information about a document. This information, called *metadata*, is extremely valuable when used correctly. For instance, a contract for a new client could contain metadata with the client's name, the contract type, or keywords that would allow anyone with sufficient permissions to quickly find the contract without needing to know where the document is saved on the network. In most environments, metadata is not available for search and retrieval actions.

Inability to Obtain an Accurate Search Result Set for Documents

If a search and retrieval process is in place, it is common for the search result set to provide either too much or too little information—or worse, incorrect responses. Moreover, an increasing amount of information is hosted on Web sites or public folders, meaning that a search for documents on a file server may not produce a complete result set.

In addition, search activities are usually performed on one data source at a time. So if possible content sources include multiple file servers, Web sites, and public folders, the user is faced with the daunting task of searching each of these locations. This activity can be time-consuming and unproductive.

Inability to Collaborate on Documents

When documents are hosted on file servers, it is nearly impossible for a team of users to collaborate effectively on document creation. For instance, it is often difficult to know who is working on the document and who has the most recent copy. Hence, most users end up e-mailing copies of a working document to other team members and asking for responses. In effect, they create versions of these documents, but often they don't take the time to note version changes inside the document itself. The inability to track previous document versions can lead to duplication of efforts or the deletion of needed information.

E-mails become the method for discussing changes to the document. The problem with this method is that an ongoing exchange of ideas needs to occur in a single location, and e-mail is not created for ongoing types of discussions. Some companies have used internal newsgroups for these conversations, but there is no connection between a newsgroup discussion thread and a particular document.

Reviewer comments can also be used, but too many comments will so clutter a document that it can become confusing to read.

Inability to Receive Notification of Changes to a Document

When a group of users are collaborating on the development of document, it is difficult for each team member to be notified that someone has updated the document without attaching the new document to an e-mail that is sent to all team members. These types of notifications are common but not very efficient. Over time, each user's inbox may hold ten or more copies of the document, with each e-mail representing a new version.

Such a system unnecessarily consumes server resources, growing the size of the mail server's database beyond what it would be if an effective KM system were in place. Moreover, users can become confused about which version in their inbox is the most recent one.

Difficulty in Implementing a Document Approval Process

After a document has been developed, the approval process may be performed on paper or in a series of e-mails passed among the team members.

Problems with document approval include the difficulty of notifying the approver that the document is ready for approval and the need for a process to formally approve the document.

If more than one person is required to approve a document, it's possible that the process will be stalled if an approver doesn't act in a timely manner. In a paper-based scenario, this means that each approver must be contacted to see who is holding up the process. Chasing after a document in a routing process is both time-consuming and unproductive.

Difficulty in Securing Documents

Currently, many environments running Windows NT or Windows 2000 secure their documents using share-level permissions, NTFS permissions, or both on a file server. The use of both types of permissions is easy to implement on a file server. But when a group collaborates on a document, it is usually best if the document can be modified by only one person at a time. File servers don't provide this type of *file locking* because each group member can copy the file to his local hard drive and then make changes independently of other team members.

In addition, it is rare that most users are allowed to access all company documents. Hence, any KM solution must provide security to all documents using permissions based on levels of access—such as read-only or change permissions—and must be able to assign these permissions to a collection of documents as well as individually.

Difficulty in Scalability

As an organization grows, so does the volume of its information. If this information is not managed correctly, it can become difficult to find documents that were easy to find when the organization was smaller. And in many organizations, if no organization-wide information technology (IT) policies are enforced, individual departments will install their own set of file servers, thus creating barriers to effective flow of information across the enterprise.

I consulted with an organization in which one department was placing documents on a Windows NT file server, another department was keeping its information in a set of Exchange public folders, and still other departments were using a workgroup model of document sharing between Macintosh computers. This organization, like others, will find that each department fights for control of its own information against an effective KM solution, all the while not realizing the overall additional costs that are incurred to the organization when information is compartmentalized along departmental boundaries. As organizations like this begin to grapple with the notion of information sharing between departments, deeply held beliefs about operating systems and the "correct" way to do things, along with the fear of unauthorized access to confidential information, stand in the way of implementing an effective KM solution.

Keys to Effective Change Implementation

Political power struggles may be an organization's largest hurdle to jump as new KM solutions are proposed. If you are in the midst of such a struggle, may I make a suggestion? Know how far you can push, and realize the limitations that exist.

For successful change to be implemented, you need five things:

- A *champion*: This is someone at the VP level or higher who can ensure that the executives are sold on the new implementation and that they will work with their managers to make the implementation go smoothly.
- A funded, approved budget: Obviously, without money, you can't purchase licenses, servers, and extended golf outings disguised as training (just kidding) for your implementation.
- Clearly defined project goals: A poorly defined goal uses vague words such as *more*, *less*, and *appropriate*. If your implementation will result in users finding documents faster, you should ensure that you have a defined method of measurement that can yield hard numbers: *23% faster* is much more meaningful than *faster*.
- Control over the entire project: This includes the ability to hire, fire, and assign project details to team members. If you're responsible for implementing the project and if you're going to be evaluated on its success, then you should have control over the entire project, including expenditures.
- Grassroots support: Believe it or not, you may need to do some work to cultivate grassroots support. Nothing is more difficult to implement than an unwanted computer system that the users view as something that is being pushed down their throat. You may need to conduct some seminars on the advantages of implementing SharePoint Portal Server.

If you have all five of these elements, you'll be successful. If you're missing any one of them, you'll have a tough time getting it done, but it can be done. For instance, if you have everything except the budget issue, you can probably get your champion to arrange for funds. If you're lacking grassroots support, you can use the positive attitude of the managers to help the users see the wisdom of a SharePoint implementation.

However, if you're missing two or more of these elements, don't even try to implement a major change. Instead, work toward gaining each element before you commence a change in your environment.

Introduction to SharePoint Portal Server

Microsoft offers compelling reasons to choose SharePoint Portal Server as your KM solution. This section introduces SPS and demonstrates how it solves the problems described earlier.

In a nutshell, SPS provides document management, collaboration, search, and portal services. Out of the box, it gives you both a development environment for customized portals and document management features. SPS also enjoys tight integration with the Microsoft Office XP suite to provide the end user a seamless experience for search, document management, and portal functions.

The term *portal* might be confusing if you're just coming into the KM area. A portal is usually thought of as an application that aggregates dissimilar sources of information and applications into a single location so that the end user can access every information source and application needed to perform her job. In a sense, a portal is a type of desktop, albeit one that is Web-based and can be accessed from any browser.

SPS provides an easy and effective method for creating corporate Web portals. When SPS is installed, it automatically installs a basic portal known as a *Digital Dashboard*, *dashboard,* or *dashboard site*. These terms are used interchangeably to describe a Web page presented to the user that is populated with *Web parts*. Together, these parts form the portal or dashboard and can be created and customized as needed.

Web parts are programs that perform specific functions and can be plugged in to dashboards with little or no additional configuration. For instance, on Networknowledge, the Internet portal that I operate, I've added the MSNBC weather Web part (Figure 1–1) from the Microsoft Web Part Gallery, which gives me current weather information for my locale. This Web part can be placed on any dashboard, offering the same functionality. In a sense, by using Web parts, you can create your own customized suite of applications that are presented to your network from a single Web page.

Web parts can be written in different ways, such as using VBScript (Visual Basic Script), XML (Extensible Markup Language), HTML (Hypertext Markup Language), ASP (Active Server Pages), or Visual Basic. Parts written in dissimilar languages can coexist on the same dashboard. Chapter 3 discusses the Digital Dashboard and Web parts more fully. It also looks at how to create customized Web parts, especially if you're not a developer.

TIP: Microsoft maintains a growing gallery of Web parts that are available for download at http://www.microsoft.com/sharepoint/downloads/webparts/default.asp.

Before writing your own Web part, consider visiting this site to see whether it has already been written. This could save you valuable time and development dollars.

Users can create their own personalized dashboards in SPS, too. As a *coordinator*—the overall administrator—for a workspace, you can force certain Web parts to appear on the users' dashboard while allowing them to select others based on personal preferences.

A *workspace* is a logical collection of documents, content sources, subscriptions, dashboards, and indexes under a single namespace. It is the highest level in the SPS document architecture. A workspace can reside on only one SharePoint server, although a SharePoint server can host more than one workspace. There are three types of workspaces:

- Document management workspaces
- Search workspaces
- Index workspaces

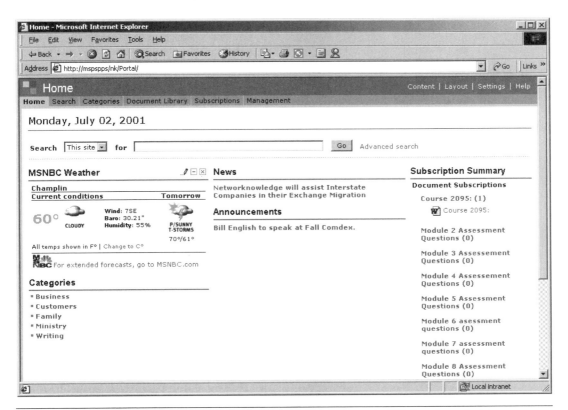

Figure 1–1 MSNBC Weather Web part on the Home dashboard of Networknowledge

Note that a document management workspace also provides search and indexing capabilities. However, in some environments it may be better to quarantine the search and indexing functions into their own workspace. This can be the case especially in large environments where many users place significant demand and stress on a SharePoint server.

The Document Management Workspace

The document management workspace hosts the document library where a company's documents are stored on the SPS server. It includes the management tools, category structure, dashboard, content sources, and a searchable index of all the information and content sources. A DM workspace can host any type of file, including spreadsheets, faxes, graphics, audio, Web, PowerPoint files, and scripts.

The Search Workspace

This type of workspace is dedicated to searching functions. The only real difference between a search workspace and a DM workspace is that a search workspace does not host documents. Instead, its primary function is to host indexes that the users can search. A search workspace can also receive indexes created inside other workspaces and sent to the search workspace for searching by users.

The Index Workspace

This type of workspace is dedicated to indexing functions. A server that performs indexing *crawls* content sources to examine the documents in the source and then build or update an index based on what it finds. Indexes created by an index workspace can be sent to one or more search or DM workspaces.

The indexing feature in SPS can crawl and build indexes from the following sources:

- Other SharePoint Portal workspaces
- Intranet or Internet sites
- Exchange 2000 and Exchange 5.5 public folders
- Lotus Notes 4.6a+ and R5 databases
- The local file system
- Shared file systems

Chapter 7 discusses the architecture of indexing.

How SPS Meets DM and KM Needs

SharePoint Portal Server offers an integrated DM environment. This section outlines some of the features of SPS and illustrates how they solve the common DM and KM problems outlined earlier.

Documents Can Be Organized Effectively

SPS gives you three organizing tools:

- Metadata: This data is represented by document profiles, which let you index and search the properties of a document, including keywords.
- Folder hierarchies: These include the physical location of the documents and any associated policies.
- Categories: Represented in the metadata, categories allow you to organize documents by subject.

Metadata and Profiles

Metadata are stored properties of the documents in the workspace. Individual metadata can be made mandatory or optional before a document is checked in to the workspace. For instance, you can customize a document *profile*: the definition of a file's metadata, which is descriptive data about the document to require users to select a category before checking in a document.

A document profile becomes a set of stored metadata that is then associated with content types. For instance, the default set of metadata for a document in, say, the Quick Links folder would be different from that in the document library. Each set of properties is grouped into a single document profile. You can think of a document profile as little more than a matrix of properties or metadata that is used to define and describe a document. The purpose and usage of the content determine the properties stored in the profile.

Like content, metadata is crawled and indexed. For instance, if a document has the property *Author* (see "The Author Role" later in this chapter), the name entered in that property will also be indexed and available for searching.

You must strike a balance between ensuring that each document has enough metadata so that it can be easily and quickly found and ensuring that users are not overburdened with the need to input so much metadata that they simply quit entering any information. Users are not likely to fill in optional properties, so you must plan document profiles before and after you've implemented your SPS network. At a minimum, you'll want your required properties to be readily visible when the profile form is loaded, so users don't spend time scrolling through a list of optional properties to find and populate the required fields before checking in a document.

NOTE: Planning issues are covered in various places throughout this book as they relate to the topic at hand.

Folder Organization

Folders are, by far, the most familiar method of organizing documents, both for you as the administrator and for your users. Folder browsing is only one method that readers can use to find a document (the other two are category browsing and searching an index). Because folders are the most familiar method for users, some coordinators are choosing to limit the Document Library dashboard from the SharePoint portal, thus forcing readers to browse for documents by category or to engage in a search process. When used correctly, these methods are faster than folder browsing.

Folders segregate content and thereby offer an attractive set of features:

- Coordinator accounts (see "The Coordinator Role" later in this chapter) can be created for different folders to increase management diversification.
- Different security models can be applied to different content in the same workspace.
- Versioning for documents can be turned on or off.
- Different profiles can be applied to different content sets, resulting in more accurate indexing of metadata.
- Different approval routes can be created for different content sets.

An SPS coordinator needs to think of folders as only one of three methods of organizing data. Hence, you should plan your folder structure more thoroughly in light of the additional functionality that folders provide. In other words, you should not create the folder hierarchy based solely on one property, such as by department or by city. Instead, you should keep in mind multiple properties and functionalities.

Yet, at the same time, as Chapter 4 suggests, your focus should not be on planning a complex folder structure as much as it should be on planning a thorough category hierarchy and set of document profiles. Folders can be created by people holding the Author or Coordinator roles, whereas categories and document profiles can be created only by coordinators. And once implemented, category hierarchies are difficult to change. In contrast, it's easier to change a folder structure because you can drag and drop bulk sets of files from one location to another. Although it is true that you can check in a large set of documents by using the same configured profile and category associations, it is usually not desirable.

Hence, even though you should carefully plan a good document folder structure, if push comes to shove, it's best to put your time into planning categories and document profiles.

Categories

Categories represent a business-oriented view of the content. Because the assignment of a document to a category is really a property in the document's metadata, you can make a document a member of multiple categories. Categories are searchable by browsing and should be created to benefit the reader, not the author or coordinator.

If you're new to managing a SharePoint Portal Server, you will probably want to create a category structure that mirrors your folder hierarchy. This is a common mistake because we are accustomed to thinking in one organizational dimension. However, if you take a long step back from your current folder structure and discuss with your users a different way of organizing information, you'll find that you can come up with a category structure that aggregates data across nontraditional content lines and allows documents held in different folders to appear together in the same category.

Table 1–2 illustrates some of the differences between folders and categories.

Table 1–2 Strategic differences between folders and categories

Characteristic	Folders	Categories
Purpose	To segregate data based on storage needs and DM needs of authors.	To organize data for readers (see "The Reader Role" later in this chapter) based on logical needs.
Primary users	Authors and coordinators—members of a team who are developing a document.	Readers and visitors to the workspace—people who are not involved with document development or creation.
Planning issues	Consider using the current folder structure to create document folders in the new workspace.	Avoid excessive hierarchy depth. Consult with readers to build initial structure, and then modify it as needed.

Documents Can Be Found Quickly and Easily

Content that is stored in the workspace can be accessed using three tools: Web browsers, Office XP, and Web folders.

Using a Web Browser to Access Documents

To access documents through a browser, you must first connect to the portal that will lead you to the documents. The default portal URL is as follows: `http://<server_name>/workspacename`. For instance, to access the workspace "marketing" on the SPS server named SPSSRV1, you would type the address `http://spssrv1/marketing`.

    If you want to go straight to the default Document Library dashboard, you would use the following default URL: `http://spssrv1/marketing/documents`.

Using Office XP to Access Documents

After a Web folder is created (more on Web folders in the next section), you can use the File|Save As menu choice to select a location within a Web folder to which a document should be saved. In addition, you can use the File|Open menu choice to open documents from a workspace location within an Office application. Moreover, the check-in and publishing DM functions are available within Office XP when you save a document to the workspace through a Web folder. This action will require the installation of the SharePoint Portal Server client.

Using Web Folders to Access Documents

Don't confuse Web folders with document folders. *Document folders* are created in the workspace to host documents. *Web folders* are a *client-side* creation that essentially routes normal local area network (LAN) traffic over port 80 to the SharePoint server.

    Web folders allow users to access the same documents whether they are sitting in their cubicles or coming into your network over the Internet. This technology offers significant possibilities for changing the way we work. For instance, Web folders let users perform some or even all of their work from home rather than commuting to the office. Although this access has been available over traditional dial-up connections or virtual private networks (VPNs), now users need only connectivity to the Internet—and not direct connectivity to your local network—to access their documents.

To create a Web folder, double-click My Network Places on your Windows 2000 or later desktop; then double-click Add Network Place. You'll be presented with the Welcome to the Add Network Place wizard (Figure 1–2). At this point, you simply type the desired URL, click Next, and then click Finish. You'll see the results by noticing a new icon pointed to your SPS server (Figure 1–3). In my example, I created a Web folder to my own SPS server at `networknowledge.com/nk`.

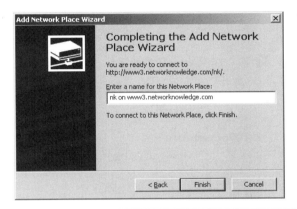

Figure 1–2 Welcome to the Add Network Place wizard

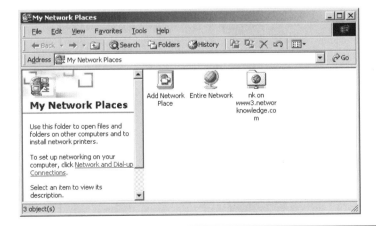

Figure 1–3 New Web folder to the NK workspace on www3.networknowledge.com in My Network Places

Creating Web Folders

If the location to which you are connecting is secured by requiring a user name and password, you'll be asked to enter this information twice: once after typing the URL and clicking Next, and again after clicking Finish. By default, after a Web folder is created, you will be presented with the contents inside the location to which the Web folder is connected.

Also, if the site is secured using Transport Layer Encryption or Secure Sockets Layer, you'll need to remember to type `https` at the beginning of your URL.

Documents Can Be Approved Efficiently

An approval process is a good way to ensure that a document is adequately reviewed before it is made public through publishing. When an author or coordinator chooses to publish a document, SPS can automatically route it to one or more people for review.

Each reviewer, called an *approver*, has the option of approving or rejecting the document.

SharePoint Portal Server offers two basic approval routes: *serial*, meaning that a document is reviewed and approved in a series by one approver after another, and *parallel*, meaning that multiple approvers review and approve the document all at once.

Documents Are Secure in an SPS Workspace

SPS uses role-based security to control access to documents and information. A *role* is one of three permission levels that can be assigned to a user. The DM functions, such as check-in, check-out, publish, and approve, are appended to traditional file access permissions, such as read, write, and change.

The three roles—Reader, Author, and Coordinator—are fixed in their permission structure and cannot be altered. Roles can be assigned to individuals or groups that reside in either a Windows NT domain or a Windows 2000 Active Directory directory service. If a user has more than one role for a folder, the least restrictive permission set is applied to that user's security context.

The Reader Role

The *Reader* role is the most restrictive role in the workspace. Readers can search for and read documents, but they cannot check out, modify, or check in documents. Readers can also execute search requests and then access content based on their security settings in the content source. Readers can view only published documents. All users have the Reader permission by default because this role is automatically given to the Everyone security group.

The Author Role

The *Author* role has all the permissions of the Reader role plus the ability to add, edit, delete, and read documents that are checked in. Authors can check out documents and execute the publish command. Authors can also create, rename, and delete document folders in the workspace. Authors cannot change the roles or the approval policy in force on a folder. A newly created folder inherits the role and folder policy settings from its parent folder.

The Coordinator Role

The *Coordinator* role is the big kahuna of the workspace. The Coordinator role has all the permissions of the Author and Reader roles plus the ability to manage the entire workspace. For instance, a coordinator can customize the dashboard site, configure workspace settings, define content sources, create indexes, configure folder security, and select the approval routing process. Coordinators can even undo a document check-out or override any approver's actions on a particular document. The user account that is used to create the workspace will be the Coordinator account for that workspace. Of course, other accounts can be added, and the original Coordinator account can be removed from the workspace security settings.

Documents Can Be Indexed and Searched Easily

A document's metadata can be indexed and then searched by users of the workspace. For instance, users can search keywords, author, date, file size, and other metadata to find the document they need. In addition to training your users on how to execute effective searches, you can take several actions as coordinator to improve the quality of search results:

- Require appropriate metadata to be entered for each document before the document can be checked in to the workspace.
- Provide categories that help organize the documents for easier browsing or retrieval.
- Configure *best bets*, which provide certain documents in all result sets when a query contains a particular word.

- Ensure that the appropriate content sources are being crawled, so users don't miss needed information or get too many unneeded hits.
- Enable Web discussions so that team members can discuss documents asynchronously.

Readers Can Be Notified of Changes to Documents

After a document has been modified, checked in, and published, notifications can be generated to interested readers to let them know that a new version of the document is available. Moreover, information held outside the workspace can also be configured to generate notifications when it is updated. Readers have the option of *subscribing* to changes in information at the document level, the folder level, or the category level. This flexibility ensures that users can remain updated about changes to documents and information.

Sometimes, the difference between a subscription and a search can be a bit confusing. However, it need not be. The essential difference is this: A *search* queries current data based on existing indexes. A *subscription* is a notification of new changes in a content source as the index is built. With a search, you find the information. With a subscription, the information finds you. Table 1–3 outlines the differences.

SPS Scales Document Management for the Enterprise

Because the search and indexing functions can be separated into dedicated servers, SPS is scalable in the enterprise. In addition, SPS allows the indexing of other SPS workspaces; as a result, as new workspaces are added to the overall SPS network, new information in those newly created workspaces can be indexed and made available to those who need it but are working in other workspaces.

Table 1–3 Differences between search and subscription

Search	Subscription
Searches past data: past-oriented.	User is notified that new data has been created: future-oriented.
New queries can be built to look at old data.	Old query notifies user of new data.
Focus is on a small, targeted query against a large mass of data.	Many content sources are queried. Results return small amounts of data.
Data is persistent.	Data is volatile.
Queries are volatile.	Queries are persistent.
Sometimes referred to as a "forward query."	Sometimes referred to as an "inverse query."

The Web-based nature of the portal ensures that users can access documents as they would any other information on an intranet, meaning that document locations do not need to be geographically close to the users who access them (although bandwidth considerations might alter this benefit in your environment). This arrangement also allows for better productivity when users are working remotely. Such functionality allows an organization to grow, increase its document reservoir, and yet ensure that all users have access to all necessary documents whenever they need them from any location at any time. All that is necessary, really, is that the user have Internet access and a browser. Very cool.

The Development Environment in SharePoint Portal Server

So far, the focus of this chapter has been on SharePoint's DM functions. But SPS is more than a DM server. It is also a development environment for customized portals that help create a collaborative solution for your company. To not know about SharePoint's development features is to miss out on some important aspects of SPS. Companies who purchase SPS only for its DM features will not utilize SPS to its fullest extent.

The portal that ships with SPS is based on the Digital Dashboard technology from Microsoft (`http://www.microsoft.com/business/dd/default.asp`). Through the portal, users can perform many of their DM tasks, including check-in, check-out, and publishing. DD applications are written to run on the Windows 2000 Internet Information Services (IIS) platform. The Web parts are stored in the Web Storage System databases.

By default, when SPS is installed, seven dashboards are also installed:

- Home
- Search
- Categories
- Document Library
- Subscriptions
- Management (visible only to coordinators)
- Document Inspection (visible only to authors and coordinators)

By default, dashboards in the SharePoint portal appear as tabs in an overall dashboard, but each one represents a distinct set of Web parts chosen to perform a collage of functions on a single Web page. The Management dashboard is available in the portal to coordinators only. The hidden Document Inspection dashboard is viewable only to coordinators and authors when they perform DM functions through the browser. Chapter 2 discusses the Digital Dashboard architecture, and Chapter 3 discusses each dashboard more fully.

The workflow features of SPS are built on a standard approval routing and publishing process that is inherent in the Web Storage System (WSS). As a result, the DM workspaces offer little support for customized workflows that ship in the box with SPS. However, if you want to customize workflows in SharePoint Portal Server, you can use the Workflow Designer for Exchange 2000 Server or the Office XP Workflow Designer. These two designers are graphical tools that can help a developer implement a sophisticated workflow process.

Therefore, if you need to use SPS and a customized workflow method, you should create Exchange 2000 public folders that exist outside the SPS workspace and enable them for workflow using the Workflow Designer. Alternatively, you can use the Office XP workflow tool.

FOR MORE INFO: The workflow tools are outside the scope of this book. To learn more about using these tools, please visit the MSDN Web site at msdn.microsoft.com.

From a development perspective, users access the workspace in one of three ways: through the portal; by using client extensions for Windows Explorer and Web folders; and by using the SPS Server Office add-in. Shared user interfaces include the SPS Document Properties dialog box and the SPS Document Edit Profile dialog box. The Document Properties dialog box displays document properties, profile information, version history, security settings, and category information.

Properties of an Office document can be "promoted" to the WSS so that they stay with a document created outside the workspace but are later copied into the workspace. Promoted properties are stored as item properties in the WSS, where they are indexed and then made available for searching by the users of the workspace.

Telecommuting and Microsoft Products

SharePoint Portal Server is one of several products that together form a well-rounded set of services to allow effective telecommuting. Think about it. How much of your job really requires that you be at the office? Look at the remote tools that are now available:

- Video conferencing
- Voice and data conferencing
- Instant messaging
- E-mail
- Chat services
- Document management
- Mobile access to personal information
- Voice calls
- Telephone conferencing
- General Internet access

The first six functions are available by purchasing Exchange 2000 Server, Exchange Conferencing Server, and SharePoint Portal Server. This type of remote access to information supports the plausible notion that many workers can now work at home, at least part of the time. Even without high-speed Internet access, you can outfit your office with voice, fax, and Internet access. Over a simple 56K line (I know, it will be slow), you can access your portal to check out a document from SharePoint Portal Server and access your e-mail using Outlook Web Access in Exchange 2000 Server. If you increase your bandwidth to a digital subscriber line (DSL) or something similar, you can realistically engage in an online video, voice, and data conference, leave an Instant Messaging (IM) client up and running and communicate using IM, attend a chat session if you care to, and conduct key elements of your work from your house.

If you need to attend a meeting with others in your company, you can use a video conference with voice and data technologies included. You and your colleagues can mark up a shared document, discuss language, and make decisions, all the while seeing one another in the browser window. If you need to use e-mail, you can do it from home using Outlook Web Access. Do you need to work on a document? You can use SharePoint Portal Server and work on documents in the public dashboards or on documents in your personal dashboard. You can use your telephone, use your fax machine, and enjoy Internet access for business research.

So, in a technically savvy company, it might be more cost-effective to outfit a room in a user's house with DSL and company-purchased equipment than it is to rent space and outfit a cubicle. I don't think we are very far away from this becoming a reality. As office costs continue to rise, companies are going to realize that their employees will be more productive and more satisfied with their jobs as they are able to work from their home, at least part of the time.

Telecommuting does not replace the need for face-to-face interaction. Personal relationships will always be necessary. Yet it's becoming clear to many people that at least parts of their job can be efficiently and effectively performed outside the office walls.

Summary

This chapter briefly outlines what SharePoint Portal Server is and how it solves many key problems in knowledge management. The following chapters take this program apart and explain its various functions. Troubleshooting tips help you with common problems that crop up when you use this program. Where appropriate, I also outline some of the problems and pitfalls of using SPS. There is much to learn, so let's get going.

CHAPTER 2

SharePoint Portal Server 2001 Concepts and Architecture

You might be tempted to skip this chapter because it's about architecture. You might expect it to be boring because all architecture chapters are boring. But you would be wrong. Architecture is both exciting and informative. True nerds find this stuff exciting. And true nerds know something "wannabe" nerds don't: Knowing how a program is put together will aid greatly in troubleshooting day-to-day problems. So, this chapter and the security chapter (Chapter 13) are probably the two most important ones in this book. This chapter drills down into how SPS is put together and looks at the Web Storage System (WSS). Let's start by discussing SharePoint Portal Server and Exchange 2000 Server.

Integration with Exchange 2000 Server

Let's start by outlining what SharePoint Portal Server is *not*. It is not a program that is Active Directory (AD)–dependent because it can work with security objects from both a Windows 2000 Active Directory and a Windows NT security accounts database. SPS should not be installed on Exchange 2000 Server (E2K); if you do, you'll find yourself without support from Microsoft. And SPS doesn't need to be installed on a Windows 2000 domain controller, although it does need to be installed on a Windows 2000 Server platform. So if you're thinking that you need Active Directory installed before you can install SPS, you'll be happy to learn that SPS is broader and more interoperable than that.

For much of the time that SPS was in beta, it was perceived to be tightly integrated with E2K. As this program has been rolled out, however, there has been a growing understanding that SPS is not tightly integrated with E2K and that, in fact, there are compelling reasons *not* to install it on an E2K server.

E2K and SPS are different programs, and the differences are not trivial. And yet they are alike in some ways. For instance, they share the WSS technology, although the WSS version that ships with SPS is a scaled-down version compared with the one that ships with E2K. Table 2–1 outlines the similarities and differences between these two products.

The one compelling reason not to install SPS on an E2K server can be summed up in two words: *no support*. If you install SPS on an E2K server, you do it at your own risk. And chances are very good that you'll permanently lose data with this configuration. Besides, SharePoint Portal Server won't even install on an Exchange 2000 Server running Service Pack 2, and if it is already installed on an Exchange 2000 Server and then Exchange is upgraded to Service Pack 2, SharePoint will cease to work. So best practice is to *not* place SharePoint Portal Server and Exchange 2000 Server on the same physical box. Just don't do it.

Table 2–1 E2K and SPS: Similarities and differences

Product Feature	Exchange 2000	SharePoint	Comment
Web Storage System	Organizes data into mailboxes, folders, and items. Data is represented as rows and tables within the database.	Organizes documents as items within folders and then organizes folders into workspaces.	Workspaces hold management folders, information categories, document profiles, and subscription information.
Document property promotion	A document's Object Linking and Embedding (OLE) properties are used to populate indexes within the store. Users then create views of these indexes within Microsoft Outlook.	A document's properties are grouped into document profiles, a standard way to describe the information (or metadata) about the document.	SharePoint's document profiles are a more standard way to view and work with a document's metadata. This method requires less sophistication by the end user when compared with creating views in Outlook to view indexes in an E2K store. Custom properties can be created and mapped between different databases.

Table 2–1 E2K and SPS: Similarities and differences *(continued)*

Product Feature	Exchange 2000	SharePoint	Comment
Indexing	Indexes information inside the store.	Indexes information from many types of content sources, including Exchange 2000 and Exchange 5.5 public folders, file shares, Lotus Notes databases, and other Share-Point workspaces.	When SharePoint is installed, it upgrades the MSSearch service found in Windows 2000.
Messaging	Provides robust messaging via the SMTP (Simple Mail Transport Protocol) service installed with Internet Information Services (IIS).	Uses the messaging service of Windows 2000 or Exchange 2000 to provide notifications to users.	SharePoint does not have its own SMTP native service. It must be provided to SPS in order for e-mail services to run properly.
Disaster recovery	Supports Windows 2000 Backup API and third-party vendors. Store supports recovery of deleted items and deleted mailboxes.	Does not support Windows 2000 Backup API. You must use the `Msmdback.vbs` script and a specific backup and restore process or use a third-party application with an appropriate agent such as Veritas Backup Exec Agent for SPS or CommVault Galaxy for SPS. No support for single item recovery after it is deleted.	This is, perhaps, SharePoint's most glaring limitation. Be sure to follow carefully the instructions on how to back up and restore SPS because if you don't, you're toast. And the utility is not intuitive.

Table 2–1 E2K and SPS: Similarities and differences *(continued)*

Product Feature	Exchange 2000	SharePoint	Comment
Integration with Active Directory	Completely dependent on AD for configuration and security.	No dependence at all on AD. Security credentials can be obtained from either a Windows NT domain controller or a Windows 2000 domain controller.	The backward compatability of this product creates a huge target market for Microsoft. When you think about it, SPS can work with either Windows NT or Windows 2000 security and can crawl Exchange 2000 and Exchange 5.5 public folders and Lotus Notes databases. The combination of these configurations must represent more than 50% of the current install base worldwide.
Storage of data	Supports as many as four storage groups with as many as five stores in each storage group.	Supports one storage group hosting one public store.	This is another downside to this version of SPS. You cannot map workspaces to different databases, nor can you quarantine a workspace in a separate storage group.
Storage limitations	Standard Edition has a 16GB store limit. Enterprise Edition has no store limit, but this doesn't help you with regard to SPS because SPS cannot be installed on an E2K Enterprise server.	No store size limit.	There is a 1,000,000-document tested limit for the store and the practical limit of meeting backup and restore times per your Service Level Agreements.
Antivirus protection	Several vendors support Exchange 2000 through the AVAPI (Anti Virus API).	Sybari Antigen is the only shipping solution at the time of this writing, but others are in development.	Very little selection, and virus protection is crucial for storage of documents.

The SharePoint Architecture

Because SPS is primarily a development environment for an enterprise-wide portal with built-in document management features, the look and feel of its architecture is different from what you may be accustomed to if you're learning SPS from the networking or operating system side of life. For instance, if you know the architecture of Windows NT or Windows 2000, you're probably accustomed to having a set of services that runs in kernel mode and another set of applications that runs in user mode, with a set of subsystems that translates calls between the two modes. Or if you know the architecture of Exchange 2000, you're acquainted with the notion that all of Exchange 2000 runs under one of two processes: `inetinfo.exe` or `store.exe`. When information is passed between these two threads, both processes use shared memory queues—called Exchange Interprocess Communication (or Epoxy) queues—to make the transfer of information very fast.

What the architectures of these two platforms—Windows 2000 and Exchange 2000—lack is a high reliance on application-layer protocols, such as HTTP or HTTP DAV (Development Authoring and Versioning), or on the markup languages, such as XML.

When SPS installs, it installs only two services: SharePoint Portal Server (`msdmserv.exe`) and Microsoft Exchange Information Store (`store.exe`). It also upgrades the search service (`MSSearch.exe`).

One of Microsoft's design goals was to build a portal that would support user interaction in terms of writing or posting information back to the portal. Microsoft views its portal solution as a *horizontal* development environment that also has an out-of-the-box *vertical* document management solution. This is a cross, really, between the competitors that Microsoft is facing. For instance, IBM has its own enterprise portal solution, WebSphere, and its own document management solution, Knowledge Discovery Server. But they are not integrated solutions, and if you called IBM sales, they would tell you that you'll need to purchase development time from IBM's Global Services in order to deploy both products in your environment.

SharePoint Portal Server is a single solution that provides both a development environment and a document management solution, and it doesn't require Microsoft Consulting Services to implement. This is a key reason, Microsoft feels, that customers will select SPS over its competitors, such as WebSphere, Oracle's 9*ia*S Portal solution, and the products of smaller vendors. SPS offers an out-of-the-box intranet solution that doesn't require a large investment in development. This product mix is high in demand, and Microsoft expects it to sell well.

One other major design goal was to keep the user interfaces to the portal as familiar to end users as possible because of the high cost of retraining. Hence, Microsoft built the SPS client into well-known tools: Office applications, the Windows shell, and the Web browser. As Microsoft moves forward with SPS and its farm of .NET servers, it is highly likely that the browser will become the main client for a number of applications that are made available through the portal. Hence, the Digital Dashboard has been written so that it can "sniff" the client browser, determine its type and version, and then present data to the browser in the most suitable method.

Server Components

SharePoint Portal Server uses four essential services: `inetinfo.exe` (IIS), `store.exe` (WSS), `MSSearch.exe` (the MSSearch service), and `msdmserv.exe` (SPS). In addition, all communication between these services takes place using either HTTP or HTTP DAV (or just DAV). Two primary interfaces are used to access data: OLEDB (Object Linking and Embedding for Databases) and EXOLEDB (Exchange OLEDB). These four services, two protocols, and two interfaces work together to produce the functionality and services we know as SharePoint Portal Server. Figure 2–1 shows how SPS is put together.

From the client perspective, interactions with the SPS workspace take place through either the browser, an application, or a Web folder. But from an architectural viewpoint, a Web folder and an application can be considered the same type of access method because both use the Microsoft Data Access Internet Publishing Provider (MSDAIPP); this provider can use either ADO (ActiveX Data Objects) or OLEDB to access data in or submit data to IIS. So when an Office application needs to read a list of folders or documents from the workspace, it binds to the MSDAIPP provider, which then uses ADO or OLEDB to submit its request to IIS. MSDAIPP then uses DAV to communicate with SPS. Information and requests flow to the SPS workspace from the SPS client through one of two protocols: HTTP or DAV. The majority of this communication is in HTTP DAV.

TIP: Because MSDAIPP requires the IIS server to support either the FrontPage Web Extender Client (WEC) or the DAV protocol extensions, you must be running IIS 5.0 or later. Versions of IIS before IIS 5.0 do not support these extensions.

When any packet arrives at port 80 on the SharePoint Portal Server, Web services examine the packet to identify it. If it is a DAV packet, Web services

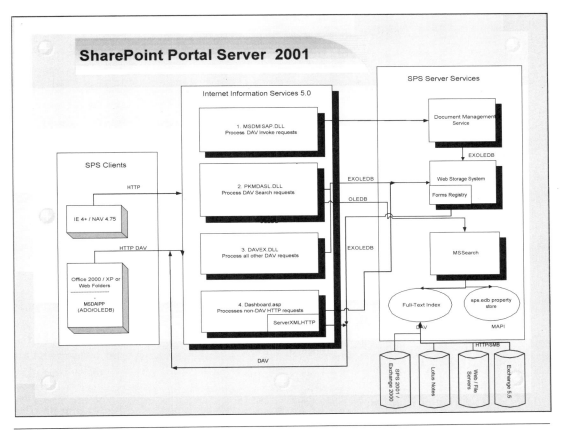

Figure 2–1 SharePoint Portal Server overview

hand it off to `pkmdasl.dll` for processing. This DLL, which is run by the `inetinfo.exe` process, processes every DAV packet in the following order:

1. Invoke command
2. Search request
3. Other

If PKMDASL finds the INVOKE command (a proprietary command that is used for DM functions) inside the packet, it hands the packet off to `mdsmisap.dll` for processing in concert with the `msdmserv.exe` component. `msdmserv.exe` then uses EXOLEDB to access information in the store, such as a document, and returns the results to the client using XML.

The INVOKE command is proprietary, so if you run a packet trace you'll see the command inside the packet. But note that it is not exposed, so you can't use it for development purposes. The switches and various uses for this command have not been released by Microsoft, nor, at the time of this writing, does Microsoft intend to do so.

If the DAV command is not an INVOKE command, PKMDASL parses the packet to see whether it contains a search query. If the packet contains a search request, PKMDASL processes the packet itself and hands it off to the MSSearch.exe process. This process then parses the search request to discern whether it is a shallow or a deep request. A *shallow* request searches the folder in focus and does not search the full-text index nor any subfolders. A shallow search request is executed against the Web store using the EXOLEDB interface.

A *deep* request, sometimes referred to as a *deep traversal*, uses the OLEDB interface to execute the request against the full-text index.

By default, PKMDASL executes all search requests as both shallow and deep, thereby ensuring that both the full-text index and the metadata associated with those documents—which are stored in the sps.edb database—are included in the search.

Finally, if the DAV command is something other than an INVOKE command or a search query, then the command is processed by DAVEX.DLL as needed. If data is needed from the Web store or if information needs to be written to the Web store, then the packet is passed to the store process (store.exe) for processing with the Web store. This assumes that the dashboard.asp component does not need to be consulted.

If the packet that arrives at inetinfo.exe is not a DAV packet, but rather is an HTTP packet (such as one that is requesting a Web part), and if the packet is intended for SharePoint Portal Server, then the packet is processed by the dashboard.asp file. This component looks up the requested URL in the packet and then communicates with the ServerXMLHTTP component to look up the forms registration for that URL in the forms database that is housed inside the WSS. Interestingly, the forms registration information is returned to IIS from the ServerXMLHTTP component encapsulated in DAV packets. This means that PKMDASL will run these response packets through its three-step parsing process.

After PKMDASL finds that these response packets contain neither the INVOKE command nor a search query, DAVEX again passes the packets to the dashboard.asp component, along with the updated information from the forms registration database. Then dashboard.asp uses ServerXMLHTTP to retrieve the requested data from the store, which returns the information to the client in the form of XML. The next section explains this process more fully.

The Digital Dashboard and the Dashboard Factory

Microsoft sometimes refers to the *dashboard factory.* This "factory" is code that resides inside `dashboard.asp` and assembles the Web parts for viewing in the browser. The `dashboard.asp` file contains the core logic for reading each Web part and deciding how best to present it in the client's browser.

The Main Files Used in Dashboard Rendering

Six files are involved in the rendering of each dashboard. Each of these files plays an important role:

- `dashboard.asp`: This is the main starting point or entry point for every dashboard. This file retrieves the dashboard's XML file from the Web store and uses either `dbview_ie.xsl` or `dbview.xsl` to render the dashboard in the browser.

- `dbview_ie.xsl`: This is the rendering file that ships with IE 5.5 and later. Earlier browsers use `dbview.xsl`. This file transforms the dashboard XML content and renders it as a Web page in the browser. The `dbview_ie.js` file is included by this file to provide JavaScript functions to minimize, restore, close, and refresh Web parts. `dbview_ie.xsl` and all other XSL sheets used by SPS point to the old XSL namespace (`http://www.w3.org/TR/WD-xsl`) instead of the new XSLT namespace (`http://www.w3.org/1999/XSL.Transform`). This means that the additional functionality of XSLT is not available in this version of SPS.

- `dbutil.vbs`: This file contains functions, subprocedures, variables, constants, and classes for use by other files. It provides core utilities for working with dashboards, Web parts, browsers, URLs, and HTTP.

- `store.vbs`: This file contains functions, subprocedures, variables, constants, and classes for use by other files. It provides core utilities for working with the Web store—getting content in and out of the store itself. It includes the `project.vbs` file.

- `project.vbs`: This file contains utility and helper functions, subprocedures, variables, constants, and classes for others to use.

- `TahoeUtils.asp`: This file contains functions, subprocedures, variables, constants, and classes for use by other files. This file has many functions that are used throughout the SPS architecture. It includes the `globalizedstrings.vbs` file.

You would be well advised to avoid modifiying these files. Microsoft has warned that, except for the `catalogs.xml` and the `dashboardextensions.vbs` files, if you modify any of these files, you'll experience problems on your SPS server and Microsoft will not support your installation.

The `dashboard.asp` file works with the ServerXMLHTTP object to access dashboard content in the database. The ServerXMLHTTP object uses DAV packets to communicate with the WSS. The dashboard and its Web parts are held in the WSS databases. The ServerXMLHTTP object is used to get Web part settings and properties that help render the Web part in the user's browser.

Here's how it works. When a user navigates to the dashboard's default URL, `dashboard.asp` obtains the list of Web parts for the requested dashboard. The `dashboard.asp` file then loops through each Web part in the list, processes each part, and renders them in the dashboard. Rendering may include executing other functions, such as running a script, performing XSL (Extensible Stylesheet Language), or following links to other sources using XMLHTTP. The `dashboard.asp` file allows rendering of a Web part to run in parallel with other queries.

The final page output from `dashboard.asp` is an XML stream of data that is then presented to the client browser. If the client is running Internet Explorer (IE) 5.5 or later, the client-side file, `dbview_ie.xsl`, is used to render the final output page. For all other browsers, the `dbview.xsl` file is used. However, you can have your own XSL file written for the XML stream that comes from `dashboard.asp`.

Content that is displayed inside the Web part can come from any number of sources, including a line of business applications, the Internet, or even a pivot table from an Excel spreadsheet. The content does not need to originate from the store, and a number of third-party vendors write Web parts that aggregate large bodies of content into syndicated, streaming, live content feeds. For instance, a news service could keep a real-time news ticker running inside a Web part that is downloaded from the news service's Web part gallery, installed in your dashboard, and written to accept multicast data streams from the news service's servers. This type of portal content and customization are available now.

The dashboard is a compilation of Web parts that are placed on the same Web page. The entire workspace that is accessed by the dashboard is really a virtual root directory inside IIS that is installed into the default Web site on the SPS server. The content of the workspace is held in the database, but the Web pages are held in the virtual root directory.

The ServerXMLHTTP object can be configured with its own proxy settings, which are stored in the registry and are independent of the server's proxy settings or the Search proxy settings. This arrangement allows an SPS workspace to have Internet connectivity while denying Internet connectivity to other services on the same server. Chapter 4 explains how to configure these proxy settings using the `proxycfg.exe` utility.

Document Management Services

Document management services (`msdmserv.exe`) lets users create, check in, check out, version, and publish documents. Using the built-in workflow process, users can also route documents for approval. Changes to published documents can result in notifications being sent to those who are subscribing to the document's parent folder or to one or more categories with which the document is associated.

All the DM functions are managed through either the Document Library dashboard, the Office client, or the IE extensions. From a user's perspective, a number of DM objects (although users don't think of these items as objects) provide the overall DM functions, as illustrated in Table 2–2.

Only HTTP DAV packets with the `INVOKE` command will be passed to `msdmserv.exe` for processing. Within a workspace, you work with document profiles, property definitions, catalogs, and two folder hierarchies: categories and documents. Access to these objects is available through the Web Folders client, and security is enforced using role-based security.

Categories and Document Hierarchies

The Document Library folder lets the team creating the documents organize them in any manner that makes sense to the team. The Categories folder

Table 2–2 DM objects and functions

Object	Function
Document profile	A method of assembling metadata about a document in a standard format.
List of possible values for a given property, such as keywords or categories	Enables the author or coordinator to select a range of predefined values for a document's metadata.
Standard or enhanced folder	Two methods of storing documents. Enhanced folders provide added DM functionality.
Categories	Provides access to methods of creating additional options for document metadata. You can also configure existing categories inside a Categories folder.
Document	Basic method of storing content and its metadata. A document is more than a file. The concept of a document includes both content and metadata.
Workspace	Central access to all the DM and knowledge management functions of SPS.

structure, however, is created by the coordinator. Categories don't replace the document folder structure. Instead, they provide a consistent set of values to describe all documents in the workspace across all the document folders. These values are added as metadata to each document to provide a rich method for document retrieval.

The difficulty most administrators face is that they tend to create a Categories folder structure that mirrors the Document Library folder structure. For a long time, administrators have used folders to create a document structure based on some type of logic, such as by topic.

But the method employed to create the document folder structure should not be mirrored by the category hierarchy. A good question to ask yourself is this: "How else would I describe my data?" When you've taken a look at your document folder structure, then find a unique answer to this question and you'll have a starting point for creating your Categories folder hierarchy.

For instance, if you've created folders inside the Document Library folder for each department, such as marketing, sales, administration, IT, and research, then don't create a Categories hierarchy that describes documents by department. Try a different method, such as by subject, end product, or some other distinguishing characteristic.

Document Folders

Documents are housed in one of two folder types: standard and enhanced. *Standard* folders support user access, categories, and building of an index by the search engine. *Enhanced* folders support these functions plus document versioning, check-in, check-out, and document approval routing. Enhanced folders require users to check out documents for editing and to publish the documents to make them visible to the readers. A standard folder can be configured as an enhanced folder, but it must not contain any documents at the time of the change.

Workspace Catalogs

Workspace *catalogs* (also known as full-text indexes) are produced by the Search service, are housed in their own files, and are available for searching in the workspace. Catalogs represent the results of searching text on one or more content sources. These catalogs are then open for searching by the user and return answers to queries in a result set. Security is applied to each item in the result set before it is presented to the user, so only those documents to which the user enjoys access are included in the final list.

Document Profiles

When working with document profiles, you need to think about three levels of information: the profile itself, the properties that make up the profile, and the various choices that you can create for selection in each property.

SPS ships with several default document profiles, such as the Base Document profile. In addition, you can create new document profiles for a group of documents so that they are described in the manner and with the data that best meets the needs of your organization. When you create a new profile, you must specify which properties the profile should contain. You can even create new properties and apply them to the profile. In effect, what you're saying when you configure new document properties is that you want particular documents described with a defined mix of data elements.

NOTE: Properties are scoped to the workspace, so when you create a new property, it can be used in any other document profile in the workspace. This can be a good thing if you want to create a customized set of properties to describe more than one set of documents. But it can also be a bad thing if a custom property is used to describe a document that the property was not intended to describe. This is why document profile creation and configuration are coordinator-level activities.

Part of creating a new document property is the opportunity it gives you to specify which data choices can be entered into the property and whether they must or may be populated before a document is checked in to the document folder. For instance, you might create a new document profile that is configured to require an entry for a category. You can then define the categories from which the author or coordinator must select.

Because every document must be associated with a profile (in other words, it must be described by a defined set of properties), it is important to plan your document profiles carefully. It is a good idea to have a process for creating new document profiles so that you strike a balance in your environment between, on the one hand, creating too many profiles with overlapping descriptions and, on the other hand, including too little information in each profile to make it of significant use to the end user.

Remember that part of a document's profile includes system-generated metadata, such as the file size and modification date. System-generated metadata is not configurable, although it is included in the workspace's index and thus can be searched by the end user.

Document Versioning

When thinking about versioning of documents, you need to think in terms of four states: checked out, checked in, waiting for approval, and published. When a document is *checked out*, the copy in the workspace is locked against further editing. Other authors and coordinators can read a checked-out document, but they cannot check it out concurrently and make their own edits. In other words, SPS forces a collaboration team to make changes to a document in serial and not in parallel. After a document is checked out, it cannot be checked out again until it is first checked back in to the workspace.

TIP: A coordinator of the workspace can undo the checked-out designation on a document. This action releases the edit reservation on the document but does not change the existing version on the server nor its version number.

When a document is *checked in*, it is unlocked and available for editing via the check-out process. Documents that are checked in can be read directly from the workspace by authors and coordinators but cannot be edited unless they are first checked out.

If an enhanced folder has been configured with an approval routing process and if the document has been issued the publish command, it will enter the *waiting for approval* state. In this state, the document is waiting to be approved according to the folder's configuration. In the dashboard, the document's status appears as *pending approval*. When the document is approved, it enters the *approved* state (also known as being *published*), and it is available for consumption by the readers in the workspace.

NOTE: Documents cannot be published without first being checked in to the workspace.

Copying Documents and Properties into a Workspace

When documents are copied into a workspace from a location outside the workspace, their properties may or may not be copied, or *promoted*, into the workspace along with the document. Table 2–3 outlines the variations of copying a document into a workspace under different conditions and the effect it has on the document's properties as the document is transferred from one context to another.

Table 2–3 Effects of copying documents and properties into a workspace

Destination of Document	Effects on Document's Properties	Initial State of Document after Being Copied to the Workspace
Enhanced document folder	Metadata is copied, and the folder's default profile is applied. Metadata that has no matching properties in the workspace is discarded.	Checked out. Documents must be checked in to be modified or published.
Standard document folder	Metadata is copied, and the folder's default profile is applied. Metadata that has no matching properties in the workspace is discarded.	Documents in standard folders are automatically available to readers. This is the same effect as publishing a document, but because standard folders do not have the document management features, it's best to say they are available rather than published.
Another workspace	Metadata is copied only on Office documents. The target folder's default profile is applied to the documents. Metadata that has no matching properties in the target folder's document profile is discarded.	The state of the document depends on whether the document is being copied to an enhanced or a standard folder.
Local folder	A limited set of metadata is copied to the local folder for Office documents. All other metadata is lost.	Not Applicable

The Web Storage System Architecture

Microsoft has released two products that use the WSS: Exchange 2000 Server and SharePoint Portal Server. The version that is used by SharePoint is similar to that used by Exchange 2000 Server. It has transaction logs, an `*.edb` database, and the Exchange Installable File System (ExIFS) kernel-mode component.

In SPS, the WSS is accessed most often by HTTP and HTTP DAV. HTTP uses a standard URL to access resources in the WSS. DAV is an extension of HTTP that allows for greater flexibility in accessing and working with resources. For instance, when a document is checked out, a `LOCK` WebDAV method is placed on the file; this method prohibits other team members from modifying the file until it is checked in, releasing the `LOCK`. Resource properties are accessed using DAV with the `SEARCH` and `PROPPATCH` methods.

DAV uses HTML to format its specific methods, such as a LOCK request, in XML text and then sends them to the WSS for processing. In addition, the WSS can process ASP scripts when accessed by clients using HTTP.

WSS API Support

The WSS in SPS supports the ADO and OLEDB application programming interfaces (APIs), and this means that you can access resources and their properties in a similar manner as you would with a relational database.

The WSS also supports a relatively new API called the Exchange Installable File System, or IFS (also known as ExIFS). If the ADO and OLEDB APIs allow for seamless access to the WSS as a relational database, the IFS allows for seamless access to the WSS as a Windows 2000 file system. By default, the M: drive is the assigned letter for mounting the IFS in SPS. After the IFS is mounted, resources in the WSS can be accessed as in any other standard file system. Unlike Exchange 2000 Server, however, this M: drive is not mounted by default. Win32 applications that save files directly to the disk can use server message blocks (SMBs) to save files to the WSS. However, note that files saved to the WSS via the IFS in SPS will not use the HTTP protocol on which many SPS services are built. Therefore, you should refrain from saving files to the workspace via the IFS because you will not be able to perform specific SPS functions on the documents or set permissions by using roles.

There are subtle but important differences in the way the WSS is implemented in Exchange 2000 Server versus SharePoint Portal Server. Table 2–4 outlines these differences.

If you find that you need to mount the M: drive, there are several ways to do it. One way is to open a command prompt and type

```
SUBST M: \\.\backofficestorage
```

Note two things about this command. First, you can use any available drive letter; you're not restricted to using the letter *M*. Second, you can mount multiple drive letters at the same time to the backofficestorage, although I can't think of a reason you'd want to do this.

If you want to permanently mount the WSS for SPS, go to the following registry key:

```
HKLM\System\CurrentControlSet\Services\EXIFS\Parameters
```

Set the driveletter value to an available drive letter.

Later, this chapter discusses the WSS folder hierarchy as viewed through both the IFS and Windows Explorer.

Table 2–4 WSS implementation differences between SPS and E2K

WSS Feature	SharePoint Portal Implementation	Exchange 2000 Implementation
Installable file system	Not mounted by default. Its use is not recommended except in limited situations because many of the document functions specific to SPS are available only if the document has been saved using HTTP or DAV.	Mounted by default, and its use is encouraged by administrators and users.
Use of drive `M:`	Used only for read-only access to the document library, FrontPage Server Extensions, and WSS development.	Used for general access to items in public folders and mailboxes. Can be used like any other file system on a file server.
Protocol support	HTTP, WebDAV, XML, IFS, ASP, and JavaScript.	HTTP, WebDAV, XML, IFS, ASP, JavaScript, MAPI, POP3, IMAP4, NNTP, LDAP, and SMTP.
API support	ADO, OLEDB, IFS	ADO, OLEDB, IFS, and MAPI.
Store support	Supports one store and a single public folder.	Standard version supports one mailbox store and as many as 19 public stores in as many as four storage groups. Enterprise version supports any combination of mailbox and public stores, up to 20 stores dispersed over four storage groups.
File architecture	Supports streaming content by using two files (an `.mdb` and an `.stm`) to make up one store.	Supports streaming content by using two files (an `.edb` and an `.stm`) to make up one store.
Transaction logging	Uses circular logging. This is not configurable.	Uses as many transaction logs as needed to perform write operations to the database. Circular logging can be enabled after Exchange 2000 is installed, but it is not enabled by default.

WSS Database Files and Transaction Logging

By default, the WSS stores its database files in the `c:\program files\ sharepoint portal server\data\web storage system` directory, as illustrated in Figure 2–2.

The database that houses all your workspace data—most commonly referred to as the *store*—really comprises two files: `wss.mdb` and `wss.stm`. The `wss.mdb` file is the public store, and `wss.stm` is the streaming file,

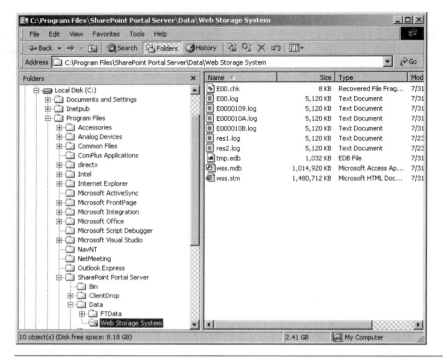

Figure 2–2 Web Storage System database files and transaction logs

which holds streaming content. The `wss.stm` file holds raw bits of data, and the meaning of those bits—their overhead and properties—is held in `wss.mdb`. This is why `wss.mdb` might sometimes be referred to as the *property* store; it hosts the metadata for all files, whether they are held in the `.stm` or the `.mdb` file.

NOTE: The `sps.edb` file (located in the `\FTData\SharePointPortalServer` directory) is sometimes referred to as the *property store for indexed documents*. When a document in indexed, its contents are placed in the index files but its properties are placed in the `sps.edb` database. The `sps.edb` database holds only the properties of indexed content.

The WSS uses a *write-ahead* method of writing information into the database because this improves performance of the server and users experience a faster write operation. This means that data is written and committed to a transaction log before it is written to the database. These same write operations are also held in the memory of the server and are written from the memory of the server to the database. The write operations to the transaction logs are used mainly to complete the WSS architecture in everyday life and to increase performance of the server. They can't be used in a recovery operation because circular logging is enforced and is not configurable.

The way that the WSS writes new or modified information to its database is not insignificant. When a write operation needs to occur, it is first written to 4K pages in memory. When the transactions are completed, they are recorded in the transaction logs. Later, at a time determined by the WSS, the transactions are written from memory back to the database.

How long the WSS waits to write new information from memory into the database is not an exact science, but here are some circumstances that will cause at least a partial flushing of the data in memory back to the WSS store:

- If the number of committed transactions reaches a certain point, the WSS will flush transactions to the databases.
- If the number of free pages in memory becomes too low, WSS will flush transactions from memory back to the database.
- If another service needs memory, the WSS will release memory to that process.
- If the store.exe process is shutting down, the WSS will first flush all transactions to the database before it allows the store.exe process to shut down.

Pages are written to the database from memory in no particular order. Furthermore, it is possible that not all the pages that represent the same file may be written to the database at the same time. The random order in which the pages are copied to disk means that a sudden loss of power could result in some pages being written to the disk for a particular file while others are not. In this case, you could end up with a corrupted database and could be forced to recover a good copy of the database using the restore script provided with SPS. You should ensure that you have adequate battery backup to your SPS server and that you are not placing this server in a location where it could inadvertently be shut down.

Each transaction log is 5MB in size, and the logs are numbered sequentially in hexadecimal. The current transaction log being used by the store process is e00.log. When it becomes full, it is renamed to the next sequential hexadecimal number, and a new e00.log is generated by the WSS. If write operations need to occur while the e00.log file is being generated, they are recorded in tmp.edb and then moved to e00.log when it is ready to go.

With circular logging, the WSS uses the same physical log files over and over, renaming them sequentially when they are reused. Rarely will you see more than five log files at any given time, not counting `e00.log`. Because transactions may be overwritten in the transaction logs before a full backup of the database can be completed, recovery of your WSS database files is limited to the last full backup. There is no recovery feature or transaction log replay into the database for transactions that have occurred since the last full backup of your databases.

The WSS and Memory Management

You might find that the `store.exe` process is consuming much more memory on your server than all the other processes. You'll probably see this by opening Task Manager, selecting the Processes tab, and sorting the list by memory usage. This is illustrated in Figure 2–3.

If you find this to be the case, don't be alarmed. You don't have a memory leak. Instead, this is by design. What you're seeing is the Dynamic Buffer Allocation (DBA) at work. The DBA monitors your server's health and functioning and decides how much of the available RAM it can allocate to the `store.exe` process even if the store process doesn't need the RAM at that time. This is done because the Extensible Storage Engine (ESE) team made a design choice to the effect that there is no sense in having unused memory on the server. Therefore, the DBA allocates to the store process all available RAM after accounting for the needs of all the processes on the server. This

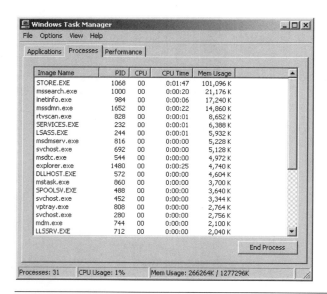

Figure 2–3 Task Manager showing memory allocation to the `store.exe` process

allocation is based on the overall paging and I/O activity, among other factors, on the server.

Should another process require additional RAM, the store process releases a sufficient amount of memory so that the other process can run efficiently and effectively. This happens dynamically and is not configurable. Remember that the goal of DBA is to improve overall system performance. It does SharePoint Portal Server no good to have allocated to itself the lion's share of the memory on the server and then have other processes excessively paging. Overall, such paging slows system performance, and this impacts SPS. Hence, don't think that DBA is going to sap your system of memory and hurt other processes running on the server.

SharePoint Portal Server Folder Structure

The WSS in SPS has one storage group hosting one public store. The single database is used to create one top-level hierarchy called SharePoint Portal Server with a domain name of `localhost`. Note that folders in the WSS can be accessed in three ways. Table 2–5 illustrates how this works.

When you use `localhost` in a URL, you may need to enter that information as a host header for the Web site hosting SharePoint Portal Server by having it accept the name `localhost`. After SPS is installed, two IIS virtual roots called Public and SharePoint Portal Server are mapped to `\\.\backofficestorage\` `localhost\SharePoint Portal Server`.

Each workspace has its own folder that is given the same name as the name of the workspace. This folder is mapped to an IIS virtual root with the

Table 2–5 Folder access methods

Protocol	Path Name / URL
Drive letter and folder path name	`M:\localhost\SharePoint Portal Server`

HTTP: URL	`http://localhost/SharePoint Portal Server`
	`http://localmachinename/SharePoint Portal Server`
	`http://DNSmachinename/SharePoint Portal Server`
	`http://localhost/Public`
	`http://localmachinename/Public`
	`http://DNSmachinename/Public`

FILE: URL	`file://./backofficestorage/localhost/SharePoint Portal Server`

same workspace name. This is what allows the workspace folder to be accessed as `http://servername/workspacename`.

The workspace Shadow folder mirrors the Documents folder for a given workspace. This is where the past major and minor versions of a document live. The Shadow folder includes all the versions of each document that have been created during the document's creation and publishing processes.

The System folder is where the workspace schema and forms registrations live. There is also a root folder for Categories and Portal content. Some of these folders are viewable through the Web Folders client. The root folder to the workspace is never viewable in any utility except through the IFS.

Here is the default folder hierarchy that is created for a new workspace:

```
.
M:\localhost
M:\localhost\SharePoint Portal Server
M:\localhost\SharePoint Portal Server\Applications
M:\localhost\SharePoint Portal Server\Applications\ec3
M:\localhost\SharePoint Portal Server\workspaces\ec3
M:\localhost\SharePoint Portal Server\workspaces\ec3\_TEMP_
M:\localhost\SharePoint Portal Server\workspaces\ec3\Categories
M:\localhost\SharePoint Portal Server\workspaces\ec3\Categories\Cat 1
M:\localhost\SharePoint Portal Server\workspaces\ec3\Categories\Cat 1\
  Cat 4
M:\localhost\SharePoint Portal Server\workspaces\ec3\Categories\Cat 1\
  Cat 5
M:\localhost\SharePoint Portal Server\workspaces\ec3\Categories\Cat 2
M:\localhost\SharePoint Portal Server\workspaces\ec3\Categories\Cat 3
M:\localhost\SharePoint Portal Server\workspaces\ec3\Documents
M:\localhost\SharePoint Portal Server\workspaces\ec3\Management
M:\localhost\SharePoint Portal Server\workspaces\ec3\Portal
M:\localhost\SharePoint Portal Server\workspaces\ec3\Portal Content
M:\localhost\SharePoint Portal Server\workspaces\ec3\Portal\Categories
M:\localhost\SharePoint Portal Server\workspaces\ec3\Portal\
  Document Library
M:\localhost\SharePoint Portal Server\workspaces\ec3\Portal\Management
M:\localhost\SharePoint Portal Server\workspaces\ec3\Portal\resources
M:\localhost\SharePoint Portal Server\workspaces\ec3\Portal\Search
M:\localhost\SharePoint Portal Server\workspaces\ec3\Portal\Subscriptions
M:\localhost\SharePoint Portal Server\workspaces\ec3\Portal Content\
  Announcements
M:\localhost\SharePoint Portal Server\workspaces\ec3\Portal Content\News
M:\localhost\SharePoint Portal Server\workspaces\ec3\Portal Content\
  Quick Links
```

```
M:\localhost\SharePoint Portal Server\workspaces\ec3\SHADOW
M:\localhost\SharePoint Portal Server\workspaces\ec3\SHADOW\Documents
M:\localhost\SharePoint Portal Server\workspaces\ec3\system
M:\localhost\SharePoint Portal Server\workspaces\ec3\system\Discussions
M:\localhost\SharePoint Portal Server\workspaces\ec3\system\Forms
M:\localhost\SharePoint Portal Server\workspaces\ec3\system\OBE
M:\localhost\SharePoint Portal Server\workspaces\ec3\system\schema
M:\localhost\SharePoint Portal Server\workspaces\ec3\system\Subscriptions
M:\localhost\SharePoint Portal Server\workspaces\ec3\system\Tour
M:\localhost\SharePoint Portal Server\workspaces\ec3\system\Users
M:\localhost\SharePoint Portal Server\workspaces\ec3\System Categories
M:\localhost\SharePoint Portal Server\workspaces\ec3\System Categories\
   Cat 1
M:\localhost\SharePoint Portal Server\workspaces\ec3\System Categories\
   Cat 2
M:\localhost\SharePoint Portal Server\workspaces\ec3\System Categories\
   Cat 3
M:\localhost\SharePoint Portal Server\workspaces\ec3\System Categories\
   Cat 4
M:\localhost\SharePoint Portal Server\workspaces\ec3\System Categories\
   Cat 5
M:\localhost\SharePoint Portal Server\workspaces\PubModels
M:\localhost\SharePoint Portal Server\workspaces\PubModels\Auto
M:\localhost\SharePoint Portal Server\workspaces\PubModels\Default
M:\localhost\SharePoint Portal Server\workspaces\PubModels\Parallel1
M:\localhost\SharePoint Portal Server\workspaces\PubModels\Serial
M:\localhost\SharePoint Portal Server\workspaces\selectors
M:\localhost\SharePoint Portal Server\workspaces\system
M:\localhost\SharePoint Portal Server\workspaces\system\All Discussions
M:\localhost\SharePoint Portal Server\workspaces\system\Discussions
M:\localhost\SharePoint Portal Server\workspaces\system\schema
```

Figure 2–4 shows the default directory structure for SharePoint Portal Server as seen through the Windows Explorer utility. As you can see, these two directory structures are very different because one is focused on the store and the other is focused on the SharePoint server files. The Bin directory holds the SharePoint Server binary files, which are the files that run the SharePoint program. The Data folder houses all the data files, including the WSS database, the transaction logs as well as the gatherer logs (these logs keep track of the successes and failures when a content source is crawled—see Chapter 7), and the full-text index.

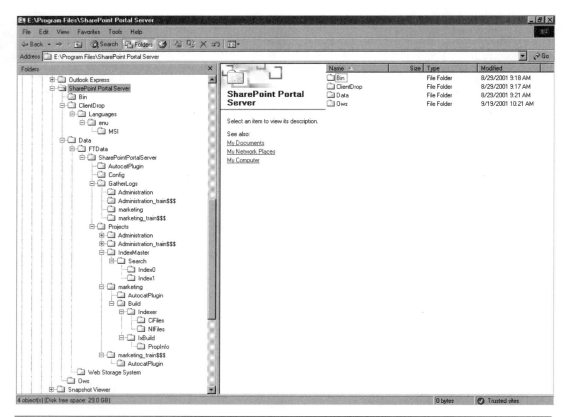

Figure 2–4 Default directory structure for SharePoint Portal Server

Summary

This chapter briefly discusses the architecture of SharePoint itself and the Web Storage System. In the coming chapters, your understanding of the how-to aspects of SharePoint will be enhanced if you've read and understood the architecture behind it. So, without further ado, let's move on to a topic that tends to pique people's interest: the Digital Dashboard.

CHAPTER 3

Managing the Digital Dashboard

The Digital Dashboard (DD) is a proprietary Microsoft technology that lets developers create custom portals, or dashboards. This chapter is written with nonprogrammers in mind—you don't need to know XML, Visual Basic (VB), or HTML to understand the contents of this chapter. However, it will be helpful if you have some basic knowledge of XML and HTML if you want to create customized Web parts.

Until the release of SPS, the DD was not viewed as a full, "real" product by Microsoft because it wasn't tied to any supported product. However, since the release of SPS with the DD technology tied to it, you can call Product Support Services (PSS) and obtain support for the dashboard. For many people, this is good news.

If you don't know much about the DD, this chapter will give you a good introduction. The default DD is being deployed in some environments as an introductory portal. A *portal* can be defined as an aggregation of entry points for accessing information and applications from a Web page that will run under existing Web server technologies. The default client for a portal is a Web browser.

As the name implies, SharePoint (a single location from which all information and applications are shared) Portal (the aggregation of services into a common set of Web pages as described in the preceding paragraph) Server ships with a default portal out of the box. This portal is also called the Digital Dashboard, which in turn comprises seven dashboards. In SPS, the seven default dashboards are both extensible and customizable. So, when you purchase SPS, you get not only a document management program but also a development environment in which you can create a customized portal for your users and customers alike.

In this chapter, you'll get acquainted with the DD technology and learn how to create a new DD, how to create and customize Web parts, and how to download new Web parts from the Internet.

Digital Dashboard Terminology

Before you can delve very far into this topic, you first need an understanding of the SharePoint Portal Server terms used to describe the dashboard.

- Dashboard site: This is the Web site, including all the Web pages, used to host the dashboards and present them to the users.
- Digital Dashboard: This is the Web page that assembles the Web parts for presentation in the user's browser.
- Web part: This is an object composed of code that either displays information, performs a function, or both. Code can be written in XML, HTML, JavaScript, and VBScript. The results of the script can be displayed in the browser using either HTML or XML/XSL. Each Web part has its own *schema*, which defines its properties.
- Web part folder: A Web part folder groups Web parts under a common schema.
- Dashboard factory: This is the code engine that resides on the server and renders the view of the dashboard to the browser based on configured properties such as layout, style, and content (see the discussion in Chapter 2 on the `dashboard.asp` file).

The DD is an efficient method of sharing information because its Web parts are reusable and extensible. For example, a Web part that presents a list of company memos that are created on one of the company's file servers can be installed into each workspace's dashboard so that no matter which workspace a user needs to use, he will see the same memo information on the dashboard for that workspace. Moreover, any dashboard can be customized and extended to include Web parts that may be of interest to the user, including stock quote tickers, a pivot table from an Excel spreadsheet, or even a weather radar display from an online weather service.

SPS and SharePoint Team Services are the first production software packages that ship with a default dashboard. Because the DD technology comprises reusable components, a Web part written for an SPS dashboard can be used immediately in an Office XP dashboard and vice versa. For a Web part to be exported to another dashboard, it must be saved in XML format and named with a `.dwp` extension.

A default DD is created when a workspace is created. The default DD allows a user to search for content, use the document management (DM) tools, use the Web discussions feature, subscribe to information, administer workspace settings, and modify the dashboard layout, styles, and content.

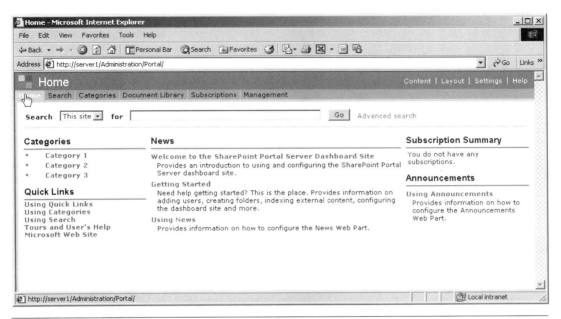

Figure 3–1 Home page for the default Digital Dashboard that installs with a new workspace

The default DD is composed of seven dashboards. Five of them are present for all users, one (Management) is viewable only to coordinators, and one more (Document Inspection) is hidden by default. These dashboards are presented as one dashboard in tabular format (see Figure 3–1). As you look at the following figures, you'll notice that each page looks like a regular Web page, but in reality, each page is a combination of Web parts designed to look a single page.

The seven dashboards are as follows:

- Home: The Home page is used to expose Web parts and other dashboards in the dashboard site. (Refer to Figure 3–1.)
- Categories: The Categories dashboard (Figure 3–2) displays the Category Information Web part and the Category Items Web part. If you have configured best bets for a category, a Best Bets Web part is also displayed. Notice that the Search Web part is displayed at the top of this dashboard and that it is accessed using the Categories tab on the Home page of the dashboard site.
- Document Library: The Document Library dashboard (Figure 3–3) displays the Folder Information and Folder Item Web parts. Again, notice that the Search Web part is displayed at the top.

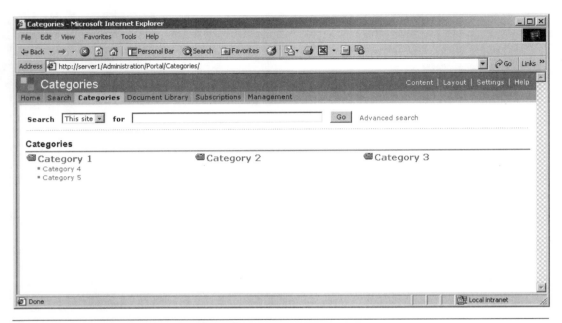

Figure 3–2 The Categories dashboard

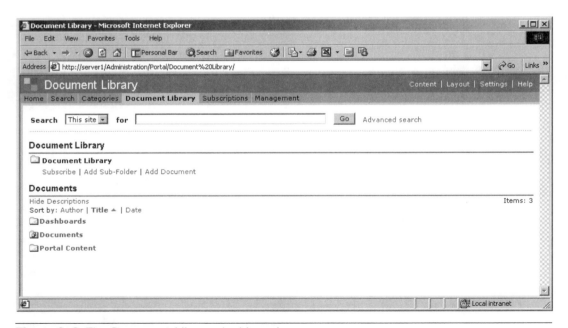

Figure 3–3 The Document Library dashboard

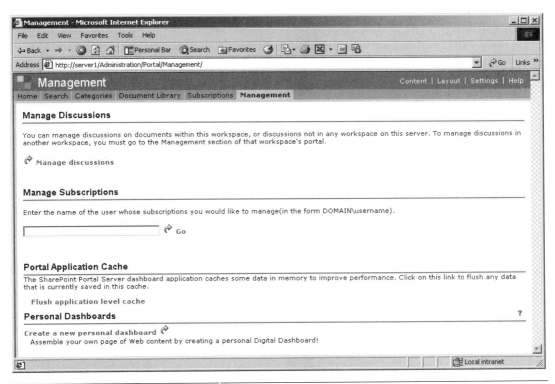

Figure 3–4 The Management dashboard

■ Management: The Management dashboard (Figure 3–4) displays management tools to the coordinator only and provides links to the Manage Discussions Web part. In this Web part, you can remove discussions associated with documents that are either internal or external to the workspace. A coordinator can also manage individual subscriptions using this Web part. Finally, this dashboard is where a coordinator can use the Flush Application Level Cache link to refresh the server's cache, which can become full at times if too many Web parts are cached on the server.

■ Search: The Search Web part allows a user to execute a search against the index in the workspace. On the Search dashboard (Figure 3–5), you will see both the Simple Search Web part and additional search options. The results of a search are displayed using four Web parts: Search Summary, Matching Categories, Best Bets, and Matching Documents.

■ Subscriptions: The Subscriptions dashboard (Figure 3–6) is used to display and manage subscriptions for your users. The subscriptions entered by

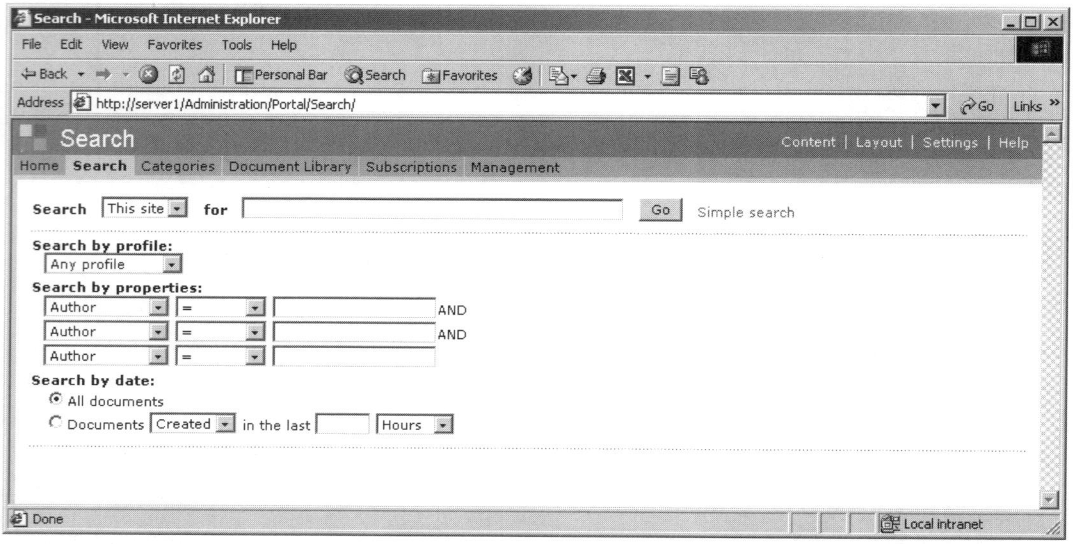

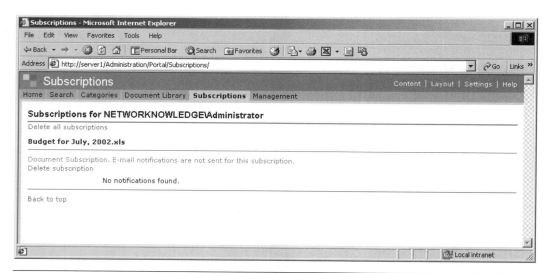

Figure 3–5 The Search dashboard

Figure 3–6 The Subscriptions dashboard

users are displayed in the Subscriptions dashboard and you, the coordinator, can manage them from there. Users have the option to clear notifications and to rerun and delete subscriptions.

■ Document Inspection: This dashboard (Figure 3–7), hidden by default, displays additional information about a document along with the Item Actions Web part. This dashboard can be seen by clicking the Show Actions link next to a document in the Document Library dashboard in the Search Results section.

The DD can be accessed by any user running a supported browser, including Microsoft's Internet Explorer 4.01 or later and Netscape's Navigator 4.73 or later. Browsers that run on a Macintosh or UNIX platform are not supported and won't work with SharePoint Portal Server.

Because the workspace is accessible from the browser, a user is not required to install the SPS client, although not doing so will mean that tight integration with the Office suite will not be available.

The folder structure of the DD can be seen under the Portal folder using the Web Folder client. You'll find the dashboards are dimmed, meaning that they are hidden by default. If you can't find them under the hidden Portal folder, be sure to use the View menu options on your Web Folder client and configure it to show hidden items. The Document Inspection dashboard is listed under the Stand-alone Dashboards folder (contents not shown).

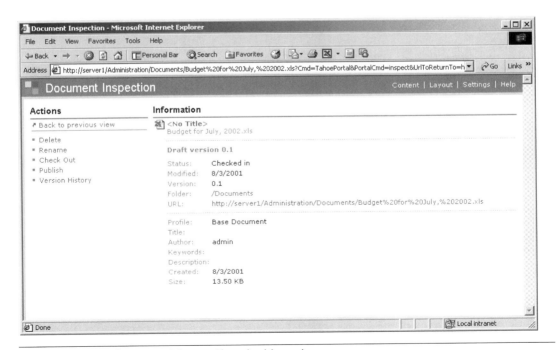

Figure 3–7 The Document Inspection dashboard

Creating a new dashboard that will appear as a tab on the default Home site is not as simple as creating a new folder under the Portal folder. Moreover, renaming a folder will not automatically rename the tabular name for that folder in the Home dashboard. The next section discusses how to customize your current dashboard settings and how to create new dashboards inside the SPS dashboard.

Customizing the Digital Dashboard

You can customize your dashboards using the default management tools that ship with SPS. Remember that these tools are available only to those who have been given the Coordinator security role in the workspace.

To customize a dashboard, click the Layout link in the upper-right corner of the home site. This action produces the Web Part Layout page (Figure 3–8). On this page, you'll see where each part is located relative to the overall page. If you want a Web part to appear in a different portion of the page, simply drag

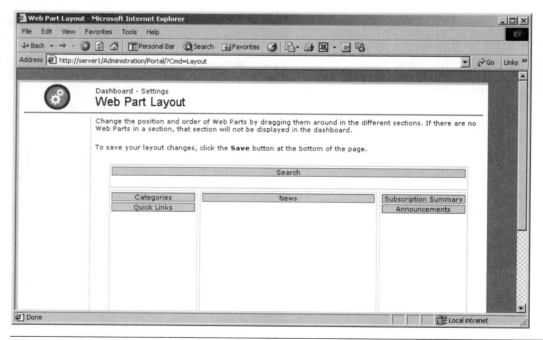

Figure 3–8 Web Part Layout page

and drop the part to the location and then click Save at the bottom of the page. You'll see the results when you next access the dashboard.

In this example, I moved the Quick Links Web part to a new location under the Announcements Web part. You can see the results in Figure 3–9. Note that this is not the page where you add or delete Web parts from your dashboard. You'll learn how to do this later in this chapter.

You can customize the DD settings by clicking the Settings link in the upper-right corner. The Settings page allows you to configure the following values:

- Display name: This is the name of the page in the title bar.
- Caption: This text is displayed above the title bar in which the display name appears.
- Description: This is for reference only. This text is not displayed anywhere.
- Auto-refresh: Here, you specify how often to refresh the dashboard. This value is in seconds.

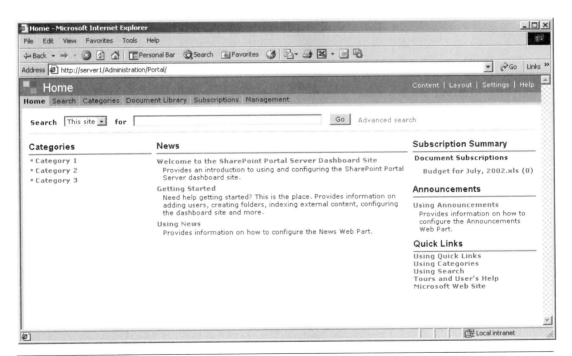

Figure 3–9 Default Digital Dashboard with the Quick Links Web part moved to new location

■ Style sheets: You select a cascading style sheet (CSS) to choose a pre-defined color package for the DD. You can also create your own CSS if you prefer.

If you click Show Advanced Settings, the Settings page will expand to include a number of important configuration options for the dashboard. Some of these options are illustrated in Figure 3–10.

■ Apply a customized cascading style sheet.
■ Specify a customized logo to appear in the title bar and navigation bar.
■ Change the order of the dashboard tabs in the navigation bar.
■ Direct the dashboard to check for updated versions of its Web parts and install them if there is a newer version on a master server.

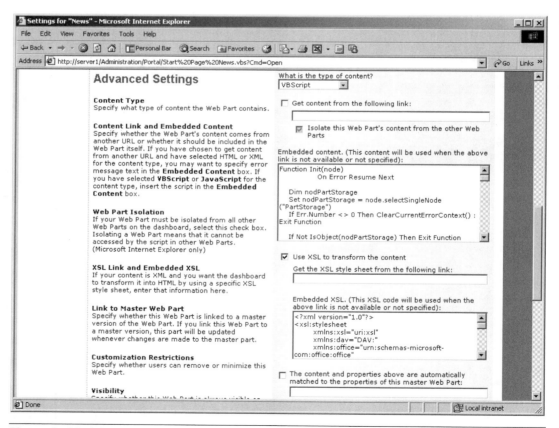

Figure 3–10 Advanced dashboard configuration options on the Settings Web page

- Specify a link for a customized Help file for the dashboard.
- Specify a location for storage of data used by the Web parts in the dashboard.

The Content page allows you to install and remove Web parts as needed. The Content page is accessed by clicking the Contents link in the upper-right corner of the Home page in the dashboard. When new Web parts are installed, they are displayed to all users by default. You can modify this default setting by clicking the Web part name, scrolling to the bottom of the General Settings page, and clicking Show Advanced Settings for the Web part. Near the bottom of the page, you'll find three user settings (Figure 3–11):

- Allow users to remove this Web part from their dashboard.
- Allow users to minimize this Web part on their dashboard.
- Make this Web part visible on the dashboard.

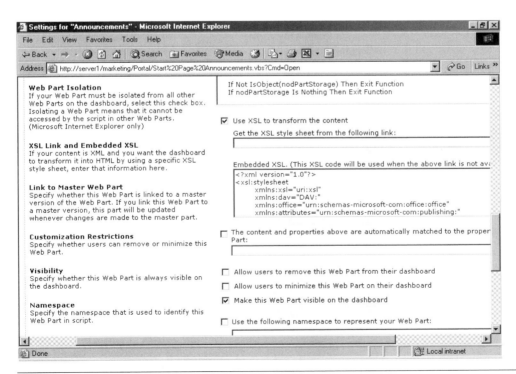

Figure 3–11 Content page for a dashboard

You should know that the wording of these settings is confusing. At face value, it seems that users can remove, minimize, or make visible Web parts in the dashboard on an individual basis. This is not the case. Only coordinators can perform these functions. This means that when you, for example, select to allow users to minimize a Web part, you're really only allowing coordinators to minimize a Web part when they are connected to the portal. Good ol' regular users won't have this option, even when the setting is selected in a Web part's properties.

From a user's perspective, Web parts are either there or they are not. They are either visible or invisible. So when you add a Web part, it's on the dashboard for all users to see.

Creating New Dashboards

SharePoint Portal Server ships with some useful management tools that allow you to create a new dashboard from within SPS. You don't need to know much programming, if any, to create a new dashboard. First, use your browser to set the focus on the dashboard in which you would like to create a new subdashboard. Then open the Contents by clicking the Content link in the upper-right part of the page. Scroll down to the bottom of the Content in the *<nameofdashboard>* Web page, and click the Create a Subdashboard link. You'll be presented with the General Settings page for your new dashboard, as illustrated in Figure 3–12. Configure the dashboard as you like, and then click Save. You'll immediately see the dashboard appear as a subdashboard in your dashboard site.

If you do this from the Home dashboard, the new dashboard will appear as another "main" dashboard to your users. So, if you want to create another main or top-level dashboard that appears as another tab in your overall portal, then create a subdashboard while focused on the Home dashboard.

After you've created the dashboard, you can populate it with Web parts from Microsoft or other vendors. You can even write your own Web parts, a subject covered in a little bit.

If you ever want to uninstall a dashboard from the default dashboard site, use the Web Folders interface to open the folders in the workspace, navigate to the Portal folder, and then delete the folder beneath the Portal folder that represents the dashboard you wish to uninstall. This action will cause the dashboard to disappear immediately. However, its tab may remain and, when clicked, will return a "Page Not Found" HTTP error message. To ensure that the tab does not appear when users refresh the Home dashboard site, flush the application-level cache in the Management dashboard (see the sidebar on page 62).

Another method of deleting a dashboard is to open its Settings and click the Delete Dashboard button. This button is available on all the dashboards except the Home and Document Inspection dashboards.

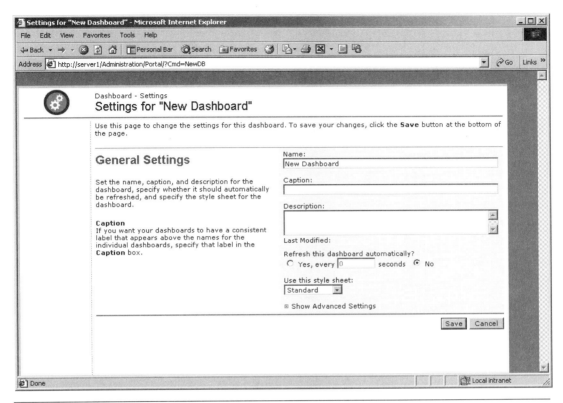

Figure 3–12 General Settings page for creating a new dashboard

SPS Dashboard Types

SharePoint Portal Server has two dashboard types: workspace dashboards and personal dashboards. Workspace dashboards are customized by the workspace coordinator, who controls the type and content of information on the dashboard. Web parts can be personalized, but only with the help of the workspace coordinator.

Personal dashboards must be allowed by the coordinator. However, once allowed, they can be fully customized by the user. Personal dashboards are held in the Dashboards folder of a workspace.

I've demonstrated how to create a new workspace dashboard, so now, let's look at how to create a new personal dashboard. First, be aware that, by default, the Web part to create a new personal dashboard is located on the Management dashboard. If you want this Web part to appear in the Home dashboard, you must export the Web part from the Management dashboard and import it into the Home dashboard.

Flushing the Application-Level Cache

To improve the performance of SPS, the store process caches some data in memory. The cache is stored and created on a Web-part-by-Web-part basis. If you make changes to data that, by default, is stored in the cache, you'll need to flush the cache to have the changes take effect. This also has an impact on permission changes to portal content. If you deny access to content that was previously available to users, they will continue to have access to the denied content until you flush the application-level cache.

Moreover, out of the box, the way the application-level cache is set up, it can work against you. If the first user to connect to content that is denied only to some users is a denied user, that permission assignment will be cached and applied to all users who try to access Web part. Similarly, if the first user to connect to content that is denied only to some users is an allowed user, that permission assignment will be cached and applied to all users.

Settings saved in the application cache are applied to all users, even if it is an incorrect application of a setting to a user. To work around this issue, perform the following tasks. First, open the Advanced settings of the Web part you need to modify. In the Should the Content of This Web Part Be Cached setting, select Per User. Save the Web part and flush the application; level cache. Now each user's settings will be saved in the application cache.

To export a Web part, open its settings under the Content link and scroll to the bottom of the page; then click the Export button. The Export Web Part to File dialog box will appear, and you can choose to save this Web part to a convenient location by specifying the directory location and clicking Save. Once you've exported the Web part, it's time to navigate back to the Home page, click the Contents link, and then click the Import a Web Part File link. Select the Personal Dashboards Web part in the Select Web Part File to Import dialog box, and click Open. By default, the Web part is set to install in the middle zone of the dashboard. You can move it to a different location by opening its settings and selecting a different zone. As illustrated in Figure 3–13, I've chosen to place this Web part in the left banner zone.

Once the Web part is located on the Home dashboard, users can use it to create their own personalized dashboards. To create a personalized dashboard, click on the link, and the General Settings page for the dashboard will appear. The default name will be the logged-on name of the user, but the user can change this if desired.

The default settings for the new dashboard are predefined by SPS and are held in the <workspacename>/portal/resources folder. Once created, the personalized dashboard will appear as a link inside the Dashboards folder

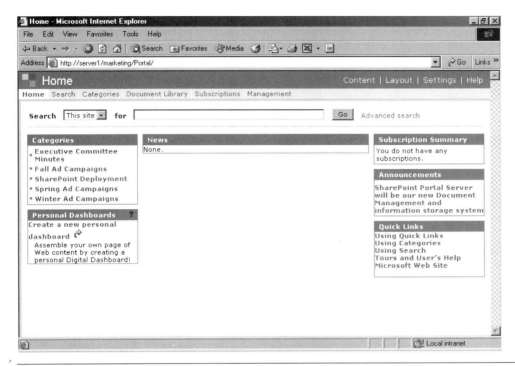

Figure 3–13 Personal Dashboard Web part in the left banner zone of the Home dashboard

on the Document Library dashboard. In Figure 3–14, I'm logged on as the Administrator for Server1, so my personalized dashboard is named Administrator.

Users can access their personal dashboard as they would any Web site: by entering the URL in the address bar of their browser, by creating a shortcut to the link on their desktop, by setting their personalized dashboard as their default Home page in their browser, or by using the link created in the Dashboards folder.

The default URL for a personal dashboard assumes the following syntax:

```
http://<servername>/<workspacename>/dashboards/<name_of_personal_dashboard>
```

Hence, for a server named Server1 and a workspace named Administration for a user named Russ, the URL to Russ's personal dashboard would be as follows:

```
http://server1/administration/dashboards/russ
```

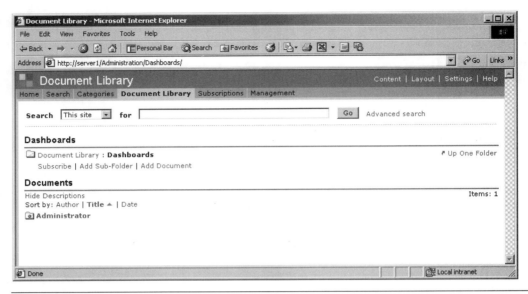

Figure 3–14 Administrator personal dashboard link

The user who creates the dashboard will be the dashboard's default coordinator. Interestingly, if a user is granted permissions to create her own personal dashboard, the workspace coordinator will have only Reader role permissions to it. The Everyone security group will have Reader role permissions, and security inheritance will be disabled by default.

NOTE: Only users who are authors or coordinators on the Dashboards folder can create personal dashboards from the Personal Dashboards Web part on the dashboard site. To give all users the ability to create their own personal dashboards, give the Everyone group Author permissions to the Dashboards folder. To disable a user from making changes to his personal dashboard, ensure that the Reader role is assigned for him. Also, to disable personal dashboard creation for all users, remove the Personal Dashboard Web part from the dashboard site.

Only coordinators can change these security settings, so if a user creates a new, personalized dashboard, she will still need to work with you, the coordinator, to change the permissions. To change permissions on a personalized dashboard, access the dashboard using a Web folder, navigate to the Dashboards folder, and open the folder. Each personal dashboard will appear as a folder. Open its properties, and then make the necessary changes on the Security tab.

NOTE: You may be wondering why I've not covered using SQL Server or Exchange public folders as a platform for hosting a Digital Dashboard for SharePoint Portal Server. The reason I've chosen not to discuss these platforms in this book is that Microsoft does not support these configurations, at least at the time of this writing. I will include a discussion of these platforms for the Digital Dashboard when Microsoft offers support for those configurations.

Creating New Web Parts

Now let's look at how to use existing HTML code to create a new Web part for your dashboard. You don't really need to be a programmer to do this, but you will need to know a few basics about HTML and XML if you're going to get into this on a regular basis. One of the main rules of thumb is that you should first try to find existing code before you attempt to write your own. Because I assume you're not a programmer, I'll demonstrate some nifty ideas to help you customize your portal.

NOTE: There are four types of Web parts: HTML, XML, VBScript, and JavaScript. As their names imply, each part can host different types of content. For instance, for pure HTML content, you use the advanced properties to configure the Web part to display HTML-formatted information. VBScript and JScript are excellent languages for passing information between Web parts on a dashboard. XML Web parts are the most versatile type because you can embed HTML code and script-based content inside XML code. You can find more information on this topic in the Digital Dashboard Resource Kit.

Adding a Google Search Web Part[1]

Many users use the Internet to conduct research. Some of the larger search engines, such as Google and AltaVista, are in regular use by users on your network. You'll need to check with Google regarding permission issues about the following demonstration, but this would be a great Web part addition to most dashboards.

First, navigate to the Google home page at `http://www.google.com`. Use your mouse to highlight the home page, right-click, and select Copy in the context menu. Then open FrontPage, create a new file, and navigate to the Normal tab. Right-click anywhere inside this tab, and select Paste from the context menu. The Google page should appear.

---

[1] Google name and graphic are used with permission.

Now, this is where it gets to be fun. Delete everything on the page except the Google graphic, the search part, and the Google Search button. Then go to the HTML page, and copy all the code to the Clipboard.

Go back to SPS, and create a new Web part by clicking the Contents link and selecting the link to create a new Web part. Name the part Google Search Web Part, and choose to have it appear in the top banner. Then, if you want the search results to appear in a different window, be sure to add the target command when specifying the source for the Web part. Here is the complete set of code for this Web part:

```html
<html>

<head>
<meta http-equiv="Content-Type" content="text/html; charset=windows-1252">
<meta name="GENERATOR" content="Microsoft FrontPage 4.0">
<meta name="ProgId" content="FrontPage.Editor.Document">
<title>New Page 1</title>
</head>

<body>

<center><img alt="Google" src="http://www.google.com/images/
  title_homepage4.gif" width="205" height="75"><br>
<br>
<form name="f" action="http://www.google.com/search" method="get"
     target="_blank">
  <table cellSpacing="0" cellPadding="0">
    <tbody>
      <tr vAlign="center" align="middle">
        <td width="75"> </td>
        <td align="middle"><input maxLength="256" size="55" name="q"
             framewidth="4"><br>
          <input type="submit" value="Google Search" name="btnG"></td>
       <td vAlign="top" noWrap align="left"><font face="arial,sans-serif"
         size="-2"> </font></td>
      </tr>
    </tbody>
  </table>
</form>
 </center>

</body>

</html>
>
```

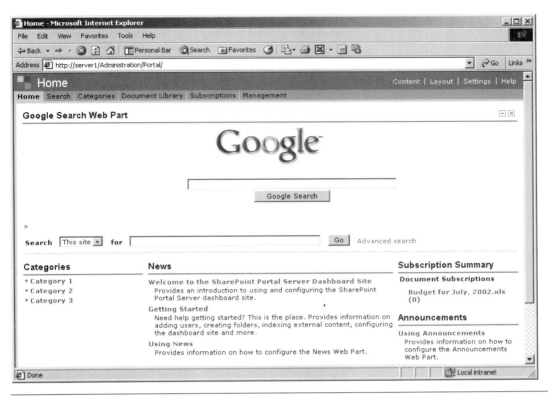

Figure 3–15 Google Web part on Home dashboard

Figure 3–15 illustrates what this Web part looks like if it is placed in the top zone of the Web page. Like any other Web part, it can be moved to another part of the dashboard to meet your users' needs, or it can be set up to start minimized instead of maximized, as illustrated here. In addition, you can place the Web part in a public gallery from which users can pull the part into their own personalized dashboards. When working with proprietary names like this on your dashboard, it is best to secure written permission.

Adding Web Parts from the Microsoft Gallery

Web parts can be imported from any source. Microsoft has a Web parts gallery that can be accessed at `http://www.microsoft.com/sharepoint/downloads/webparts/default.asp`. On this site, you'll find a host of Web parts developed by third-party vendors and many that were developed by Microsoft, such as MSNBC Weather. Remember that you must have configured the ServerXMLHTTP object's proxy settings to import Web parts from the Internet. To learn how to configure these settings, please see Chapter 4.

In the Content link from a dashboard, you'll also find a link to a smaller Web Part Gallery, and that link automatically connects to a smaller list of Microsoft Web parts that can be downloaded quickly into your portal. This list of Web parts is represented in the larger Web parts link mentioned in the preceding paragraph.

To add a Web part from the Microsoft gallery, click the Contents link, and then click the Microsoft Web Part Gallery link. This will take you to a Web parts gallery location on Microsoft's Web site. Select the Web parts you want to use, agree to the licensing agreement, and then let them download and install. This happens automatically. Then click Save, and *bing-badda-boom*, the Web parts are installed into your portal.

Table 3–1 lists the free Web parts that are available for download from Microsoft's site. All these Web parts are found in the Default Web Part Gallery. You might find other locations that offer Web parts as well.

Table 3–1 Free Web parts from Microsoft's Web site

Web Part	Function
Content Viewer	Used to view a file, folder, or Web page within a Web part on the DD
Date Header	Displays current date at the top of your portal Web page
Microsoft Office Spreadsheet	Excel spreadsheet in a Web part*
Outlook Calendar	Used to view personal calendar in the mailbox*
Outlook Contacts	Used to view personal contacts in your mailbox*
Outlook Messages	Used to view personal e-mail*
Outlook Notes	Used to manage personal notes*
Outlook Tasks	Used to manage your personal to-do list*
Simple HTML Viewer	Simple HTML editor
Web Links	Used to create and manage a custom list of links
MSN Encarta Reference	Used to search the *Encarta* reference encyclopedia or dictionary
MSN MoneyCentral Stock Ticker	Used to view stock information and financial headlines
MSN Search	Used to search the Web
MSN MoneyCentral Search	Used to search MSN MoneyCentral Search for news and information

*Requires Office XP and IE 5.0 or later

Table 3–1 Free Web parts from Microsoft's Web site *(continued)*

Web Part	Function
MSN MoneyCentral Stock Quotes	Used to look up stock quotes
MSNBC Business News	Used to view the latest business news headlines
MSNBC Stock News	Used to view stock headlines about your personal list of stocks
MSNBC Stock Quote List	Used to view a customized list of stock quotes in one Web part
MSNBC Weather	Used to view your local weather

Most of the other Web parts at `http://www.microsoft.com/sharepoint/downloads/webparts/default.asp` will require you to do one or more of the following: register with the Web part owner, pay for the Web part, or copy HTML code to your server and finish creating the Web part yourself. Many Web parts are proprietary to Microsoft's own product, and thus the Web part is not useful to you unless you're running Microsoft's application.

Creating a Personal Contacts Dashboard

This section demonstrates how to create a dashboard that can appear in either the default dashboard site or a personal dashboard that is dedicated to holding each user's contacts database. Users could also use these instructions to create a Contacts dashboard inside their personal dashboard. Such a dashboard might have its own set of subdashboards, each one dedicated to a certain type of contact, such as customers, vendors, professional contacts, or employees. By the way, you'll need to have installed Office XP Professional and Internet Explorer 5.0 or later before you can create a Contacts dashboard.

The first step is to navigate to the Home dashboard and create a subdashboard as described earlier in this chapter. A sample name for this dashboard might be "My Contacts." Next, import the Contact Web part from Microsoft's Web Part Gallery and configure its advanced settings to force the Web part to run maximized in the center banner.

Once the Web part is saved, the first time you connect to the dashboard, the Office XP Outlook client installation wizard will start asking whether you want to connect to an Exchange Server for e-mail. Click No and then click Finish. Soon, you'll be connected to the Contacts Web part on the dashboard. Note that I'm assuming here that you already have an Outlook profile created. If not, then select Yes in the wizard and connect to your exchange server.

This gives you a subdashboard whose contact information is personalized to each user based on her logon information. This configuration gives her her own Contacts list from her personal mailbox on the Exchange 2000 Server. What I've described here is not a company-wide contacts list that can be shared by all users in the organization. That's described next.

Creating Outlook Functionality in a Default Company-Wide Dashboard for Each User

To expand on the previous discussion, it might be desirable to have your users use the dashboard for their common Outlook tasks instead of opening Outlook itself. For instance, the following Outlook Web parts are ready for download from Microsoft's Web Part Gallery:

- Tasks
- Journal
- Messages
- Contacts
- Calendar

The Messages Web part includes inbox, outbox, drafts, and sent items functionality. We are accustomed to seeing these functions as separate folders in the Outlook client, but all of them are presented in the same Web part for the dashboard. The Calendar Web part includes day, week, and month views. By default, all these Web parts are generated with the setting that allows the user to minimize the Web part if necessary. Figure 3–16 illustrates these Web parts in a customized Outlook Tools dashboard.

TIP: If you want to create a link on the Home dashboard that invokes the user's local Outlook program outside a Web part or the dashboard, use the following: for Outlook XP, `outlook://inbox`, and for Office 2000, `outlook:inbox`. For quick invocation of the Outlook client from within the portal, you could place such a link in the Quick Links Web part.

You can name the dashboard "My Mailbox" or "My Outlook" or some other name that your users will easily recognize as the location where they can find and perform many of their mailbox functions.

Now, suppose you want to place a company-wide Contacts folder or company-wide Calendar folder on your portal for overall contact management or scheduling information. How do you do this? Really, it's simpler than you think.

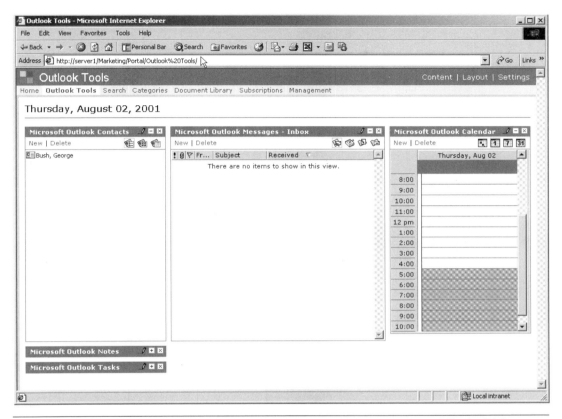

Figure 3–16 Outlook Web parts in a single dashboard with the Notes and Tasks Web parts minimized

First, open the browser on your SharePoint Portal Server and enter the following URL:

```
http://<servername>/public/applications/workspace
```

Then create a new folder by right-clicking the Applications folder, selecting New Folder, and then configuring the type of folder you want to create. If it's a Calendar folder, select Appointment Items. If it's a Contact folder, select Contacts. Click OK and ensure that the folder has been created successfully. Next, right-click the new folder and select Open in New. Then copy the URL from the address bar of the new window. Create a new Web part, and then paste the URL into the Get Content from the Following Link property. Choose Isolate, and make any other configuration changes you desire. Save it, and there you go. You'll now have a Web part that displays overall company contacts or schedules that are hosted within SharePoint Portal Server.

But suppose you don't want to create a *new* folder because you already have this information sitting in a public folder in Exchange. How do you get that same public folder to appear in a Web part? Following is the code[1] to help you do that.

ASP code to query WSS with ADO:

```
<h3>Retrieving contact details using ADO</h3>
<%
set rsContacts = Server.CreateObject("ADODB.Recordset")
set conn = server.CreateObject("ADODB.Connection")
sConnection = "Provider=Microsoft Exchange OLE DB Provider;Data
Source=http://pctim/public/public contacts" conn.open sConnection
sQuery = "SELECT ""urn:schemas:contacts:fileas"", " sQuery = sQuery +
  """http://schemas.microsoft.com/mapi/email1emailaddress"""
sQuery = sQuery + "FROM scope('shallow traversal of ""http://pctim/
  public/public contacts""')" sQuery = sQuery + " ORDER
BY ""urn:schemas:contacts:fileas""" rsContacts.Source = sQuery
set rsContacts.ActiveConnection = conn
rsContacts.open
response.write "<table border=1>"
for iCount = 1 to 10
Response.write "<tr><td>" + rsContacts.Fields(0) + "</td>"
Response.write "<td>" + rsContacts.Fields(1) + "</td></tr>"
rsContacts.MoveNext
next
response.write "</table>"
rsContacts.close
conn.close
%>
```

ASP code using WebDAV:

```
<h3>Retrieving contact details using WebDAV</h3>
<%
set senddoc = createobject("MSXML2.DOMDocument")
set responsedoc = createobject("MSXML2.DOMDocument")
strURL = "http://pctim/public/public contacts/"
Set pi = senddoc.createProcessingInstruction("xml", "version=""1.0""")
```

---

[1] Published in Application Development Advisor (www.appdevadvisor.co.uk). Code is used with permission.

```
senddoc.appendChild pi Set node = senddoc.createNode(1,
"searchrequest", "DAV:") Set senddoc.documentElement = node Set node2
= senddoc.createNode(1, "sql", "DAV:") node.appendChild node2
Set query =
  senddoc.createTextNode("select""urn:schemas:contacts:fileas"",""http://
  schemas.microsoft.com/mapi/email1emailaddress"" from """ & strURL & """
  ")
node2.appendChild query
Set req = CreateObject("MSXML2.XMLHTTP")
req.open "SEARCH", strURL, False, "yourdomain\yourusername",
"yourpassword"
req.setrequestheader "Translate", "f"
req.setrequestheader "Content-Type", "text/xml" req.setrequestheader
"Depth", "0" req.send senddoc
set responsedoc = req.responseXML
response.write "<table border=1>"
Set objNodeList = responsedoc.getElementsByTagName("a:prop")
For i = 0 To (objNodeList.length - 1)
Set objPropNodes = objNodeList.item(i).childNodes
response.write "<tr>"
For j = 0 To (objPropNodes.length - 1)
Set objNode = objPropNodes.item(j)
Response.Write ("<td>" + objPropNodes.item(j).text + "</td>")
Next
response.write "</tr>"
Next
response.write "</table>"
%>
```

Using Office XP in the Portal

Microsoft Office documents can be saved as individual documents or as Web parts and then published on the dashboard. This means that documents, such as memos, budgets, vacation schedules, project schedules, and so on, can be published immediately on the dashboard. Depending on how you publish the information, it also can be dynamically updated in the portal as the source document is updated.

I'll demonstrate how to save an Excel spreadsheet as a company news item that outlines a fictitious budget for the Networknowledge company. You open Excel, create your budget, and save it as a Web page (Figure 3–17). In this example, I've chosen to publish the file, and that invokes the Publish as Web Page dialog box in Excel, as illustrated in Figure 3–18. When you select AutoRepublish Every Time, Excel updates your Web part each time the original file is saved. After making this selection, click Publish.

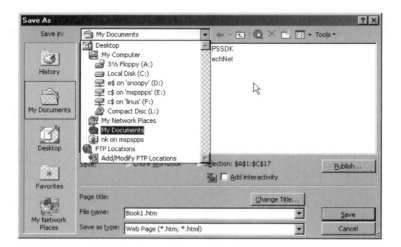

Figure 3–17 Saving the Networknowledge budget as a Web page. Notice that I'm using the client-side Web folder option to specify where I'd like this document to be saved.

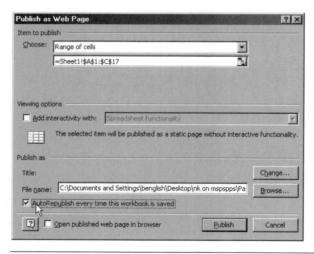

Figure 3–18 Publish as Web Page dialog box in Excel

After you click Publish a second time, the document's profile appears (Figure 3–19). After you configure the document's profile, it is saved to the News folder in the workspace and appears as a news item in the dashboard (Figure 3–20).

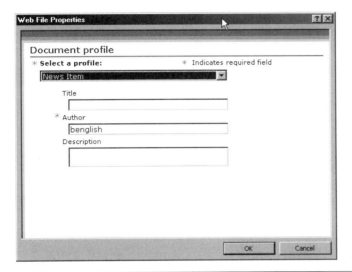

Figure 3–19 Configuring the document's profile

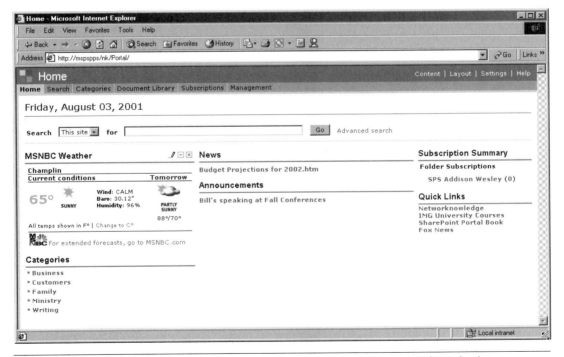

Figure 3–20 Networknowledge budget document appearing as a news item in the NK workspace

Now, not only can you save documents directly to the workspace using Office XP, but you can also create Web parts whose functionality comprises an Office XP document. To use Office XP to create a Web part, you must save the document to a personal dashboard. To demonstrate this, let's create a spreadsheet called "Current Sales to Date" that will appear, not as a news item, but rather as a Web part on the Home dashboard. Such a Web part could be used to keep users up-to-date on inportant information.

The first step is to create the Web part on your personal dashboard and then import it to the Home dashboard. In my example, I'll create a new personal dashboard, which I'll name Bill (that's creative, eh? <g>). Then you save an Excel document to the dashboard as a Web part.

When you save the document to your personal dashboard as a Web page, you're presented with the Web File Properties dialog box asking you to create a new Web part on your dashboard. I'll name the sample new Web part "Current Sales Figures." Then you click Save (Figure 3–21). Now you have a new Web part that can be imported to the Home dashboard for everyone's viewing pleasure.

Note that you do not need to save the file as a Web part. Interestingly, if you save it as a good ol' Excel spreadsheet, the Web part will be created, but when it attempts to load in the user's browser, the user will be asked if he would like to open the file from its present location or save the file locally. Hence, if you want to create a Web part composed of an Office document *and*

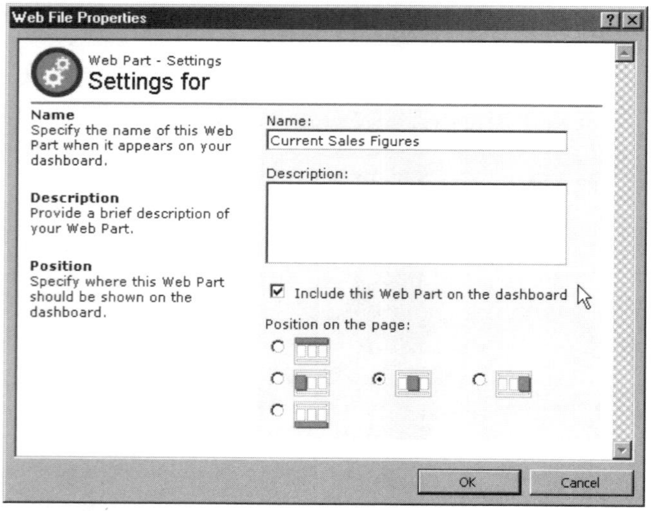

Figure 3–21 Web File Properties dialog box

want to make that document available for download from within the Web part, then don't save the document as a Web page. Instead, save it as a native document. Then, when the Web part is built in the user's browser, he will be given the choice to either view or download the document.

The Resource Kit and the Digital Dashboard

Some cool resource kit tools and Web parts ship with the SharePoint Portal Server Resource Kit. This kit can be purchased or found online at `http://www.microsoft.com/sharepoint/techinfo/reskit/default.asp`. One section on Web parts is different from the Web part galleries I've been discussing here. These Web parts are available for use for free from this location.

The resource kit contains several Web parts that I discuss here. I don't discuss them all, but there are a few I'd like to point out.

Add a Link to the Dashboard Site Home Page

This Web part allows users to add announcements, news items, and quick links directly to the portal (Figure 3–22). Even though the Web part can be published on the Home dashboard, you'll still need Author or Coordinator privileges to modify the portal content. There is also an option to remove content in these folders, and that option uses the Web folders client. This is a handy Web part to make available to those who configure portal content. Very nice.

Announcements Authoring Tool

This Web part updates the standard Announcements Web part that ships with SPS. It lets you create content without the use of FrontPage or Word. A script must be run, and then a Web part must be imported to make this work.

You'll encounter a couple of screwy things. First, if you're importing this into the Home dashboard, you'll find that in the layout view of the dashboard, two Announcements Web parts will appear. There will also be two Announcements Web parts in the Content listing of the Home dashboard. Yet, from the browser, you'll see only one Announcements Web part (Figure 3–23). In this updated Announcements Web part, there is a link called Add New Announcement. This link invokes a screen in which you can create a new announcement title and give it a description and an abstract along with start and end dates. If you want to edit the announcement, you can call up a simple text editor with some

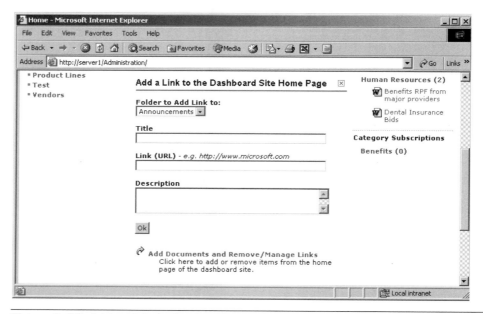

Figure 3–22 Add a Link to the Dashboard Site Home Page Web part

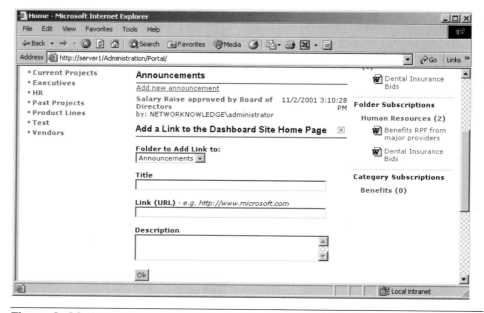

Figure 3–23 Announcements Authoring Tool Web part

graphics capabilities, allowing you to create visually stimulating and interesting announcements. Use this tool to spruce up your announcements. Note that you'll need Author privileges to create a new announcement using this tool.

Category Management

This Web part allows you to manage Web parts using the portal instead of the Web folders client. Install this Web part on your dashboard if you need to manage categories from various computers, some of which do not have the SPS client installed.

Server Content Source Status Tool

This one is cool. With this tool, you can see the current status of all your content sources from one location (see Figure 3–24). This Web part installs cleanly and gives you a visual representation of the content source's status in a neat table. This part is dynamic, so as you add and delete content sources, information will be updated in the Web part.

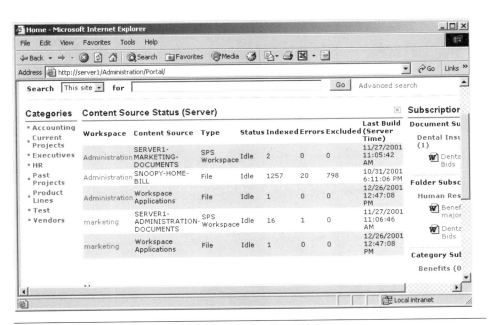

Figure 3–24 Server Content Source Status Tool Web part

Document Status

This Web part shows to each user the documents that she has checked out, which ones are awaiting her approval, and any documents she has authored that are awaiting the approval of others.

To install this Web part, you first run a script and then import the Web part. Once installed, it will appear as a Web part, by default, in the left column of your Home dashboard. The title of the Web part will change to reflect the choice of document status you want displayed. The default is Checked Out to You. Use the drop-down arrow to make a different selection. It's recommended that you install this Web part on the Home dashboard (Figure 3–25).

Property-Based Browsing

This tool extends the Advanced Search Web part by allowing it to search on list values. I recommend that you install this Web part on the Search dashboard. Figure 3–26 illustrates this Web part. Possible choices are listed in the Choose a Value drop-down list. If no matching document exists, this will be displayed.

Interestingly, if you choose a property to search on and there are no matching documents, the Web part will automatically give you a second drop-down

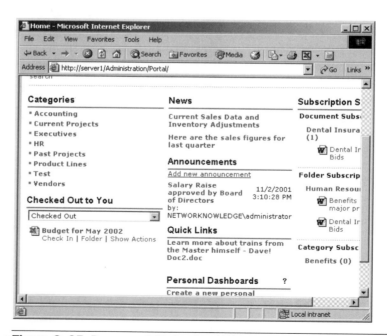

Figure 3–25 Document Status Tool Web Part

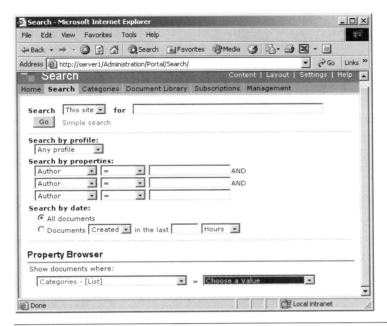

Figure 3–26 Property-Based Browsing Web Part

box, where you can choose a different property to search on. The second property search will be combined with the first in an AND Boolean search string, meaning that the document must meet the search criteria for both the first and the second query strings.

New tools are often released by Microsoft. Be sure to regularly check Microsoft's Web site for new tools at `http://www.microsoft.com/sharepoint/techinfo/reskit/default.asp`.

Summary

Working with Web parts in the DD is not difficult, and you don't need an extensive programming background. As this technology grows, you'll want to stay abreast of the public Web parts that are being created. Microsoft maintains its own Web Part Gallery, and it provides links to a more extensive gallery that comprises third-party vendor Web parts. This link can be found at `http://www.microsoft.com/sharepoint/portalserver.asp`.

Creating a dynamic and effective portal solution is no small task. Much of the work goes on behind the scenes—talking with managers and users about how they would like to see the portal developed and understanding what kinds of functionalities are necessary to enable your users to perform their jobs effectively. Chapter 4 outlines some planning issues that you should consider before you ever put a CD-ROM in the CD-ROM drive, and Chapter 5 explains how to install SharePoint Portal Server. It's going to be fun, so read on, my friend.

PART II

Planning and Installation

Planning for SharePoint Portal Server 2001

Like Chapter 2, this is another chapter that you might feel you can bypass. Again, I encourage you not to do this, because this chapter has important information that will help you correctly implement SharePoint in your environment and thus reduce the support your SPS implementation will need.

Planning issues have become paramount in the world of Microsoft products. When Windows NT 4.0 and earlier versions were the reigning operating systems, you could pretty much botch a Windows NT 4.0 installation and still come out okay at the end of the day. This enabled many clueless consultants to perform adequately. However, this is not true for Windows 2000 and Windows .NET Server installations, nor is it true of SPS. You must know what you're going to do before you do it. Doing your planning work will result in a better-run SPS environment and one that will meet the needs of your organization.

This chapter focuses on several important topics. First, it covers how to plan for an SPS deployment. Second, it discusses capacity planning issues. Third, it looks at how to plan for SPS with the Web store in mind. Then it turns its attention to planning for and implementing SPS over the Internet.

NOTE: Security planning issues are covered in Chapter 13.

Planning Your SharePoint Portal Server Deployment

A good deployment plan will help you streamline your document management processes and present a dashboard to your users that will effectively help them do their jobs. In planning for SPS, you need to look at the server, network, portal and dashboard, document folder, category, and client planning issues.

Server Planning Issues

Out of the box, SPS can be used in various ways. First, it can be used mainly as a document management product that allows groups to collaborate on the development of documents though the check-out, check-in, publishing, and approval functions. Or it can be used mainly as a server that indexes content held in various content sources, which are then searched by users using the Search Web part. Third, it can be used mainly as a turn-key intranet and portal solution. A single server can perform all three of these functions, or these functions can be quarantined onto different servers. This means that you need a good understanding of how your SPS server will be used before you can do much other planning.

Every installation is unique, so here are the core issues to consider when planning your server topology. First, take a look at the number of users and the number of documents that will be hosted in your SPS environment. A high number of both might indicate a need for multiple document management (DM) servers. If you need to host multiple document sets on multiple workspaces spread out over multiple servers, then you might need to somehow tie all these workspaces together for search and indexing purposes. Remember that workspaces can cross-search one another, and this functionality will help users find documents that have something in common and are also hosted in different workspaces. The ability to cross-search workspaces ties them together into a unified body of knowledge that is available to all users in your company (assuming that all users have the Reader role on each workspace).

Second, look at the number of searches that will be conducted on your SPS server. Even in smaller environments with relatively few documents, you might find that it's best to install an SPS server used only for searching. The greater the number of search requests, the more likely it is that you'll need an SPS server dedicated to this function.

Third, you must decide how many workspaces you'll have and whether all of them will be hosted on a single physical server or dispersed over a range of servers. Remember that there is a supported limit of 15 workspaces per server. Although you can install more than 15 workspaces on a single server, this configuration isn't supported by Microsoft Product Support Services. So, if you're worried about the load that users will place on your server, it won't do any good to create multiple workspaces to separate the indexing, searching, and DM functions because all of them will be using the same physical server resources.

It does make sense to have multiple workspaces on a single server when you need different category structures for different departments or divisions. It also makes sense when you want your company's mission-critical documents to reside in a separate workspace for security, indexing, and search purposes.

It makes sense to host your SPS installations on multiple servers if the load will be more than a single server can handle. Other considerations might include political issues, such as a department wanting to install its own SPS server, or geographical considerations, such as placing an SPS server near those users who will access it most often.

Top 10 Planning Issues

Here's a handy checklist of planning issues to help you ensure that you've not missed an important planning step:

- Basic setup and configuration
- Taxonomy, categories, and profiles
- Client setup
- Management of workspaces and servers
- Backup and restoration of a workspace (and server duplication)
- Security and virus protection
- Document management
- Configuring content sources
- Index server setup
- Deployment topology planning

Using this list, you can easily begin to develop an overall plan for your new SPS environment. If you already have SPS deployed on your network, you can use this list to hone your ongoing plan to ensure that you don't omit key areas.

The Big Picture: Deployment Scenarios

Microsoft proffers four SPS deployment scenarios: group document management, group search, corporate search, and search and aggregated document management. But even though these scenarios are helpful, I've found them to be somewhat arbitrary. In reality, you'll have three functions (DM, search and indexing, and portal use) correlated with three basic demand scenarios (low, medium, and high demand). Generally, if any one of the three functions will experience high demand, you'll probably want to quarantine that function on a separate server and not just a separate workspace. This is because a high-demand environment will stress the physical server, which may be best managed by dedicating a server to the task.

If you expect the other functions to experience a medium amount of demand and if the server's physical resources can handle the stress, then I suggest placing the higher-demand function in its own workspace but on the same server with other workspaces.

Of course, low-demand environments are the most easily managed from a resource standpoint because they present little opportunity to maximize the server's resources.

Remember, *you decide what is low, medium, and high* demand for your environment. Microsoft doesn't do this for you. If you're looking for specific capacity planning numbers, see "Capacity Planning Your SharePoint Portal Servers" later in this chapter.

Table 4–1 may aid your understanding of how to deploy the three main functions of SPS given the three different demand levels.

One area not discussed in Microsoft SPS planning white papers is heavy use of the portal. In my estimation, as the portal replaces the desktop (no, I'm not kidding), SharePoint administrators will be faced with the prospect of separating out high-demand portal functions to individual servers. As with the search and DM functions, which are routed through IIS, it stands to reason that heavily accessed Web parts could place as great a drain on IIS as does heavy DM use or heavy search use. As Web parts become increasingly common, they will also become increasingly complex, expanding their functionality and services. As users become accustomed to using Web parts in place of certain

Table 4–1 Demand levels and SPS core functions matrix

Function	Low Demand	Medium Demand	High Demand
Document management	You can implement DM with other SPS functions on a single server.	You may need to use multiple workspaces on a single server or multiple workspaces hosted by multiple servers.	Seriously consider hosting multiple workspaces over multiple servers.
Search and indexing	You can implement this with other SPS functions on a single server.	You may need to use a single workspace for search and indexing features. This may or may not be best to host on the same physical server with other SPS functions.	Seriously consider placing the indexing of content sources on one physical server, having users search the indexes on a second physical server and having portal and DM functions hosted on other physical servers.

Table 4–1 Demand levels and SPS core functions matrix *(continued)*

Function	Low Demand	Medium Demand	High Demand
Portal use	You can implement this with other SPS functions on a single server.	Stress-test your IIS services to determine how many users can access the ASP pages before adverse effects take hold. Consider hosting often-accessed Web parts on a separate portal. The downside is that users may be forced to enter multiple URLs to access different functions of SPS.	Consider creating a unified portal that will redirect users to other Web pages hosting the high-demand Web parts. Also, consider ways to minimize the number of URLs users must access to gain entry to all SPS functions, including search and DM functions.

applications, users will place greater stress on IIS services that are not related to DM and search functions. Hence, there will be an increased need to view the portal itself as a core function of SPS that may need to be transferred to individual servers or even a farm of servers.

Network Planning

The first step in network planning is to ensure that you are running TCP/IP. If you run any other protocol for SPS, you'll soon be installing TCP/IP. Second, you can install SharePoint Portal Server 2001 in a Windows NT 4.0 or Windows 2000 domain. If it is installed in a Windows NT domain, you must configure a Windows 2000 server as a member of the domain in order for SPS to work with the domain's security accounts database. Also, if you want to use a fully qualified domain name (FQDN) together with index workspace propagation, both the index server and the destination SPS server must be in a Windows 2000 domain.

If the SPS server is to be made available over the Internet, be sure to install SPS in the language of the workspaces you'll need. For instance, you cannot install the French version of SPS and then create an English workspace. You can, however, install the French version of Windows 2000 and then install the German version of SPS. In other words, the workspaces must be in the same language as the SPS platform, but the SPS operating system does not need to be in the same language as the Windows 2000 operating system.

Finally, if you create a workspace in one language, you can add content from another language and have that content indexed and crawled by a client of that language. For instance, you could create a workspace in French, add English documents to the workspace, and access them using the English client to SPS.

NOTE: Subscription notifications are always generated in the workspace language. There is no support for a separate client language for subscription notifications.

Portal and Dashboard Planning

Because your users will see the Digital Dashboard (DD) often, it would be wise to carefully consider how it will be configured. However, before you begin configuring your portal, you must first assess your existing content, identify the needs and habits of your users, and then outline your deployment goals.

NOTE: The term *portal* is used to denote a single location from which users can access all the information and applications needed to perform their jobs. *Digital Dashboard* is a Microsoft term used to describe the technology used by Microsoft to build a portal. In real life, the terms *portal* and *dashboard* are sometimes used interchangeably, and I will do the same in this section. If I refer to the *Digital Dashboard*, you can assume I'm referring to Microsoft's technology. But if I refer to a *portal* or *dashboard*, you can assume that I'm referring to a portal developed using DD technology.

Here are some key questions to ask during the assessment phase for the dashboard:

- Who produces the company's content?
- Who manages the company's content?
- Where is it stored now?
- What content, if any, will you be migrating to SPS?
- How will the content be migrated?
- What is the purpose of the content?
- Is it structured or unstructured content?
- Who are the current users of the content?
- How do they find relevant documents currently?

If you can't answer these questions satisfactorily, perhaps you should consider taking a user survey, which might include questions such as these:

- What are the three most often accessed information sources you use to do your job?
- What type of content do you normally work with—database, Office document, e-mail, customized application in a public folder, other?
- How do you normally access this information?
- What sources of information would you like to have more easily accessible?
- How would you prefer to find your information?
- What information could be included in the portal that would help you perform your job more effectively?

Questions like these can give you rich information as you plan your dashboard. Look for common threads in the responses, which are likely to be varied. If it's impossible to pin down a set of common threads, you may need to rewrite the survey to obtain better information.

You should also be planning structured training for your users on how to use the portal and the core Web parts. For example, they should know how to use the Search Web part to find information using a keyword search, using a customized search, or by browsing through the category or folder hierarchies. Because users are accustomed to searching for information using the browsing method, most of their training should be in browsing categories or using the Search Web part.

You might also find that users have a difficult time tracking revisions to documents that are passed around in e-mails. If they do, teach them how to use the document versioning feature. The check-out, check-in, and publishing features are not as intuitive as you might think. Users should receive specific training on these DM functions so that you don't get an avalanche of Help desk calls after SPS is implemented. Moreover, approvers should be trained on how to approve or decline documents awaiting their approval.

If you find that information must be displayed quickly for the entire organization, use the Announcements and Quick Links Web parts on the Home page of the portal to quickly display information on the Home dashboard. If users who are collaborating to develop a document cannot find a private place in which to work on it, be sure to host their content in enhanced folders in the workspace.

If you find that the standard portal configuration that installs with SPS does not fully meet your needs, consider installing or deleting Web parts as needed. To learn how to install or remove Web parts from the dashboard, please refer to Chapter 3. Also, be sure to check out the Web parts in the SharePoint Resource Kit and other vendor-specific Web parts that might enhance your users' productivity.

Document Folder Structure

Once you've gathered your data and have made some decisions about the dashboard, category, and folder hierarchies, it's time to start preparing the workspace to hold the content and accept client calls for it. Remember that the workspace can be accessed using a Web browser, Windows Explorer, and, when the client extensions are installed, Office 2000 or higher. If you want to support only the browser, don't install the SPS client. However, this means that the extensions for the Office products will not be installed. If you don't install the SharePoint client on your own workstation, you won't be able to manage the workspace very well because most management activities are accomplished through the Web Folders client.

One warning here: You really can't decide how to create the document folder hierarchy until you've first learned about how your company creates and organizes information. If you implement an incorrect, intricate document folder hierarchy, fixing it could prove to be time-consuming. And as you'll read in a moment, my advice is to spend less time on the document hierarchy and more time on the category and keyword lists.

When you create a new folder structure, it is wise to bear in mind the differences between standard and enhanced folders. Documents held in standard folders can use role-based security, document metadata, category assignments, and indexing of both the content and the metadata. Documents held in enhanced folders can use these features plus the collaboration functions: versioning, check-out, check-in, approval, and publishing. Documents in standard folders are automatically published in whatever state they are in, meaning that there is no document privacy during development. Except for those documents that can be viewed publicly, you should plan to develop documents in enhanced folders to provide the additional functionality and privacy.

There is one exception to that advice: When you're hosting compound, or multipart, documents, they can be developed and hosted only in standard folders. A *compound* document contains linked or embedded data from other programs. If your users need privacy while developing these documents, you must instruct them to develop each part of the document as a separate document in an enhanced folder, with a view to joining the parts into a compound document only when it is time to publish it. You must then use a standard folder to host the compound document.

When planning your folder hierarchy, you must also understand how folder inheritance works. Unless otherwise specified, a new child folder inherits all the permissions and settings of its parent folder. This arrangement also applies when you drag a folder into the workspace from another location. To break this inheritance, you enable or disable the folder's inheritance settings. Therefore, if you need to create a new permission setting on a folder and have that setting apply to all the documents therein, you first disable inheritance on the folder, then create the permissions structure, and then have those permissions applied to all the subfolders. Documents in a folder automatically inherit permission changes from their parent folder. For more discussion on how to do this, please refer to Chapter 6.

When planning your document folders, also keep in mind which documents need to be routed through an approval process and which do not. Note that the approval process is configured at the folder level and not the document level. This means that every document in a folder configured with an approval process must be routed through the approval process before it can be published and made available to the general user population. If you have a department or group that works with a range of documents, some of which undergo approval and others that do not, you must create separate folders for each set of documents.

Remember, too, that only enhanced folders can be configured with an approval routing process. So if you are working with compound documents that must be approved, you must perform some gymnastics to route the various document parts through the approval process. Best practice here is to create the document parts in an enhanced folder that is not configured for approval, and then either route the completed document manually or through e-mail, or route the individual parts of the document through separate routing processes. Then when everything is approved, copy the document to a standard folder, where it will be published. To learn more about approval routing, please see Chapter 8.

Document Profiles

Document profiles are configured at the folder level, and each folder must have at least one associated default document profile. You can have as many document profiles associated with a document folder as you like. Planning for document profiles and their properties depends on how you structure the document folders in the workspace. Here are some questions to ask yourself about document profiles:

- Does the base document profile have sufficient properties to describe your documents, or should you create more properties for it?
- Instead of using the default profile, would it be better to simply create a new document profile altogether?

- Which properties on each profile should be required to be populated, and which can you allow users to choose whether or not to populate before the document is checked in?
- Which properties can have multiple values?
- What should those multiple values be?

The base document profile contains the title, author, keywords, and description properties. You may need additional information, such as category assignments or an internal tracking number.

You may also want to survey your users to see whether they use other descriptive patterns that could be turned into document profiles. Any survey is no small task, and this one is no exception. However, such a survey might greatly aid your awareness of what is needed in your environment to help the users to find their documents more quickly and easily.

If you make extensive use of categories, you'll likely make them a required property in your document profiles. In most environments that use required properties, you'll want to provide a list of values from which the users can select instead of allowing them to enter their own values. Using a list avoids inconsistencies in the entered values and improves the search process for all users. It requires some planning to create a controlled vocabulary, but you can make this a manageable task by asking for your users' input.

Content Sources

When you're planning for content sources, be sure to add the sources that host content used by your users. Although this might seem obvious, it's really not. It's possible to inadvertently add too much content to the workspace by not properly restricting the depth and breadth of Web content crawls or by adding an entire public folder tree instead of selected public folders held within a larger tree. It's also possible to miss content sources on the Web or a file server that are necessary for a user to conduct business. Be sure to pay close attention to this area by asking your users where *all* their content resides.

A content source represents a location outside the workspace where content is stored. Content sources are accessed by a URL, not by an IP address, except for file shares, which are accessed by a UNC (Universal Naming Convention). Content sources can be Web sites, ftp sites, Exchange 5.5 and 2000 public folders, Lotus Notes databases and other SPS workspaces, and any other resource accessible via a URL. A searchable index of all content in each content source can be created and made available via the Search process for reading, but not for check-out, editing, and check-in functions. Only documents stored in the local workspace are available for document management functions.

Once you've configured your content sources, you'll need to look at how often they should be updated. Updates from the content sources will update the index to include new material.

To improve the speed of searches and yield shorter, more accurate result lists, you can limit the scope of searches. You might want to plan on offering scopes to your users to help them obtain the results they need, but in a shorter list. For more information on how to set scopes, please refer to Chapter 7.

Categories

Categories provide you with an additional method of organizing your documents. Documents that are similar in some respect but are located in different folders can be found based on their common property. For instance, a television news station might decide to list each of its stories in separate documents on a one-folder-per-newscast basis. But the lead story might also be assigned to the Lead Story category, thus allowing an editor or producer to find all the lead stories in a given date range.

It's also helpful to associate a document with multiple categories. For instance, a story on dog grooming might be associated with the following categories: dogs, pet care, human interest, and animal ownership. A search on any one of these categories would include the story on dog grooming that was recently aired.

Hence, categories serve two purposes: They provide a centralized structure for finding information, and they provide a consistent set of values that can be added to documents as metadata.

Categories are the more important hierarchy to be used to find information. By contrast, document folders are the more important hierarchy to secure and develop your information.

Every workspace contains a category hierarchy. The top of the hierarchy is labeled Categories, and default subcategories are nested inside. You can delete these subcategories and replace them with your own structure. Be sure to consult your users about a category structure that will make sense and be user-friendly. On the dashboard, each category link will lead you to see any subcategories, any configured category best bets (discussed in Chapter 7), and documents assigned to the category.

One problem is that the category structure you initially develop might mirror the folder structure. To avoid this, here's a useful set of questions to ask:

- How is your information currently organized? By department? By project? By subject?
- Does your current file system directory structure represent an organization by department, project, subject, or some other method?
- How many levels of subcategories do you want your users to navigate?
- How many levels of subcategories will your users navigate before giving up or complaining?
- Do you need to configure any best bets for a category?

Questions like these will help you form your category structure, so a good way to start is to look at how you currently organize your data. In many environments, the directory structure is built by subject. If this is the case, you can use the directory structure to help you figure out your category structure because categories tend to organize information better by subject than by other methods. Then create a document folder hierarchy that is distinct from the category structure, such as creating document folders for each department.

Three Ways to Organize Your Documents

A file server gives you only one dimension or method of organizing information. Directory hierarchies reflect the physical storage of files on the server.

SharePoint Portal Server offers three dimensions of document organization. First, document folders represent the physical storage of documents in the Web Storage System (WSS). Second, document profiles allow you great flexibility in assigning metadata to documents and using each piece of metadata as a method of organizing documents. Third, categories allow you to organize documents based on their subject content in a structured method.

Document folders are the most familiar method of organizing documents. Document folder structures can be implemented by authors and coordinators and may be used by readers to find documents, although this isn't the recommended method of finding them. Document folder hierarchies are easy to use by everyone, but for readers it is not the most efficient method of finding documents in the workspace.

Segregating content by document folders allows you to implement dissimilar security structures and different approval processes for different sets of files. It also allows for different coordinators to manage different folder hierarchies. However, it's possible that commonly used names will result in conflicts across the workspace.

Document profiles let you assign metadata to a document when it is checked in. Metadata, stored as properties attached to documents, enhances their searchability. A document's profile is determined by the purpose if its content, and the metadata should accurately describe the document to such a degree that it can be found quickly in a search query.

Implementing profiles can be tricky. The larger the profile, the better chance you have of using accurate metadata that can be searched quickly. On the flip side, however, large document profiles consume additional space in the database and require more processing power from the server and may not be populated by busy users.

Categories represent a business-oriented view of a document's content. Categories can be optimized to benefit readers based on the document's subject matter. Categories should be developed with the reader in mind, whereas document folder structures should be developed with the author in mind.

The point of using three different methods is to make a large number of documents available quickly to both readers and authors alike, albeit via different means.

The best way to start building meaningful, usable structures is to *start with what you have, and build on it*. For instance, if your files are sitting on a file server but are organized in the directory hierarchy based on subject matter, use the directory structure as a starting point to build your category structure. Then meet with the prospective authors to discuss how they would like the document folder hierarchy to work. Be sure that these two structures don't mirror each other.

Also, look at the type of metadata that is already being developed and used in your organization. Adopt that usage as a starting point to help users develop their metadata into meaningful document profiles.

Understanding the different purposes of the folder structure, document profiles, and categories will aid you greatly in your planning efforts.

FOR MORE INFO: In the Microsoft literature about document organization, you'll often find the word *taxonomy*. Be sure to search on this word for additional information on planning issues for SharePoint Portal Server content.

Client Issues

There is no individual client application that works with SharePoint Portal Server. The client components of SPS are extensions to Windows Explorer and Office applications. The extensions produce menu items in Office applications and in Windows Explorer that allow for integration with SPS functionality.

Other applications can be used to store information in the workspace, but they cannot include the SPS-specific menu commands. You must use Windows

Training Your Users

It is common for a company to purchase new, expensive hardware and software packages, get them deployed, and experience a load of new Help desk calls from users who don't know how to use the new software correctly.

This is a training issue, pure and simple. If people know how to use a software product, they tend to use more of the product's features and you will experience more ROI (return on investment) on the software.

Deploying SPS is no exception. You should include significant training time in your deployment budget for all the users. All of them will need training on the Search, Category, Quick Links, and Announcements Web parts. If you have added customized Web parts, users may need training in those parts as well.

A smaller group will need training on the Document Library dashboard. They'll need to know how to check out, check in, publish, and approve documents. They'll need to gain familiarity with the interface and learn to think differently about document management.

I'm a bit biased because I'm a trainer as well as an author and consultant (does this sound like a sales pitch? <g>). But I've trained hundreds of system administrators in nearly every part of the country, and one common thread I find is that the average system administrator spends too much time putting out fires caused by users who inadvertently cause a problem because they were not properly trained on the software.

So be sure to include training as part of your deployment budget. Having users who know how to use the SPS software to their advantage will go a long way toward a successful implementation.

Explorer or a Web browser to perform SPS document management tasks on documents created by these other applications.

More than likely, you'll be using SPS to host documents created by applications other than Office applications. In this case, you'll need to plan on training your users on how to use Explorer or the Web browser to perform DM tasks.

Capacity Planning Your SharePoint Portal Servers

Before you can capacity plan your servers, you must first decide on a deployment option. The number of workspaces, content sources, indexes, and user demands will dictate how many SPS servers you'll need and the type of load that will be placed on them.

In many first-time—or what I sometimes call "greenfield"—deployments, you must guess the overall stress that will be placed on your servers. If your installation is a new one, please be sure to read Chapter 12 for information on how to track server health and gain the data necessary to predict trends on your SharePoint server's performance.

Next, you must determine benchmarks for your servers. By *benchmarks*, I mean hard numbers that, if sustained for a predefined period of time, will require action on your part.

Here's how to determine benchmarks. First, take a look at the maximum amount of load each server can handle, and then throttle that back to at least 75 percent. That number represents the amount of stress that a server is allowed to sustain. Anything over this, and your accounting office will need to write a check for something: new memory, a new processor, maybe even a new server. So you should, over time, track the amount of stress on each SharePoint server and then create benchmarks that say when it's time to purchase more resources to manage the increased load.

You'll also want to create benchmarks to indicate when an index becomes too large. As the number of documents increases in a workspace, so does the size of the index, and that will result in longer search times. Using scope limits on searches will help, but at some point, even this action will not be effective in minimizing search times if the index is too large. If the search times become too long for your users, you may need to consider dedicating a server to indexing and search functions. And if the result list is too long, containing a number of false positives, you should plan on refining more narrowly focused search scopes.

Benchmark Numbers Published by Microsoft

Most smaller and many medium-sized businesses will plan on deploying a single server, at least at first. And most businesses will not ever reach Microsoft's benchmarks for a SharePoint server deployment. But some will, and for them, Microsoft has published some good information.

First, Microsoft says that a single SharePoint Portal Server implementation can store as many as 1,000,000 document versions. That's a whole lot of documents, folks. Even if we give each document five versions in the workspace, we're still talking about 200,000 documents. Personally, I'd hesitate to put 1,000,000 document versions in a single database, primarily because of the size of the WSS stores required to host this many documents. Restore times could be very long with this number of documents. To be on the safe side, I suggest that you cut this number way back to something under 200,000 or else have a hot spare server that is ready to go should your SPS server experience a disaster.

You might wonder why I suggest limiting the number of documents to less than 200,000. Well, one of the main reasons that Microsoft went to a multiple database structure in Exchange 2000 from Exchange 5.5 was that the restore times were, literally, an entire day or longer in environments where the Exchange databases were exceptionally large—say, larger than 40GB. This was unacceptable to many of Microsoft's customers because a restore procedure always takes longer than a backup procedure and because the databases are not available for use during a restore procedure and thus, users were unproductive, sometimes for 24 hours or longer.

Couple a long backup restore time with the general uneasiness of putting all your documents in a single public folder housed in a single database, and you start to understand why, even if you can, you would not want to put 1,000,000 documents or versions in the same database. You've probably heard the phrase "Don't put all your eggs in one basket." *Load balancing* your documents over a number of servers is about the only way to ensure that you don't put all your eggs in one basket. Creating multiple workspaces on the same server doesn't help you here; all those workspaces are still housed in the same database on that server.

Think of what would happen if all your documents were sitting on a SharePoint server and the database became corrupted and needed to be restored. Think of the uncomfortable feeling you might get knowing that this database contained 100,000 documents and its loss would represent a significant economic loss for your company.

I submit that lack of productivity due to internal document loss is a more costly type of lack of productivity than the loss of e-mail, although this is not true in all circumstances. So let's suppose you have 100,000 documents sitting *in a single public folder that is hosted in a single database* (because that's all the SPS Web Storage System is), and the database size is 50GB—and you now get to restore that database. How long will it take? Hours. And if the restore procedure fails for some reason? Then you get to start all over again. Can you hear your manager now, asking you when the database is going to be up and running? Can you hear your manager telling you that the CEO wants to know when the database will be live again? You don't want this scenario, do you? I didn't think so.

So I suggest that one way to know when you need another SharePoint server is when the database size gets to the point that it is too large to be restored in the window of time agreed on by you and your manager. For instance, let's say you and your manager agree that the company will not be without loss of SharePoint services for more than 4 hours. Now let's suppose that you're able to restore the full-text index and the `wss.mdb` file at a hard disk write rate of 1MB/sec and that your workspace database is 40GB. How long will it take to restore this database? Approximately 1.2 hours. In addition, I always recommend that whatever the Service Level Agreement (SLA) window is, you plan on taking at least half the time to perform diagnosis and start a restore procedure. It is always best to ensure that the database sizes remain below a level that can be restored within 50 percent of the SLA window. In our example, you're okay because 2 hours for diagnosis plus 1.2 hours for the procedure is less than the 4-hour SLA window.

Second, Microsoft recommends that a single SharePoint server not crawl more than 3.5 million documents. The bandwidth needed to perform this action would be tremendous, especially if most of the documents were out on the Internet. Again, I recommend that you not approach this limit with a single server performing all the crawl functions. This would be a heavy load for one server, and the possibility exists that a single server may not finish crawling 3.5 million documents before it's scheduled to start crawling those same documents again.

Third, Microsoft recommends not having more than 10,000 licensed users connecting to (and presumably using on a regular basis) a single SharePoint server. In larger deployments with multiple processors and gigabytes' worth of RAM on a server, you may be able to inch toward 15,000 users on a single portal. But you must monitor this to know when you have too many users accessing a single portal.

Here are some other recommended numbers from Microsoft:

- Maximum number of documents per server: 500,000
- Maximum number of document versions per server: 1,000,000
- Maximum number of documents included in the index per server: 3,500,000
- Maximum number of documents per folder: 200 (up to 3,000 if rendering is not an issue)
- Maximum document size: 50MB
- Maximum number of versions per document: 1,000
- Maximum number of subscriptions per workspace: 100,000
- Maximum number of document profiles: 500
- Maximum number of content sources: 100
- Maximum number of role security assignments per folder: 600
- Maximum number of categories: 500

Determining Hardware Requirements

Microsoft offers a formula for estimating an overall load on a SharePoint server by including the following elements:

- The number of users in the organization.
- The number of active users each day, expressed as a percentage of the total number of users.
- The number of operations (not site hits, but page views) by the active users each day.
- The number of hours each day that most activity occurs.
- A *peak factor*, which estimates the extent to which the average throughput of the server is exceeded by user demand. This number is expressed as a value between 1 and 4. By definition, the average throughput is always set to 1. The peak factor represents the highest relative proportional deviation from the norm, or the largest spike in activity that can occur. Be definition, this number is 4. The formula assumes that whatever represents an average throughput on your server (expressed as a value of 1), you won't experience a spike in activity larger than four times the average throughput. This makes sense if you look at a bell curve because very rarely does any measurement occur for any standard that is larger than 4 standard deviations from the mean.

The result of running these numbers is expressed as a number of operations per second, based on the formula that looks like this:

$$\frac{\text{number of users} \times \text{percentage of active users/day} \times \text{number of operations/active users/day} \times \text{peak factor}}{360{,}000 \times \text{number of hours per day}}$$

The number 360,000 is determined by 100 (for percent conversion) × 60 (the number of minutes in an hour) × 60 (the number of seconds in a minute).

Hence, a company with 800 users, 80 percent of whom are active, and who have an average of 20 operations each day during an 8-hour period and an assumed peak factor of 4, would have the following result:

$$\frac{800 \times 80 \times 20 \times 4}{360{,}000 \times 8}$$

Result: The predicted peak throughput is 1.77 operations per second.

Microsoft recommends a quad processor 500MHz Pentium III with 1GB RAM for a peak throughput of 1.0. In this scenario, you might consider purchasing a second server and load balancing your data and user calls across two servers. Essentially, your goal is to reduce your operations per second to less than 1.0.

However, if you need to stay with one server, Microsoft recommends that you purchase a quad processor 700MHz Pentium III with 2GB of RAM if your predicted peak throughput is 1.3 operations per second. Moreover, any operation that takes longer than 10 seconds is considered too slow. Interestingly, more than a few people have complained that it can take as long as 20 or even 30 seconds to *open the portal itself* in the Web browser. In this case, you definitely need additional hardware, better bandwidth, or both.

If you'd like some hard numbers to work with, here they are. The base installation of SPS is 150MB. The first workspace consumes an additional 50MB. Each additional workspace consumes an initial 20MB of disk space.

Documents in a standard or enhanced folder with 10 properties use 12K of disk space for metadata storage, 30 percent of document size for index storage, and 100 percent of document size for document storage. So to store a 1MB document with 10 properties, you'll need 1.312MB of disk space. Each version of a document in an enhanced folder will need its own allocation of disk space.

For RAM, plan on a base of 256MB with an additional 100MB for each set of 100,000 documents stored in the workspace or available in the index. The total size of the backup is the combination of the full-text index and the `wss.mdb` file. The index will grow at a size equal to 30 percent of the documents added to the workspace.

Obviously, the hard numbers here are not complete. You will need to monitor your own SharePoint servers to determine the effects of certain actions. To learn more about how to monitor SharePoint Portal Server and to read about the Microsoft Web Application Stress (WAS) tool, please consult Chapter 12.

Improving the Performance of the Dashboard Site

As mentioned in the preceding section, many people have complained about the slowness of opening the portal. You can do a couple of things to speed up portal performance. First, enable full-page caching for each dashboard in your site. To do this, you must first run the `portalperf.vbs` script and then set the cache setting for all Web parts to All Users from the Web Part Settings page. The syntax is as follows:

```
Cscript portalperf.vbs http://servername/workspacename/portal/
  dashboardname fullpage enable
```

This action allows Web parts to be placed in the SharePoint cache, and this means that the dashboard can load more quickly because the Web parts are taken out of the cache rather than the store process. Don't enable full-page caching for the Categories and Document Library dashboards because they have multiple views that don't work properly with full-page caching. It's recommended that you cache only for the Home dashboard.

Second, ensure that you have not enabled the automatic refresh for dashboards. Automatic refreshing of the dashboard in the user's browser can result in unnecessary traffic between the server and all the users. Be sure to turn off this setting in the General Settings portion of a dashboard's properties.

Third, use the All Users Cache for Web Parts setting in the advanced properties of a Web part. This setting enables the Web part to be produced from the cache for every user instead of executing the Web part for each user who connects to the portal. However, the problem with this setting is that users who have been denied access to content in a Web part will gain access if the first person who uses the Web part has permissions to the content and this security setting gets cached for all users. Best practice is to use this setting only on Web parts that do not give access to secured content.

Fourth, on Web parts and dashboards that use a cache, set the time-out value as high as possible. A high value reduces the traffic between the server and clients because the Web part is refreshed less often.

A fifth method of decreasing dashboard response times lies in working with the dashboard definition caching. You can use this cache to group a common set of Web parts and dashboards that is available to a common set of users. The first user in the group who connects places the Web parts and dashboards in a cache automatically (this happens on the server and is transparent to the user), which is then made available to other users in the same group. After two hours, the cache expires and a new definition is created the next time a user from the group accesses a Web part or dashboard in the set. You'll need to run the `portalperf.vbs` script with the following syntax:

```
Cscript portalperf.vbs http://servername/portal/dashboardname
  dashboarddef enable
```

Remember that you can cache subdashboards associated with a dashboard according to the first user who visits the dashboard. Be sure to move key subdashboards into the correct positions to be either included or excluded from this feature.

A sixth method of improving dashboard performance is to run the ASP engine in-process. This is a setting in the IIS Default Web Site Properties dialog box. To do this, right-click the default Web site in the Internet Services

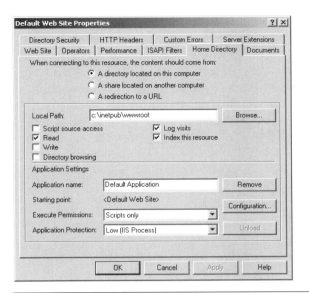

Figure 4–1 Setting the IIS process to Low

Manager, click Properties, and then click the Home Directory tab. Change the Application Protection setting from Medium (pooled) to Low (IIS Process) (Figure 4–1). One caution, however, is in order. The Low setting will allow a single malfunctioning Web part or script to take down the entire IIS process. Be sure to configure recovery options for the World Wide Web Publishing service to ensure that the process restarts properly if a failure occurs.

Tuning the ASP Engine

To help the ASP engine run more efficiently for your environment, you might consider tuning several parameters. First, take a look at the `ASPProcessor-ThreadMax` registry setting. This setting specifies the maximum number of ASP requests that can be processed simultaneously. The default is set to 25. If you have ASP applications that make numerous calls to external sources, consider raising this thread value.

The `AspRequestQueueMax` registry setting specifies the maximum number of concurrent ASP requests that are permitted into the queue. The `AspQueueConnectionTestTime` setting looks at the length of time a request has been sitting in a queue, and if it has been there longer than this configured value, ASP first checks to ensure that the client is still connected to the server before processing the ASP request. The default is 3 seconds. Adjust this value to ensure that IIS doesn't process a request that has been abandoned by the user.

The `AspScriptEngineCacheMax` setting specifies the maximum number of scripting engines that ASP pages will keep cached in memory. The default is 125. Make sure you increase this number if you're getting error messages indicating that an ASP couldn't run a script on a busy server.

The `AspSessionTimeOut` setting specifies the default amount of time (in minutes) that a session object is maintained after traffic between the client and server ends. Because maintaining sessions requires memory on the server, consider lowering this value to make your applications more scalable on your server. The default is set to 20 minutes.

To configure any of these values, run the `adsutil.vbs` script from the `\inetpub\adminscripts` directory with the following syntax:

```
Adsutil.vbs set w3svc /AspSessionTimeOut <new value>
```

Note that such a configuration change will apply to all Web sites on the server because this changes values at the Master WWW properties level.

Planning and Implementing SharePoint Portal Server across the Internet

Out of the box, SharePoint Portal Server does not work over the Internet, nor can it be accessed over the Internet even if you use the correct FQDN or IP address. This is because the workspace has its own proxy server settings, which allows an administrator specify which proxy server the dashboard should use.

When accessing an SPS server, you'll need to pay attention to the following points:

- You will need the NetBIOS name of the computer. The default method of accessing the workspace, `http://server_name/workspace_name`, uses the NetBIOS name of the computer, not its host name. (And you thought that with Windows 2000, you didn't need NetBIOS anymore!)
- You'll also need an internal FQDN and an external FQDN. Each must be unique but may use the same domain name. They can be made unique by using different server names.
- The internal FQDN uses the NetBIOS name instead of the host name in the server name portion of the FQDN. If you are not using WINS (Windows Internet Naming Service) on your local network or if your

DNS service is not configured to support NetBIOS, then your users must use the FQDN of the SPS server to access the workspace.
- The external FQDN uses the host name you wish to use on the Internet. Alias names here are okay.

After gathering this information, you're ready to start configuring SharePoint to work over the Internet. The first step is to configure the proxy settings on the ServerXMLHTTP object, which has its own proxy settings for the workspace apart from the settings relied on by other applications that might be installed on the server. To configure these settings, you use the command prompt and the `proxycfg.exe` utility. There is no graphical interface for configuring this object.

By default, the proxy settings for the ServerXMLHTTP object are configured the same as the server's proxy settings when SharePoint is installed. But if you need to use SharePoint to crawl content sites on different servers or over the Internet and if you're not using a proxy server in your environment, then you'll need to configure the ServerXMLHTTP object using the `proxycfg.exe` utility.

Using the `proxycfg.exe` Utility

To run `proxycfg.exe`, open a command prompt and navigate to the SharePoint /Bin directory. Type `proxycfg`, and you'll see the current proxy settings. Then use the utility to configure the proxy settings according to the switches explained in Table 4–2.

The `proxycfg` utility has much more flexibility than meets the eye. In addition to knowing when to use the –d, -p, or –u switch, you can also configure the ServerXMLHTTP object in the following ways.

First, if you want to associate a certain protocol with a certain proxy server, the syntax is as follows:

```
<protocol>=http://<proxy_name>:<port_number>
```

Valid protocols that can be used here are HTTP and HTTPS. If you want the SPS server accessed over the Internet using SSL (Secure Sockets Layer) instead of HTTP, you would type the following:

```
https=http://proxy_server_name:443
```

Note that in the command itself, you don't use "HTTPS" to specify the name of the proxy server that is using SSL instead of HTTP (rather counterintuitive,

Table 4–2 `proxycfg.exe` utility switches

Switch	Syntax	Comment	Security Issues
-d	proxycfg -d	Allows the SPS server to bypass all proxy servers. If you don't have any proxy servers on your network, you'll need to use this switch.	Port 80 or 443 will need to be open on your firewall for Internet users.
-p	Proxycfg -p proxy-server-list optional-bypass list	This switch specifies one or more proxy servers that exist on the network. The optional bypass list can enumerate the proxy servers that should be bypassed.	Port 80 or 443 will need to be open on your firewall for Internet users.
-u	Proxycfg -u	Sets the ServerXMLHTTP proxy settings to be the same as those of the currently logged-on user, which are found in the Internet Explorer profile. Auto-discovery and script-based proxy configuration settings are not supported by the `proxycfg` utility.	—

if you ask me). Note also that if you're using the default port number for the specified protocol, it is not necessary to specify the port number. However, if you want to use a different port number for that protocol, you must specify the port number and ensure that the port is open on your firewall. Finally, host names and IP addresses can be used, as long as they are known locally to the SPS server.

You can also specify a default proxy server for all protocols that are not assigned a particular proxy server. For instance, if you wanted to specify Server1 as the SSL proxy server and Server2 and Server 3 as the proxy servers for HTTP, you could enter the command in the `proxycfg` utility as follows:

```
https=http://server1 server2 server3
```

Because no port numbers are specified, the default port numbers are assumed. And because the HTTP protocol is not specified and because servers are listed using a space-delimited string, Server2 and Server3 become the servers offering proxy services over HTTP.

At times you may want to specify that the proxy server be bypassed for certain domain names. The wildcard character "*" can be used in a pattern to specify that connections to a domain name bypass the proxy server. Connections to other domain names that don't fit this criterion will be routed through the proxy server. For instance, if you wanted to bypass the proxy server when connecting to the Networknowledge.com domain from your SPS server, you would type

```
*.networknowledge.com
```

Again, if you need to list multiple domain names, separate them with blank spaces or semicolons in the proxy bypass string. The `<local>` designation bypasses any proxy server in the list whose host name does not contain a period.

So, to put this all together, following are some sample scenarios and commands that might be of help to you.

Scenario 1: If you are physically cabled to get to the Internet through your proxy server, the following command will perform this function for you. Assume that the name of the proxy server is proxy1.

```
proxycfg -p proxy1
```

In this command, ports 80 and 443 are assumed, and both HTTP and SSL traffic from the SPS server will be routed through proxy1. No servers are listed in a bypass list, so requests to host names without periods will also be routed to proxy1. Figure 4–2 shows what this will look like in the command prompt. Notice that the bypass list is empty, as indicated by the `-not set-` designation.

Scenario 2: If you are using proxy services for your users but you're physically cabled so that the Internet can be directly accessed and if you want to bypass the proxy server on your network to allow traffic to and from the SPS server, use this syntax:

```
proxycfg -d
```

Scenario 3: If you do not have a proxy server and need to access both local and Internet locations, enter this command:

```
Proxycfg -d "<local>"
```

Scenario 4: If you have one proxy server that performs HTTP services (proxy1) and a second proxy server that performs SSL services over port 4400 (proxy2)

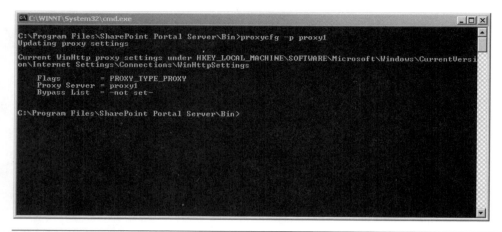

Figure 4–2 Routing all HTTP and HTTPS requests through a specified proxy server using the `proxycfg` utility

and if you want all local intranet sites and any site in the Networknowledge.com domain to bypass both proxy servers, here is the command you would enter:

```
Proxycfg -p "http:=proxy1 https:=proxy2:4000" "<local>";
*.networknowledge.com
```

Other scenarios exist in the real world, and I don't have space to give the command for each one, but hopefully I've covered the more common scenarios and given you one instance of a not-so-common scenario.

Completing Your Internet Implementation

After configuring your SharePoint server using the `proxycfg` utility, you must ensure that you have a DNS entry created for the external name of your SPS server. This might seem obvious, but sometimes we forget the obvious when we implement new technologies.

Next, you need to create a new Web site in IIS for each security model that you'll need. For instance, if you have a group of documents that need to be made available to all readers using HTTP and Anonymous access, and another group of documents that need to be available to a group of authors using HTTPS and Basic authentication, then you'll need two Web sites: one for each security model. For more information on how to create a new Web site, please consult the Internet Information Service Resource Kit, or *How to Set Up and Maintain a Web Site, Second Edition* by Lincoln Stein. Remember that, by default, the SPS Web site will use Windows Integrated Authentication. To use SPS over the Internet, you must use either Basic or Anonymous authentication.

NOTE: If you use the Anonymous security setting, users who access the dashboard with this security setting will not be able to create subscriptions from the dashboard site.

To enable Web discussions over the Internet, you must edit the registry and import a key into the `adsutil.vbs` file. Web discussions allow users to discuss the document as a whole or to comment on particular parts of it. Discussions can be viewed and remarks entered from either the browser or an Office application.

The key you'll want to navigate to (using the `Regedit` command) is

```
HKEY_LOCAL_MACHINE\SOFTWARE\Microsoft\Office\9.0\Web
Server\1 registry key
```

After you are there, perform these steps in order:

1. Save the key as `EnableDiscussions`.
2. Rename the number 1 folder to the number of the Web site in which SPS is hosted. Typically, the default Web site is number 1, the administrative Web site is number 2, and the SPS Web site is number 3. This assumes that you created Web sites on the server other than the default Web sites when you installed Windows 2000 before SPS was installed.
3. Import the file you saved as `EnableDiscussions`. You do this by highlighting the Web Server parent folder and then importing the file. This will cause another key (named `1`) to be installed in the same directory (Figure 4–3).
4. Edit the properties of the server root URL in folder 3, and change its value to the Internet FQDN for the SPS server. You do *not* type the name of the workspace here; type only the FQDN.
5. Restart the server.

Troubleshooting Internet Connectivity to Your Dashboard

As with all software products, there is more that can go wrong than you might initially anticipate. Table 4–2 lists these problems and explains how you can fix them.

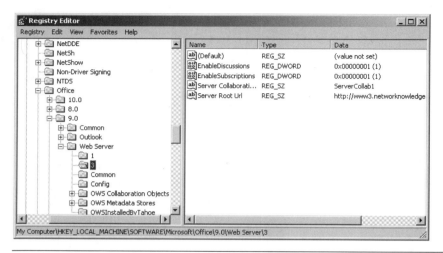

Figure 4-3 Second Web discussions key created in the registry

Table 4-3 Troubleshooting tips for using SPS over the Internet

Problem	Resolution
Denied access to the server	Check the authentication methods. Make sure they are either Basic or Anonymous on the SPS Web site.
HTTP Error 401	If using Anonymous, add the Internet Guest account as a Reader on the hidden Portal folder in the workspace.
HTTP Error 424	After configuring the proxy settings, you must restart the server. Also, if you get this error when using SSL but not when using HTTP, make sure the IIS application protection is specified as Low for the virtual directory for the workspace in the SPS Web site. For information on how to configure this setting, see the IIS Resource Kit.
HTTP Error 519	Ensure that you have enabled Web discussions on your SPS server.
HTTP Error 500 or you're unable to map a Web folder to the workspace	Ensure that you have not selected the Check That File Exists check box on the public and workspace virtual directories in the SPS Web site.
Unable to perform discussions	Ensure that the execute permissions are set to Scripts and Executables on the MSOffice virtual directory on the SPS Web site.
HTTP Error 11004 Host not found	Ensure that DNS is configured correctly.

Risks of Opening Your Portal to the Internet

After you have created the Web site and correctly configured DNS and the ServerXMLHTTP object, your SPS server should be accessible from the Internet. However, before you jump for joy, you should be aware of a number of warnings.

First, most worms and viruses are caused by malformed packets that attack IIS in one way or another. When Microsoft releases a security hot fix to combat these worms and viruses, it does not guarantee that the fix will work with all installations of SharePoint. In other words, you can't be certain that a hot fix for a particular security breach in IIS will work seamlessly with Share-Point because there is no guarantee that Microsoft completely regression-tested the hot fix before releasing it. So the best practice here is to set up an offline SPS server that is configured (at the software level) exactly like your production SPS server. Then install the security patch against the offline server and run it through a series of internal tests. Such tests might include the following:

■ Accessing the server from the local area network

■ Accessing the server from the Internet (or through its FQDN)

■ Accessing the server from an Office application

■ Accessing the server from the Web folder client

■ Running a script that creates, checks in, and publishes a series of documents, perhaps in the range of 200 to 500 documents

■ Allowing the Search process to index these new documents

■ Using the Search process

■ Using each Web part on each dashboard

Perhaps you have thought of other tests that could be run, but the point is that you should develop an internal testing method to ensure that the security fix applied to the server does not interfere with any of SharePoint's functions.

A second warning is that if you install some of the Outlook Web parts, then for each computer from which a user attempts to use them, a local Outlook profile must be created. Hence, a user who dials in to the Internet and then accesses his Outlook dashboard will need to have his Outlook profile already stored on the local computer, or else it will need to be created over the dial-up connection. I probably don't need to tell you that using the Outlook Web parts over a 56K dial-up connection is slow, but to make users create the Outlook profile is not likely to lead to a positive end-user experience. So even though the SPS portal can be accessed over the Internet, some users may have a slow experience of it.

The second warning leads to a third warning. In planning the look and feel of your Home dashboard, be aware that the more Web parts you place there, the longer the download time. This sluggishness can be especially noteworthy if some of the Web parts offer application functionality. Be sure to test and assess the download time of your dashboards as it relates to the slowest type of Internet connection to your portal.

A fourth warning is security-related. If you open your portal to the Internet, chances are pretty good that you'll open it using port 80 and HTTP. Be sure to consider carefully the implications of using the Anonymous account in this configuration. If you give anonymous access to the portal over port 80 using HTTP, then, by default, everyone on the Internet will be able to read all published documents in your workspace. Remember that the Everyone security group is given reader permissions at the root of the Document Library folder. A better name for this group would have been Anyone, which more accurately portrays how wide the scope of this group is. Anyone who can make a network connection of any type to any part of your network will become a member of the Everyone security group and can read all published documents in your portal.

A fifth warning is that Web discussions are not held as part of the documents, so any security you apply to the documents is not inherited or applied to the Web discussions about those documents. Moreover, Web discussions cannot be secured, so use them with caution.

A sixth warning has to do with license compliance. Every device that connects to your SPS server requires a client access license (CAL) in order to be in compliance with the licensing agreement. If you open up your portal to the Internet for general use, then estimating how many licenses you need may be a bit of a problem. Fortunately (or unfortunately, depending on how you view it), Microsoft has not included a counter in the Performance Monitor application to tell you how many CALs you need specifically for SPS. However, under the Web Service performance object in Performance Monitor, you can use the Current CAL Count for authenticated users to see how many CALs are being used by simultaneous connections to your Web service, but you're not able to specify the SPS Web site as an instance for this counter. I honestly don't know how you'll know how many CALs you'll need if you're opening up your portal to the Internet—if you're going to open it up for general consumption. If you're opening up the portal only for certain customers who are required to log in, then you should have a good idea as to how many client licenses are needed for those customers.

A seventh and final warning comes from Microsoft itself. You are advised not to run the Windows 2000 Internet Server Security Tool on any server after installing SharePoint Portal Server. Doing so may completely disable your dashboard site and render it useless.

Tuning the Web Storage System

This section discusses ways to make the WSS work a bit better and faster given certain scenarios. (For an overview of the Web Storage System, please consult Chapter 2.)

First, if you want to increase the number of DAV threads that SPS can process simultaneously and thereby increase its throughput, modify the following registry key:

```
HKLM\System\CCS\Services\MSExchangeIS\ParametersSystem
Parameter:  ChildExecutionThreadFactor (Reg_DWORD)
Default Setting:  Does not exist.
Recommended Setting:  A factor of four doubles the amount of threads
  available to service requests.
```

By default, the number of DAV threads allocated is two times the number of system processors plus 1.

If you find that you are running out of database sessions, you'll need to make an adjustment. The default maximum number of database sessions is 40. These can be used up quickly if you're running lots of user sessions, subscription notifications, crawling content sources, and so on. You'll know this is happening because you'll see messages to this effect, as well as request time-out messages, in the Event Viewer. Adjust this key:

```
HKLM\Software\Microsoft\ESE98\Process\InformationStore\System Parameter
  Overrides
Parameter:  LogBuffers (REG_SZ)
Default Setting:  40 (though it won't appear as such)
Recommended setting:  Increase to between 60 - 100.
```

After making a change like this, be sure to monitor your server to see whether the error messages go away in the Event Viewer and whether the additional database sessions are using too much RAM.

If the WSS just seems slow, consider increasing the log buffers on the server. Before information is written to the transaction logs, it is first written to a log buffer on the server in 4K page sizes. The default value of 84 represents the number of log buffers that can exist as SPS exists out of the box. On a high-demand server, this number will be much too low, forcing the server to write information to the transaction logs faster than it normally would. In high-demand environments, increase the number of log buffers to 9,000 or more. Do this in the following registry key:

```
HKLM\Software\Microsoft\ESE98\Process\InformationStore\System Parameter
  Overrides
Parameter    LogBuffers
```

SharePoint Portal Servers with more than 1GB of RAM may need to adjust the size of the store database cache. The hard-coded cache size for the information store is 900MB, meaning that the store process can use as much as 900MB of RAM to temporarily store information. By monitoring the Performance Object/Process, Counter/Virtual Bytes, and Instance/Store counters in Performance Monitor, you can obtain an accurate value representing the amount of virtual address space that the store.exe process is using. On a server using the /3GB switch in the Boot.ini file, this value in Performance Monitor should always be less than 2.8GB. For servers not using the /3GB switch, this value in Performance Monitor should never be greater than 1.8GB. If you see Performance Monitor values that exceed the recommended values, do not increase the store database cache size. However, to the extent that the values are less than the recommended limits, you can increase this cache size value in the registry.

For instance, if you are not using the /3GB switch in Boot.ini and your Performance Monitor shows that you're using 1.5GB of RAM, you can safely increase the store database cache size by 300MB.

FOR MORE INFO: See the TechNet knowledge base article Q266096 for more information on the /3GB switch.

If you really want to increase the performance of the WSS, ensure that your transaction logs have been placed on a physically separate drive that does nothing except host the WSS transaction logs. The sequential read/write architecture of the transaction logs reduces head seek time significantly in the WSS, thereby returning control to the end user much more quickly. To move the transaction log files, use the catutil.exe from the resource kit.

Summary

This chapter discusses the important planning issues and explains how to configure your SPS server for access from the Internet. You've also learned how to configure the `proxycfg` utility. And you've learned about important issues to consider when opening your portal to the Internet, even if you limit traffic to selected parties.

Chapter 5 discusses how to install SharePoint Portal Server. It describes the changes it makes to your server and includes troubleshooting tips for failed installations.

Installing SharePoint Portal Server 2001

If you were to pull out the SharePoint Portal Server CD-ROM and run the installation program (assuming you had all the installation requirements met), you'd probably think that installing SPS is easy. A piece of cake. And you'd be right.

Well, sort of.

If you limit your definition of an installation to making sure the binary and database files are set up and ready to go, then yes, installing SPS is easy and quick. Painless, too.

But if your definition of an installation is broader and includes understanding why you made the installation selections you made and knowing how your server has changed because of the installation, then no, installing SPS is not so simple. There are planning issues to resolve, a new site in IIS to understand, and the architecture of the Web Storage System to understand. In addition, there is a client to SPS to be deployed. And you need to ensure that you don't attempt to install SPS with incompatible software.

Hence the need for a chapter on installing SPS. You can use this chapter as a learning tool or as a reference for failed installations. Either way, you'll find useful information that will help you plan, understand, and troubleshoot your installation of SharePoint Portal Server.

Planning for the SharePoint Installation

Before you can perform an installation, you must first make sure that your servers and clients are ready for SPS. Because SPS is one of the .NET servers, it is not fully compatible with all the client operating systems currently being used, and the server files can be installed only on a Windows 2000 Server or later platform.

You will get the most bang for your buck if you are running a pure Windows 2000 environment, both on the server and on the client. However, many environments are not so pure, so here's the scoop on each operating system and its integration with SharePoint. Bear in mind that access to the portal (dashboard) is available from all Intel-based platforms via the browser.

- Windows 95: This platform has no support for either the server or the client installation. If you're running mainly Windows 95 clients and you want to install SPS, my advice is to upgrade the clients to Windows 2000 or at least Windows Millenium.
- Windows 98: This platform has no support for installing the server, but it has limited client support for the Web folders. I say "limited" because the Windows 98, Windows ME, and Windows NT platforms do not support coordinator functions such as scheduling updates, configuring content sources, and any administrative task using the Microsoft Management Console (MMC) or Web views.
- Windows Millennium: You cannot install the server portion of SPS on this platform, and, like Windows 98, it has limited support for the SPS client.
- Windows NT 4.0, SP6A: There is no support for installing the server on either the workstation or the server NT platform. There is limited support for the SPS client, and the limitations are the same as for Windows 98.
- Windows 2000 Professional: This platform has no support for installing the server files. The SPS client enjoys full support and functionality on this platform.
- Windows 2000 Server or Advanced Server: This is the platform on which you can install the server files for SPS. You need to have previously installed Windows 2000 Service Pack 1. The SPS client can also be installed, and it will enjoy full functionality.
- Windows 2000 DataCenter: This platform has no support for installing either the SPS client or the SPS server.
- Windows XP: You cannot install the server portion of SPS on Windows XP, but the SPS client enjoys full support and interaction with an SPS server when installed on a Windows XP workstation. You will need Service Pack 1 or higher of the SPS client on a Windows XP workstation.
- Macintosh (all versions): This platform has no support for installing either the SPS client or the SPS server.
- UNIX (all versions): This platform has no support for installing either the SPS client or the SPS server.

Also, SPS supports only two browsers: Microsoft's Internet Explorer (4.x or later) and its arch rival, Netscape, starting with version 4.7x. SPS must also be running on a Windows operating system in order to connect to the portal. The Macintosh, Solaris, UNIX, and Linux operating systems are not supported.

Finally, note that those clients who upgrade to Windows XP from Windows 98 and Windows NT Workstation where the SPS client was already installed may encounter random or intermittent connectivity problems. Be sure that after an upgrade, you reinstall the SPS client.

Server Prerequisites

SPS can be installed only on the Windows 2000 Server platform, but even such installations may have serious issues. Be sure to check the readme file on your SPS Server CD-ROM for the latest in hot fix and service pack information as it relates to Windows 2000. At the time of this writing, the first thing you need to do is to upgrade to Service Pack 2 or higher for Windows 2000. If for some reason you can't do this, then please read the rest of this paragraph. It could save you serious headaches. If you have installed Service Pack 1 for Windows 2000 and you cannot install Service Pack 2 or later, be sure to reference Q291340 and Q286360 for updates that need to be installed with Service Pack 1. If you are running Service Pack 2 and cannot install Service Pack 3 or later, then be sure to reference Q291340 for an update that should be installed after Service Pack 2. Finally, if you are running Service Pack 1 and cannot install Service Pack 2 or later *and* if you have installed the Windows 2000 hot fix as outlined in Q269862, then you'll need to *remove* this hot fix before installing SPS.

The second thing you need to do is to ensure that the Windows Remote Registry service is running.

Third, make sure that the default Web site on the Windows 2000 Server on which you wish to install SPS is configured to accept calls on `localhost` over port 80. The setup program checks only the first entry in the Advanced Settings box of the default Web site if multiple entries exist. So be sure that the first entry allows for this type of access to the site.

Fourth, for best performance, ensure that SMTP is installed in IIS. This enables e-mail notifications to function in the subscriptions component.

Hardware Recommendations

You're likely to find various opinions about the kind of hardware you should have on hand. Much of this decision is based on your estimates of user demands and stress levels, so it's hard to pinpoint a minimum hardware configuration.

However, after working with several companies on SharePoint implementations, both large and small, I've arrived at the following minimums that I recommend:

- Dual Pentium 4/1GHz or higher
- 1GB of RAM
- 200MB of free disk space for program installation
- 2GB of free disk space for data files
- 100Mbps adapter
- Fast hard disks (and I mean fast)

This is way above the minimums that Microsoft recommends. For instance, it recommends a single processor with 256MB of RAM as a minimum, and 300MB minimum for data files. But this seems low unless the number of users being serviced is small (fewer than 25) and their activity is not persistent or demanding on the SPS server.

On the client side, have at least a Pentium III/500MHz or later processor with at least 128MB of RAM, Internet Explorer 5.0 or later, and Office 2000 or later. Again, my hardware recommendations might seem to some to be a bit much, but I've yet to meet a user or administrator who was hurt by having too much power for applications.

You might also want to reread "Capacity Planning Your SharePoint Portal Servers" in Chapter 4. That section outlines the Microsoft formula for deciding how much processing power is required for SPS to run efficiently.

Hardware Configuration of an SPS Server

Now let's look at an ideal scenario in which you build a server without budget constraints. In that way, you can calculate the kinds of trade-offs you're looking at in building your real-world implementation.

First, mirror the boot and system partitions. In Microsoft's world, the *boot partition* contains all the operating system (OS) files that run the OS. The *system partition* is the partition that contains the boot files. So if you switch the logical meaning of these words in your head, you've got it!

For improved performance of Windows 2000, place the `pagefile.sys` file on a separate disk.

Second, quarantine the transaction log files on your SPS server to their own mirrored pair of disks. The transaction logs exist for the Web Storage System, and it's crucial to store them on their own mirrored pair. Why? It's because the performance of SPS is directly related to how fast transactions can be written to the logs. Because writes to the logs are sequential, the heads on the disk will write and then stop at the next location where they will write again. This arrangement significantly reduces disk seek time, which in turn means that transactions are written faster to the logs. This means that control is returned to the user more quickly, resulting in a better user experience of SPS.

Note also that the disks on which you place the transaction logs should be the fastest disks you can afford. How fast? Fast! I won't give you an RPM number, but you should select the fastest disks that you can afford. 'nuff said.

Finally, don't place your transaction logs on a RAID5 (disk striping with parity) volume. The calculation of the parity information will slow down SPS more than does placing the transaction logs on a single, but slow, disk.

Here is the optimum disk structure for a SharePoint Portal Server:

- `C:\` drive: mirrored pair, system and boot partitions
- `D:\` drive: single disk, `pagefile.sys` file
- `E:\` drive: mirrored pair, WSS transaction logs
- `F:\` drive: RAID5, WSS databases

Moreover, this entire discussion also applies to the other main database, the `sps.edb` database. It has its own set of transaction logs (`MSS*.log`) and is used to hold the property information of documents indexed by SPS.

Server Coexistence Issues

If SharePoint Team Services is installed on the server where you want to install SPS, you must first uninstall Team Services and delete the following registry key:

```
HKEY_LOCAL_MACHINE\Software\Microsoft\Office\9.0\Web Server
```

If you choose to install SharePoint Team Services after you have installed SharePoint Portal Server, you will lose some functionality:

- Subscriptions enabled by using the Office collaboration toolbar will not generate notifications.
- All discussions stored in Team Services will be lost.
- Discussion items will not be included in the index and thus will not be available for searching.

If you are running any of the following, SPS will not install:

- Exchange 5.5 or earlier
- Exchange 2000 Enterprise Edition
- Any version of Microsoft Site Server
- Windows 2000 Cluster Service
- Microsoft Office Server Extensions (OSE)

SharePoint and SQL Server

If you install SPS on a server running SQL 7.0, or SQL 2000, the existing MSSearch service will be upgraded. The search service can be shared by more than one application on a local machine. In addition, SPS upgrades the full-text index on the server the next time the MSSearch service is started.

To upgrade the existing full-text index successfully, you'll need 120 percent of free disk space relative to the size of the largest full-text index on the hard disk. Depending on the size of the index, this upgrade could take several hours. Hence, before you begin installing the SPS Server, be sure to check the size of your largest full-text index and then ensure that you have the required free disk space.

NOTE: Installing SPS on a SQL Server cluster is neither recommended nor supported by Microsoft.

If you install SPS on a SQL 7.0 Server and then decide to uninstall it, the MSSearch service and the full-text index will not automatically be rolled back to the pre-SPS version. To go back to the previous version of MSSearch, you must use the SQL setup program to uninstall and reinstall it. This will force the full-text indexes to be re-created after the earlier version of MSSearch is installed.

SharePoint and Windows 2000 Domain Controller

If you are planning to install SPS on a Windows 2000 domain controller, think again. Members of the Local Administrators security group on a member server have full access to information in the workspace, even if they are not assigned the Coordinator role in the workspace. This right is not configurable and cannot be revoked. However, on a Windows 2000 domain controller, there is no Local Administrators security group, so if a coordinator makes a mistake or removes the Coordinator role from all the coordinators in a workspace, you will not have the backdoor of a Local Administrators security group to resolve security issues.

You cannot remove all coordinators from a folder—that would cause document lockout and loss of management of that folder—but a coordinator can still make serious security mistakes without realizing it, such as inadvertently removing all users from a folder's permissions. If such mistakes occur, there is no backdoor on a domain controller because, unlike the NTFS file system, SPS has no concept of ownership of files, and domain administrators cannot take ownership in order to change permissions on a folder or file. However, if SPS is installed on a member server and a coordinator takes unwise security actions, they can be changed by any member of the Local Administrators security group. This group's permissions even override the Deny role on items in the workspace.

NOTE: Members of the Local Administrators security group have full rights to all documents, published and unpublished, in the workspace, even if their user account is granted only the Reader role and even if their user account is expressly given the Deny role on a document. The only way to prevent a user who is a member of the Local Administrators group from having such pervasive permissions is to remove that user from the group.

Installing SharePoint Portal Server

You install SharePoint Portal Server by running the SharePoint Portal Server Setup wizard. Be sure to log on as a member of either the Local Administrators or Domain Administrators security group. Also, be sure to stop all antivirus software or else the setup will fail.

Place the SPS CD-ROM in the CD-ROM drive, and let the autostart bring up the initial splash page. Notice that you can choose to install the server or client to SPS. This section discusses the installation of the server component, so select Server Installation and then proceed from there (Figure 5–1). If you don't want to use the setup wizard, you can double-click `setup.exe` in the Server folder on the SPS CD-ROM.

Setup will load installation components into memory and then display the Welcome to Microsoft SharePoint Portal Server 2001 Setup screen. Your only choice here is to click Cancel or click Next. After you click Next, the following screen shows the license agreement.

Figure 5–1 Initial SharePoint splash screen with installation choices

Once you've agreed to the license agreement (have you ever seen a licensing agreement with which you did not agree?), you're presented with the product key code input screen, where you enter the product key code.

The following screen is the Installation Folders screen, where you're given a chance to specify where you want the program files and data files installed (Figure 5–2). Note that these files need not be on the same partition. There is also a button called Disk Information, which brings up a summary of all the logical partitions on the server and lists each partition's size and available space. Use this button to inform yourself if you are unsure where to place the program and data files or if you want to recheck your planning decisions before committing to the locations.

Remember that the path names have a maximum length of 100 characters and can contain only lowercase ASCII characters. Moreover, a root path, such as `G:\` or `T:\`, is not allowed, but something like `G:\SPInstall` or `T:\SPSInstallation` would be acceptable.

After making your folder selections, you're presented with the SharePoint Portal Server Indexing Settings screen, where you can specify the security context in which content external to the workspace should be crawled (Figure 5–3). Moreover, you must specify an e-mail address that others can contact if problems occur when SPS crawls their site. The contact address can be either an individual or a group e-mail address. This information can be configured

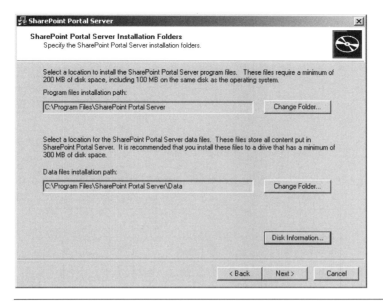

Figure 5–2 SharePoint Portal Server Installation Folders screen

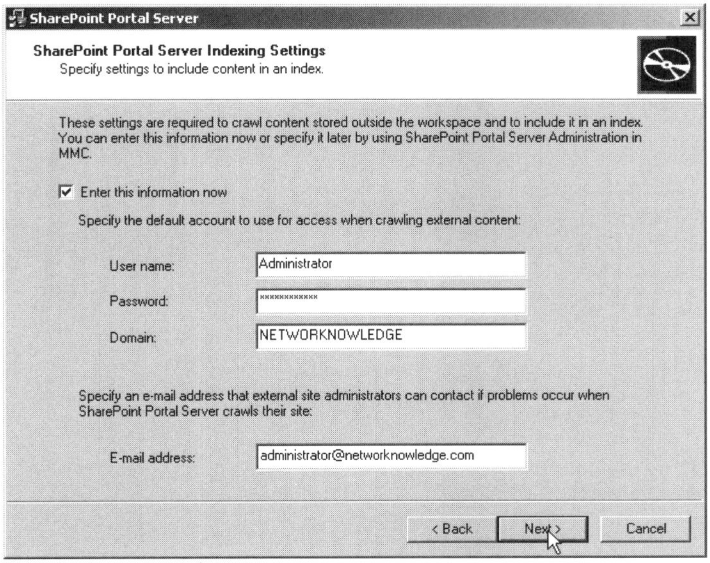

Figure 5–3 SharePoint Portal Server Indexing Settings screen

later, after the workspace is created, but it's easier to do it during installation. Enter the information, and then click Next.

When you click Next, setup has all the information it needs to begin installing files in the locations you specified. It will copy some setup files to your local hard disk and then begin the installation of the Web Storage System, Microsoft Search, and SharePoint Portal Server. Status bars for each set will inform you as to each component's progress (Figure 5–4).

NOTE: Installation of the server components also includes installation of the client components on the server. To install the client components on workstations on your network, please refer to "Installing the SPS Client" later in this chapter.

After the components are finished installing, click Finish on the Finish Installing SharePoint Portal Server 2001 screen. Setup will take you immediately to the Welcome to the New Workspace wizard. This move is logical because there is little point in installing SharePoint without also installing a workspace. Some verbiage on this screen offers a synopsis of workspaces. Read it if you like, and then click Next. The New Workspace Wizard screen will appear, and this is where you name and describe the first workspace for your SPS server (Figure 5–5).

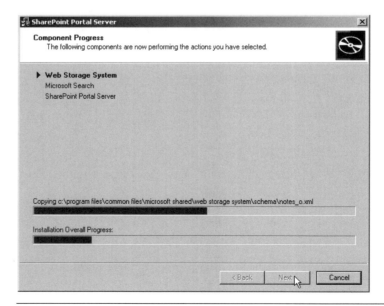

Figure 5–4 Component Progress screen

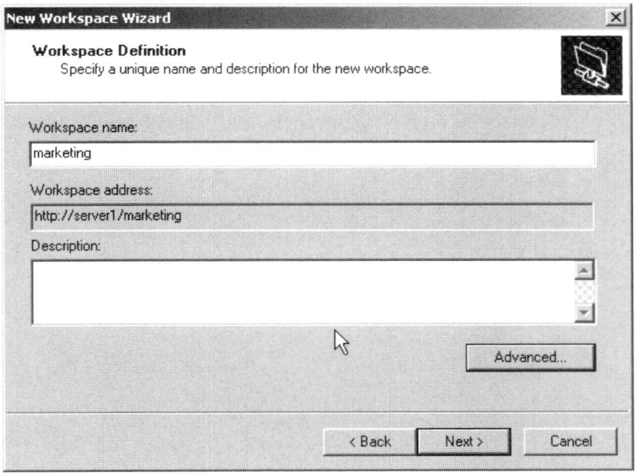

Figure 5–5 New Workspace Wizard screen

TIP: You'll learn how to create multiple workspaces in the following section.

Remember that workspace names can consist only of lowercase ASCII characters and cannot include the space character nor the following:
: \ ? * < > % / | ” { } ~ [ ] ! ( ) = ; . , @ & +

In addition, the workspace name cannot exceed 25 characters in length. The workspace name must also be unique on the server or with names of index servers from which this server receives propagated indexes. Workspace names cannot be edited after creation, so be sure to choose the correct name now.

When you type the name of the workspace, the Advanced button will become active. This is where you can choose to make this workspace an index-only workspace. The index generated will then be sent to the destination workspace, which you must supply in the Specify the Destination Workspace Address input box (Figure 5–6). The destination workspace will then be dedicated to search functions, and the workspace you're creating will be dedicated to indexing functions. The destination workspace must exist before you create the index workspace, and the name of the index workspace cannot be the same as the name of the destination workspace.

After entering the required information on the workspace name and advanced settings and then clicking Next, you'll see the Workspace Contact screen, where you type the workspace contact name and e-mail address. Enter the appropriate information, and click Next.

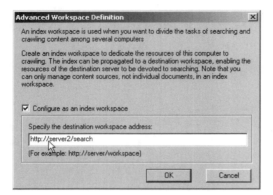

Figure 5–6 Advanced Workspace Definition screen

The Completing the New Workspace Wizard screen will appear, showing a summary of the choices you've made. The Back button will be active so that you can return to the previous screens and make changes if you like. When you click Finish, the workspace wizard will create a new workspace and a new Web site in IIS. This process takes longer than you might think, so be patient.

Once the new workspace has been created, setup will automatically open three screens:

■ Configure Your Workspace Getting Started Help
■ A Web folders view of the workspace
■ A dashboard view of the workspace in the browser

Once these windows open successfully, you'll know that SharePoint has been installed correctly. If they do not, please refer to "Troubleshooting Failed Installations" later in this chapter.

Installing Additional Workspaces

To install more than one workspace, you use the SharePoint Portal Server Administration snap-in, which is found, by default, under the Administrative Tools menu on the Windows 2000 Server.

Open the snap-in, expand the SharePoint Portal Server container, and right-click the SharePoint server you wish to create a new workspace on. Point to New, and select Workspace (Figure 5–7). This will invoke the New Workspace wizard discussed previously. The wizard will run exactly the same as it did during the new installation of SPS, and you will be able to create a new workspace on your SharePoint server. Microsoft supports as many as 15 simultaneous

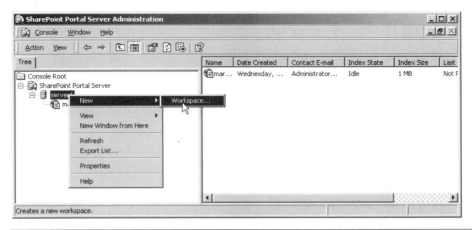

Figure 5–7 Creating a new workspace in the SPS Administration snap-in

workspaces on a single server. To ensure that the server has enough hardware resources to serve the additional demand and stress, a wise administrator will monitor the SharePoint server before adding workspaces.

Unattended Server Installations

If you are installing a large number of SharePoint servers, you may need to perform unattended installations on some servers. When you install SPS using the unattended mode, no dialog boxes appear. This type of installation allows you to install identical configurations of SPS on multiple machines.

To run the unattended installation, first create an .ini file that contains the settings needed for the unattended installation. You can create this file using any text editor, wherein you manually type all the information. But why do that when you can simply run the SPS setup program, which will automatically create the /createunattend switch and the .ini file? Then you can use a text editor to modify the file as needed.

It is a bit unnerving that when you run setup with this switch, it will look and feel as if SPS is being reinstalled on the server. Bear in mind that even though it looks that way, it really isn't being installed on the server. Only the .ini file is being created. The command syntax is as follows:

```
X:\path_to_setup_file\setup /creatunattend: /path filename.ini
```

If you plan to use this technique on different servers with different storage configurations, be sure to modify the installation paths in the .ini file for each unique storage configuration so that the installation goes off without a hitch. It is not recommended that you modify the installation paths for either the WSS or the Search process.

Performing a Remote Installation of SPS

SPS can be installed through the use of Windows 2000 Terminal Services. This allows you to connect to a remote server and then perform the installation from a file share. Be sure that you use the Universal Naming Convention, and not a mapped drive, to connect to the installation share point. Problems will arise if you try to install SPS through a mapped drive via Terminal Services.

Another option is to copy the source files to the local hard drive of the remote machine and then perform the installation from the local files on the remote server. Although this is not a popular option, it is something to consider if you can't get the installation to work properly through Terminal Services and a shared installation point for the source files.

Installing the SPS Client

The client for SPS is little more than a set of extensions to Windows Explorer and Office applications. There is no individual client application for SPS. These extensions integrate certain verbs into the client operating system so that there is a seamless interactivity between the client and the SharePoint server.

To integrate the Office application with SPS, you must be running Office 2000 or later. There is no support for integration of the Office applications with SPS from older versions. The SPS client is automatically included in the Office XP suite.

Installing the SPS client is painless and straightforward. To install the SPS client on a workstation, connect to the installation share point that has the client installation files, and run `setup.exe`. The client files are installed into the `c:\program files\sharepoint portal server\clientdrop\languages\language` directory. Alternatively, you can install the client files by running `setup.exe` from a CD-ROM that contains the client files.

There are no user-configurable options in the client setup program. In addition, before setup begins to install the client files, it first runs a check of the local workstation to ensure that the client computer is running a supported operating system and that other installation requirements are met, such as having Internet Explorer 5.0 or later installed on the workstation.

If the installation requirements are not met, setup will halt with an error message indicating the missing requirements. The only exception to this relates to the Microsoft Data Access Component (MDAC). The minimum version required for installation is 2.5. If an earlier version is found, the client installation program will install MDAC 2.5, Service Pack 1.

NOTE: Do not attempt to use the Web folders client provided in Windows 2000 or Office 2000 if the SPS client is not installed on the client machine. The SPS client updates the Web folders client to include document management features, such as check-in, check-out, and so on. Working with documents using a non-SPS client Web folder will give you unexpected results.

If you plan to use *only* the browser to connect to the dashboard, you need not install the client components. However, if you do install the client components, here is what will be installed on the workstation:

- The client Web folders upgrade.
- The Office 2000 Component Object Model (COM) add-in. This component adds the publishing verbs, such as *check in*, *check out*, and *publish*, to the installed Office applications.
- SPS Collaboration Data Objects (CDO) extensions. This component installs cdoex.dll, which contains Exchange CDO extensions.
- Microsoft Data Access Components.

Registry entries for the SPS client are entered in the HKEY_LOCAL_MACHINE tree, not under the HKEY_CURRENT_USER tree. Hence, the Office COM add-in will not be displayed in the Office interface, as are other add-ins. This means that you cannot remove the Office 2000 COM add-in for troubleshooting purposes.

NOTE: If the SPS client is installed on a workstation and then you install Office 2000 SR1, you'll likely receive an Internal Error 2318 message. The fix for this is to install the Office SR1 before installing the SPS client.

After you install the client components for SPS, you must add a Web folder that points to the workspace(s) to which the client needs connectivity. The default address of the workspace is http://server_name/workspace_name. Use the Add Network Place utility in Network Neighborhood's properties to create this Web folder.

Unattended Installation of Client Components

You can perform unattended installation of the client components by using either Systems Management Server (SMS) or by using Windows Installer in Windows 2000. Alternatively, the program can be pushed down to the workstation using Group Policies in Windows 2000. The program will appear under the Add/Remove section in Control Panel. There are more than a few known issues with the use of Group Policies to install the client to SPS, so be sure to do a search in TechNet on these issues before using Group Policies to install the SPS client.

Uninstalling the SPS Client

The client components can be uninstalled by using the Add/Remove program in Control Panel on the local workstation. Uninstalling the client components removes all components except the upgrade to the Web folders.

Server Updates When SPS Is Installed

When SPS is installed, it creates the folder structure outlined in Table 5–1.

The Web Storage System is also installed with SPS. By default, here are the files and what they do:

- E00.chk: This file keeps track of which completed transactions in the transaction logs have been written to the database on the file and which have not.
- E00.log: This is the current transaction log file.
- E*******.log: These files represent the most recent generations of the transaction log series. Because SPS uses only circular logging, you will rarely see more than five transaction logs in this directory at any given time.
- Res*.log: These are the reserved transaction log files that are used only when the partition runs out of disk space. When this occurs, both files are converted to transaction logs, committed transactions in memory are flushed to the database and recorded in the transaction logs, and the WSS halts.
- Tmp.edb: This is a temporary transaction log file that is used to record transactions when the current E00.log file is being renamed and a new E00.log file is being created. After the new E00.log file is created, transactions written to the tmp.edb log file are written to the new E00.log file.

Table 5–1 Folder structure of SPS

Folder Location	Purpose
C:\program files\common files\system\mssearch\bin	Binary files for the search process
C:\program files\common files\microsoft shared\web storage system	Program files for the WSS
C:\program files\sharepoint portal server\data	Root data directory for SPS
C:\program files\sharepoint portal server\data\web storage system	Folder that hosts the WSS data files, including the databases and transaction logs
C:\program files\sharepoint portal server\data\ftdata	Root of the Search application folder hierarchy for the portal and the full-text index
C:\program files\sharepoint portal server\help	Location for the Help files
C:\program files\sharepoint portal server\bin	Location where the SPS program binary files are installed
C:\program files\sharepoint portal server\OWS	Contains files that work with the IE and Office clients
C:\program files\sharepoint portal server\clientdrop\languages\language	Hosts the client installation files
C:\program files\microsoft integration\sharepoint portal server	Contains the program error and setup logs and a location for update information and documents
C:\program files\sharepoint portal server\data\ftdata\sharepointportalserver	Contains the full-text index, transaction logs, and other information

- Wss.mdb: This is the rich-text portion of the data. This file holds property information about documents and data in the Web store. This file is inextricably linked to the next file, wss.stm.
- Wss.stm: This is the streaming file that holds all the non-rich-text information. All the data said to be held in the Web store is held in this file together with wss.mdb.
- SPS.edb: This database file is used to host the property store for the full-text index.
- MSS*****.log: These are the transaction logs for the sps.edb database.

The transaction logs are numbered in hexadecimal. Creating the first workspace consumes approximately 24MB for the .mdb file, 12MB for the .stm file, and 25MB for the initial transaction logs. When multiple workspaces are created on the same server, they are all held in the .mdb and .stm files. At the time of this writing, SPS does not support the ability to create multiple databases on the same server and then create a mapping between workspaces and individual databases. You must take care in planning how much information you want housed in a single database even if it is hosted by multiple workspaces.

The SPS Web Site

During the installation of SPS, a new Web site is created that has several virtual directories, some of which map to the WSS. When you go into IIS Manager, you might find red stop sign symbols over the icons for these virtual directories. Because the WSS in SPS starts after the services for IIS during a server boot process, the virtual directories are not available to IIS when it is starting its services. To clear these stop sign symbols, stop and restart the IIS Web service. However, this action is not required to make SPS work correctly. Even though the stop sign symbols appear, the virtual directories are working with IIS as they should. These symbols do not represent a critical error or situation.

In Figure 5–8, notice that the SPS Web site installs as a series of virtual directories, including

- Exchweb
- SharePoint Portal Server
- Public
- Name of workspace

The Exchweb virtual directory hosts the files needed for Outlook Web Access (OWA). This might come as a surprise, but OWA is included in the SPS installation. There is no immediate use for OWA in SPS, but it's there. One reason postulated is that it was too difficult to pull OWA out of the WSS because the WSS used in SPS is so similar to the one used in Exchange 2000 Server. Beyond that, I've yet to see, read, or discuss with someone else a significant reason for the existence of OWA in SPS.

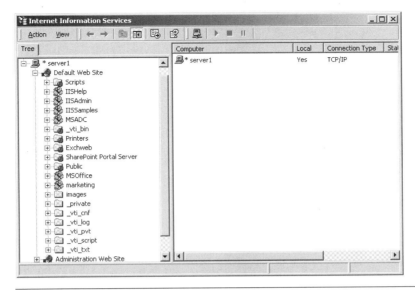

Figure 5-8 IIS default Web site with SPS virtual directories

Troubleshooting Failed Installations

If you're reading this section, it means you're probably not having a good day. SPS doesn't install, or else it has installed and now you're having unexpected problems. This section describes some of the problems that others have encountered installing SPS and explains how they resolved them. It also discusses some of the unexpected results of installing SPS and how to fix those problems, too.

Uninstalling SharePoint Portal Server

You can uninstall SharePoint Portal Server by rerunning the Setup wizard and choosing the uninstall option as opposed to the repair option (more on the repair option in a moment). Uninstalling SPS does the following:

- Removes all application files
- Removes registry entries
- Removes the uninstaller
- Does not install earlier versions of core components
- Removes client components

Individual components of SharePoint cannot be uninstalled and then rein-stalled. It's an all-or-nothing proposition. Uninstalling SPS leaves the machine with updated core components for the Microsoft Foundation Classes Library (MFC), Open Database Connectivity (ODBC), and Data Access Objects (DAO) DLLs.

All workspaces and all data in the workspaces are also removed when SPS is uninstalled. Be sure to save all your critical data to another server before uninstalling SPS.

Repairing SharePoint Portal Server

There may be times when you need to repair the binary files for SPS without having to recover the data in the WSS. For this eventuality, Microsoft has pro-vided a method of repairing the SPS program files. Repairing SPS reinstalls all SPS binary files and registry keys. It also starts the WSS reinstallation process but does not modify any existing data or the WSS during this process. You will not be prompted for any information, such as installation directories.

If you repair the server components of SPS, the client components on the server will also be repaired. The repair process requires at least one free net-work drive letter on the local server. If no free drive letters are available, the repair process will halt and fail. You will also need to reinstall all SharePoint service packs after performing a repair process.

Troubleshooting Log Files

Before we discuss specific problems and solutions, let's look at some trouble-shooting files that you might check if your installation has failed.

First, check the Application Event Log for errors. Then use these event notices as background for reading entries in the log files.

Second, check the `eventlog.txt` and `errorlog.txt` files, which are located (by default) in the `c:\program files\microsoft integration\ sharepoint portal server\logs` directory. The `eventlog.txt` file (Figure 5–9) contains a verbose listing of all setup actions, both successful and failed. If the installation failed, this file will be found in the `%temp%` directory.

The `errorlog.txt` file contains any errors encountered during setup, even if setup was successful. This same information also can be found in `eventlog.txt`. If you have a failed installation, `errorlog.txt` is the first file you should check to see what kind of setup errors you encountered. For failed installations, this file will be located in the `%temp%` directory.

The `setup.log` file is a summary of the major components installed and their versions, and it states whether or not the installation was successful. Error messages for failed installations also are found in this file. It is always

```
eventlog.txt - Notepad                                              _ □ ×
File  Edit  Format  Help
[08/29/01,09:50:08]  Setup.exe: GetGlobalCustomProperty(B51015E7-26A5-4c8f-B871-26ABA9BEFB65
[08/29/01,09:50:08]  Setup.exe: LoadSetupDatabase()
[08/29/01,09:50:08]  Setup.exe: in InternalRegisterSetupService()
[08/29/01,09:50:08]  Setup.exe: in InternalRegisterSetupService()
[08/29/01,09:50:08]  Setup.exe: IsRunningUnattended
[08/29/01,09:50:08]  Setup.exe: AddGlobalCustomProperty
[08/29/01,09:50:08]  Setup.exe: IsRunningUnattended
[08/29/01,09:50:08]  Setup.exe: inside ISetupManager::LoadHelpManager()
[08/29/01,09:50:08]  Setup.exe: in InternalRegisterSetupService()
[08/29/01,09:50:08]  Setup.exe: in InternalRegisterSetupService()
[08/29/01,09:50:08]  Setup.exe: ISetupManager::LoadCommandLineMgr() completed
[08/29/01,09:50:08]  Setup.exe: in InternalRegisterSetupService()
[08/29/01,09:50:09]  Setup.exe: ISetupManager::LoadSetupLog() completed
[08/29/01,09:50:09]  Setup.exe: ISetupManager::RunIntro() starting
[08/29/01,09:50:09]  Setup.exe: inside ISetupManager::LoadDependencyMgr()
[08/29/01,09:50:09]  Setup.exe: in InternalRegisterSetupService()
[08/29/01,09:50:09]  Setup.exe: inside ISetupManager::LoadCDInfoMgr()
[08/29/01,09:50:10]  Setup.exe: GetCustomProperties()
[08/29/01,09:50:10]  Setup.exe: get_CustomProperties()
[08/29/01,09:50:10]  Setup.exe: in InternalRegisterSetupService()
[08/29/01,09:50:10]  Setup.exe: inside ISetupManager::LoadTemplMgr()
[08/29/01,09:50:11]  Setup.exe: in InternalRegisterSetupService()
[08/29/01,09:50:11]  Setup.exe: inside ISetupManager::LoadDiskInfoMgr()
[08/29/01,09:50:12]  Setup.exe: in InternalRegisterSetupService()
[08/29/01,09:50:12]  Setup.exe: inside ISetupManager::LoadUIManager()
[08/29/01,09:50:13]  Setup.exe: in RegisterSetupService()
[08/29/01,09:50:14]  Setup.exe: in InternalRegisterSetupService()
[08/29/01,09:50:14]  Setup.exe: GetGlobalCustomProperty({0DC70217-9545-11D2-ACD4-00C04F8EEBA
[08/29/01,09:50:14]  Setup.exe: IsRunningUnattended
[08/29/01,09:50:14]  Setup.exe: GetGlobalCustomProperty({AA62DF98-3F2C-11D3-887B-00C04F8ECDD
[08/29/01,09:50:14]  Setup.exe: in InternalRegisterSetupService()
```

Figure 5–9 `eventlog.txt` file from a new installation of SPS

located, by default, in the `c:\program files\microsoft integration\ sharepoint portal server\logs` directory.

The `spsclisrv.log` file contains verbose setup logging for the installation of the client components. This file is located in the `c:\program files\ microsoft integration\sharepoint portal server\logs` directory.

The `Exchange Server Setup Progress.log` file is held in the root of the operating system drive and contains verbose setup information for the installation of the WSS and its core components.

Troubleshooting Specific Problems

Now let's look at some specific problems you might encounter.

You Cannot Connect to the SPS Workspace from Windows 98, Windows ME, or Windows NT

If you try to use the Web folders shortcut or the Open command in an Office 2000 application, you may receive this error message:

```
You have attempted to connect to a SharePoint Portal Server. To use the
document management features of SharePoint Portal Server, you must
install Outlook Express 5 (or later).
```

This error comes from having an old version of the `inetcomm.dll` file. Install Internet Explorer 5.0 or later, and this error should go away. Because IE 5.0 is installed by default with Windows 2000, this error will appear only on older desktop operating systems.

After You Install SPS, Outlook Express No Longer Works

Reboot the server. Outlook Express will start thereafter.

You Get Internal Error 2755 When Trying to Install the SPS Client Components

You'll get this error if you're trying to install the client to SPS via Terminal Services (TS) and you've mapped a drive inside TS to the client installation share. To get rid of this error, use a Universal Naming Convention (UNC - `\\server_name\share_name`) to connect to the shared files rather than map a drive inside TS.

Setup Stops with Error 0xC0070002

You usually receive this error when you're attempting to uninstall or repair SPS and the Exchange 2000 Server administration tools have been previously installed and then uninstalled. To fix this problem, please follow the instructions in Q295721.

Event 20488: Cannot Create a New Workspace

You might also receive this error message:

```
The process cannot access the file because it is being used by another
process.
```

Be sure to disable virus scanning during both the installation of SPS and workspace creation.

You Cannot Install SPS Because a Subcomponent Failed

The error message may look like this:

```
Setup failed while installing subcomponent OLEDB protocol with error code
0xc103798A.
```

This can occur on a Windows 2000 Server that was upgraded from Windows NT 4.0. The solution here is to manually register the `oledb32.dll` file with the following command:

```
Regsvr32 oledb32.dll
```

Other Errors

Many other errors you're likely to encounter can be avoided as follows:

- Do not attempt to install SPS when logged on with cached credentials. This will result in a VAIfy error.
- You must have at least one drive letter free during the installation or repair of SPS, or else the installation will fail.
- Be sure that your date and time synchronization is accurate with the SNTP (Simple Network Time Protocol) Server.
- Ensure that the Cache ISAPI Applications setting on your default Web site is enabled, that the WWW service and IIS Admin Service are started, and that HTTP keep-alives are enabled.
- IE proxy settings must not use automatic settings, and if there is a proxy server, you must specify the Bypass proxy server for local addresses.

Summary

This chapter explains how to install, uninstall, and repair SharePoint Portal Server. It also discusses the issues surrounding successful and failed installations and suggests ways to improve your chances of experiencing a successful installation of SPS. Next, we turn our attention to the administration of SharePoint Portal Server. Chapter 6 looks at how to work with documents and document folders.

PART III

Administration

Working with Documents and Document Folders

Document management (DM) is one of the two compelling reasons to purchase SharePoint Portal Server (the other being the SPS development environment). The DM features are the driving force behind many decisions to purchase and implement SPS.

When viewed only as a DM program, SPS falls short of its competitors, such as PCDocs or Lotus Notes Knowledge Discovery Server. Feature for feature, these competitors outperform SPS in a number of areas. Yet SPS is being implemented far and wide because of its portal abilities and tight integration with the Office XP suite of applications. Investing today in SPS is a commitment to what SPS will become in the future, and managers are making this decision banking on the hope that the DM features will be much improved in future releases.

Based on my conversations with IT managers in the field, there is not universal enthusiasm for SPS, especially when it comes to large-scale DM deployments that require complex security structures. SPS is being implemented anyway, however, and IT managers are waiting for updates in future service pack releases while scrambling to find developers to write customized code to help them overcome its shortcomings.

But in spite of this gloomy picture, SPS has features that constitute a good, basic DM solution. Many smaller companies implementing this portal product will find that SharePoint Portal Server 2001 meets their needs.

This chapter dives into what SPS offers in DM functionality. There may be more here than what you might initially expect. But I'm sure that at some point you'll wonder why Microsoft didn't do this or that with DM. You won't be alone. However, it would be good to remember that this is a 1.0 product and will be improved and tweaked in the coming service packs and revisions. So let's get going and take a look at how DM functionality works in SPS.

Managing Document Folders

Documents in an SPS workspace are held in document folders in the Web Storage System. Because a folder structure can be created that mimics a file server's directory structure for documents, it's easy to confuse the folder structure with that of a file server. Please don't fall for the idea that the Document Library dashboard is little more than a Web-based front end to a traditional file server structure. Nothing could be further from the truth.

Standard and Enhanced Folders

One feature that separates document folders from traditional folders in a file directory structure is that a document folder can be either standard or enhanced. A standard document folder can support public documents but does not support check-in, check-out, and publishing. Enhanced folders support these functions, which help a team collaborate on the development of a document.

Standard folders have limited functionality because they offer little in the way of support for document collaboration. The main reason to create and use standard folders is that they are the only type that hosts compound or multipart documents, such as a Word document that has an embedded Excel spreadsheet or an HTML document with relative links. Enhanced folders cannot host these types of documents. Collaboration on compound documents must be performed either on each part of the document in an enhanced folder or be performed outside the SPS workspace using traditional methods.

Because standard folders do not support collaboration features such as checking in a document before publishing it, documents that are placed in a standard folder are immediately public. Hence, such a document is immediately viewable by all users in the workspace who have at least the Reader permission.

Documents held in an enhanced folder must be checked out before they can be edited. While a document is checked out, it can be viewed by other team members, but it cannot be checked out and modified. This means that SPS 2001 has no support for the simultaneous, multiple checking out of the same document. Documents must be edited in serial, not parallel. Such an architecture eliminates the need to merge document changes into a single master document and force an individual to deal with conflicts in document changes.

Each time a document is checked out, a new, full, working copy is created that is a child of the version that was last checked in. The check-out action forces the author to create a copy of the document on the local hard drive; after modification, this version is copied back to the workspace to become the most recent version of the document.

NOTE: Throughout this discussion, I refer to an author performing the DM functions. Coordinators can also perform these same functions. However, for discussion purposes, when I refer to an *author*, I mean any user who has been granted either the Author or Coordinator role for the documents in question. For a discussion of the SharePoint security roles, please consult Chapter 13.

The check-in action converts the working copy of the document held on the author's local hard drive to the most recent draft version, which is stored in the workspace on the SPS server. Once checked in, the document is available to other authors for that folder. Because those given only the Reader security role on the document's parent folder can see only published documents, readers cannot view a document that has only been checked in. When checking in a document, authors can choose to initiate the publishing process, which, if so configured, also triggers the approval process.

The publishing action creates a new, primary version of the document and sets that version as the default, approved version available to those with the Reader, Author, or Coordinator security roles. Only checked-in documents can be published.

Some administrators have complained that they are not allowed to simply click a document in the workspace to open it, make changes, and then save it back to the workspace. This limitation is by design. First, when you click a document in the workspace, it naturally opens in the browser and not in its native application. You can view a document opened in the browser, but you cannot make changes to it because the browser is not the document's native application. Second, if someone could quickly open the document, make a change in the browser, and then close it back to the workspace, it would bypass the formal DM process. Errors could occur in which two users opened the document at the same time and created conflicting changes. So don't look for a way to modify a document in the workspace on the fly. Document modifications *require* you and your users to follow the DM process of check-out, modify, check-in.

The default Documents folder is an enhanced folder. By default, every new folder that is created in the workspace inherits the folder type and security structure of its parent. Hence, by default, all document folders in the workspace will be enhanced folders unless you manually configure a new folder to be a standard folder.

When you change the folder type from enhanced to standard or vice versa, the folder must be empty. So to change the folder's type, you must first remove all its documents. Then you open the folder's properties and either select or clear the Enable Enhanced Folders check box, as illustrated in Figure 6–1. Note that this view is available only to authors and coordinators in the Web folders view. It's not available through the dashboard view.

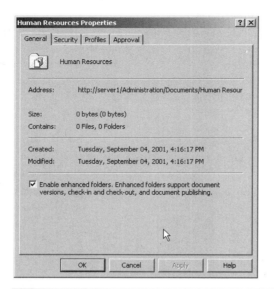

Figure 6–1 Folder properties displaying the Enable Enhanced Folders check box

Administering Document Folders

The administration of document folders includes creating and configuring the folders to meet the needs of your workspace users. As with many SPS workspace administrative activities, there is more than one way to perform an administrative task. Working with document folders is no exception.

Document folders can be created in the dashboard or the Web folders view, as you prefer. To create a new document folder using the dashboard, navigate to the folder in which you want to create a new subfolder. This means that to create a new top-level folder in the Document Library dashboard, you open the Documents folder and then click the Add Sub-Folder link, as displayed in Figure 6–2. Clicking this link brings up the Create a New Folder Web page (Figure 6–3), where you type the name of the new folder and then click Create. If you change your mind, you can click Cancel to cancel the operation.

A new document folder can also be created in the Web folders view. Simply right-click inside the window that is focused on the folder in which you want to create a new subfolder. Then point to New and select Folder (Figure 6–4). A new folder will be created and ready to be named inside the window. Name the folder, and you'll immediately see it in the dashboard view. You should know that document folders are immediately available for use after they have been created.

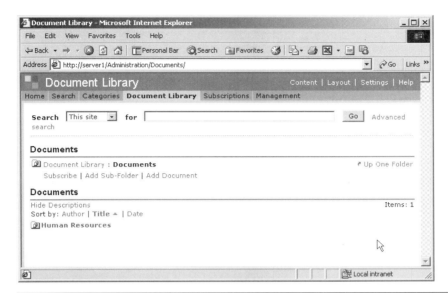

Figure 6–2 Add Sub-Folder link in the Document Library dashboard

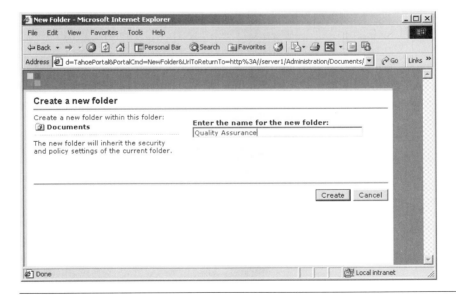

Figure 6–3 Create a New Folder page

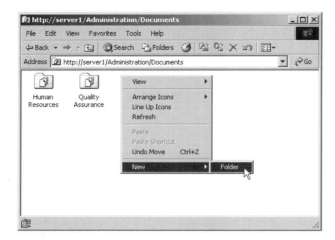

Figure 6–4 Creating a new document folder in the Web folders view

In the Web folders view, you can rename or delete a document folder using its context menu. Right-click the document folder, and choose the action you need. You cannot rename or delete a document folder using the dashboard.

For faster access, end users can use this context menu to create shortcuts to a document folder. The shortcut is automatically placed on the user's desktop—a handy feature for those who often access a particular document folder and don't wish to navigate the document folder structure repeatedly throughout the workday. Shortcuts honor the security settings on the document folder and do not bypass any change that's made in security settings. Hence, a user who creates a shortcut to a document folder and whose permissions to the folder are later removed will not lose the desktop shortcut. However, when the shortcut is invoked, a logon dialog box will appear asking the user for credentials to access the folder.

Users can also create a shortcut in the dashboard by right-clicking the document folder and selecting Copy Shortcut. Thereafter, the user can place the shortcut on her desktop by using the Paste Shortcut command from the desktop context menu.

In the Web folders view, it's easy to move document folders around. For instance, you can drag and drop one document folder into another one. Or you can use the Cut and Paste commands, cutting a document folder and then pasting it into a different part of the hierarchy. You can move folders when they're populated with documents.

NOTE: Chapter 13 discusses security settings on document folders, and Chapter 9 explains document publishing and approval. Working with document profiles is discussed later in this chapter in "Creating and Managing Document Profiles."

Administering Documents and Document Versioning

If any part of the SPS program will require end-user training, it is this part. Your users will need to learn not only how to use the dashboard interface to find and work with documents but also how to think differently about document management.

For instance, this book is being written using SPS as the DM solution (seemed like a good idea to use the product I'm writing about, eh?). And the excellent editors at Addison-Wesley and the team of technical editors were gracious enough to adjust their traditional editing process to accommodate the use of SPS in the production of this book. The most difficult change was that the editing had to be done serially instead of batching the chapters for each section, e-mailing them to all the editors at the same time, and then having the chapters sent back to me for review. With SPS, a level of coordination had to be implemented in order to make the editing flow smoothly.

So learning how to work with the DM functions of SPS is not difficult. But some unanticipated workflow and cultural adjustments may also need to be made. Be prepared to manage the "people" part of this technology.

The Web Folders Client

In the 1990s, documents were managed using folder shares and mapped drives. In fact, we taught our users to put their important files on the server for backup, and they connected to the server through a share on a folder.

If the 1990s were the decade of local area networks (LANs), folder shares, and mapped drives, this first decade in the new millennium will be the decade of the Internet, Web folders, and connectivity to information from any device at any time from any place. Increasing numbers of users will be using the Internet to access their information on the LAN or on Internet-based servers, and that is where Web folders come into play.

You can think of Web folders as a method of creating a mapped drive to a URL and routing what would normally be thought of as LAN-based traffic over port 80. Now, what really happens is not a drive mapping over port 80—but that is the experience of the end user. Architecturally, a Web folder is an interface for managing folders and documents using Web-based technologies, such as a browser.

In SPS, Web folders are used primarily by coordinators and authors, not readers. In other words, they are used mainly for administrative purposes. The Web folders client in Windows 2000 will be updated when the SPS client is installed on the workstation. Thereafter, a Web folder will need to be created to the workspace so that users can use it for saving and opening files inside an Office application.

In Windows 2000, you can create a Web folder by opening My Network Places on the desktop and double-clicking the Add Network Place icon. This will invoke the Welcome to the Add Network Place wizard. Type the URL you wish to connect to (Figure 6–5), click Next, and then click Finish.

You can also create a Web folder to the root Documents folder in the workspace or to any document folder whose entire path name contains no spaces. For instance, if you create a folder titled "Quality Assurance" in the Documents folder and then try to create a Web folder to it, you would use this URL:

```
http://<server_name>/<workspace_name>/documents/quality assurance
```

When the Web folders client reads this URL, it will stop parsing after the word *quality* because there is a space in the URL; and because there is no folder under the Documents folder named "quality," it will default to creating a Web folder to the Documents folder.

To work around this, be sure not to include spaces in your document folder names. For instance, to create a folder to host documents on the rate of accidents in a manufacturing plant, name it "AccidentRates" and not "Accident Rates."

Figure 6–5 Entering the URL for the administration workspace on Server1

In that way, users can create a Web folder to this folder and work with documents directly in the folder from their Office application.

NOTE: The entire document folder path must be free of spaces in order for users to create Web folders to a document folder deeply nested inside the document folder hierarchy. Even using the "%20" space filler will not ensure a Web folder path to a folder name that has spaces.

Users can create desktop shortcuts that point to a Web folder. These shortcuts allow the user to drag and drop documents into a Web folder location. To create a shortcut to a Web folder, right-click the Web folder inside My Network Places, and choose Create Shortcut from the context menu. A second copy of the Web folder will appear in the window; this copy will have the same name and the next increment number for that shortcut. Then you can drag and drop the shortcut to the desktop, and users can drag and drop files into the document folder on the SPS server.

To save time, you could simply drag the original Web folders client icon to the desktop and bypass creating a shortcut to it. But this would remove the Web folders client from the My Network Places window and place it on your desktop.

Using Web Folders over the Internet

An immediate use for Web folders is to allow users who are away from the office to access the folders over the Internet. But don't limit your thinking to those who travel. Think also of those who could regularly perform part or most of their job from their homes. In the near future, telecommuting will be a normal part of many people's job description. If your company needs additional office space, consider telecommuting as a way to control overhead costs while increasing the number of employees on your network.

Troubleshooting Web Folders

If your users are having problems connecting to the workspace using Web folders, one of the first lines of defense is to flush the application cache on the Maintenance dashboard. Another method of clearing the cache is to reboot the server.

If clearing the application cache doesn't solve your problem, you'll need to use the Network Monitor utility to analyze the packets that are being sent between the client and the server. If you don't see any HTTP traffic, it means that either the server is down or you've typed the workspace URL incorrectly. If the NetMon trace shows HTTP traffic but returns errors, it means that the server being accessed is not configured to accept MSDAIPP Web folder connections using the HTTP DAV protocol. You'll know this because the first GET request from the client will be met with an "HTTP 1.1: 404 Object not found" error message. In this scenario, be sure that the FrontPage extensions on the SPS server have been installed correctly and that you're running IIS 5.0 or later.

Adding Documents to the Workspace

Documents can be added to the workspace in several ways. First, I'll describe how to add an individual document to the workspace, and then I'll describe how to perform bulk importation of documents.

Individual documents can be added to the workspace in one of three ways: through the dashboard, through Web folders, and through an Office application.

Adding a Document Using the Dashboard

To add a document to the workspace using the dashboard, navigate to the desired document folder, and then click the Add Document link (Figure 6–6). This will invoke the Add a Document Web page (Figure 6–7). You can browse to select the document from your local hard drive or from a network location.

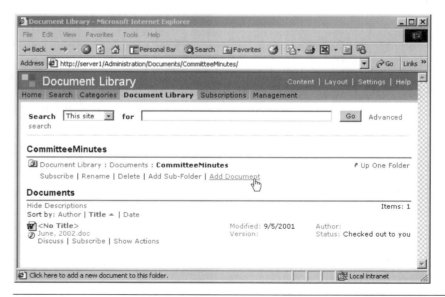

Figure 6–6   Add Document link in the dashboard

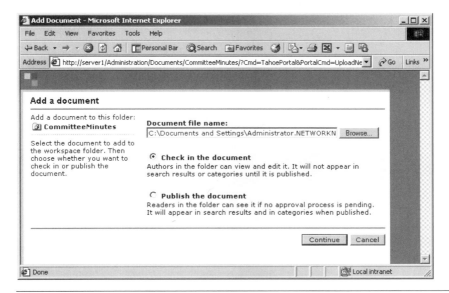

Figure 6–7 Add a Document Web page

After the document is specified, the entire path to the document will automatically be added to the Document File Name input box.

When you add a document to the workspace, you can also check the document in, or even publish it if you like, by selecting the appropriate radio button. In this interface, you cannot choose to add a document without either checking it in or publishing it. The radio buttons in Figure 6–7 require that you choose one or the other. This is different from using the Web folders, discussed in a moment.

After making your selection, click Continue. The document's profile will appear on the Version Comments page (Figure 6–8). You must apply a document profile to a document when you check it in to the workspace. After typing the information—some of which may be required—click Save at the bottom of the page, and the document will appear in the workspace.

Adding a Document Using Web Folders

Using Web folders, adding a document is as simple as using a drag-and-drop or cut-and-paste method. Open the Web folders client to the workspace, and navigate to the desired document folder. Then open a second window using Windows Explorer or My Computer, and navigate to the source document. Once you have the two windows open, you can drag and drop the source document into the window that is focused on the document folder, or you can right-click

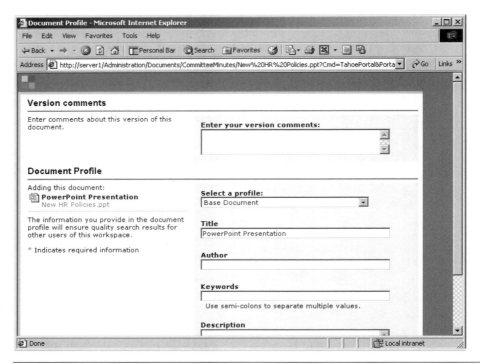

Figure 6–8 Version Comments Web page, where you apply a document profile to a new document

the source document, select Cut, change your focus to the target document folder window, right-click, and select Paste. Either method will create a copy of the source document in the document folder.

Documents copied in this manner are copied as checked-out documents. This allows for bulk operations. You can select multiple documents and then drag and drop them to the desired folder. Or if you select a source folder, all its documents and subfolders will be copied into the workspace. Once documents are copied to the workspace, you can perform a number of administrative actions on them using the context menu, as illustrated in Figure 6–9.

Checking in the documents in bulk saves administrative effort. The only downside is that when a group of documents is checked in, all of them will get the same document profile, including author and title. If you need to associate a different title with each document, you can't check in the documents in bulk.

So if you have 10,000 documents that need to be imported into the workspace, and if each one needs a unique title, then you must perform 10,000 check-in operations. This task can be scripted by a developer.

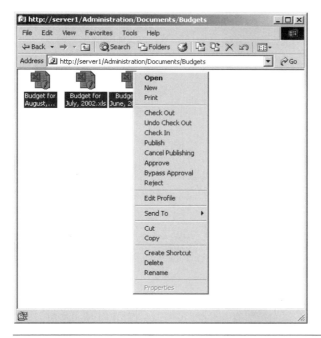

Figure 6–9 The context menu for bulk import of documents supports numerous administrative functions.

Documents can be checked out, published, approved, and rejected using this same context menu. Coordinators can use this menu to cancel a published document, approve a document that was rejected by the approvers, bypass the approval process, reject a document that is undergoing an approval process, and retrieve a document that has been checked out. These actions can be committed to one document or a group of selected documents.

Adding a Document Using an Office Application

When you save a document from an Office application, you can use the Save As command to navigate the document folder hierarchy using the Web folder as a client (Figure 6–10). In this figure, the Committee Minutes document for August 2002 is being saved to the CommitteeMinutes document folder. Because the Web folder is targeted at the root document folder in the workspace, it doesn't list the CommitteeMinutes subfolder in the Save In dropdown list. This arrangement could present problems for your users if they accidentally choose the wrong subfolder in which to save their document.

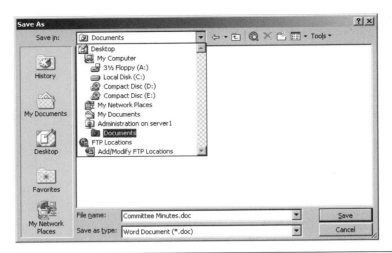

Figure 6–10 Save As dialog box in Word 2002 illustrating the use of Web folders for saving documents to the SPS workspace

Hence, you should consider creating multiple Web folders clients to each document folder in which a user regularly saves documents.

When you click Save, the Web File Properties dialog box will appear, asking you to choose a document profile for the document (Figure 6–11). When you click OK, the document will be copied to the workspace.

Now comes the interesting part. When you try to close the document—either by exiting from Word or by closing the document—you'll be asked whether you want to check in the changes to the document or leave the document checked out. If you choose to leave the document checked out, the document in Word will close, and that will be all.

However, if you choose to check in the document, you will get the Version Comments Web page shown earlier, where you can click the Publish This Document After Check-in check box (Figure 6–12). Clicking this check box will automatically publish the document after it has been checked in. You can also enter version comments to inform other authors of information about the document when they open the document's profile.

NOTE: A *thicket* is a set of files and folders that is created when a document is saved using the Save As a Page command in an Office application. You can save Office thickets only to standard folders unless you use the Office 2000 Web Archive add-in, which allows you to use this command to save your information to a single file using MHTML.

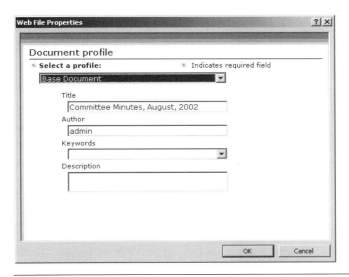

Figure 6–11 Web File Properties dialog box, where you apply a document profile to a document being saved to the workspace

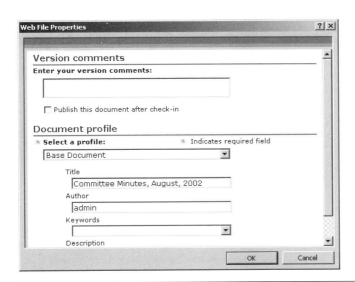

Figure 6–12 Version Comments Web page with the Publish This Document After Check-in check box

Administering Document Versioning

SPS implements a two-tier versioning model. Each document enjoys one of two version series:

- *Primary* (or *public*) version series: This is the set of versions that is approved for public use and viewable by readers. Only the most recent version of a document is viewable by readers. These versions are also termed *major* versions.
- *Secondary* (or *draft*) version series: This is the set of versions that are "under construction." This version series is available only to authors and coordinators. Readers cannot view draft versions of documents, nor do draft versions appear in the result set of a search request. These versions are also termed *minor* versions.

The current architecture of SPS versioning does not support tree branching, which allows multiple draft versions of the same draft series to become new, primary versions of new document version series. Instead, in SPS, documents follow a single version path, with SPS maintaining a full-text version of each document in the Shadow folder.

SPS uses a simple versioning scheme for all documents in the workspace. Version numbers are appended in a set of parentheses following the name of the document, in the following format: (#.#). The number to the left of the dot (.) is the current primary (or major) version number, and the number to the right of the dot is the current draft (or minor) version number. Each check-out increments the draft version number, and each publishing action increments the primary version number by 1.

Hence, if a document's current version number is 2.6, it means that the document has been published twice and the current published version has been checked out (and presumably modified) six additional times. When a new version of this document is published, its version number will become 3.0.

Previous versions of a document can be accessed in one of two ways. First, the Web folders client can be used to open the properties of the document (Figure 6–13). From this location, you can view

- The document version
- The date and time that the document was checked in or published
- The name of the user who created the document version
- Version comments
- The document profile that was specified at the time of check-in

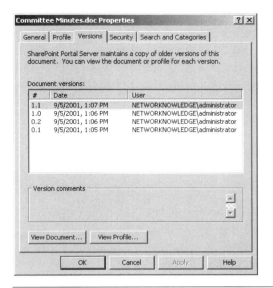

Figure 6–13 Document properties showing past versions of a document

The Shadow folder that holds these documents can be found using the Web folders client of the workspace. Inside the Shadow folder, you'll find a mirror image of the document folder structure and all the versions of each document, including the most recent version (Figure 6–14). When a document is deleted, all its previous versions are also deleted.

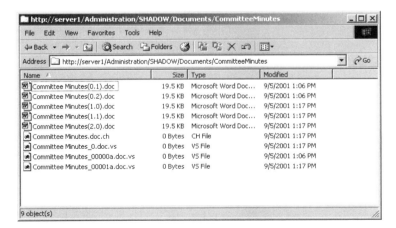

Figure 6–14 Listing of all previous versions of a document in the Shadow folder

The second way to view the version histories of a document is to use the Show Actions link beneath the document in the dashboard and then choose the Version History link from the Document Inspection dashboard. The document's version history will be displayed, along with a link to each version. This list in the dashboard is identical to the list in the Web folders client view.

Version Pruning

By default, version pruning is not turned on; an unlimited number of primary versions can exist on the workspace. However, you can specify a maximum number, from 1 to 999. Each time a document is published, its primary number is incremented by 1. Versions that are older than the specified value are permanently deleted from the workspace, including all draft versions of the primary version. The value that you set does not affect the number of draft versions, only the number of primary versions that are stored in the workspace.

To turn on version pruning, in the Web folders view double-click the Workspace Settings icon inside the Management folder. At the bottom of the General tab, you'll see a check box labeled Number of Major Versions Retained Per Document, as illustrated in Figure 6–15. Select this check box, and then type the desired number.

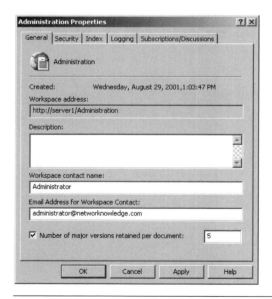

Figure 6–15 Configuring the workspace to retain the five most recent primary versions of published documents

You may be wondering whether there is another way to retire or expire older documents. Without writing a customized script, the answer is no: SPS has no other native way to expire, retire, terminate, discontinue, fail, wither, extinguish, delete, remove, or otherwise get rid of a document in the workspace.

When you specify a new version pruning number, SPS does not automatically check every existing document in the workspace. Instead, the new value will be applied to each document version series only when a new version of the document is published. If you want to reduce the amount of disk space that is being consumed by old document versions, you must force a publish operation on each document series that violates the new version retention policy. Best practice is to configure version pruning before you import a large number of documents, so that the value is enforced from the beginning.

This is a real sticking point for a number of SPS administrators. Especially in larger environments, they can envision their workspace hard disk space getting out of control quickly because of both the number of primary documents and the number of draft versions of each one. In the absence of an automatic removal mechanism, it is possible that a server's disk space will be eaten up with outdated versions of documents. My advice is to either set the number low—say, between 2 and 4—or hire a developer to write a script that fires periodically and deletes documents based on their modified date, size, or some other type of document metadata.

Document Actions in the Dashboard

Inside the dashboard, some cool document management features are available to your users, whether they are readers, authors, or even coordinators. This section focuses on these actions and explains how they work. First, however, a couple of housekeeping items are worth noting.

First, remember that you can't work on a document's profile or properties as long as the document is checked in to the workspace. To make such changes, you must first check out the document.

Second, the title of the document that appears in the dashboard is different from the name of the document. The title itself is configured in the document's profile during check-in. If you don't train your users to enter a title, you will get a list of documents similar to the one illustrated in Figure 6–16. Notice that `June, 2002.doc` has no title, and this fact, unfortunately, is the most prominent item about the file that is presented in the title view for these documents.

Beneath each document in the dashboard are three links to it: Discuss, Subscribe, and Show Actions. The Show Actions link invokes the Document Inspection dashboard, which displays two Web parts: the Actions Web part,

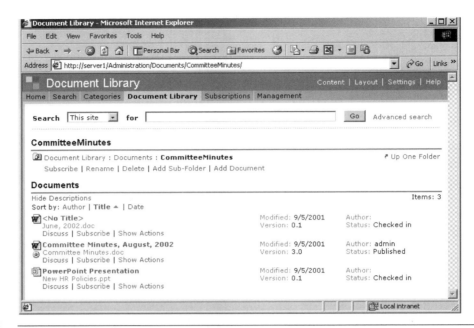

Figure 6–16 How a document with no title is presented in the dashboard

which shows the actions that can be performed on the document, and the Information Web part, which shows detailed information about the document. You can use the Document Inspection dashboard to check in, check out, publish, delete, and rename a document.

NOTE: When you choose to rename a document, you are changing is file name, not its title. The only way to change the title is to check out the document and then, during check-in, give it a new title.

To check out a document, click the Check Out link in the Actions Web part on the Document Inspection dashboard; then follow the instructions on the Check Out a Document Web page. Essentially, you right-click the document link and choose to save the file to your local hard drive.

Once a file has been checked out, the Actions Web part for that document will contain a link, available only to coordinators, to undo the check-out. If this link is chosen, the most recent version of the document in the workspace will be checked in, and its version number will be decremented to the version before the document was checked out.

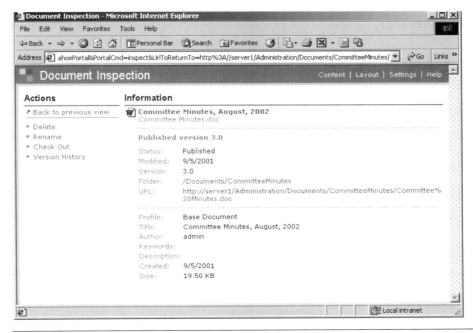

Figure 6–17 Document Inspection dashboard

Using Categories to Find Documents

Most users are accustomed to finding documents by browsing a directory structure on a server, and this means that their first instinct is to browse the document folder hierarchy to find their documents. Many SPS administrators are trying to move users away from browsing to using the other two main SPS tools: categories and searching. In fact, some administrators are even deleting the Documents dashboard, forcing their users to find documents without browsing.

This section covers how categories can be used to find documents. Chapter 7 discusses the search process in detail and illustrates how to use the Search Web part to find documents. Chapter 8 discusses how to work with categories from a planning and administrative perspective. So as you read this section, if you find yourself wondering how I created the category structure in the example, please refer to Chapter 8.

To find a document using categories, click a top-level category hierarchy; this is found on the Categories Web part, which is, by default, on the left side of the Home dashboard. Each word or phrase that you see in the Categories Web part is a link to all the subcategories that have been created beneath it.

The top-level categories do not (and in most environments, should not) have any type of peer-to-peer relationship to one another.

There is also a Categories dashboard that allows access to the same category hierarchy. This view of the categories is a bit better than that provided by the Web part because, unlike the Web part view, the default in the Categories dashboard is to display the first two levels of categories, as illustrated in Figure 6–18. Such a view can eliminate at least one click for users because they can begin their search at the second level instead of the top level, as in the Categories Web part.

The downside to using the Categories dashboard to access a category hierarchy is that if there are more than five second-level categories, only the first five (in alphabetical order) appear; the others are available by clicking the More link (shown in Figure 6–18). The More link invokes the Categories Web part, with its focus on the category level referenced by the More link. The Categories Web part displays all the categories, as illustrated in Figure 6–19.

Figure 6–19 also shows the "John Somebody" name listed as the contact for this category. This entry is the default entry; you can change it by accessing the category's properties in the Web folders view and entering the name and e-mail address of the contact person for this category. This is illustrated in Figure 6–20.

Documents that match a category structure will be displayed, along with the other categories. Any subcategories will be listed in the Categories Web

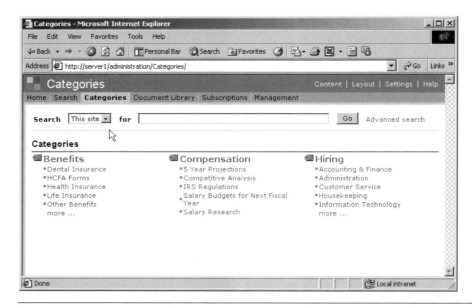

Figure 6–18 Listing of categories on the Categories dashboard

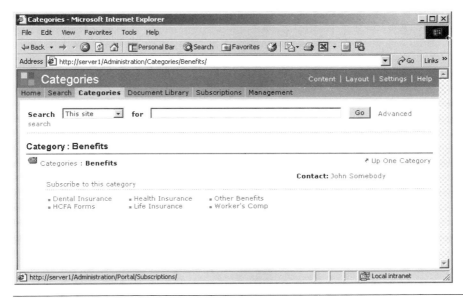

Figure 6–19 Categories listed in the Categories Web part

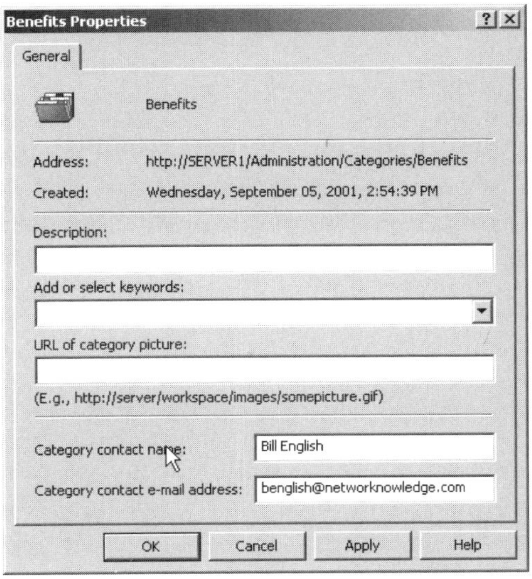

Figure 6–20 Configuring the contact person for a category in the category's properties

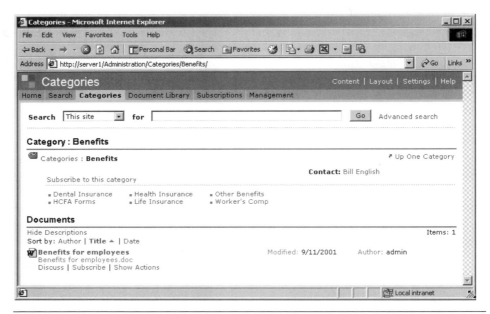

Figure 6–21 Benefits category listing subcategories plus a document assigned to this category

part, and the documents associated with that category will be listed in the Documents Web part beneath the category. Figure 6–21 shows how the documents are listed. Notice that the Documents Web part—which resides in the Documents dashboard, as discussed earlier in this chapter—is invoked here, complete with the various available document actions: discussion, subscription, and the publishing actions.

Folder Properties and Inheritance

Folder properties, profiles, and permissions are inherited by lower-level folders and files. By default, new folders and files inherit their parent's permissions. This is similar in concept to the inheritance of the ACLs (access control lists) in the NTFS file system. When a new folder is created beneath a parent folder, all security role configurations are exactly the same for the child as for the parent folder.

When changes are made to a folder's properties, the changes are inherited by all child folders and files. If inheritance is deselected by a child folder, any subsequent changes to the child's properties or security configurations do not affect its parent's configurations.

Approval policies are inherited by a child folder when it is created, but subsequent changes to the approval policies of the parent folder are not inherited by the child folders.

You can see folder properties in the Web folders view by right-clicking the folder and choosing Properties. Four tabs—General, Security, Profiles, and Approval—constitute each folder's properties.

The General tab lists the URL of the folder along with its size, creation date, last modified date, and the number of folders and files it contains. The General tab also contains the check box to configure the folder to be an enhanced folder, which is the inherited default in every SPS workspace. An enhanced folder allows files to be checked out, checked in, and published. Clearing this check box makes the folder a standard folder, which is useful if you want to work with Office-based compound documents in an SPS workspace.

The Security tab (Figure 6–22) is the location where you set security roles for the folder, its files, and its subfolders and files. You also use this tab to block security inheritance by clearing the Use Parent Folder's Security Settings check box. Security settings configured here can be forced to all lower-level folders and files by selecting the Reset All Subfolders to Use These Security Settings check box.

FOR MORE INFO: For more information on security in SPS, please consult Chapter 13.

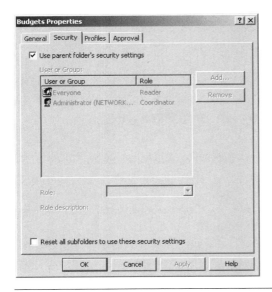

Figure 6–22 Security tab from a folder's properties

Figure 6–23 Profiles tab from a folder's properties

On the Profiles tab (Figure 6–23), you configure one or more profiles to be available for documents that are developed inside the folder. At the bottom of this tab, you choose the default profile for all files saved in the folder. As additional profiles are created, they will be available on this tab for addition to the folder's properties. The next section explains how to create new document profiles.

On the Approval tab (Figure 6–24) you configure approval routes and approvers for the documents in a folder. Notice that these properties are configured for all files in a folder and cannot be configured on a file-by-file basis. Publishing and approving documents are discussed in depth in Chapter 8.

Creating and Managing Document Profiles

One of the key components of finding documents quickly using the Search Web part is to have the correct metadata—descriptive document information—associated with documents. This metadata is exposed and configured using document profiles. A well-planned document profile yields rich search data to help users to find a document quickly and easily.

It is important not to miss this point: The main goal in creating good document profiles is to make it easier and faster to find the document's content through its collection of metadata. Metadata is stored with a document but is not a part of it.

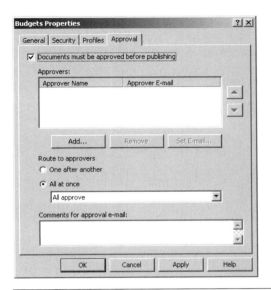

Figure 6–24 Approval tab from a folder's properties

Information that is configured to be part of a document's profile can be created and altered in the SPS graphical interfaces. When a new property is configured for a document profile, that property amounts to an addition to the schema of the workspace.

The technical aspects of creating document profiles are easy, as you'll see in a moment. However, the planning that goes into a document profile must be extensive because a good set of profiles is the result of excellent planning. In other words, if users are to find the right documents quickly, those documents must be described correctly, and such descriptions are the result of a collaborative effort between the SPS management team and users.

For instance, suppose you're implementing SPS for a law firm that specializes in divorce and bankruptcy cases. Before you create the profiles for the firm's documents, you should first sit down with those who will interact with the documents in the workspace and ask them what kinds of data they would use to describe the documents. You'll be surprised by some of their answers. But knowing how your users think *about* their own documents is the soil from which excellent document profiles are grown.

Profiles are presented to users through the `pubform.asp` file on the server. This ASP (Active Server Pages) page will appear whenever a document is checked in to an enhanced folder or added to a standard folder. The form that is presented is identical whether a user is checking in the document from an Office application, a Web folders client, or the browser. Microsoft strongly advises against customizing `pubform.asp`. If you do so and problems arise as a result, you will find yourself without support from Microsoft.

To create a new document profile, you open the Document Profiles folder under the Management folder using the Web folders client, and run the Add Document Profile wizard. When you first open this folder, you'll find four default profiles automatically installed with SPS: Announcements, Base Document, New Item, and Web Link. Each of these profiles is used to describe the type of document suggested by its name. Each document type can have multiple profiles created to meet the needs of those who use the workspace.

The Add Document Profile wizard can be invoked in this folder. The wizard starts with a Welcome screen; clicking Next takes you to the Document Profile screen (Figure 6–25). Here, you type the name of the profile and then choose one of the existing profiles as a template. In this example, I'm creating a new Human Resource profile to describe the various HR documents in the workspace. So I type *Human Resource* in the Name input box and select the Base Document as my template.

NOTE: The profile name must be unique and cannot contain the following characters:

: \ ? \ # * < > / | " ~

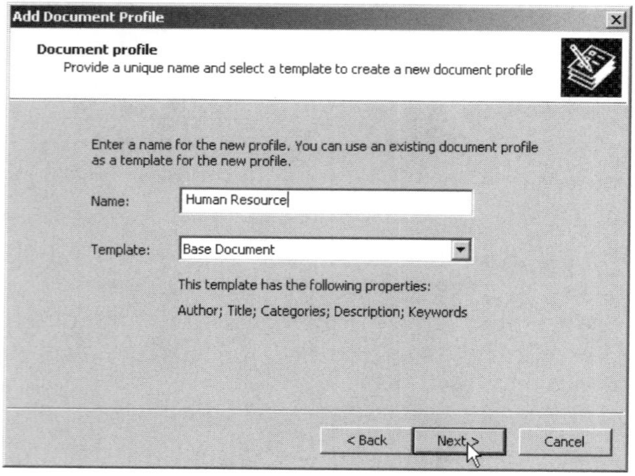

Figure 6–25 Document Profile screen in the Add Document Profile wizard

When you click Next, the Select the Properties screen appears (Figure 6–26). On this screen, you select the properties to be used to describe these documents. If you wish, you can choose from a predefined list of properties:

- Author
- Categories
- Company
- Description
- Keywords
- Link
- Manager
- Subject
- Title

Following each default property is the word *System* in parentheses. This is to remind you that this property was created by the SPS system and not by a coordinator. The property type is listed (more on this in a moment) and whether or not it is required.

The Required field indicates which properties must be filled in by an author when checking in a document. For instance, if a document is being checked in to the workspace and the Required field of the Author property for the chosen profile is set to Yes, then SPS will not allow the document to be checked in until the Author field in the document's profile contains a name. It's obvious that SPS is not smart enough to tell the difference between a string

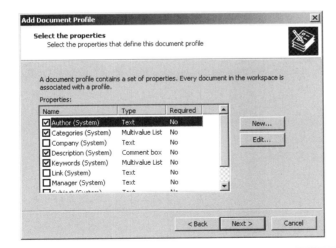

Figure 6–26 Select the Properties screen in the Add Document Profile wizard

of random letters and a proper name. So it's probably more accurate to say that a required field must be populated with at least one character, but for practical purposes, it's best to say that the field must be filled in with the needed information before SPS will check in the document.

A coordinator can create new properties for inclusion in the new document profile. When the New button is clicked, a simple Create New Property dialog box appears asking for the field name, the type of data that the field will hold, and whether the new property will be required.

The property types that can be used are as follows:

- Text: A Text property type creates a simple text field that holds as many as 55 characters on a single line.
- Number: This property type allows users to type a numeric value only.
- List: This property type provides users with a list of possible values, which you can create in advance and from which they must select a single value. Users can also be allowed to create their own values on the fly, but this opens a can of worms related to data quality and consistency across documents.
- Multivalue: This property type provides users with a list of possible values, which you can create in advance and from which they can select multiple values. This type is used for keyword properties. Again, users can create their own values here, but it is not recommended.
- Date: This property type provides users with a Date entry field.
- Comment box: This field allows users to enter a Comment as long as 255 characters, including spaces. Free-form text is allowed in the comment box.

When you've created your customized field, click Next to go to the Configure the Property Order screen (Figure 6–28). This screen allows a coordinator to determine the order in which the properties are listed in the document profile. For instance, some coordinators may decide that it's best to list the

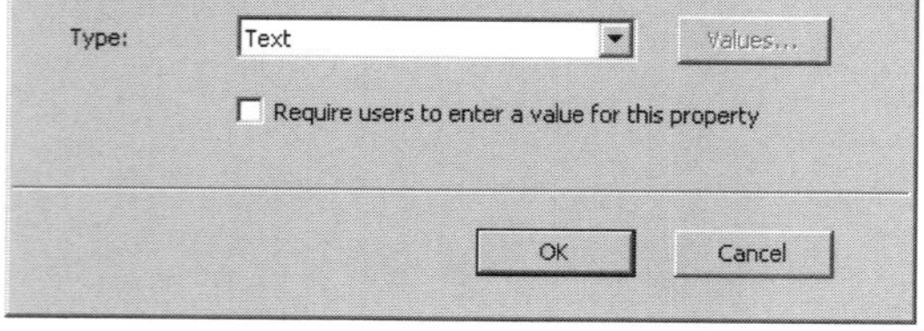

Figure 6–27 Create New Property dialog box

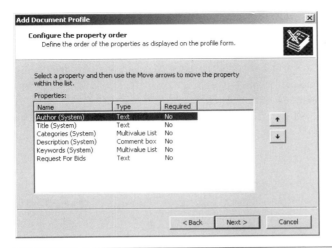

Figure 6–28 Configure the Property Order screen in the Add Document Profile wizard

required fields at the top of the profile; this makes it easier for users to type the required information without having to scroll down the list to find the required fields.

After you've chosen the order in which you want the properties to appear, click Next to go to the Finish screen and finish the wizard. Your new profile will appear in the folder. To make this new profile available for use with documents, you must add it to the list of possible profiles in the folder's properties on the Profiles tab (refer to Figure 6–23). By default, the new profile will appear there, but you must select the check box next to the profile to activate it for the documents in that folder.

Configuring a List of Keywords

The Keyword property is a default property on the Base Document profile. Its default setting is to allow users to type their own keywords if they don't appear on the list of configured keywords. Moreover, the list of keywords is blank, meaning that out of the gate, the Keyword property is essentially an open text box in which users can type any value they desire.

Like categories, the Keyword property should include a well-planned list of values that accurately provide a description list that users can search against to find documents. The planning for keywords is as important as the profile and category planning. When combined with profiles and categories, keywords allow you significant flexibility in how documents are described, and they provide a method of using dissimilar description schemes to form a cross-matrix that can be used to find documents.

To create or modify the keyword list for the Keyword (or any other multi-value) property, click the Edit button for the Keyword property and then click the Edit Values button on the General tab of the Keyword attribute. On the Values screen (Figure 6–29), you can type a keyword in the Enter a New List Value input box, and then click Add. Once the word has been added to the keyword list, you can move the word up and down the list using the arrows to the right of the list box.

This tells you two things. First, the list is not automatically sorted, nor can it be sorted in a method other than manually. Second, because it's not automatically sorted, you have the flexibility of placing the more commonly used keywords at the top of the list, freeing users from the need to scroll through a list to find an often-used keyword. The choice is entirely up to you, and that affords you the opportunity to tune the list to meet your users' needs precisely.

Also, if you want to confine the users to using only the list of keywords that you provide, be sure to clear the Allow Users to Enter Values Not in the List check box. Doing so denies users the ability to enter their own keywords when checking in a document.

With the multivalue and list types, users are presented with a list of possible values from which to choose. These types are special in that they have associated dictionaries. Don't go trotting off to find these dictionaries in some other location. You can find and edit them only on the Values screen as just described. Each property can have only one dictionary associated with it.

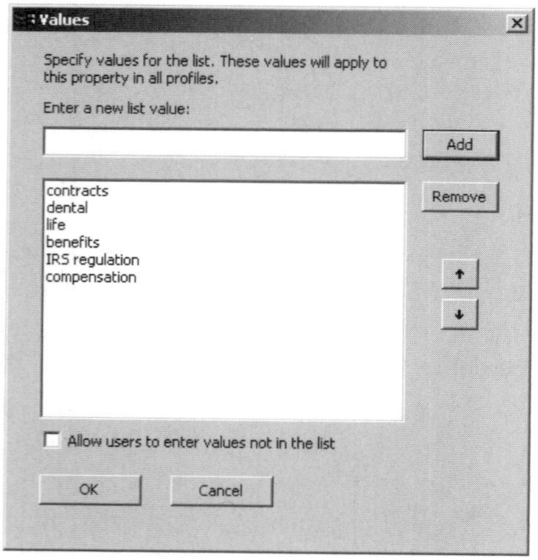

Figure 6–29 Values input area for creating a list of keywords

Property Promotion and Demotion

Recall that document metadata is held in a document's profile. However, SPS isn't the only program that works with metadata. The Office suite of applications works with metadata, too.

Document metadata, in an SPS workspace, is held as additional columns on the document row in the WSS database. When users are working with an Office document outside the SPS workspace, this same metadata is stored for the document in OLE storage. To make sure that the document's metadata is synchronized between these two areas—the OLE storage outside the workspace and the property store (`wss.edb`) in the SPS workspace—you use the concepts of promotion and demotion.

The property data will be synchronized if the property names match. For instance, if you have a property on an Office application called Author and you ensure that there is an Author property on the document profile in SPS, then the value entered in the Office application for Author will be available when the document is moved to the SPS workspace and checked in. When a value for a property is set in an Office application and then reappears for that document in the SPS workspace, it is known as property *promotion* because the property was promoted from the Office application into the workspace.

Conversely, when a property is created in the workspace and then reappears in an Office application, it is said to have been *demoted* because the property was demoted to the stand-alone Office application. Hence, if you change the value of a property on a profile form, the next time you view that property in an Office application, it will contain the new value.

When you initially copy a file into a document folder from a location outside the workspace, the default profile for that folder will define the document's metadata. In this instance, if the profile for the document folder does not contain a property that was populated in the Office application, that value will be lost when the document is checked in to the document folder. Later, should that document be copied from the workspace and then opened in the Office application, that property will not reappear because it was lost when the document was checked in to the document folder.

If you check out a document, open it with an Office application, change one of the properties, and then check that document back in, the new value for the property will be promoted into the workspace.

If you copy a document from one workspace to another workspace, all the Office properties will travel with the document and will appear when you check in the document's metadata in the new workspace. Any properties that were defined for the document in the source workspace that are not defined the same way in the target workspace will be lost.

If you save a document to the workspace using the IFS (Installable File System), only the Office properties will be saved with the document in the workspace. Any customized properties for that document will not be saved with the document because you used the IFS, and not the recommended methods described earlier in this chapter, to save the document.

Promotion and demotion are not supported for any files other than those native to Office applications. This means that `.htm` and `.txt` files, for example, are not supported. You should also know that multivalue, custom properties that are created in the workspace will not appear in the Office application because Office does not support these properties. This does not apply to the Keyword property, which is supported by Office.

Also, the Comments property in Office is promoted to the Description property in SPS, and vice versa.

Troubleshooting Tips

I've compiled some errors that seem to crop up every so often for administrators. I don't pretend that this list is exhaustive, but, hopefully, it will help more than a few people who are having problems with their workspace.

If you are getting an error message involving the `INVOKE` command or an error executing an `INVOKE` query, ensure that Internet Information Services (IIS) has continuous virtual server IDs. To do this, run the `\inetpub\ adminscripts\adsutil enum /p w3svc` utility, and take a look at your virtual server IDs. If there are any gaps in the numbers, create a new virtual server using the IIS Administration tool.

If your users are getting a login box when they attempt to open or read a document that has been published and you are certain that they have the correct permissions for this document, be sure that you are running Office 2000 SR-1 or later. Older versions of Office 2000 try to open the document with read/write privileges, and if the user is assigned the Reader role, a logon box will pop up asking for a user account that has write privileges. Canceling the dialog box forces Office 2000 to open the document in a read-only form, something that readers can do. This problem is fixed in SR-1 and Office XP.

More than a few administrators have wondered how they can associate an icon with a particular file extension in the dashboard. Here's how. I'll use a PDF file as an example. First, create the icon as a GIF file in either 16×16 or 32×32 pixels. Then name it `PDF16.gif` or `PDF32.gif`. Remember that the filename comprises both the file extension and its size. Then use the Web folders client to put the icon in the `/Portal/resources/DocTypeIcons` folder. Then restart the MSSearch and MSDMSERV services. The icon should now be associated with the correct files in your workspace.

If you want to hide the Document Library dashboard from the portal for some users, use the Web folders client to navigate to the hidden folder named Portal; then configure the security on the Document Library dashboard to allow only the desired users to have access to it. If a user is not listed in the security settings, the dashboard will not be available. Be sure to turn on per-user caching for the dashboard, too.

If you want your users to be able to get to the portal by typing only its name (such as `http://server`), create a `default.htm` file in the default Web site using the following code:

```
<html><head>
<title>Workspacename</title>
<meta http-equiv="refresh" content="0; url=http://servername/
  workspacename">
</head>
<body>
<h3>One Moment Please….</h3>
<p>You are being redirected to Workspacename.
</body>
</html>
```

Note that in this code, the number zero (0) represents the number of seconds users will wait before being redirected. You can set this value to any number you wish.

Summary

This chapter focuses on document management tasks. As you have learned, DM is straightforward in SPS, and it represents a basic set of functions that will be helpful for many smaller businesses. You have also learned how to create and manage document profiles and how to ensure that metadata on existing Office documents is copied into the workspace by ensuring that the same metadata field exists in the SPS workspace.

Chapter 7 looks at how to crawl, index, and search content sources in SharePoint Portal Server 2001.

Managing the Workspace and Search Settings

In Chapter 6, you learned about document management, versioning, and profiles. This chapter focuses on two important concepts: day-to-day management of the workspace, and working with search settings.

When looking at workspace management, you can do a number of things to customize the workspace, such as adding users, setting roles, setting notifications, and configuring subscriptions. All these activities directly impact the users who will be accessing your workspace.

It's important to understand how to use the search options and how to create, edit, reset, and propagate an index. Being able to find a document via the search process is extremely important for your users, so you must know how to manage the search process and the indexes to meet your users' needs. The benefit of including full-text indexing and Search services is that users can quickly locate documents and data. And the Search service that ships with SPS can search any content type, provided that an appropriate protocol handler and IFilter (index filter) are installed for that data type.

This chapter outlines the search architecture, discusses the Search Web parts, and then describes various workspace management tasks.

The Search and Index Service Architecture

Understanding the MSSearch service, which provides search and indexing functions, is fundamental to managing a SharePoint Portal workspace. SPS provides a crawling and search service that supports full-text searching and the Structured Query Language (SQL) query grammar. The MSSearch service (hereafter referred to as the search service) can crawl both content and metadata at the following locations:

- Intranet sites
- Internet sites
- Exchange 2000 public folders
- Exchange 5.5 public folders
- Lotus Notes databases
- SharePoint Team Services Web sites
- Other SPS workspaces

Searches can be executed in a query that requests both metadata and document content. For instance, you could execute a query looking for the phrase *out in left field* in documents that are greater than 3MB in size. The search service will search for the phrase *out in left field* in the catalogs and search the sps.edb database for the 3MB property size.

Out of the box, SPS supports the searching of Office, HTML, plain text, and TIFF files. At the time of this writing, you can get IFilters from Adobe for its PDF files and from Corel for WordPerfect documents. (IFilters are discussed in more detail in "Configuring and Managing Microsoft Search" later in this chapter.) And if necessary, you can implement your own IFilter for a particular document type.

The Search service also provides linguistic support for 11 languages, including

- English
- German
- French
- Italian
- Spanish
- Dutch
- Swedish
- Japanese
- Simplified/Traditional Chinese
- Korean
- Thai

If you're indexing content in a language other than these, SPS uses a neutral wordbreaker component (discussed later in this chapter) to provide a basic level of indexing.

NOTE: Bear in mind that even though the search service has wordbreaker and stemmer support for 11 languages, the workspace itself can be configured for only six languages: English, Japanese, German, French, Spanish, and Italian.

Remember that the product language does not need to match the language of the server operating system. For example, you could install an English workspace on top of a Windows 2000 operating system that is running French. However, the SPS server and its workspaces must all be in the same language. There is support for adding content to a workspace that is in a language different from that of the workspace. For instance, an English workspace can hold Thai folders and documents.

The default query that runs through the Search Web part on the default dashboard uses probabilistic ranking and attribute weighting to return results. The default query performs two parallel queries: one on normal document matches, and the other on best bets, which have been configured to return a predetermined set of documents for a query based on category or keyword assignments. The results of the query are displayed on the dashboard based on their rank, with the top five best bets appearing first in the list.

Subscriptions and the Persistent Query Service

Until the release of SPS, the only way to find information was to have the user execute a search query against a set of indexes. Now, using subscriptions in SPS, you can have the information find the user. Subscriptions give users a way to be notified when changes are made to data that the user is interested in. Subscriptions are managed by the persistent query service (PQS), which is part of the gatherer service. The PQS matches documents against queries as they are indexed, and when a match is found, users are notified of the new information or change in the content source.

Users can subscribe to documents, folders, categories, and searches. Notifications can be viewed on the Subscription Summary Web part or on the Subscriptions page of the Subscriptions dashboard. Notifications can appear on the dashboard or can be e-mailed to the users, or both.

The PQS is sometimes called a *reverse query processor* when compared with the search process. The analogy is this: A search query evaluates a specific query against a large number of content sources, such as documents. The opposite happens with the PQS: It evaluates a large number of queries against a specific content source.

One instance of PQS runs for each workspace because each workspace has its own configured PQS. The PQS is configured by the subscriptions generated by the users and fires when documents are indexed. During this process, PQS evaluates each document against the set of rules (or subscriptions) to determine whether any documents match the rules created by existing subscriptions.

With folder and file subscriptions, the PQS evaluates a document's discussion items as well as its contents. Items are handed to the PQS plug-in during the crawl phase of the search process.

Planning Subscriptions and Notifications

Because the PQS is the component that identifies changes in content for which the user must be notified and because that identification can occur only during the crawl phase of indexing, there are notification latency issues you should be aware of.

First, the time lag between reindexing of content sources directly impacts the timeliness of user notifications. For instance, if you index an external file server only once each week, it could be days before a user is notified that a document has been modified. One of the goals of your planning process should be to balance the overhead of the indexing process against the needs of your users to have timely notifications. If fast notifications are important, it is best to create an aggressive schedule of indexing, which will allow document changes to be evaluated by the PQS so that users can be notified of the changes.

Second, if the PQS is evaluating an index that is being propagated from a dedicated indexing server, the latency time will increase commensurate with the indexing and propagation schedule of the indexing server. Be sure to account for this latency time. (For more on propagation, see "Propagating an Index between Workspaces" later in this chapter.)

Third, full builds of the index will result in unnecessary notifications because every document is passed through the PQS, which generates a notification if it matches the rules, whether or not there has been a change. This problem highlights an architectural nuance: It's not the change in the document that causes the notification. Instead, notification is triggered when content in the content source matches a subscription rule. Incremental builds index only new or modified information, so users perceive that they receive a notification only when information has been modified or a new document has been added to the content source. But you should understand that it's not the *newness* of the information that generates the notification; it's that the content *matches* the subscription rules.

Hence, as a planning issue, you must balance competing interests: fast, timely notifications of changes in external content sources versus an up-to-date, full-text index versus generation of unnecessary notifications. Here are two rules of thumb to help you in this balancing act:

- In most environments, the search process is more important to the overall organization, whereas notification is more important to individual users and specific documents. When in doubt, do what is best for the overall organization.

■ If a group of users needs fast notifications and most of the other users do not, consider creating a separate workspace for those users and ramping up the indexing schedule to meet their needs.

Subscriptions and the Windows 2000 Scheduler Service

The Subscription Summary Web part on the Home dashboard is the location in the portal where notifications are displayed on a per-user basis. (Do not confuse this with the Subscriptions plug-in.) This means that only those notifications for the currently logged-on user will be displayed in the Web part. Notifications on the dashboard are available immediately.

The timing of notifications is handled by the Windows 2000 scheduler service, and you can configure the timing. Hence, notification tasks can be scheduled in the Control Panel|Scheduled Tasks area of Windows 2000. For instance, if you open the Scheduled Tasks in Control Panel, you'll find that there are five default scheduled tasks per workspace on the server:

■ Workspace MSTS-CSM notification calls the `startbuild.vbs` script and is configured for each index update interval that is configured for each content source. Hence, if you have three content sources and have both an incremental and full updates scheduled, you should see six MSTS-CSM entries.

■ Workspace applications notification is configured to fire every 30 minutes.

■ Workspace daily subscription notification is configured to notify, by default, at 4 AM every day.

■ Workspace immediate subscription notification, by default, fires every 5 minutes.

■ Workspace weekly subscription notification, by default, fires every Sunday night at 10 PM.

If the defaults don't work for you, you can configure each task to run at the time you prefer. You can also enter additional scheduled tasks, such as sending notifications at the time a user logs on, but additional scheduled tasks won't appear as a choice when a user creates a subscription. For that reason, any task you create will have limited value. These tasks are illustrated later in this chapter.

Table 7–1 shows the components of the search service.

Table 7–1 MSSearch service components and their primary functions

Search Service Component	Primary Function
Search engine	Executes the query against the index.
Index engine	Processes text chunks and metadata that are filtered from content sources. Decides which metadata information is written to the full-text index.
Gatherer	Manages crawling based on rules that tell it which content sources to crawl.
Wordbreaker	Component shared by the search and index components. Breaks compound words and phrases into single words. When a user executes a search, the query is passed through a language-specific wordbreaker to ensure that the request is executed in similar terms as were used to build the index being queried.
Stemmer	Component shared by the search and index components. Generates inflected forms of a word to be included in the index. When a user executes a search, the query is passed through the language-specific stemmers to ensure that the request is executed over a similar scope of variations on a word as was used to build the index being queried.
Filter daemon	Performs several functions. Receives requests from the gatherer service and executes them using the correct protocol handler to access a content source and then uses the correct IFilter to filter the file. It creates a stream of data consisting of text chunks and properties and returns that stream to the gatherer component.
Protocol handlers	Provides access to content sources in their native protocol and exposes the content for filtering by the IFilter.
IFilter	Reads the content from a content source in the source's native format and filters the content into text chunks and properties, which the filter daemon passes back to the gatherer component.
Content sources	Configured location of data that the search service crawls for content.

The Gatherer Component

The *gatherer* component is the core component in the `MSSearch.exe` process. It runs inside this process, is multithreaded, and is responsible for the overall crawl process. The gatherer process interacts with the filter daemon process (`mssdmn.exe`) to receive data streams from crawled documents. Note that because IFilters are susceptible to error and looping, the filter process runs independently of the search process, thereby allowing the filter process to be terminated without the need to terminate the search process. A set of shared memory queues is used by both processes to read and write data and pass commands between the processes.

Each workspace has its own gatherer process and full-text index. The full-text index for a workspace is called the *workspace catalog*. Each gatherer process maintains its own rules, plug-ins, logs, and performance statistics.

The crawl process can be started in several ways: manually, by schedule, or in response to a notification from a file store. Such a notification is based on a subscription created by a user in the workspace.

Initial connection to a content source is based on the existence of a working *protocol handler*. This component is used to connect to the content source. For instance, if the content source is accessed using a URL, the HTTP protocol handler is used. The protocol handler does not access the documents themselves; that is the responsibility of the IFilter.

Even though initial connection to a content source is through the protocol handler, after the gatherer process receives a URL from the content source, the URL is initially passed to the filter daemon process, which is responsible for management of all the IFilters. The appropriate IFilter for the content source then calls the appropriate protocol handler to connect to the content source. After successful connection, the IFilter begins to extract data in the source's documents.

The gatherer process uses a shared memory queue to work with the IFilters to request that a crawl begin and to receive text chunks and metadata properties. Once the data is received from the IFilter, the gatherer service runs the data through a series of internal components, called *plug-ins* (such as the PQS plug-in), before the data is relayed to the index engine.

In this version of SPS, the gatherer saves a document's properties in a property store (`sps.edb`) that is separate from the SPS document store. The *property store* is a table of properties and their values, which can be retrieved and sorted. Each row in the table represents a different document in the full-text index. The property store enforces document-level security roles, and this is where a document's role-based security configuration is held.

The Index Component

Once the data stream is received from the gatherer, the index engine uses wordbreakers and stemmers to break down the text chunks. The wordbreaker breaks the chunks into phrases and words, and the stemmer is used to generate inflected forms of a word. Noise words (such as *and*, *the*, or *a*) are removed because they offer no indexing value, and the catalogs are updated to reflect the new changes in the content sources.

During client execution of a query against an index, the query is passed through the same wordbreakers and stemmers to enhance the effectiveness of the search. This ensures that the same words and inflections that were used to build the index are also used to perform searches against it.

When a property value query is executed, the index is checked to see whether there is a match. If there is a match, the properties for those documents are retrieved from the property store and then are rechecked to verify the match before being returned to the user.

Improving Query Performance

Sometimes, users complain that it takes too long to get a result set back from a search request. More frequent, however, is the complaint that they can't find what they want—meaning that the result set is not an effective set for use in their work.

The good news is that you can take steps to improve the performance of the search service and the quality of the result set. Table 7–2 outlines some performance factors and lists the actions you can take to improve upon them.

Table 7–2 Ways to improve query performance

Query Factor	Ways to Improve Performance
A high number of documents and content sources (sometimes called the *corpus*)	As this number increases, the amount of time to index and return quality results to the user may also increase. Try reducing the number of documents in the index to improve performance. Weed out, if possible, any unnecessary documents in your index.
Search terms used	The rarer the search term, the faster the search. Consider educating your users to use rarer terms instead of more common terms.
Searching metadata	Document metadata is held in the property store and thus must be read from the store in order to fulfill the query request. A large number of metadata requests can result in slow performance.
Server resources are used by non-SPS services	If the search service must compete for server resources, users will experience a slow response from the SharePoint server. Ensure that you have enough resources on your server to handle the anticipated user load on SPS services along with any other services you might have.
The size of the result set returned to the user	Specify a limit on the maximum number of rows returned by the search service. Doing so improves performance because the search service does not need to compile a large list of items for the result set.
Ranking results by properties	Ordering result sets by rank does not degrade performance. However, ordering results by any other property causes the query to access the property store to retrieve that value for each item in the result set. This can significantly decrease performance.

IFilters

Out of the box, SPS contains IFilters for Office, HTML, text, MIME, and TIFF files. The Windows 2000 Indexing Service has its own set of filters, and SPS will use them if it doesn't have its own filter. However, if an SPS-specific filter is available, SPS will use it in place of the Windows 2000 filter.

To find out which file extension associations are registered on your server, you can run the `filtreg.exe` utility from the Tools|Support folder on the SPS server CD. This utility walks through the registry and displays a list of file extensions and their associated filters.

Protocol Handlers

Each protocol handler's information is stored in the registry in the following location:

```
HKEY_LOCAL_MACHINE\Software\Microsoft\Search\1.0\ProtocolHandlers
```

The protocol handler that is selected for a content source is based on the prefix of the URL. For each supported URL, a separate ProgID (Program ID) is stored in the registry; this ProgID corresponds to a DLL (dynamic link library) that is used by the gatherer to crawl the content source. The ProgIDs are also registered in the `HKEY_CLASSES_ROOT` and are associated with the correct DLL.

To learn more about the prefixes for content sources, please consult Chapter 9.

The Index and Property Store in Brief

The *index* holds information in compressed format. The index by itself can be used for content searches. When a search is executed that involves both content and properties, the property store is also queried. The property store holds properties of the indexed content.

You should plan on the size of your indexes being about 30 percent of the size of your content sources.

The full-text index is really composed of word lists, shadow indexes, and master indexes. *Word lists* are just that—lists of words that are stored in memory. Queries of word lists are the fastest method of returning results to users because no disk activities are involved. Because word lists are volatile and can consume considerable amounts of RAM, information doesn't stay in a word list for very long. When indexing is completed, information is moved from a word list to a shadow list.

Shadow lists, also known as shadow indexes, are compressed, disk-space structures that hold permanent information. Creation and access times are longer than for a word list, but the trade-off of having information permanently in place is worth the cost. Once created, shadow indexes cannot be modified. Therefore, as new word lists are created and then written to disk to form shadow indexes, query time will increase because of the growth in the number of shadow indexes.

A *master merge* is a compilation of all the shadow indexes. By default, master merges occur daily at midnight if a certain number of documents have been indexed or if disk space becomes sparse, or both. You cannot manually force a master merge in the user interface, which is something that I think Microsoft should address either in a service pack release or in the next version of SharePoint Portal Server.

To adjust the number of minutes after midnight that the master merge will run, you modify the following registry key:

```
HKLM\Software\Microsoft\Search\1.0\CatalogNames\SharePointPortalServer\
    workspace_name\Indexer:ci:MidnightMasterMergeTimeDelta
```

Type the number of minutes after midnight you'd like the merge to begin, and this code will schedule the master merge process to run around other activities that might be ongoing at midnight.

Day-to-Day Workspace Management

The first part of this chapter has been dedicated to explaining the search and indexing architecture. My hope is that you've read that part and are now ready to focus on workspace management. I'll briefly shift focus to discuss security issues in the documents area, and then I'll outline a way to think about the workspace as a unit. Next, I'll talk about subscriptions and notifications. After that, we'll return to the search process from a management perspective.

One of your regular administrative activities is to apply security to document folders. This is one area where SharePoint Portal Server has significant flexibility: SPS can use security principles from either a Windows NT 4.0 security accounts database on a primary domain controller (PDC), or from a Windows 2000 Domain Controller (DC) Active Directory (AD) service directory. Although SPS must be installed on a Windows 2000 server, the latter can be a member of a Windows NT 4.0 domain, which will allow SPS to use the security principles from the PDC. To see how to work with security in SPS, secure document folders with user accounts, and understand the role-based security in SPS, please see Chapter 13.

Other daily workspace management tasks include not only setting security on document folders but also working with subscriptions, notifications, and Web discussions.

What Is a Workspace?

When you're thinking about the workspace as a concept, it is important to understand how a workspace is put together. You can think of a workspace as having three parts: collaboration tools, data, and a framework that allows the collaboration tools to work with the data.

In terms of the framework, there are several ways to build a robust workspace that is extremely useful for users. For instance, categories can be used to build an excellent framework in which to find and view data. Document profiles can be used to build a different type of framework: one that comprises metadata that can be indexed and searched. Categories and document profiles are the two main ways that a workspace is constructed to allow the collaboration tools to work effectively with the data. Another way to think about this is to think of the categories and metadata as providing multiple, but dissimilar, methods of organizing the data that exists in the workspace.

You might think that the document library hierarchy is another framework, but it is really more of a method of holding data. The data in the workspace is held, essentially, in two locations: the document library and the search index. Any other data that is available in the portal is held in another location, no matter how the data is accessed.

The collaboration tools that are used to work with the data include Web discussions, subscriptions, and the document management tools. Subscriptions are really the client side of notifications, but they produce a collaborative effect in that the notification can inform users dynamically when an event has occurred.

Managing Subscriptions

Subscriptions are the only way for a user to know when a content source has been updated without the user manually checking for changes. There are four types of subscriptions: file, folder, category, and search. File and folder subscriptions are available either through the dashboard or an Office 2000 or later application. Category and search subscriptions are available only through the dashboard site.

A notification is generated in response to a subscription on content that has changed. Hence, a notification is not generated simply because it exists,

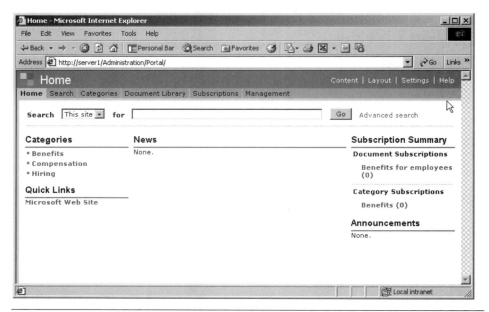

Figure 7–1 Subscription Summary Web part on the Home dashboard

but only when content has changed for which a subscription has been created. Notifications can be viewed either in the dashboard site or in an e-mail, or both.

On the Home dashboard, the Subscription Summary Web part is in the upper-right portion (Figure 7–1). In addition, a Subscriptions dashboard is created as part of the default portal. This dashboard hosts a single Web part, Subscriptions. This Web part displays each user's own subscriptions and notifications.

There is also a Manage Subscriptions Web part on the Management dashboard, which is available only to coordinators. This is illustrated in Figure 7–2.

Subscriptions for the dashboard can also be viewed using the Web folders client (Figure 7–3). The problem here is that although you can see them, there isn't much you can do with them from an administrative viewpoint. They are simple files with numbers. So, unlike many other administrative functions in Share-Point Portal Server, the Web folders client is not very helpful in this instance.

Creating Subscriptions to Internal Content

Now let's look at how to create a subscription for each type.

To create a file subscription, navigate to the file in the dashboard, and then click the Subscribe link beneath the filename (Figure 7–4). This action registers a subscription for you in the workspace, and it will appear in the Subscription Summary Web part on the Home dashboard.

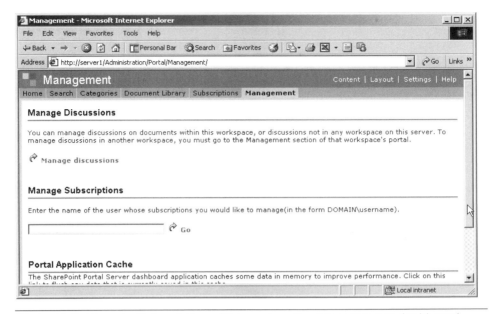

Figure 7–2 Manage Subscriptions Web part on the Management dashboard

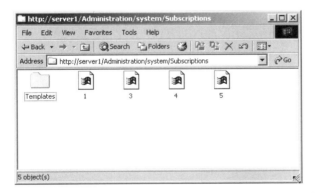

Figure 7–3 Viewing subscriptions using the Web folders client

To create a folder subscription, use the Document Library dashboard to navigate to the document folder that you want to subscribe to. Then, on the folder's Action toolbar, click the Subscribe link (Figure 7–5).

To create a category subscription, use the Categories Web part on the Home dashboard (or the Categories tab) and navigate to the category for which you wish to create a new subscription. Click the Subscribe to This Category link (Figure 7–6), and a new subscription will be entered for you in the workspace.

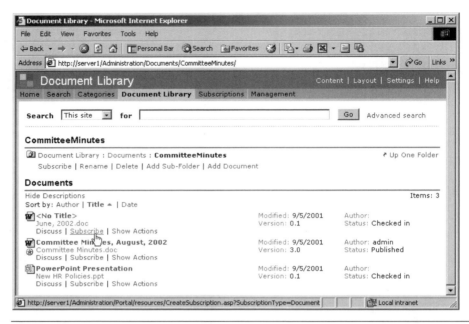

Figure 7–4 Creating a file subscription for a document in the dashboard

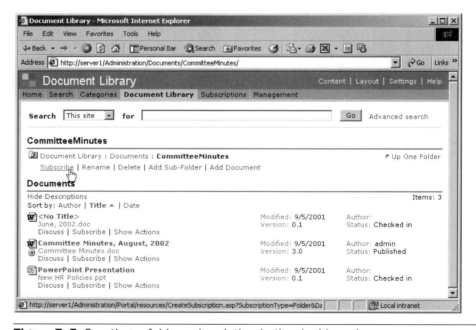

Figure 7–5 Creating a folder subscription in the dashboard

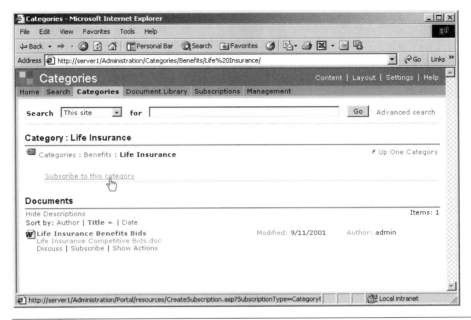

Figure 7–6 Creating a category subscription in the dashboard

To create a search subscription, first execute the search. It's not enough to enter the search data. The query must be executed so that the PQS knows what rules to apply when filtering documents. After you have executed the search, the Search Summary Web part will contain a Subscribe to This Search link (Figure 7–7). Click this link, and the subscription will be entered.

Each subscription that is created by a user will show up on the Subscription Summary Web part in the Home dashboard when that user logs on. Subscriptions are displayed by type, as illustrated in Figure 7–8. You can see that document, folder, category, and search subscriptions are all listed inside the Subscription Summary Web part. Each listing beneath the type heading is a link that will take the user directly to the Subscriptions dashboard and the item on that dashboard that contains information about the content source.

NOTE: For a user to use subscriptions in the dashboard, the user must have Reader permissions. Coordinators and authors also have this permission by default because those roles include all the permissions of the Reader role.

Subscribing to external content is really no different from subscribing to internal content. In all instances of creating a new subscription, you'll be presented

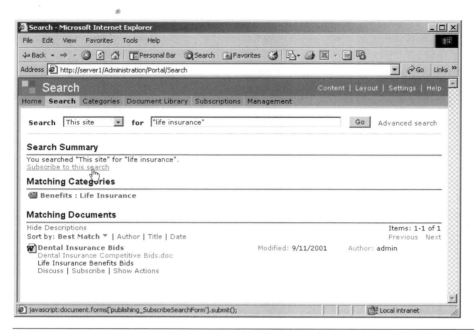

Figure 7–7 Creating a search subscription in the dashboard

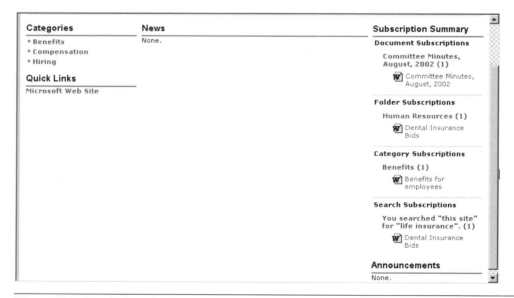

Figure 7–8 Displaying the four subscription types in the Home dashboard

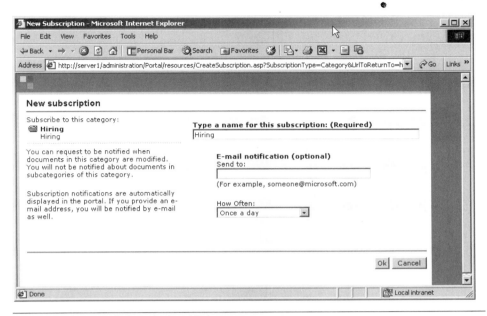

Figure 7–9 New Subscription Web page

with the New Subscription screen (Figure 7–9), which outlines your subscription options. First, you can type a name for the subscription that is unique and personalized. This name is placed in the Type a Name for This Subscription input box. A name for the subscription is required.

Second, you can input an e-mail address to which a system-generated notification can be sent. The e-mail address must be in Simple Mail Transport Protocol (SMTP) format. Third, you can specify how often you wish to be notified by choosing one of the following from the How Often drop-down box:

- Once a day
- Once a week
- When a change occurs

Don't be fooled by the last choice. More than a few people have chosen this and then modified a document to which they had subscribed, only to find that they weren't immediately notified of the change. The last choice really means that when the PQS becomes aware of a change, it will generate a notification immediately. If e-mail has been chosen, a notification will be sent immediately. If the PQS runs across 20 such changes to 20 different content sources, then one e-mail will be generated with 20 inline notifications.

This is why some people choose to be notified once a day or even once a week; all the notifications come in one batch, instead of multiple notifications. Note that dashboard site notifications always appear immediately. There is no notification latency once the PQS filters the modified document. Also, dashboard notifications persist until the user manually removes them.

You can configure these three notification options in Control Panel. If you open the Windows 2000 Task Scheduler, you'll see several notifications that are created on the SPS server automatically during installation. Each scheduled task spawns `pkmntfy.exe` on the server, retrieves the subscription results, and sends e-mail notifications as directed.

The tasks in the Windows 2000 Task Scheduler can be broken down into two types: index builds and subscription notifications (Figure 7–10). The tasks that begin with *MSTS-CSM* are index builds and are the results of your administrative actions in manually configuring when you want indexing to run. The tasks that begin with the word *workspace* are notification schedules that represent the three notification choices in the New Subscription Web page (shown earlier in Figure 7–9). If you want to modify this list so that users receive notifications on schedules not offered in the default list, a developer must change the code for the New Subscriptions Web page and create a new scheduled task. But note that Microsoft does not support the modification of its Web pages or Visual Basic (VB) scripts in SPS.

All the workspace tasks appear in Task Scheduler. By default, one index build task and three notification tasks are shown. For each workspace that you create on your server, you'll create four new scheduled tasks.

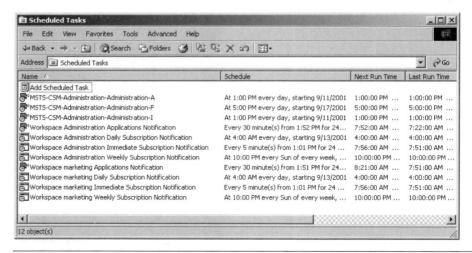

Figure 7–10 Scheduled tasks for SPS in Task Scheduler

If you plan on hosting multiple workspaces on your server, you should be aware of the need to stagger the default schedules. For instance, the daily e-mail notification is scheduled to produce the e-mails at 4 AM every day. If you have, say, six workspaces on your server, you may not want all the e-mail notifications for all six workspaces to be generated at the same time. Wisdom suggests staggering the schedules so that you don't overload your server at any given time. Best practice is to create a schedule sheet outlining when each workspace will perform each task. Care must be taken to ensure that none of these tasks occurs during a backup operation. Although they can be fired during backup, I try to avoid it because I like to have as idle a server as possible during backup so that the image is as accurate as possible when it finishes.

Using the Office Collaboration Toolbar to Create Subscriptions

You can create subscriptions from within Internet Explorer by invoking the collaboration toolbar from the View|Explorer Bar|Discuss menu. When invoked, it will appear as a toolbar at the bottom of the browser. It displays a Subscribe button, which you click to open the Document Subscription dialog box (Figure 7–11). Here, you can subscribe to either a file or a folder, but not a category or a search query.

The advantage of using this method for file and folder subscriptions is that you have more conditions to work with:

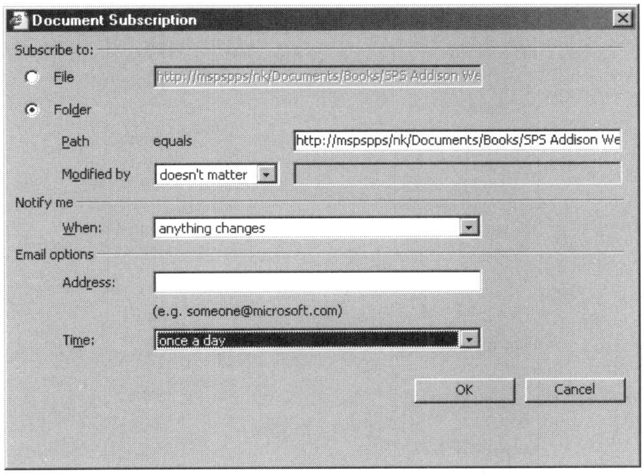

Figure 7–11 Document Subscription dialog box

- Anything changes: covers any of the changes in the rest of this list
- A new document is created: the same as a document modification
- A document is modified: applies to both files and folders
- A document is deleted: supports only files, not folders
- A document is moved: does not support files or folders
- A discussion item is inserted: supported on both files and folders

The e-mail address and notification options are the same as described earlier. However, in contrast to a dashboard subscription, no address resolution is performed.

TIP: If you modify the security settings for the Web site that hosts the workspace to allow Anonymous access, users will not be able to create subscriptions through the dashboard.

Using Subscriptions

Subscription results will appear in the Subscriptions dashboard. On the Home dashboard, under Subscription Summary, you will see a number in parentheses—such as "(1)"—next to a subscription, indicating that a change has occurred to the content source.

On the Subscriptions dashboard, you receive a bit more information, as illustrated in Figure 7–12. Here, you see that the Dental Insurance Bids document

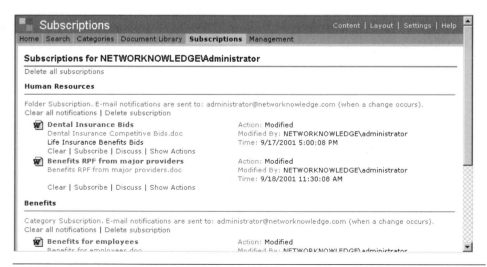

Figure 7–12 Subscriptions dashboard showing notifications

has been modified, as indicated on the right side of the screen with the word *modified* next to the Action label. You can also invoke a Web discussion about this modified document, clear the subscription, show the publishing actions for this document, or change your subscription rules by clicking the Subscribe link. Search subscriptions (subscriptions that are created after a search query has been executed—this is not shown in Figure 7-12) will list a Rerun Search action, which, when clicked, executes the search associated with the subscription. The results of a rerun search query will display document, but not category, matches.

Notice that near the top of this dashboard, you can delete all the subscriptions with one action. But don't confuse this action with clearing all the notifications, something you can do for each subscription type by clicking the Clear All Notifications link. Next to this link is the Delete Subscriptions link, which allows you to delete all the subscriptions within a certain subscription type.

Subscriptions are displayed in this dashboard (in order from newest to oldest) even if there are no active notifications. Notifications are also listed in order from newest to oldest.

Coordinators can view and manage all subscriptions and notifications for all users in the workspace. On the Management dashboard, a coordinator can type a user name in the Management Subscriptions Web part. This action brings up all the subscriptions for that user, and the coordinator can take management actions on these subscriptions.

Be sure to enter the domain name ahead of the user's name: `domainname\` `username`. If you put in only a user name, the local security account database will be referenced rather than the domain account database in AD.

Also, when you view a user's subscriptions using this Web part from the Management dashboard, you will see only the user's subscriptions, not the notifications.

E-Mail and Notifications

When you install SPS on a Windows 2000 server, the default setting is to use the local SMTP mail server that ships with IIS. If you want to point SPS to use an Exchange 2000 server or some other SMTP server, open the server Properties tab in the SPS Administration Microsoft Management Console (MMC). Type the name of the server in the SMTP Server input box. Remember that all workspaces will use this e-mail server, so be sure to stagger your schedule of e-mail notifications if you are running multiple workspaces. Also, if the SPS server is dedicated to content indexing, this setting will be ignored.

If you're having problems with e-mail notifications, it means that your SMTP server is not configured properly. If you're unsure, open a telnet session to your SMTP server over port 25 and see whether you can send a message. If you can, it means that your SMTP server is working fine. To test this, open a command prompt and type the following (be sure to press the Enter key after each command):

```
Telnet
Set local_echo
Open Server_FQDN  25 [where Server_FQDN = the SMTP server's fully
  qualified domain name]
Ehlo
Mail from: username@domainame.com
Rcpt to: username@domainame.com
Data Text of the data entered here
. [Type a single period and then press the Enter key]
```

You should then receive a message saying that the mail was queued for delivery. If you can't send mail using these commands, there may be a configuration issue with your SMTP server. If e-mail still isn't delivered, you should check to ensure that you have spelled the SMTP server name and domain name correctly.

In addition, users may become confused about when subscriptions fire on documents. Be sure to let them know that their subscriptions apply only to published documents and not to documents that have merely been checked in. Team members who are collaborating on a document are not notified when a document is checked in, but they are notified when it is published.

Finally, it is possible that you have reached the limit on the total number of subscriptions for your workspace. The default is 5,000. If this limit is reached, the next person who attempts to create another subscription will receive an error message indicating that the workspace quota has been reached.

Quotas and Notifications

Here are the default limits on notifications when a workspace is created:

- Per user: 20
- Per workspace: 100,000
- Per subscription: 20

The notifications per subscription is limited to 100, and the default is 20. Quotas are enforced at the time a subscription is created. If you reduce the quota number and a user already exceeds the new quota limit, the user will be allowed to remain over the limit until enough subscriptions are manually deleted to bring the user within the quota limits. Whether a user is *at* or *over* a quota, new subscriptions cannot be created.

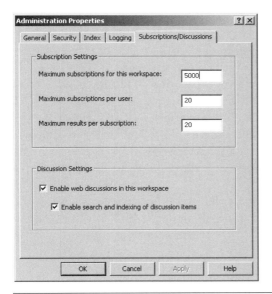

Figure 7–13 Subscriptions/Discussions tab in the SPS MMC

Notifications are removed in one instance: when new notifications arrive for a subscription that has already reached its notification quota. In this instance, SPS selects which notification to throw away based on the following:

- If it's a file, folder, or category subscription, the oldest notification is thrown away.
- If the subscription is set for e-mail notification, SPS will throw away the lowest-ranked notification, whether or not the notification has been sent.
- If the subscription is not set for e-mail notification, SPS will throw away the lowest-ranked notification, even if it is a new notification.

These settings are configured on the Subscriptions/Discussions tab in the SPS MMC workspace properties, as illustrated in Figure 7–13.

Configuring and Managing Microsoft Search

One of the primary features of SPS is the advanced search engine (MSSearch) that installs when you install SPS. The two core elements of the Microsoft search process are the indexing process and the gatherer process. The indexing process was introduced with Index Server 1.0. Version 2.0 shipped with the

Windows NT 4.0 option pack, and the next version, 3.0, shipped with Windows 2000 as the indexing service. The first version ran as an ISAPI application. Later versions ran as a service in kernel mode of the operating system.

The gatherer process was introduced with Site Server 3.0. In SQL 7.0, the gatherer was bundled with the index engine to create a more comprehensive search service. Version 2.0 of this service shipped with Exchange 2000 Server and SQL Server 2000. The current version, 2.1, ships with SPS.

If you are familiar with Site Server, don't look at the search engine in SPS as an upgrade to the functionality you enjoyed in Site Server. SPS does not include all the previous features of Site Server, nor does if offer any upgrade tools or upgrade paths.

MSSearch really provides portal users the ability to search an index of content from dissimilar sources. How the index is built is discussed earlier in this chapter. Four primary tasks create the index users will search:

- Configuring MSSearch to index content sources
- Crawling the content
- Filtering the content to create the index
- Searching the index

Before anything else, you must have a content source that has content to index. The content sources that SPS can crawl include Web servers, file systems, Exchange 5.5 and Exchange 2000 public folders, Lotus Notes databases, and other SPS workspaces. You create content sources inside the Management|Content folder of the workspace when viewed using the Web folders client. For more information on how to create a content source, please consult Chapter 9.

Once a content source is created, you must configure the index engine to crawl the content source. The search services look at the content source and then retrieve documents from it. Protocol handlers help retrieve the document in its native format.

Index filters (IFilters) take the data streams from the documents in their native format and break them into text chunks, which are then transferred to the indexing engine. Both the content and its properties are indexed and then stored for later retrieval. SPS ships with IFilters for Office documents, HTML pages, TIFF files, MIME files, and text files. IFilters can be written by third-party vendors, such as Adobe, and are fully compatible with SPS.

Included in the properties indexed is the document's access control list (ACL). This means that the ACL permission set can be applied to search queries to ensure that users see only those documents to which they have permissions. This is explained more in Chapter 13.

Finally, after the content has been indexed, it is queried by portal users using SQL syntax. The query result is a list of all matching results, ordered according to their relevance to the query words. The Search Web part in the portal is used by clients to search the index for desired documents.

Configuring the Search Process

You use the SharePoint Portal Server Administration MMC to manage some of the SPS search settings. To open this MMC, right-click your server's name and choose Properties. In the box that appears, you can configure the following search values:

- Search contact
- Search resource usage
- Site hit frequency rules
- Time-out settings
- Default content access account
- Proxy server
- Data locations

It's important to configure the *search contact* because when the search process crawls a Web site, in the header of the packets sent to the site is the e-mail address of the search contact. If the crawling process is having an adverse effect on the target Web site, the e-mail address gives Web site administrators a person to contact about the problem. You must provide this address when creating a content source. This address can be modified at any time on the General tab, as illustrated in Figure 7–14. Note that the SMTP server e-mail address is not related to the E-mail Address input box, even though the two appear next to each other. Hence, the SMTP server entered in the SMTP Server input box need not host the e-mail address in the E-mail Address input box. Instead, you use the SMTP Server input box to specify which SMTP server should be used to generate notifications.

Second, the bottom half of the General tab (refer to Figure 7–14) has settings that control *resource usage* by the search process. Because both the indexing and the searching processes run on an SPS server, both are available for configuration on this tab. Use the slider controls to select the desired value.

The default is to balance resource usage between background and dedicated. The descriptions are not terribly intuitive, so here goes: The farther to the left you move the slider control, the more you are choosing to use the server's resources for applications running in the background. This means that applications running in the background have a higher thread priority for the server's resources than do applications running in the foreground, or desktop.

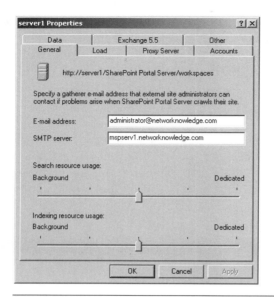

Figure 7–14 The General tab of a server's Properties dialog box in the SPS MMC

Similarly, if you move the slider control to the right, you are choosing to focus the server's resources on the search or indexing threads. This gives these processes a higher thread priority than those running in the background. If you are running other significant applications (I know, are *any* applications insignificant? <g>), you should avoid setting the controls to dedicated or near-dedicated for either process. Otherwise, you may deprive those applications of the server resources they need.

Third, when SPS is crawling content sources, it's probably a good idea to tell the indexing process how often to request a document and how many documents to ask for in a single request. These values are configured using the *site hit frequency rules*. These rules also tell the indexing process how long to wait between document requests. You use these rules to avoid overloading an external site with document requests. If you fail to pay attention to this value, the administrator of the content source may deny you access to the content.

By default, the indexing process asks for five documents in each request. When considering a change in values, you'll probably want to decrease the number of documents requested from an external source. For internal sources for which you are responsible, you can increase this value to build the index more quickly.

To change this value, navigate to the Load tab (Figure 7–15) and click Add, which will invoke the Add Site Hit Frequency Rule dialog box (Figure 7–16). This box is more complicated than you might think, so let's discuss how to create these rules.

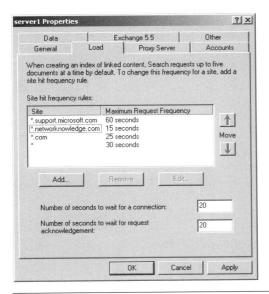

Figure 7–15 Load tab in SPS server's properties

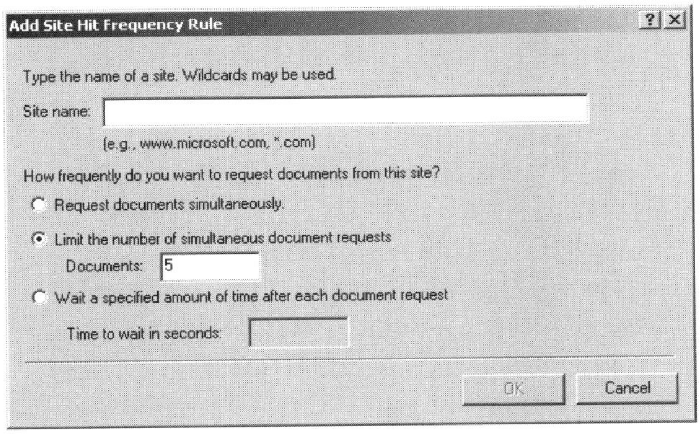

Figure 7–16 Add Site Hit Frequency Rule dialog box

First, you can set rules for individual sites, or you can use the wildcard character "*", in the site names to set rules on multiple sites. Table 7–3 explains how to use the wildcard character in site hit frequency rules.

Remember that site names are evaluated in order, so the first matching site name will apply. Hence, you'll probably want to ensure that any site rules that apply to the * site name should be the last rules in the rules list on the Load tab.

Table 7–3 Wildcard characters in site hit frequency rules

Use of the Wildcard Character in a Rule	Purpose and Effect
*	Use this to apply the rule to all content source sites. This will include intranet sites.
.	Use this format to apply the rule to all content sites that have a dot in the name. This may or may not apply to an intranet site.
*.sitename.com	Apply this rule to all the sites in the *sitename.com* domain. An example of this would be *.networkknowledge.com.
*.top-level-domain	Apply this rule to all sites that have the same top-level domain name, such as *.com, *.org, *.web. Rules are specific to a site, such as www.networkknowledge.com. Hence, if you create a rule for the *.com domains and also create a rule for www.networkknowledge.com, then the *.com rule will not be applied to the www.networkknowledge.com domain.

In my example (shown earlier in Figure 7–15), I placed the most specific rule using the wildcard character at the top of the list. The most general use of the wildcard character * is at the bottom, meaning that for a content source located on an `.org` domain, the last rule would be the only rule that applies.

In Figure 7–16, if you click Request Documents Simultaneously, you will instruct the indexing process to use all its allocated system resources to request as many documents as possible simultaneously. This option also tells it to request these documents continuously (in an uninterrupted flow) and not constantly (in a uniform flow). In this way, there is no delay between document requests. Select this option only when you know that the content source can handle a barrage of requests over sufficient bandwidth.

The second option, Limit the Number of Simultaneous Document Requests, allows you to specify the maximum number of documents in any single document request. Finally, Wait a Specified Amount of Time After Each Document Request instructs the indexing service to back off the configured value (in seconds) before sending another document request. When you combine this option with the value specified in the second option, you can instruct the indexing service to be considerate of content sources' bandwidth and overall capacity to field requests from your indexing service. Note that to combine two or more values in this field, you must create separate rules for each configured value. For instance, if you want to limit the crawl process to retrieve three documents at a time and have the gatherer wait five seconds between document requests, it would require two different site hit frequency rules.

Fourth, you can configure two *time-out settings* on the Load tab (shown earlier in Figure 7–15). You use these connection wait times to specify how long the indexing service should wait to establish a connection with a Web site or server or send an acknowledgment request. If you set the values too high, the indexing server will waste time waiting to connect to a site that no longer exists, is down, or is otherwise unavailable. If you set the time too low, the indexing server may not have adequate time to establish a connection with a server that is up and running. So it's best to set your wait times between 10 seconds and 2 minutes (120 seconds).

Also, if the indexing service encounters 32 or more consecutive time-outs to a server, it will mark the server as unavailable and will not process any more requests for that server for 10 minutes.

Fifth, you set the *content access account* on the Accounts tab (Figure 7–17). The Default Content Access Account is the security context in which the indexing process will attempt to crawl external content sources. The Propagation Access Account is the security context that will be used to propagate workspace indexes to other servers. This account must have administrator privileges on both SPS servers and must be configured *before* the index is built. Failing to pay attention to this detail will require that the index be rebuilt before it can be propagated to a new workspace.

Sixth, you'll use the Proxy Server tab (Figure 7–18) to make *proxy server* configurations for the search process. By default, the search process uses the

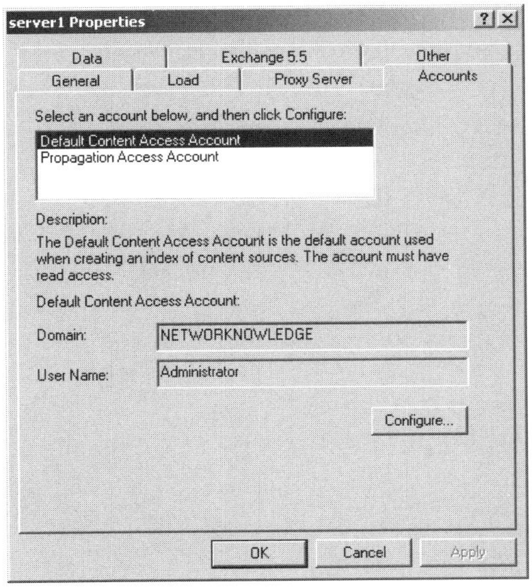

Figure 7–17 Accounts tab in server properties

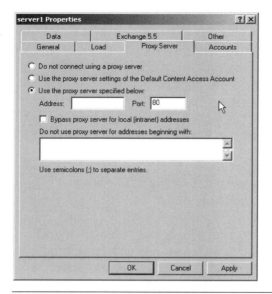

Figure 7–18 Proxy Server tab in server properties

proxy settings of the security context of the Default Content Access Account, but you can change this on this tab. You might wonder how these settings are affected by the settings on the `proxycfg` utility (explained in Chapter 4). The `proxycfg` tool is used to set proxy settings on the XMLHTTP object. The tab under discussion here is used to set proxy settings for the Search service. Neither of these proxy settings has any effect on the Internet Explorer or browser proxy settings. So, in essence, each SPS server has three proxy settings: browser, search, and XMLHTTP.

Finally, the Data tab (Figure 7–19) lists the locations of all your logs and databases. Table 7–4 lists these default locations.

As you highlight each database or log location in the Server Data and Log Files display box, a short description will appear under the Description label. These are self-explanatory and aren't covered here. Below that, you can set the location for these log and database files by following these steps:

1. Highlight the files you wish to move.
2. Click the Browse button and choose a new location.
3. Click OK.
4. Click Apply and watch the files move.

Pretty cool, eh?

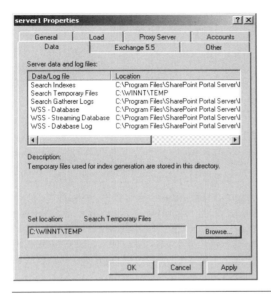

Figure 7–19 Data tab in server properties

While the WSS files are moving, the databases are not available, and anyone trying to get to the portal will receive a "page cannot be found" error message. If you change the directory for the search files, the files themselves are not moved. Instead, you're telling the search process to use the new location the next time an index is created. If you want to move the current index files, you must use the Catutil utility.

Table 7–4 Data tab in server properties

Data/Log File	Location
WSS .edb database	C:\program files\sharepoint portal server\ data\web storage system
WSS .stm database	C:\program files\sharepoint portal server\ data\web storage system
WSS transaction logs	C:\program files\sharepoint portal server\ data\web storage system
Search gatherer logs	C:\program files\sharepoint portal server\ FTData\sharepointportalserver\gatherlogs
Search indexes	C:\program files\sharepoint portal server\ FTData\sharepointportalserver\projects
Search temporary files	C:\winnt\temp

The destination location you choose must be a hard drive; a zip drive or floppy drive will not be allowed by SPS.

Whenever a workspace index is created, a log file for that index is created that contains pertinent information, such as record access errors and index creation data. The gatherer logs contain information about the URLs that have been accessed during the indexing process. This log will contain errors, successes, and URLs that have been, by rule, disallowed access.

To view this log, you use the content source object inside the Management| Content Sources folder in the Web folders view of the workspace (Figure 7–20).

NOTE: Logging exclusions as well as successes will generate a much greater number of entries than logging successes only. Also, you must be using the Web content folders view instead of the Windows classic view under the Tools|Folder Options menu. If you use the classic view, you won't be able to see the gatherer logs on the crawling information in the left column because that column won't be there.

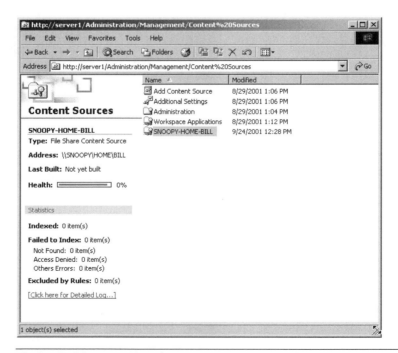

Figure 7–20 View of the gatherer logs from the Web folders client

If you click the Click Here for Detailed Log link, you'll find a wealth of information about the URLs that are being accessed, the number of errors and successes, and other pertinent information about the gatherer's experience in crawling this content source. However, this isn't the only way to view the gatherer logs.

To view the gatherer logs outside the Web interface to the workspace, use the `gthrlog.vbs` utility. Be aware, though, that it's difficult to read the log files using Notepad or some other text editor. The `gthrlog.vbs` utility is located, by default, in the following directory and is installed with SPS during a normal installation:

```
Program files\common files\microsoft shared\mssearch\bin
```

The generic usage of this utility is as follows:

```
Gthrlog.vbs "path_to_log_file_and_log_file_name"
```

Table 7–5 lists the switches for this utility.

When this command is run, you will receive the output in a series of popup boxes with an OK button for each line in the log file. Clicking OK through all these boxes is not fun, so I recommend that you include commands to send the output to a text file. Use the following command:

```
Cscript Gthrlog.vbs "path_to_log_file_and_log_file_name"
>c:\gatherlog.txt
```

Note that although this command appears to be two lines (because of the length limits of the printed page), in fact it's a one-line command.

You should receive a text file similar to the one in Figure 7–21.

Table 7–5 `gthrlog.vbs` utility switches

Switch	Purpose
/b	Order by descending time stamp
/n	Display any messages that don't match the filter
/t	Specifies the transaction type
/e	Specifies the error mask
/s	Specifies the transaction status
/u	Input the URL that contains any wildcard characters, such as * or ?

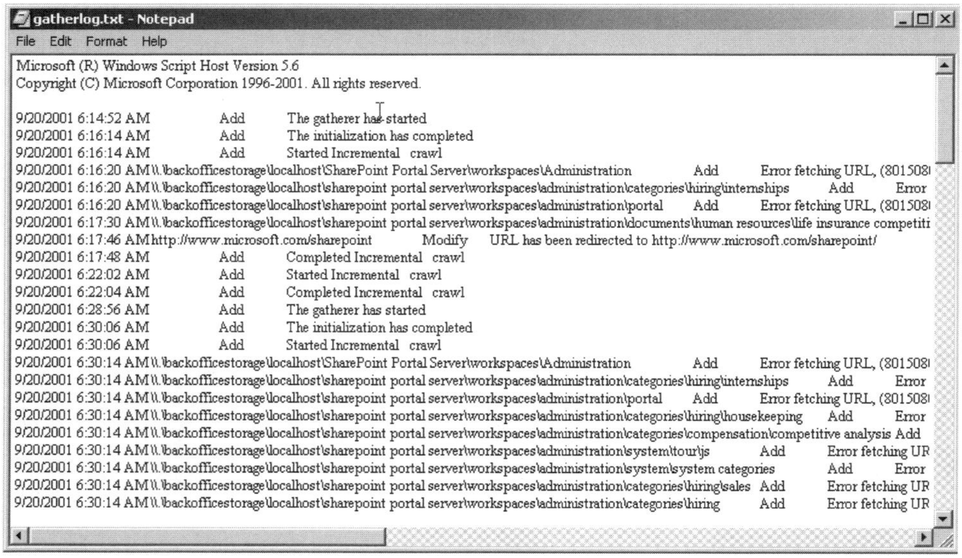

Figure 7–21 `gatherlog.txt` file output from using the `gthrlog.vbs` utility

Configuring Index Builds

This task is one of the more important responsibilities of your administration of an SPS workspace. You have several options for specifying how and when indexes are built. Your choices here will directly impact the quality and relevance of the result sets returned to your users.

It is a good idea for the workspace coordinator to monitor the state of the indexes regularly. Using the Web folders view and the SPS MMC, you can view the build status and read about any errors that were encountered during the build process. SPS supports four types of indexes: full, incremental, adaptive, and notification. Let's discuss each one.

Full Indexes

A *full* update of the index instructs the gatherer to follow all the links for all content specified in all the content sources for the workspace. A new index is built, regardless of the past crawling history on any given content source. New content will be added, old content will be deleted, and URLs that don't connect to content will be discarded.

NOTE: The first build of an index for a new content source is always a full build.

Full builds of an index will likely peg the processor at 100 percent utilization, so you can assume that they are very resource-intensive. Given this, you should not plan to perform full updates to your index except in the following circumstances:

- Whenever the update rules for a workspace are modified
- If you rename a category
- If you modify the noise word file or register new IFilters or protocol handlers
- If you retrain the Category Assistant (see Chapter 8)

In addition, keep in mind that a full build of the index is automatically initiated after you reset the index. And remember that each notification will be re-sent during a full index build of any content source.

Incremental Builds

Incremental builds are not nearly as time-consuming or pervasive as a full index build. During an incremental build, only those documents that have been modified or added to the content source since the last build are filtered. Content that has been deleted is also deleted from an index during an incremental build. You'll likely use incremental builds every day to keep your index up-to-date, whereas you'll use full builds less often.

Incremental updates do not crawl content that has been excluded by rules that are set on the Properties page of the Content Sources folder. For example, if you exclude certain file types that were previously included in the index, an incremental update will not recognize the new rules; this means that it will continue to index those file types. If you want to ensure that newly excluded file types are not included in future indexing, you must first run a full build of the index. Subsequent incremental index builds will then honor the new exclusion rules.

Notification Builds

A *notification* build configures a content source to notify the gatherer service when a change to content has occurred. The gatherer then crawls the content and updates the index as appropriate. Notification updates are enabled by default for NTFS and SPS workspace content sources and can be disabled if desired. Currently, only NTFS and SPS content sources can be configured for this type of index build.

Adaptive Updates

In an *adaptive update*, the gatherer keeps track of how often the information in a content source has changed and uses an algorithm to compute the probability that the information has recently changed. Only those documents that are considered likely to have changed are crawled by the gatherer service. By default, all non-notification content sources participate in adaptive updates.

As more statistical samples become available to the gatherer service through a growing number of index builds, this type of update is supposed to improve system performance by ensuring that only those documents most likely to have changed are actually crawled.

The first time an adaptive update is run, you can consider it to be the equivalent of a full update. The second adaptive update on a content source is really like an incremental update. In theory, you won't notice any system performance improvements until the third adaptive update, which is the first opportunity for the gatherer to use comparative information to decide which documents are most likely to have been modified.

If you start with incremental updates and then switch to adaptive updates, you'll find that system performance will improve immediately because the adaptive algorithm will have a number of samples to use in its calculations. Adaptive updates are faster than either incremental or full updates.

Adaptive updates, however, have an obvious huge downside: Some documents that are rarely modified might be missed during the next and even subsequent updates. Remember, an adaptive update crawls only those documents identified by the algorithm, whether or not the document has actually been modified. To work around this problem, the gatherer service checks the time stamp on documents that have not been crawled for at least two weeks and indexes them if they're past the two-week interval. This interval is not configurable.

Unless you are willing to use indexes that might be incomplete, I suggest staying away from adaptive updates and sticking with the tried-and-true incremental and full updates. Adaptive updates are enabled or disabled in each content source's properties on the Configuration tab but are scheduled on the Scheduled Updates tab in the Additional Settings of the Content Sources folder. All adaptive updates for all content sources will run at the same time.

Configuring Search Rules

There are three basic types of search rules: site path rules, mapping rules, and file type rules. Good configuration of these rules will ensure that the content sources that you add to the workspace are used and updated most efficiently. This is also the location where you can tweak the rules to give your users the best possible set of results from a search query. These rules are configured in the Additional Settings icon in the Content Sources folder.

To configure the first set of rules, the site path rules, click the Site Path button on the Rules tab in the Administration Properties dialog box. *Site path* rules allow you to determine the type of information that is included or excluded from the index. For instance, you might want to exclude all the content in the `networknowledge.com/funstuff` pages but still include the information in the `networknowledge.com/funstuff/practicaljokes` page. Site path rules let you customize your configuration so that you can exclude from the crawl process certain pages and folders in a hierarchy while including children of excluded information.

To create a new rule, click the New button that is found in the Site Paths dialog box; then type the path, using the wildcard character "*" to broaden the scope of the path if desired. Then choose to either exclude or include the path in the rule. If you choose to exclude the path, you're finished configuring the path. However, if you choose to include the path, you're really saying that you want to customize the path in some way. To customize an included path, click the Options button. Figure 7–22 illustrates the Create New Site Path Rule dialog box.

Clicking the Options button gives you several choices (Figure 7–23). First, you can override the default content access account for a specific site and choose either Basic or Windows Integration Authentication (WIA) as the authentication method. Second, you can enable complex links, which will instruct the gatherer service to follow links by using parameters that follow a question mark in the link. Third, you can suppress indexing to prevent documents in the path from being included in the index. However, links *from* these

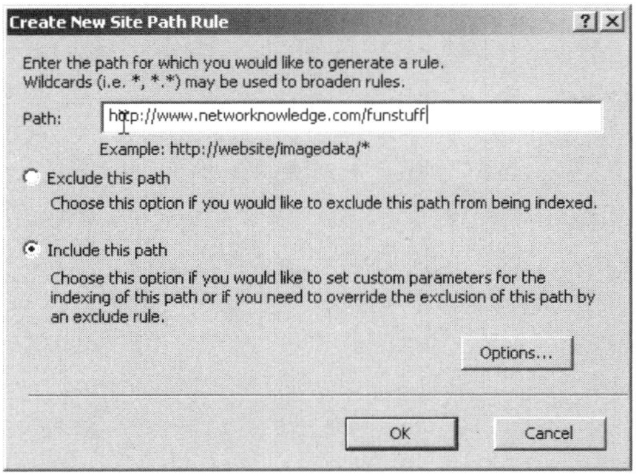

Figure 7–22 Create New Site Path Rule dialog box

Figure 7–23 Site path rule customizations

documents are still followed, and those target documents will be included in the index.

Note that the name of the server in the site rule is not resolved to the IP address for that machine. Instead, the host name of the server is matched to the URL in question. Therefore, if your content source is set up with a URL to one host name of a server but your site path rule specifies a different host name for the same server, then the rule will not be processed because the host names cannot be matched. To put it a different way, DNS is not involved in matching different host names between the site path rule and the content source based on a common IP address.

Managing Index Builds

You can manage index builds from either the Web folders client or the SPS MMC. However, you can manage individual content sources only from the Web folders client. When using the SPS MMC, you right-click the workspace name, point to All Tasks, and then select the type of build you wish to initiate. Depending on current activity in the workspace, you'll be offered the following choices:

- Delete workspace
- Start adaptive update
- Start incremental update

- Start full update
- Pause
- Resume
- Stop
- Reset index

Pausing an update means that any URLs not yet crawled remain in system memory. Because they remain in memory, the indexing can resume later from the point where it was paused. *Stopping* an index kills the URLs in memory, effectively defining the entire index build as the work up to the point of the stop command.

When you *reset* an index, you are emptying the index and asking the indexing service to start over. Statistical information about previous index builds is retained, however, for use with adaptive updates. Resetting an index forces a full build to occur. Therefore, you should not reset the index unless you know or suspect that your index is corrupted or if users are able to view data to which they should not have access. Resetting the index will immediately deny their ability to see restricted data.

To work with an individual content source, open the Web folders client to the workspace and navigate to the Management|Content Sources folder. Right-click the folder, and select the action you desire. From here, you can start a full build or incremental update, or you can stop an index build that is in progress.

The best way to monitor a crawl action in progress is to use the Web folders client to view the individual content sources. The information is displayed in the left column. Refer to Figure 7–20, presented earlier.

Propagating an Index between Workspaces

If you have a large number of content sources to crawl, you should seriously consider dedicating a single workspace (and server) to the task of crawling and indexing. SPS provides this feature. Coordinators can create a workspace that is fully dedicated to content indexing. Sometimes, you'll see this server referred to as a *dedicated content indexing* (DCI) server.

Users do not search the workspace of the DCI server. Instead, the DCI server's index is copied to, or *propagated*, to the workspace that the users search. Once this is done, the index is available to receive search queries from workspace users. Any given workspace can receive as many as four propagated indexes.

Categories can be assigned to incoming indexes by having the coordinators first create a shortcut to the external content and then assigning categories to the shortcut. This allows category browsing to work with both local and external content in terms of category browsing.

If you have a customized schema for your target workspace, you'll be happy to know that for schema synchronization purposes, the DCI workspace acts as a client to the destination workspace, updating its cache and schema to match those of the destination workspace.

To create a DCI server, it is best to install SPS on a separate server. During the SPS installation, select the Advanced button on the Workspace Definition screen of the installation wizard. This will invoke the Advanced Workspace Definition screen, illustrated in Figure 7–24. Select the Configure As an Index Workspace check box, and then type the workspace name of the destination workspace to which you want the index to be propagated.

NOTE: The indexing and destination workspaces cannot be on the same physical server. SPS will enforce this restriction when you create the indexing workspace.

After you type the URL of the destination workspace, you'll be prompted to type the propagation account user name and password. Remember that this account must have write permission for both workspaces and should be a Coordinator-level account. After typing this information, you can finish the wizard to create the indexing workspace.

When naming your DCI workspace, keep in mind two things. First, the DCI workspace name must be different from the destination workspace name, and, second, the DCI workspace name can be the same as any other DCI workspace name that is propagating to the destination workspace. But if you

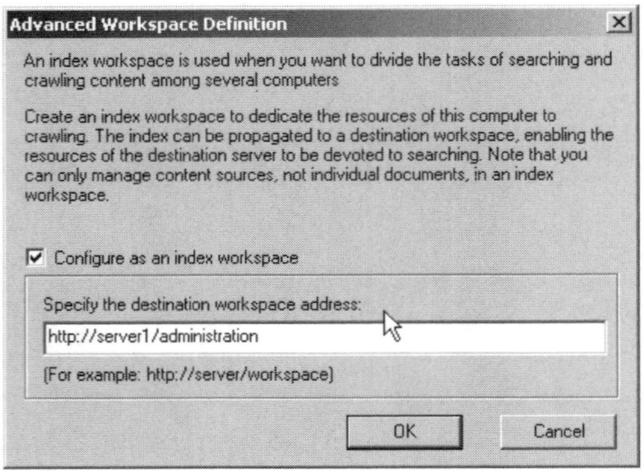

Figure 7–24 Typing the destination workspace URL during the installation of a DCI server

do the latter, the search projects (see Chapter 9) will be overwritten by the most recent propagation, and your users will never have a full set of indexes from all the propagation servers against which to execute a query.

Also, before you propagate an index to another server, be sure that you have at least 100MB of free disk space for the new index plus the size of the catalog that will be propagated. And if you are going to propagate the index through a firewall, you must have the server message blocks (SMBs) ports open on your firewall, and this means opening up the NetBIOS ports 137 and 139 plus a random port for the end point mapper.

After the DCI server has completed its build, the index can be propagated manually or on a scheduled basis. The first time an index is propagated, a search project will be created in the default search project location. The name of the search project will be the name of the DCI workspace.

To manually start the propagation, right-click the workspace in the SPS MMC of the DCI server, point to All Tasks, and then choose Propagate Index. To schedule index propagation, you can schedule index builds on the server or you can create a script using the method `IKnowledgeCatalog::PropagateNow`. Please refer to the SPS Software Development Kit (SDK) for more information on this method.

During the propagation of the index, no method is available to pause or stop it; however, it can be canceled. Immediately before propagation starts, the indexing service in the destination workspace will pause and will continue its work after the propagation process has been completed.

If you ever want to eliminate a propagated catalog from being available to your users, you should delete the DCI workspace that is generating the propagated catalog. This action will automatically delete the catalog on the destination server. If you delete the DCI workspace and find that the propagated catalog still exists on the destination server, use Catutil to delete the orphaned catalog.

Searching for Content Using the Search Web Parts

The default portal that installs with SPS contains two Search Web parts: Simple Search and Advanced Search. The Simple Web part (Figure 7–25) has a drop-down list for choosing the search scopes, as well as an input box for typing the search query.

Search *scopes* give users a way to define both the range and the depth of searches in the workspace. Hence, a user can either trim or expand the number of documents against which the query is matched. For example, suppose

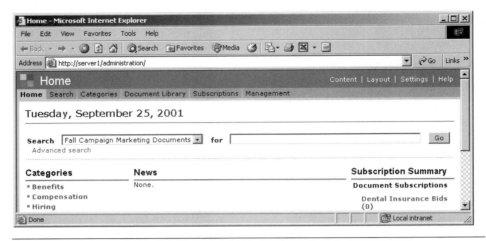

Figure 7–25 Simple Search Web part in portal

you have a large number of marketing documents related to an upcoming campaign for the fall quarter. You could create a search scope called Fall Quarter Marketing Campaign and ensure that only the fall campaign marketing documents are included in the scope. This will enable your users who need a fall campaign marketing document to find it without having to search the entire workspace index.

A search scope can be associated with one or more content sources. The default scope is This Site, which includes all content sources and published documents in the workspace. A search scope name can contain as many as 60 characters.

NOTE: A given document cannot belong to more than one scope at any given time. A document's scope membership is based on the most recently crawled content source. For instance, if document1 is referenced by two different content sources and if each content source is associated with a different scope, the most recent crawl process for a content source is the scope in which the document will be found.

To create a new search scope, navigate to the Advanced tab of a content source's properties and type a new name for the scope. You will be prompted to rebuild the index in order to make the new scope active.

Depending on where you are in the portal, the contents in the drop-down list may change. For instance, if you are in the Categories dashboard and use the Simple Search Web part, you'll be given the choice This Category. However, if you are on the Home dashboard, you won't find this choice in the drop-down list.

When typing search terms, you can type a single word or a phrase in quotation marks, such as "customer responses." You can type multiple single words (a phrase without quotation marks is treated as multiple single words, meaning that a document that matches on any given word will be in the result set), but the result set will likely have too many *false positives*: documents that match the search criteria but aren't really relevant or useful to you. Obviously, the quality of the result set is directly related to the quality of the search request. And remember that wildcard characters—such as * or ? or %—are not allowed in the search terms or property names. Using these characters will yield an empty result set. The box can accept a search query of unlimited length. The search terms are executed as a free-text query.

The Advanced Search Web part (Figure 7–26) gives you a search tool that's more powerful and flexible than the Simple Search Web part. With the Advanced Search Web part, you can refine your search query by searching by profile, properties, and date. The profile search allows you to specify documents that are described by a certain profile. This option eliminates documents that fall outside the chosen profiles.

When searching by properties, you can drill down into a specific property (and not just the profile) that is defined in the workspace. You can combine as many as three properties in the same search query. You can also define the date range for the document, either by the date the document was created or by the date it was last modified. Smart users can cut their document browsing time considerably by using the Advanced Search Web part.

Free-Text Queries

With free-text queries, you can type a group of words or a complete sentence as part of the overall search query. When you do this, the indexing service will find the pages that best match the words and phrases in the query. The indexing service is more interested in finding documents that match the meaning, rather than the exact wording, of the search query. And because SPS uses free-text queries, the indexing service will ignore Boolean, proximity, and wildcard operators. For more information on free-text queries and the ways it differs from Boolean, pattern matching, and other query types, please see the section Files and Printers in the *Windows 2000 Advanced Server Manual*, which can be found in the Manuals section in TechNet under the Windows Product Family Top Level Book.

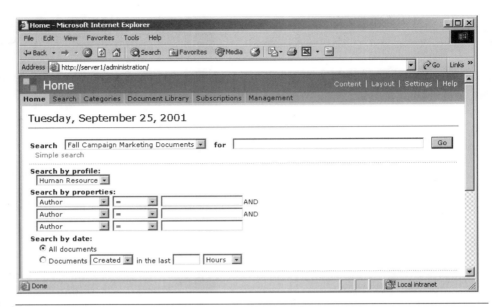

Figure 7–26 Advanced Search Web part in portal

It's worth noting a couple of things here. First, when you test the Advanced Search Web part, even though the interface says "AND," any fields that are left blank will not be included in the search query.

Second, according to tests run at this end, if you publish a document and then search for a word in that document, it will be immediately available and will appear in the result set. This is true even if you haven't run an incremental or full build. However, if you search for that same word using the Contains comparison operator, the document will not appear until a new build has been created by the index service. This is also true of the other comparison operators except the equal sign (=) operator.

Your users will experience such behavior as inconsistent, and you should be proactive in overcoming this perception through training.

Table 7–6 shows several comparison operators.

By combining these comparison operators, you can create a complex search query and narrow the result set so that it includes as few false positives as possible.

Table 7–6 Comparison operators

Operator	Meaning
=	Search will find documents that have the exact string of characters entered.
>	If you search for "Author > M", search will return author names that start with *N* through the end of the alphabet.
<	If you search for "Author < M", search will return author names that begin with the letters from *A* through *L*.

Summary

This chapter skims the surface of managing the search process, subscriptions, and notifications. There is much here to digest and learn. Most of what is presented in this chapter will have direct, daily effects on your users. A similar area is the way you set up and manage categories. In fact, it's so important that I've dedicated an entire chapter to it. So let's continue in Chapter 8 and learn about how to create and manage categories as well as how to publish documents.

Publishing, Approving, and Categorizing Documents

If you're like most system administrators, you understand that when you take a new position with a new company to run its network, a period of time is required to learn about the network. Each network has its own personality, and it takes time to learn what the former administrator did to make it work (or break it, in some instances <g>). Often, learning a new network requires you to think outside your box, to view familiar concepts in new and different ways. Working with categories calls for the same kind of thought process.

When you begin to set up a category structure for your users, you will be faced with an awesome challenge. This chapter, short as it is, is aimed at enabling you to create category hierarchies more effectively and more quickly as a result of reading it.

Setting up a category structure is one of the most important administrative acts you will undertake as coordinator for a workspace. This might sound a bit dramatic, but it's the unvarnished truth. I can say with 100 percent certainty that you will always be questioning the taxonomy that you've implemented. So now that I've built up your confidence just a bit <g>, let's get going.

This chapter discusses four important topics: how to plan for categories, how to create categories (this one's easy), how to configure categories, and how to manage categories.

But first, a short lesson on the architecture of categories. Categories are really search results. When users open a category in the dashboard, they are really performing a query that is associated with an underlying *search folder*, which is really a grouping of documents based on their shared category assignments. The query simply filters the folders for the selected category and returns those documents to the user in the dashboard. Because of this architecture, category names must be unique in the workspace.

Planning for Categories

Planning for category creation is not the same thing as creating directory structures for a large number of files on a file server. For instance, I once managed a group of servers for a well-known international chemical research company. When I took over the network, I inherited a file server that had nearly 20GB of original research in areas that I knew very little about.

The directory structure had been set up according to subjects: coating, filming, reactions, production, and so on. Each top-level folder was assigned a contact person in the network for management. Each contact person was responsible for the entire directory structure beneath his or her assigned top-level folder. About the only thing I did (well, it wasn't the *only* thing I did) was to create new top-level folders from time to time when the director of the division requested additional disk space and gave me a folder name and contact. The default administrator account and the contact were given Full Control NTFS permissions on the top-level folder.

This process might sound familiar. It's likely that you have implemented some type of file server directory management that, like my experience, features a collaborative management effort between you and selected users on your network.

Creating a category structure does not work this way, nor would you want it to. You, the coordinator, are solely responsible for creating a category hierarchy or group of hierarchies. The information for this process comes from consultation with your users, but the category structure is implemented entirely by you.

When it comes to mapping out a plan for category hierarchies, you should first stop and take a hard look at how you're managing files now. Are they arranged by subject? Department? Department and then subject? You should understand not only *what* the current system is but also *why* it was created the way it was. This is important because an effective category hierarchy reflects how your users think about their documents and not necessarily the content of the documents. Usually, current directory structures indicate one method of how users think about their information.

Creating category hierarchies that reflect how people think about documents suffers from a significant problem: Often, there is little commonality among your users. Some of them think about documents based on their department affiliation. Others think about documents based on the documents' topics. Still others may think about documents based on the documents' authors. The problem is that each of these methods is valid, so how do you choose which approach to take? SharePoint Portal Server solves this dilemma by allowing you to create competing, dissimilar category hierarchies for your documents. Each document can be a member of multiple categories, thus allowing the document to be found through different category searches. Remember that categories provide a flexible way to both *describe* and *find* documents. If you lose sight of either of these functions, you probably won't create an optimal category structure for your environment.

One company that I've been working with has a goal of ensuring that all documents can be found within three clicks of the mouse. This is a formidable task because they have more than 10,000 documents that will need to be checked in and categorized. The company has a daunting task ahead of it, one whose solution will reside in an effective category structure. To be successful, the coordinators will be creating several shallow, but wide, sets of category hierarchies. The trade-off is this: Users will need to navigate a plethora of categories, especially at the second level of the hierarchy, in order to find their documents, but at least they won't be browsing a deep and cumbersome directory structure on a file server. The company is betting that the new hierarchy plan will save users time and make them more productive.

So when you're creating your plan, the first step is to decide what kind of metadata is needed to accurately describe the documents in different ways. What follows is a quick list to help stir your thinking:

- Subject
- Department
- Division
- Project name
- Project number
- Customer
- Season
- Product line
- Production plant
- Type of research
- Region
- Dates
- Quantities, such as dollars, marks, pounds, and so on
- Method of communication

The list doesn't include things such as author or title because these are already defined in the SPS default document profiles and are indexed for searching purposes. Categories complement a document's metadata and, in fact, become a part of it. But categories do not reflect all the metadata for a document, nor should they: Categories are a method of building additional structures around your data to enable your users to find documents more quickly.

Furthermore, there is confusion among SharePoint administrators about the role of categories versus the role of the document folder hierarchy. To aid your understanding in this area, following is some advice that SPS administrators have offered me:

- Model your folder structure after your company organization chart because it likely best reflects the security contexts of the documents. Use categories sparingly until you and your users have worked with SPS for a substantial amount of time.
- Don't implement a rich set of categories until your users are *very* familiar with the concept of categories and have received substantive training on how to use them. Users are accustomed to a folder hierarchy and usually prefer something they are familiar with.
- Consider using a rich set of keywords before implementing a rich set of categories. Users are more likely to search based on a keyword than to browse a category list.
- Do an extensive test of a sample category structure, and then plan to reimplement the tested structure in a production environment. Test for at least 180 days with a pilot group of users.

As you can see, these four administrators understand one basic principle: Once a category structure is implemented, it is hard to change. So go slow, be careful, and be willing to rethink your structure many times.

Now let's work out a hypothetical example to illustrate these concepts. Let's assume you're the coordinator for the Administration workspace on Server1 for the `trainsbydave.com` Web site and store. Your company sells trains over the Internet and through selected walk-in stores around the country. The Administration workspace is designed to hold documents for all administrative personnel, including those in human resources, accounting, and management. This example contains seven hierarchies of categories, represented by the seven hierarchies in the portal workspace:

- Accounting
- Current Projects
- Executives
- HR
- Past Projects
- Product Lines
- Vendors

Notice that each department has a category hierarchy, as do current projects, past projects, product lines, and vendors. Hence, a document that outlines the demographic characteristics of a new target market could be assigned to categories in the Executives, Current Projects, and Product Lines hierarchies. Moreover, a job description document could be assigned to categories in the Executives, HR, Current Projects, and Accounting hierarchies.

By assigning the document to multiple categories in different hierarchies, you improve the chances that it will be found when needed. For instance, the demographic document may be needed by the folks working in product development to better understand the target market for the product they are creating. In addition, this document might be needed by the executives to discern whether the new marketing campaign is going to reach those defined by the demographics. Those who are developing the new product would be more likely to search for the document based on the product it is associated with, whereas those responsible for product management might more likely search under the product's marketing campaign.

Based on this little amount of information, you've probably come up with better (or at least different) ways of creating categories for this hypothetical example. If you did, it should indicate just how difficult it is to implement a category structure that makes sense to most of your users.

The solution is to plan your categories to give different users in your company different methods or ways of describing the company's documents so that they can use multiple methods of searching.

Creating Categories

By default, every SPS workspace contains a category structure, creatively named Category 1, Category 2, and Category 3. Categories appear as links in the workspace; when a category is chosen, the Web page shows subcategories, best bets, and documents assigned to the category.

Only coordinators can create new categories. To create a new category, use the Web folders client and navigate to the Categories section of the workspace. Then use the File|New|Category menu selection or right-click inside the Web folders client, point to New, and choose Category from the context menu. Either way will create a new category, which you must name.

You'll see an animated graphic while the system creates the new category. It's cool the first time you see it. Thereafter, it's pretty boring.

When a new category is created, the workspace schema is also updated to include the new category value in its overall workspace definitions.

Once you've created a new category, you can create an unlimited number of subcategories inside it. However, practically speaking, you won't want to create thousands of categories in any hierarchy because navigation would become too cumbersome. The resource kit recommends no more than 500 categories aggregate, but some environments will exceed this. I recommend a wider, shallower structure versus a deeper, narrower structure. Overall, the former will result in fewer clicks for your users to find a document, and this would be a good thing.

When you delete a category, you're also deleting all its subcategories. Categories can be renamed but can't be moved within the hierarchy. When a category is deleted, all the associated documents must be updated to reflect the loss of the association. Similarly, when a category is renamed, all the documents must be retagged, which can take considerable time and consume precious system resources. Best practice is to perform this type of administrative action during off-peak hours.

Configuring and Managing Categories

The best place to start this discussion is to look at a category's properties, which can be viewed by right-clicking a category and then choosing Properties. Figure 8–1 illustrates the single-tab properties page for the Executives

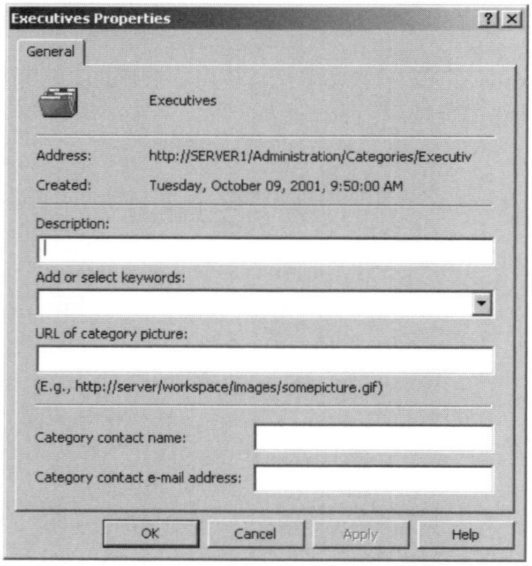

Figure 8–1 Executives category properties

category. Notice that you can type a description to communicate to your users the meaning and purpose of this category.

You can also associate keywords with this category to assist users in searching for data. If you'd like to use a special category icon to help users understand what the category is referring to, you can specify the icon's URL in the box labeled URL of Category Picture.

The category contact person and e-mail address are displayed in the dashboard. A Mail to link lets users send e-mail to the category contact. Being specified as a category contact does not imply any special permissions to manage the category. Figure 8–2 illustrates how a category description and contact information are displayed in the dashboard.

TIP: If you have multiple workspaces on the same server and you create categories with the same name, you can use the category hierarchy to browse documents in both workspaces. This also requires index propagation between the workspaces.

As with any object in the workspace, you can assign permissions to a category. These permissions apply only to creating, renaming, deleting, and mov-

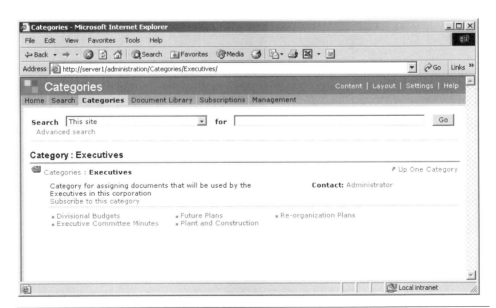

Figure 8–2 Executives category in the dashboard with description and contact information

ing categories. Category permissions are not another layer of permissions for the documents associated with a category. This separation of permissions gives you administrative flexibility in determining who can manage the categories without being concerned about leaking sensitive information to the category administrator.

It would be nice if category permissions were exposed in the user interface, but unfortunately they are not. Instead, they are inherited from the workspace security settings. This means that you can configure category security only at the workspace level, using the workspace security roles. A coordinator will have full permissions to manage categories. People who have been assigned the Author and Reader security roles can only read categories; they have no permissions to manage them.

Documents can be associated with categories in one of two ways. First, if you use the Web folders client to open a document's properties, you'll find a Search and Categories tab where you can choose the categories with which the document should be associated (Figure 8–3). This tab is displayed only to coordinators.

You can also associate a category with a document during the check-in process on the document's profile form. Authors will use this method to assign documents to categories. This is illustrated in Figure 8–4.

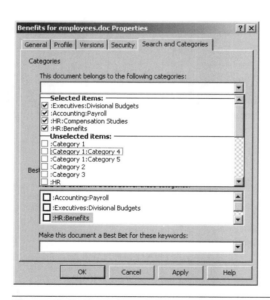

Figure 8–3 Search and Categories tab in a document's properties

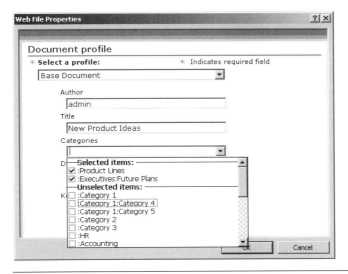

Figure 8–4 Assigning a category to a document during check-in

Best Bets

The Search and Categories tab has a place to configure a best bet (shown earlier in Figure 8–3). Best bets are documents that are assigned to appear when users select a particular category. The idea is to select documents that are highly relevant to the category and that would be on most people's list of documents they would expect to see when they browse that category.

There are two types of best bets: keyword and category. *Keyword* best bet documents will appear whenever the configured keywords are used in a search query. *Category* best bet documents will appear whenever the category is browsed. For instance, I've chosen to make the `Budget for June, 2002.xls` file a best bet for the Divisional Budgets category. You can see in Figure 8–5 that this document appears as a best bet when the Divisional Budgets category is browsed. Also, this document will appear whenever the word *budget* is used in a search query.

Using the Category Assistant

If you have a large number of documents but don't have the time or workers to manually assign them to categories, you can use an SPS feature called the Category Assistant (CA). This technology automatically categorizes crawled documents.

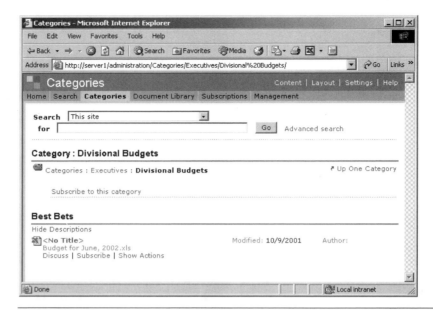

Figure 8–5 The `Budget for June, 2002` file appearing as a best bet for the Divisional Budgets category

NOTE: The Category Assistant does not work well with any language other than English. If you're working outside an English-speaking country, you will likely find the CA to be less than desirable, and you'll probably end up assigning categories manually.

To make the CA work properly, you must first *train* it to associate certain document types—based on a document's contents, not its filename extension—with certain categories. Then, when new documents are added to the workspace, they are auto-categorized accordingly. The success of this technique depends entirely on the CA's training; good training leads to good automatic categorizations, and vice versa.

To train the CA, you open the properties of the Categories folder using the Web folders view of the workspace (Figure 8–6). Then click on the Train Now button, and the CA will proceed to auto-categorize current documents into categories.

In Figure 8–6, you can see that the sample population of documents was not large enough to train the CA. Hence, the training has ended, and an error message was returned to this effect. Note that you can categorize documents

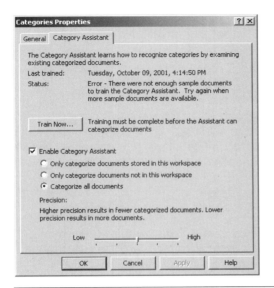

Figure 8–6 The Category Assistant tab in the Categories Properties dialog box

that originate either inside or outside the workspace or choose to categorize all documents defined by all content sources.

The CA trains itself by comparing a list of words in each already categorized document with the list of words in newly crawled documents. When there is sufficient overlap, the crawled document is automatically added to the category holding other documents whose content has a similar list of words. Based on this category-to-document comparison, the CA provides a confidence number that reflects the document's relevance to the assigned category.

To complete the training, the CA requires at least ten documents per category. If you create an elaborate category structure, you'll need at least ten documents associated *with each category* before the CA can run properly. There is no provision or support for training each category individually.

You can set the CA's precision level at the bottom of the Category Assistant tab (refer to Figure 8–6). If you set this value high, the CA will require a more complete and thorough match before associating a document with a category. This means that some documents will not appear in the category where you would otherwise wish it to appear. Setting this value low means that the CA will work with a more lenient set of match criteria and will add more documents to each category. The problem is that when browsing categories, you could be presented with a number of false positives: documents that match well enough to be added to a category they don't really belong with.

If you don't like how the CA has assigned a particular document to a category, you can override it by clearing the Display Document in Suggested Categories check box on the Search and Categories tab in the document's properties. This will set the `issuggestedcategoryused` property to `FALSE`.

FOR MORE INFO: To learn more about how auto-categorization works, please see the document "Inductive Learning Algorithms and Representations for Text Categorization," by Platt et al., at the following URL: `http://research.microsoft.com/users/jplatt/cikm98.pdf`.

NOTE: The CA can categorize content external to the workspace.

Another feature that Microsoft has implemented is the ability to assign categories to shortcuts that link to URLs and other content sources. This is most clearly seen when you create quick links on the Home dashboard. In my example (Figure 8–7), I created a quick link to `http://www.foxnews.com`. I also assigned this link to the Category 1 category, and this means that when this category is browsed, this link will appear as one of the results. Also, if the

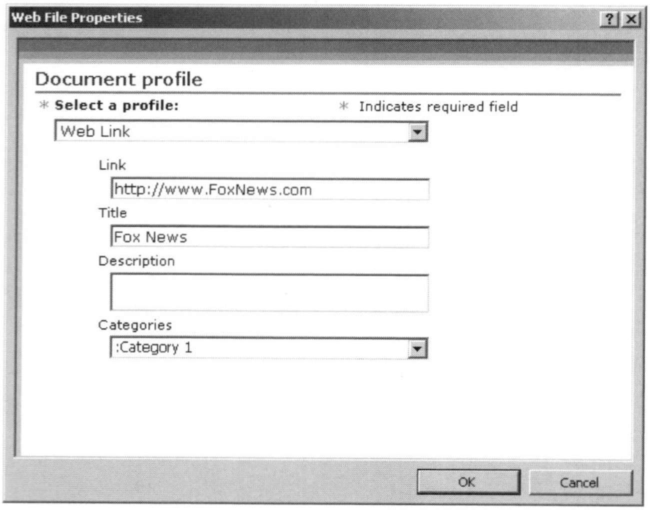

Figure 8–7 Assigning a Web link to a category

link points to a Web page, the first page of the site will be crawled and indexed, meaning that any words that appear in the Web page will appear in a result set of a search query that encompasses words found on that site.

Figure 8–8 illustrates how a category will appear when there are documents that have been assigned as best bets for that category and other documents whose metadata has been associated with that category. Here, two documents have been configured as best bets for the Cash Flow Forecasting category. These documents appear under the Best Bets Web part. Another document is associated with the category but is not a best bet, and it appears in the Documents Web part. Hence, in Figure 8–8, the dashboard has four Web parts: Search, Category, Best Bets, and Documents. If no documents had been configured as best bets for this category, the Best Bets Web part would not have appeared.

For each document, you can click the Show Actions link to initiate a Web discussion, create a subscription, or show the allowed actions on the Document Inspection Web page. Also, you can subscribe to the category and thereby be informed of any changes to published documents in the entire category.

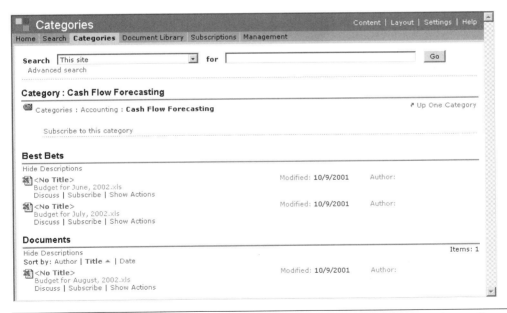

Figure 8–8 A category that has assigned documents as well as documents configured as best bets

Publishing and Approving Documents

In a collaborative environment, where documents are developed by more than one person, you often need to route new documents through an approval process. SharePoint Portal Server facilitates this collaborative process through an approval routing feature that is native to SPS when you install it.

The approval feature is invoked only after a document has been developed. During its development, only those users who are actively working on the document can open and modify its contents. In may cases, you may want to ensure that only the document's authors, and not the larger user community, can find it in the portal. This protection of documents during development is at the heart of the document management process of checking out and checking in documents.

After reading this chapter, you may think that mastering DM isn't very difficult—and you'd be right. However, don't forget that the DM functions present significant training issues for your users. Don't deploy SharePoint Portal Server in the absence of an end-user training program.

We'll look at the two SPS collaborative functions: publishing and approving documents. However, to understand the publishing process, you first need a basic understanding of the security roles in the workspace.

Security Roles in SharePoint Portal Server

The publishing, approval, and other collaborative functions of SPS are implemented using three security roles: Coordinator, Author, and Reader. These roles are assigned by you to users in the workspace at the folder or workspace level. Each role has a permission set that you can't modify. If a user holds more than one role on a folder or workspace, the most lenient permission applies. For instance, if the Everyone security group has the Reader role on the Corporate folder, and Tom, a user in the domain, has the Author role on the Corporate folder, Tom will enjoy Author role permissions on the folder and all the documents therein, unless he's specifically excluded on one or more documents in the folder.

SPS can work with security principles either from a Windows NT security accounts database or from a Windows 2000 Active Directory directory. It's a fine distinction, but important to note, that SPS does not have its own user accounts for its workspaces, but it does have its own role-based security model. Hence, the server on which you install SPS must be a member of either a Windows NT domain or a Windows 2000 forest in order for SPS to pull those security principles from the databases and assign them roles in the workspace. For more information on security, please see Chapter 13.

The Coordinator role has the permission to manage the entire workspace. A user with the Coordinator role can perform workspace-wide and administrator-level functions, such as customizing the Digital Dashboard, managing indexes, managing categories, and configuring content sources. At the folder level, a coordinator can add, delete, and modify folders and documents as well as create the approval process and override denials, approvals, and check-outs. The coordinator is the big kahuna and rules the roost.

The Author role has permissions to add, edit, delete, and read documents in a folder. In an enhanced folder, this role also has permission to publish a document. An author can create, delete, and modify folders but can't change a folder's permissions or approval policies. This is why you, as an administrator for a SharePoint Portal Server workspace, should not be as concerned about the document folder structure in your workspace: Authors can create and delete folders as needed to aid them in their role as developers of documents. Your focus should be on creating an excellent category and keyword list.

The Reader role has permission to search for and read documents. By default, all users (that is, everyone in the Everyone security group) have this role. Only published documents can be viewed by those who hold the Reader permission. Hence, during a document's development, if it is only checked in to the workspace but not published, it can be viewed only by those who hold the Author or Coordinator role, not by those who hold only the Reader role.

Each workspace provides permission inheritance, and this means that permissions set on one object in the hierarchy are, by default, inherited by all the objects at a lower level (child objects). You can block permission inheritance by configuring the child object not to use its parent's security settings. Moreover, you can configure security settings on one object to apply to all subfolders and documents.

The Publishing Process

Collaboration on documents is performed by those who hold the Author or Coordinator role, not by those who hold the Reader role. Collaboration tools include the check-out and check-in features, which allow a document to be checked out of the workspace, modified, and then checked in to the workspace for other team members' consideration.

Because a document may incur many versions during development, it is important to train your users to understand that a checked-out document is a copy of the most recent version of the document. When a document is checked out, the team member saves the checked-out version on the local hard disk or home directory before making modifications to it. When the team member checks the document back in to the workspace, the checked-in copy becomes the most recent version, and the document's version number is incremented on the server. Team members can't overwrite a checked-in or published document without first checking it out. However, they can view, and can engage in Web discussions about, a document that has been checked out.

This means that, unlike other document management programs, SharePoint offers no method for parallel document check-out with a method of merging all the modifications made to a document back into a single document. In other words, two people cannot check out a document at the same time, make their own modifications, and then expect their changes to be merged with the other changes after both have checked in the document. Even though this type of functionality is available in Exchange 2000 Server's public folders, it is not implemented here in SharePoint Portal Server.

Remember that publishing a document is different from checking it in or out. Publishing makes the document available to those assigned the Reader role, which is, by default, the Everyone security group. Whenever you work with the Everyone group, you should think "anyone" because anyone who can connect to your server will automatically become a member of the Everyone group. This includes users from within your organization and users who come into your network from the Internet.

Although authors who have checked out a document can modify their local copy of it, authors and coordinators can still publish the most recent version of that document on the SharePoint Portal Server machine. Authors and coordinators can view checked-in documents, whereas users with the Reader role can view only published documents.

SPS lets users with appropriate permissions publish a document after it has been checked in or during the check-in process. Let's look at two ways of publishing a document: publishing with and without an approval process.

Publishing Documents with an Approval Process

Many organizations require that a document be approved before it is made public. For example, before a human resources (HR) department distributes a benefits manual to all employees, the HR manager must approve the manual's contents. If the HR team developed the manual in SharePoint Portal Server, you can give the HR manager the Approver role to require him to approve the document before you publish it and make it available to all the users in the company. By using the portal, you don't actually distribute the manual.

Instead, you use e-mail to notify users that the manual is ready for previewing, or you place an announcement on the Home page of the dashboard and provide a link directly to the document. And this brings up another point: Although only one person can check out a document at any given time, multiple readers can view a published document simultaneously through the portal.

The Approver role is its own type of security role. Those assigned the Approver role are not required to have the Author or Coordinator role. Being an approver is a separate function that's specific to the folder and its documents. Unlike the other security roles, the Approver role doesn't have an associated permission set per se, but it does give an approver the ability to read a document that is in the approval process *even if the approver has not been granted any of the other security roles for that document.* This ability to read a document during the approval process is unique and allows you to make any user an approver without the need to ensure that the approver also has a set of minimum permissions to the folder. The one requirement for approvers is that their user account must reside in the same domain as the SPS computer or in a trusted domain.

Only a coordinator can configure who will be approvers on a given document folder. Approval options are set on a folder-by-folder basis, not on a document-by-document basis. Moreover, a coordinator can override the approval process and publish or not publish a document, regardless of what the approver or approvers do. This allows you the option of getting a stuck document through the approval route in case one of the approvers is on vacation or is too swamped to approve the document and move it through the routing process. Moreover, it also allows a document to be halted in the approval process by having you reject it even though others are approving it. This could be the case when a document is ready for publication and is undergoing the approval process but must be halted quickly because new information has made it inaccurate or obsolete.

To set up an approval process, the coordinator must configure the approval requirement on an enhanced documents folder. To configure the approval process, right-click the folder in the Web folders client, select Properties, and then click the Approval tab (Figure 8–9). Type the names of approvers for the folder's documents, and then type their e-mail addresses. I know you're going to ask whether there is any type of name resolution to an e-mail address, and the answer is no. Even though the user might be hosted on a local Exchange server, SPS does not query Active Directory (AD) to obtain a primary e-mail address for users entered on this tab.

Next, you configure a notification message for the approvers. Create a message that will work in most situations, and remind the approver that once a document is approved, it will be made public. Your message could also include

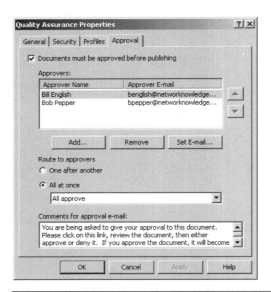

Figure 8–9 The Approval tab in the document folder's properties

a description of the routing process and a list of the other approvers, if desired. Because approval is set on a folder-by-folder basis and is uniform for each individual folder, this may be a handy way of informing those charged with approving various kinds of documents of the specific routing process for the document linked in their e-mail.

Finally, select either parallel- or serial-routing topology. Again, there is a lack of robustness here. Your choices are limited to what you see in the screen. There is no method of selecting a "majority wins" process, designating that one person must approve and then any one of an additional four must approve, or saying that any two out of five must approve. The logic necessary to support these choices is simply not in the code for this 1.0 product. If you've worked with other DM solutions, you're not going to find this to be a feature. But it's a start, and this is what is in SPS.

SharePoint Portal Server automatically sends an e-mail message to the approvers when an author initiates the publishing process by choosing to publish the document. When approvers click the link to the document in the e-mail (Figure 8–10), the Document Inspection dashboard appears (Figure 8–11). This screen outlines the actions that can be taken on the document, identifies the reviewers, lists the type of routing process that has been configured for this document, and provides other document information. If approvers wish to see the actual document, they click the document link in the Document Inspection dashboard, and this opens the document in the browser for review. The

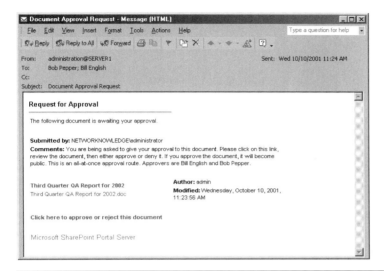

Figure 8–10 Approver request e-mail

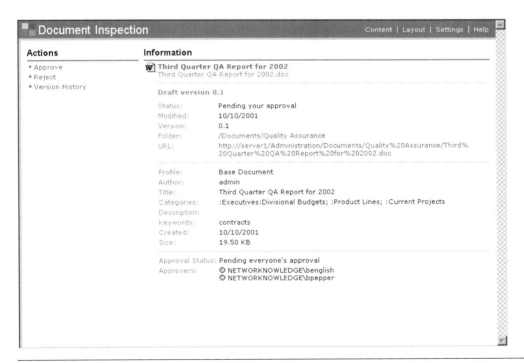

Figure 8–11 Document Inspection dashboard for a document awaiting approval

version history of the document is also available so that approvers can reference previous versions and compare them to the pending version.

When the approvers are ready, they can approve the document. Whether the document is approved or rejected, there is no automatic notification by e-mail to the author(s) of the document indicating the approvers' action. This means that you need to implement a policy for approvers to notify those who are in a need-to-know position that the document has been approved or rejected.

An approver can approve a document from the e-mail message that Share-Point Portal Server automatically generates, from the workspace, or from the dashboard site. While the document is awaiting approval, its status shows in the workspace as Pending Your Approval. After the reviewers approve the document, its status changes to Published. If the document is rejected, it is marked as checked in.

Publishing Documents without an Approval Process

If the coordinator hasn't configured the folder to require approval, an author or the coordinator can publish the document at any time. To eliminate the approval requirement, you clear the Documents Must Be Approved Before Publishing check box in the folder's Properties dialog box (shown earlier in Figure 8–9).

Documents can be published from the dashboard, from an Office application, or from the Web folders client. To publish documents individually, use the dashboard. However, if you want to check in a group of documents that you're migrating from another server, use the Web folders client, which lets you check in and publish documents in bulk. For a bulk check-in, select all the documents in the Web view, right-click those documents, and choose Check In from the context menu.

Publishing from the Digital Dashboard

To publish the document from the Digital Dashboard, you first create the document in Microsoft Word 2000 or later and then save it to your local hard disk. Then navigate to the document folder in which you wish to publish the document, click Add Document, and type the name of this document and its path in the Document File Name input box, as Figure 8–12 illustrates. Clicking Publish the Document tells SharePoint Portal Server to publish the document as soon as you add it to the folder. If you don't want to publish the document immediately, choose Check in the Document. You must select one or the other option. If you choose to check in the document, then authors and coordinators

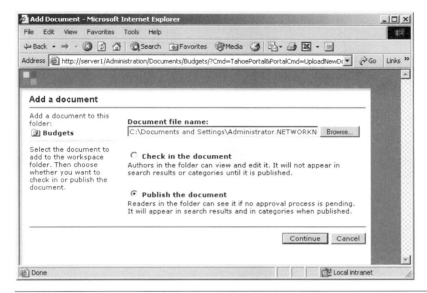

Figure 8–12 Publishing a document in the dashboard

will continue to have access to it to make any necessary changes before publishing it, but readers will not be able to see it in the dashboard and it will not appear in any search result set.

Publishing from an Office Application

Documents also can be published directly from an Office application. This requires Office 2000 or later (one more good reason to upgrade to the latest Office products). To publish directly from an Office application, first create the document in the application (I've chosen PowerPoint for this illustration), and then click Save As and choose the workspace in which to save the document (Figure 8–13). Drill down in the workspace to the correct folder—in this example, the Company Presentations folder—and then click Save. In the Document Profile box, shown in Figure 8–14, type the appropriate information about the document. If more than one profile is configured for this document folder, you can select which profile you'd like to use. Remember, all documents saved in SPS have a profile, and it provides metadata that SPS can categorize and search for fast document retrieval.

Now you have several options—and your users will need training to deal with them. If you choose to save your document but not to close it, SharePoint Portal Server returns control of the document to you in the Office application.

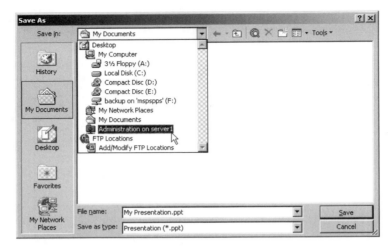

Figure 8–13 Workspace selection in the Save As dialog box from an Office application

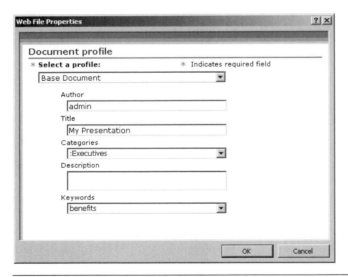

Figure 8–14 Document Profile box during the Save procedure of a document from an Office application

However, if you choose to close your document, SPS asks you to either check in the changes or keep the document checked out. At this point, if you choose to check in your document, you're then presented with the Check In dialog box (Figure 8–15), where you can modify the document's profile, select a new

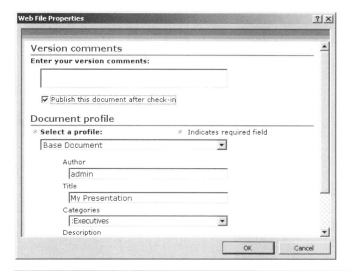

Figure 8–15 Check In dialog box

profile, enter version comments, and click a check box to publish the document after you check it in. If you choose to publish the document after check-in, SPS publishes it directly from the Office application.

Publishing from a Web View

To publish documents from the Web view, you must first create a shortcut to the workspace on the Web server on the client machine. A shortcut to a Web server is called a Web folder (don't confuse this shortcut with a Web link shortcut on the dashboard discussed earlier in this chapter). To create a Web folder, double-click My Network Places on your desktop, and then double-click Add Network Place to invoke the Welcome to the Add Network Place wizard. In the location input box, type the URL of your workspace. In most environments, you probably will type a full URL (for example, `http://hostname.domainname.com/workspacename`). In my example (Figure 8–16), I've typed `http://server1/administration`.

In the next screen, the wizard lets you give the Web folder a unique name in the form `virtualdirectoryname` on `servername`. In this example, the default name is `administration` on `server1`.

After you create the Web folder, you open a Web view by double-clicking the Web folder in My Network Places or by creating a shortcut to the Web folder on your desktop and using that to open the client to the workspace. Then drill down to the document you want to publish, right-click the document, and

Figure 8–16 Add Network Place wizard to create Web folders client to the Administration workspace on Server1

click Publish. The document must be checked in, and you must have either Author or Coordinator permission to publish a document in this way.

After a document is published, it remains published until you remove it from the workspace. In addition, it will automatically appear in the index and is viewable in the dashboard by all users. SharePoint Portal Server doesn't include an expiration feature. To place time limits on published documents, you must either have a developer write code to remove documents, or you must track documents and remove them manually. About the only way to eliminate published documents without writing code is to limit the number of published versions of a document that SPS will retain in the workspace. (By default, this value is unlimited.) You can configure this number on the General tab of the workspace Properties dialog box. This number also affects the number of unpublished versions, so for each published version of a document you allow to be saved in your workspace, there can be an unlimited number of unpublished versions that were used to develop the published version. You cannot limit the number of unpublished versions of a document in the workspace. And because each version is saved as a full-text version, you'd better have plenty of disk space to hold all these versions.

To check in a group of documents, you can perform bulk check-in or publish functions using the Web folders client. However, this technique has serious drawbacks. I'll first illustrate how to check in a group of documents and then point out the glaring shortcomings of importing documents into the workspace using a bulk method.

First, you can drag and drop a number of documents into the workspace. Find the documents in their source location, and then choose the group of

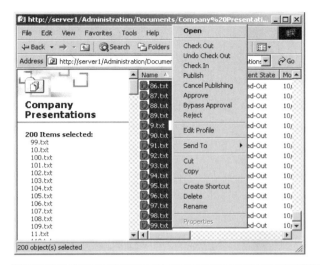

Figure 8–17 Selected list of documents in the Company Presentations folder

documents you wish to import. In this example, I'm importing 200 text files to the Company Presentations folder in the Administration workspace. I used Network Neighborhood to navigate to the source location for these documents and then performed the drag-and-drop operation. Now, all 200 files are in the Company Presentations folder but are checked out, which is the default state for files that are imported into the workspace.

In Figure 8-17, I've highlighted and right-clicked the documents, and the context menu has appeared. Notice that I can check in, publish, approve, or reject the documents or edit their profiles. If I were to click Publish, the Document Profile screen would appear; after I typed the appropriate information, each document would be published.

The huge problem with bulk imports is that whatever you type in the Document Profile screen is applied identically to all the files in the group at the same time. This means that if you type a document title, it will be applied to all the files selected (Figure 8–18). So if you need a unique title for each document in your workspace, you're left with one of two choices: Either check in and publish each document manually (where's the phone number for that temp agency?) or hire a developer to write specialized code to add the correct document title to each document when it is checked in. Frankly, neither is an attractive choice, but this is the reality.

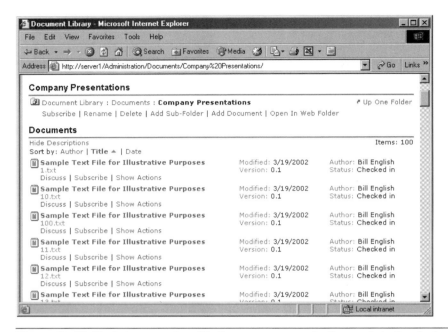

Figure 8–18 Text documents with the same name in the portal after being checked in using the bulk method

Summary

This chapter discusses how to manage and plan for categories and how to approve and publish documents in SPS. When it comes to categories, be sure to spend adequate time planning your category hierarchies before you implement them. And make sure that the hierarchies that you implement will be understood and usable by your users.

When it comes to publishing and approving documents, be sure that you give adequate training to your end users about how and when to use the DM functions. Nothing will kill an SPS implementation faster than a series of bad user experiences that result from inadequate training. When used properly, the DM capabilities of SPS will provide your organization with a much improved DM system over your current file servers.

Chapter 9 discusses how to import information into your workspace and illustrates how to access information on the different types of servers, including Exchange and Lotus Notes.

Importing and Managing External Information

One of the most attractive features of SharePoint Portal Server is its ability to crawl and index information that exists outside the workspace. Having external information appear in a search result set along with workspace documents means that the end user will have a much more comprehensive set of information to work with.

SPS would not be much of a knowledge management program if it didn't address the reality of important information existing in dissimilar types of documents, coupled with the fact that this information rarely exists in a single location for any given organization. Mission-critical information usually exists in a number of document types—Office, AVI, JPEG, and so on—and on various platforms: Exchange, Web servers, file servers, Lotus Notes servers, and so on.

Moreover, it's not enough to be able to access the document's information. Often, critical information about these documents can improve both productivity and information flow in an organization.

One challenge faced by many organizations is the difficulty of moving from their current methods of holding information to using a robust KM program such as SharePoint Portal Server. Not only does the organization need to rethink how it views its information, but it also needs to provision the desktop and train its users to work with the dashboard. Such an investment of time and money is not taken lightly by most of those who write the checks and call the shots.

When I teach the Microsoft class (course number 2095) on SharePoint Portal Server, students often confuse the SPS document management features with the documents that appear in a result set. Bear in mind that just because SPS can crawl and index external content, this does not mean that the document management functions (check-in, check-out, and publishing) can be performed on external content. The DM functions can be performed only on content that exists in the workspace, whereas the crawl and indexing functions can be performed on both internal and external content. To index content from an outside source, you must ensure that you have an IFilter installed for that particular type of content. IFilters are discussed in detail later in this chapter and are also referenced in Chapter 7.

Documents that are held on a file server can be accessed by SharePoint Portal Server. Microsoft uses server message blocks (SMBs) to create shares through which files are exposed to others on a network. Other operating systems—such as Novell Netware (when Gateway services are installed), IBM's OS/2, or Samba (UNIX)—support SMBs. SPS can crawl files exposed through a file share on these operating systems.

However, if you are familiar with Site Server 3.0, you'll remember that it was able to perform schema mapping between custom properties found in HTML meta tags and Office document properties using the `schema.txt` and `gathererprm.txt` files. The current version of SPS does not support schema mapping using these text files.

This chapter illustrates how to create and manage content sources for an SPS server. But first, let's discuss how the gatherer process works.

The Gatherer Process

Chapter 7 discusses the gatherer service as it relates to the larger search and index architecture. Here, I take a more practical approach and outline the sequence of events for this service. The gatherer service (`mssdmn.exe`) works with the Search service (`MSSearch.exe`) to crawl and index information located in content sources. At a detailed level, the gatherer process flows as follows:

1. The crawl is initiated, and a URL is passed to the gatherer service from the content source. The gatherer service parses the prefix of the URL to determine which protocol handler and IFilter should be used (protocol handlers are discussed later in this chapter).
2. The gatherer service loads the appropriate IFilter.
3. Any crawl restrictions are enforced, such as site path rules or crawl depth limitations.
4. Crawl history is referenced to ensure that the same content source is not crawled twice in the same crawl session, or *project*.
5. The URL is then checked for site hit restrictions. If there are none, the URL is placed in an active queue. If restrictions exist, it is placed in a delayed queue.
6. The correct protocol handler is loaded based on the URL prefix.
7. The gatherer service connects to the content source using named pipes.

8. The document's metadata is retrieved but not passed to the gatherer service.
9. The correct IFilter is employed to open the source document.
10. The data in the document is filtered and streamed out of the document by the IFilter. This thread loops through the data in the document to read it and stream it to the gatherer service on the SPS server. Metadata is also passed to the gatherer during this step.
11. The data is streamed to the gatherer plug-in.
12. The gatherer performs word breaking on the data.
13. The filtered properties and data chunks are passed through other plug-ins, such as the PQS, auto-categorization, and indexing (discussed later in this chapter), before being indexed by the search process.
14. The indexing engine then does several things:
    a. Normalizes the text
    b. Removes noise words
    c. Creates the index for full-text searching (located, by default, in the `\program files\sharepoint portal server\data\ ftdata\sharepointportalserver\Projects\foo\ indexer\cifiles dir`)
15. When step 14 is finished, the URL is taken off the crawl queue, marked as complete, and logged.
16. The next URL is loaded from the active queue, and this process starts over again.

If there are any significant errors, the event is flagged and the transaction is aborted. Moreover, a retry number is associated with a URL, and if that number becomes too high, the URL is aborted for that reason, too.

NOTE: The gatherer process indexes only the first 16MB of a file. If the file is larger than this, the remaining information is not crawled, and a message to this effect is placed in the gatherer log file. The 16MB limit is not configurable.

The gatherer process is unique to the workspace. This means that if you've installed multiple workspaces on your SPS server, you'll have multiple gatherer projects running. Each workspace has its own set of gatherer logs and performance statistics. Be sure to stagger the crawl start times between content sources and workspaces so as to minimize the potential of bottlenecking your server's network subsystem unnecessarily.

How you get at the content sources is a major concern in SPS, so let's take some time to discuss how content sources are created.

Creating Content Sources in SharePoint Portal Server

A content source to a file share or a Web site is the easiest type of content source to create. First, open the Web folders client to the workspace and double-click the Management folder. From there, you'll see the Content Source folder, which you can double-click to reveal its contents, including the Add Content Source wizard. When you double-click this wizard, you'll be greeted with the Welcome screen and then the Content Source Type screen (Figure 9–1). As you can see, you're free to select any of the following:

- A remote SharePoint Portal Server workspace
- With Service Pack 1 installed, any SharePoint Team Services Web site (not shown)
- Exchange 5.5 Server Public Folder
- Exchange 2000 Server Public Folder
- Lotus Notes 4.6a/5R or later databases
- Any file share
- Any ftp site
- Any Web page or Web site

The choice you make here will determine how the balance of the wizard will run. Let's discuss how each content source type will be created.

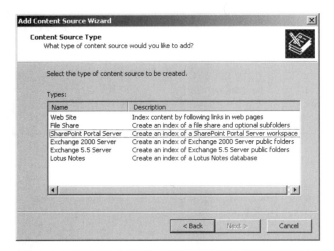

Figure 9–1 The Content Source Type dialog box in the Add Content Source wizard

SharePoint Portal Server and Web Sites

When creating a content source that is another workspace on either the local or a remote SharePoint server, you must type the URL of the folder that you want to crawl and index. In the example (Figure 9–2), I've created a content source to one of my other SharePoint servers. The syntax is as follows:

```
http://servername/workspacename/foldername
```

Moreover, as you can see in Figure 9–2, you can specify whether you want only the contents of the target folder indexed or its contents along with all the contents of its subfolders. This action is configured using the two radio buttons under the Create an Index Of location on the Add Content Source screen.

TIP: It's a good idea to navigate to the target folder and then copy the URL from the browser and into this screen. Doing this will not only give you the correct URL but will also ensure that the folder can be accessed using your logged-on security context.

The next screen will use the URL as its default name. More than likely, you'll want to change this default name to something a bit more friendly. Then, on the Completing the Add Content Source Wizard screen, you'll see a

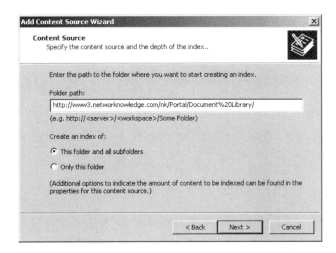

Figure 9–2 Typing the URL for a new workspace content source in the Add Content Source wizard

marked check box that will start indexing this location immediately. You can clear this check box if you prefer to wait until later to start populating your indexes with the information in this new content source.

A Web site is created in the same manner and has the same options available as those for creating a content source.

File Share

Creating a content source to a file share is very similar to that of a Web site and a remote workspace. The screens are the same, but you type the path to the remote source differently. Instead of using a URL, you type a Universal Naming Convention (UNC):

```
\\servername\sharename\foldername
```

The crawl of the content source will fail unless you type a folder name inside the share that acts as the starting point for the gatherer service to crawl the remote information.

Exchange 5.5 Public Folder

SPS can crawl and index information sitting in an Exchange 5.5 public folder, regardless of its service pack level. Items crawled in an Exchange 5.5 public folder include the message content and its properties as well as any Office attachments. If the Office documents have custom properties, these will be indexed if they also exist in the SPS workspace schema.

NOTE: The Search service does not index embedded contents within messages, such as an embedded PowerPoint graphic in a message body.

Only one Exchange 5.5 server can be crawled by a SharePoint server, even if the SharePoint server has multiple workspaces. As a planning issue, if you have multiple workspaces that need to crawl multiple Exchange 5.5 servers, you must install a separate SharePoint server for each Exchange 5.5 server that needs to be crawled and indexed. It is here that public folder replication can help you: Replicate all the public folders that need to be crawled to one Exchange 5.5 server, and then crawl that server. To learn more about public folder replication, please see Chapter 8 of *Developing Applications with Exchange 2000* by Scott Jamison.

Before you create a content source to an Exchange 5.5 public folder server, you must first configure SPS with the Exchange server information.

Some SPS literature calls what I'm about to describe "enabling" this feature. Don't be confused if you read that. Entering this configuration information *is* "enabling" this feature. The first step is to type the Exchange 5.5 server information in the server's properties into the SPS MMC (Figure 9–3). In addition, the Outlook 2000 client must be installed on the SPS server to give it a MAPI (Messaging Application Programming Interface) client with which to work. If you don't do these things, the content source creation wizard will fail for an Exchange 5.5 server.

You must type the following before you can create an Exchange 5.5 content source:

- The Exchange server name
- The Exchange site name
- The Exchange 5.5 organization name
- The OWA Server name (will default to the Exchange server name)
- The access account information

The access account must have Admin privileges on the Site and Configuration containers in the Exchange 5.5 organization. In addition, some (not all) of the Microsoft literature suggests that the site and organization names are case-sensitive. If you're having trouble connecting, ensure that your capitalization

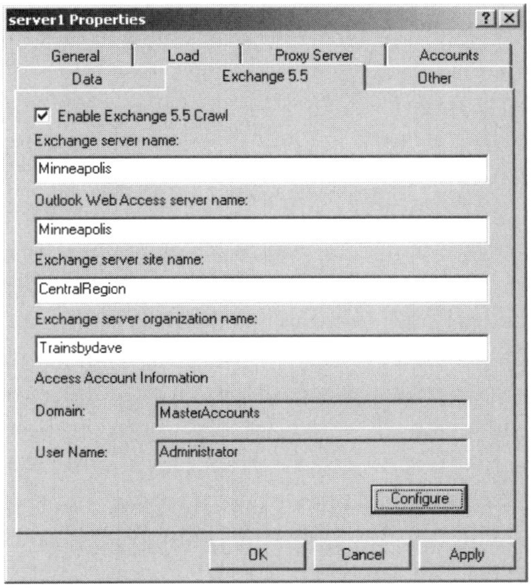

Figure 9–3 Enabling the Exchange 5.5 crawl feature in the properties of a SharePoint server

matches that of the site and organization names. If nothing else, this will eliminate at least one variable in your troubleshooting process.

Only *after* you have installed the Outlook 2000 (or later) client on the SPS server and have configured the server with the Exchange 5.5 server information are you ready to create a content source to an Exchange 5.5 server.

When you run the Add Content Source wizard and select Exchange 5.5 as the data source, you must provide a path to the public folders you want to crawl. The path matches the folder's hierarchy and starts with the `exch://` designation. Each folder in the hierarchy should be separated by a forward slash (/). Hence, if you wanted to crawl the `memos` public folder on `Server1`, the correct syntax would be as follows:

```
Exch://Server1/public folders/all public folders/memos
```

If you want to crawl all the folders in an Exchange 5.5 hierarchy, end your syntax with `all public folders` and ensure that there is a trailing forward slash:

```
Exch://Server1/public folders/all public folders/
```

Exchange 2000 Public Folders

Because both Exchange 2000 Server and SharePoint Portal Server use the same underlying Web store database engines and architecture, it should come as no surprise that the gatherer in SPS will use HTTP and Web DAV to crawl content from one or more Exchange 2000 public folders. This is why no pre-configuration is required, as there is for Exchange 5.5 Server. Simply run the Add Content wizard and type the correct path, and the gatherer service will crawl the information without additional configuration.

The user account security context to be crawled must have read access to the information. And unlike Exchange 5.5, you can crawl multiple Exchange 2000 servers from a single SharePoint server, something that negates the need to have public folders replicated for the express purpose of ensuring that they are in one location for the gatherer service. Also, private mailboxes can be crawled, raising the possibility that departmental mailbox content could be indexed and made available to users in the workspace. Finally, if the content classes match between the Exchange 2000 Server and the SharePoint Portal Server, an item's metadata will be crawled, too. However, the schema that takes precedence here is the SPS schema, not the Exchange 2000 schema.

The syntax for crawling an Exchange 2000 public folder is similar to that of Exchange 5.5, except that you'll use HTTP and specify the hierarchy path a bit differently. To crawl a public folder named `memos` on `Server1` in the `administration` public folder tree in an Exchange 2000 organization, the syntax would be as follows:

```
http://server1/public/administration/memos
```

To crawl a departmental mailbox named `admin` for the Administration department, the syntax would be as follows:

```
http://server1/exchange/admin
```

Remember that the default content access account used to crawl an Exchange 2000 Server is the one specified for the entire server. To use a different content access account, you must specify a separate path rule for each unique security context you wish to employ.

If you are working with redirected URLs, you must specify a different site path rule for each unique URL in the redirection.

Lotus Notes

To add Lotus Notes, as with Exchange 5.5 Server, requires advance planning and configuration. As with Exchange, you must install a Lotus Notes R5 or later client on the SharePoint Portal Server. Such a client will allow you to crawl Lotus Notes (LN) 4.6a, R5, or later databases. Also, you must configure the LN client to use an account that has Reader access to the databases that you wish to crawl.

To connect to the LN server using a secure connection, you must create a mapping between the LN user account and a Windows NT security account. This is because the security model used in Lotus Notes is different from the one used in either Windows NT or Windows 2000. Because of this incompatibility between the LN platform and the Microsoft platforms, when content is crawled on an LN server, the security settings for that information are re-created in the SPS workspace. For each LN user name you use to crawl information in an LN database, you must map it to a Windows NT user account so that SPS has a familiar account to work with in creating the security on the crawled content. Note that SPS has no support for crawling information that has been encrypted by LN in an LN database.

When the content source crawls an LN database, you can choose to either honor or dishonor the security settings of the LN database. Here are the implications of both choices:

■ If you choose not to honor the security settings on the LN database, only that information that is public in the LN database will be accessible for crawling and indexing. This means that if the database contains secured information that should be included in the index, it will be missed, and your users will not receive a full set of information.

■ If you choose to honor the security settings on the LN database, you must crawl the secured content with an account that has access to the information. Moreover, this account must be mapped to a user account, as described previously. This means that the secured content in the LN database will be crawled and indexed using the Windows security principle, and the permissions will be applied to the content using that principle. Be sure you have secured this content appropriately in your Windows environment.

■ If you are unsure whether you should or should not honor the LN security settings, best practice is to honor them. This will allow you to access all the information in the database and make it available to your end users.

Honoring LN security settings requires a bit more work. You must create an LN view containing both the LN and Windows user names. The view should be sorted on the LN user name, not the Windows user name, and it must be marked as a shared view so that all clients can access it.

After you have made your choices, you are ready to run the Lotus Notes Indexing Setup wizard. This wizard is located in the SharePoint Portal Server Administrator snap-in. Open the server's properties, go to the Other tab, and you'll see the Lotus Notes Setup Wizard button. You need run this only once per server, and remember, every LN database that you crawl will use the same settings you typed here in the wizard.

The wizard asks you for the following:

■ The location of the `notes.ini` file
■ The location of the notes installation directory
■ The LN user password

If you don't want to honor the security settings of the LN database, you must select the check box labeled Ignore Lotus Notes Security While Building an Index, as illustrated in Figure 9–4. In addition, you'll need the following information:

■ The name of the LN server that has the user account mapping, a view of this mapping, and the view name
■ The name of the LN database
■ The name of the columns in the view that map to both the LN and the Windows user names

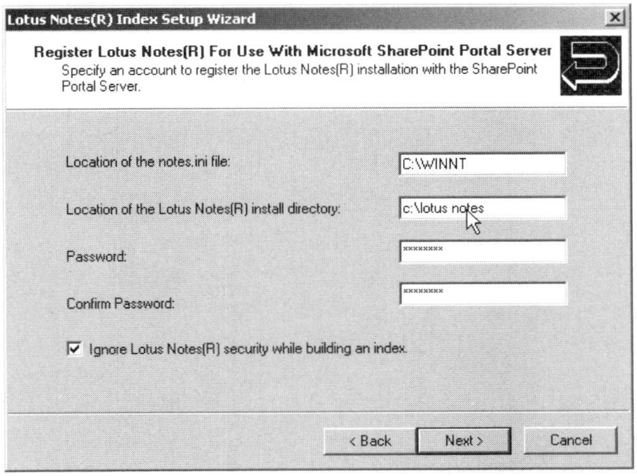

Figure 9–4 Ignore Lotus Notes Security check box in the Lotus Notes Setup wizard

After you have run the setup wizard, run the Add Content Source wizard and chosen the Lotus Notes server, choose a database, and then map the profile properties to field names in the LN database. What you're doing here is mapping metadata in the LN database to metadata in the SharePoint database.

The list of possible LN servers is produced by the content wizard by reading the `notes.ini` file. If the server isn't listed in that file, it won't appear as a possible server in the content wizard. If the server doesn't appear in the list of possible servers, you can type the name of the server manually.

After you choose the server, its databases will appear in a list, and you can pick which database you wish to crawl. However, you should note that databases on the LN server that do not reside in the `\Lotus Notes\data` directory will not be enumerated in this list. This is because the LN documentation recommends that databases be placed in this category, so SharePoint looks only in this directory for databases.

When you specify field-name-to-document-profile mappings, only those fields that are actually mapped will be included in the index. This means that rich metadata may be lost or not included if you don't get the fields mapped correctly. Reconfiguration will be necessary if the security changes on the LN database. Moreover, if you change the account that is used to crawl the LN databases, or if this account's security changes, or if the user account mappings change, you'll need to restart the MSSearch service to reflect these changes.

SharePoint Team Services

When you install Service Pack 1, a protocol handler for SharePoint Team Services (STS) is automatically installed that allows SPS to crawl documents hosted in an STS site. The syntax for crawling such a site is as follows:

```
STS://sitename/*
```

You must overcome a couple of quirks before an STS crawl will be successful. First in line is the account under which you'll access the STS site. You must ensure that you've done the following:

1. Create an account in the domain that will be used specifically to crawl the STS site.
2. Add this account to the STS site using the Administrator role.
3. Either use this account as the default content access account or set up a site path rule to the STS site specifying that this account should be used when crawling the STS content.

Now you can crawl and index lists in STS, but there are some gotchas. First, by default, if a term appears more than once in the same list, the list as a whole will appear in the result set only once. In other words, not every instance of the queried word results in a separate instance of the word in the result set, unless you edit the registry as follows:

```
HKLM\SOFTWARE\Microsoft\Search\1.0\CatalogNames\SharePointPortalServer\
   workspace_name
```

Add a `DWORD` value called `STS-ListBehavior`, and then enter the desired numeric value:

- 0 = List content is not included in the index and will not appear in any result set.
- 1 = The list as a whole is included in the index, but not every individual instance of a word in the list appears in the result set. This is the default setting in Service Pack 1 for SharePoint Portal Server.
- 2 = All list items in all lists are indexed. Each instance of a term results in a separate item in the result set. This configuration is the only one that allows secured lists to appear in a result set.

There are two other items to consider when you're crawling and indexing an STS site. First, if a list's security is modified, the modification won't appear in the SPS index until the list's cache is refreshed or until SPS performs another crawl, whichever comes first. To have security changes reflected immediately in SPS, restart the `MSSearch.exe` process and then crawl the STS site again.

Second, use the `domainname\authorname` syntax to search for authors in an STS site. Typing only the author name will not yield the results you're looking for.

Managing Content Sources in SharePoint Portal Server

When you're indexing external content, creating the content source doesn't mean that your job is finished. As you might suspect, you must configure the content sources and, at times, troubleshoot them as well.

If you have a content source that is pointed to a Web site, one of the first things that you'll want to change is the crawl depth. The default is to create an index of the site and to link to all pages. This means that any link on any page is followed even if it points to a page outside the site. Hence, if you crawl a public site that has any link anywhere to a search engine, you'll end up indexing the entire Internet. I know disk space is cheap these days, but I don't think you can purchase enough disk space to index the Internet.

So if you have a content source pointed to a Web site, be sure to navigate to the Configuration tab in the Web site content source's properties (Figure 9–5) and select either This Page Only or a Custom setting with which you are comfortable. In this way, you can control the number and scope of pages that are indexed. The range is 0 to 32,767. You can also configure whether the crawling will "hop" or "jump" to another site linked to by the target site and continue crawling that site, too.

To configure a file share content source, you can create an index of either the folder itself or the folder plus all its subfolders. You don't have the option to pick and choose the folders in an overall directory, nor do you have a crawl depth that you can configure as with the Web site content source. This option also doesn't exist on Exchange public folder content sources.

One other thing: By default, SPS does not contain a schedule to crawl and index content sources (although when you first create a new content source, you are prompted to initiate a full index of it). Hence, if you don't set up a schedule to do this, you might manually start a crawl and index process on an external content source only to find later that new information at that source is not appearing in your index. Be sure that you have configured regular indexing intervals for your content sources to fire; otherwise, you'll be forever having to

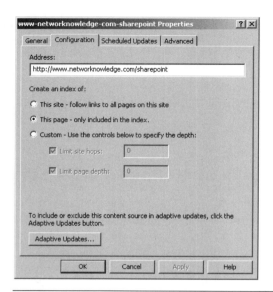

Figure 9–5 Configuration tab in Web site content source

go in and manually start the process on all your content sources. As you might suspect, that would not be a lot of fun.

To configure a schedule for your content sources to fire, use the Scheduled Updates tab in the content sources properties to schedule either incremental or full updates, as warranted by your environment.

To summarize, when you run the Content Source wizard, there are four important items that you should remember to configure after the content source has been created:

- Configure your hops and depths as appropriate.
- Associate your content source with a search scope as appropriate (discussed in the next section).
- Schedule the updates.
- Use site path rules as needed.

The wizards won't tell you to configure these items, but you should take a couple of moments to ensure you have them configured appropriately for your network.

Configuring Search Scopes

A search scope gives you a way to define one or more content sources that you want your search to be limited to. This allows you to expand or contract the range and number of documents to be searched, and that makes searching more efficient for that scope. By default, all the content sources belong to the "this site" search scope.

You can assign multiple content sources to a single search scope. Scope names can be as long as 60 characters and should be employed when you wish to carve out a range of documents from a larger group of content sources for searching.

To configure a scope, navigate to the Advanced tab in a content source's properties, and enter the scope name (Figure 9–6). I've typed two names: SharePoint and Security. To type the name, start typing in the Search Scope input box. The drop-down list will reveal the names already entered.

This list will also appear as search options in the Simple Search Web part on your dashboard, as illustrated in Figure 9–7.

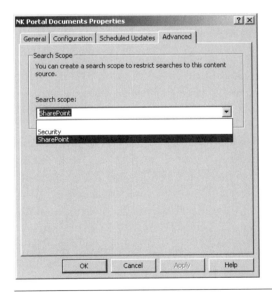

Figure 9–6 Drop-down list of the two scopes I've created in my SPS site

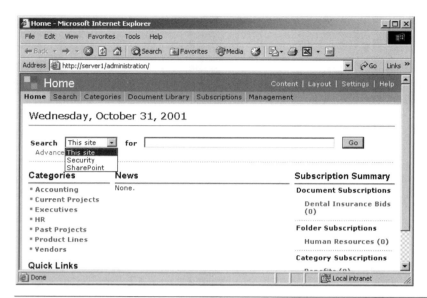

Figure 9–7 Search scopes in the Simple Search Web part in the portal

Security and Content Sources

The gatherer—the core component of the MSSearch process—connects to an SPS or Web content source using HTTP. Either Basic, Anonymous, or Integrated Windows Authentication (IWA) can be used to validate the security account under which the gatherer service is running to the content source. By default, the gatherer service, when connecting to a content source using HTTP, will use IWA. If you want the service to use Basic authentication, you must create a site path rule, as discussed in Chapter 7.

If you need to use Basic authentication, which is required to connect to file systems on UNIX and Novell platforms, but still need security when data is transferred over the line, you can use Transport Layer Security (TLS), also known as Secure Sockets Layer (SSL), to encrypt the data during transport.

NOTE: In one version of the Web folders client, SPS will be unable to crawl other content sources using Basic authentication if the access account does not have a password. In this scenario, the crawl will fail with the error code "80040e4d – Authentication failed" in the gatherer log. To avoid encountering this error, ensure that you have a password defined when using Basic authentication.

To crawl content sources in a nontrusted domain, you'll need to consider one of two workarounds. First, you can use a site path rule to specify the authentication method and credentials used to access the content. This is the preferred method because if the remote domain is not trusted, chances are good that you have little, if any, control over its administration. The second method uses pass-through authentication by creating identical accounts and passwords in each domain. This approach assumes that you have considerable control over the remote domain. In many scenarios, this second alternative is not possible because of administrative constraints.

Working with IFilters

IFilters are special dynamic link libraries that expose the contents of a data document as raw bits for extraction by `MSSearch.exe`. They open data streams to the data documents and then group the bits into chunks that can be indexed. For example, the HTML IFilter opens an HTML document, strips out the tags, and then streams out the raw text for indexing. Any additional information found in the meta tags—for example, the title—will be indexed as metadata. IFilters are registered to a document type and not to a protocol. This means that regardless of the protocol used to access the data file, the IFilter can open the document and allow its data to be indexed.

SPS ships with IFilters for the following document types:

- Office documents
- HTML
- TIFF
- Text
- MIME

Other document vendors, such as Adobe, also make IFilters available for their products. Most likely, by the time this book hits the shelves, more IFilters will be available. At the time of this writing, the following IFilters are available:

Product	Location
Adobe Acrobat	`http://www.adobe.com/support/downloads/detail.jsp?ftpID=1276`
AutoCAD	`http://www.cad-company.nl/ifilter/`

WordPerfect	`http://www.corel.com/support/ftpsite/` `pub/wordperfect/wpwin/61`
RTF	`http://www.microsoft.com/sharepoint/` `techinfo/reskit/RTF_Filter.asp`
XML	`http://www.microsoft.com/sharepoint/` `techinfo/reskit/XML_Filter.asp`
DWG	`http://www.cad-company.nl/support/` `_downloads/DWG-IFilter/` `form_download_dwg_ifilter_basic_us.htm`
MP3	`http://www.hitsquad.com/smm/programs/` `MP3_Ifilter`

NOTE: An IFilter for Visio is expected to be released soon but was not available at the time of this writing. Also, you can check `http://www.sharepointcode.com` to find a list of other IFilters that might be available. If you find an IFilter that you want to use, be sure to place the appropriate GIF file in the `doctypeicons` folder. Chapter 6 describes how to do this.

Interestingly, Windows 2000 registers its own IFilters for its own use. However, if there is an SPS version of an IFilter, SPS uses that one instead of the ones provided by Windows 2000.

The TIFF (Tagged Interchange File Format) IFilter is used to filter scanned or faxed documents. By default, it is installed in a disabled state, although even in this state it will find important file metadata, such as filename and last modified date. When it is enabled with the optical character recognition (OCR) option, it will attempt to look at the TIFF document and see whether it can recognize any characters to include in an index.

OCR is resource-intensive, so the TIFF IFilter doesn't scan and index a single-paged document larger than 1MB. Multipaged documents are always scanned, regardless of their size. The OCR scan is performed in a single thread, meaning that if there are multiple TIFF documents to scan, they will be loaded by the search process and then scanned in serial, not parallel, as would be the case if it were a multithreaded operation.

Because the TIFF filter can scan faxed documents, they need to appear to the OCR feature right-side up. Sideways or upside-down images don't work very well for character recognition. So Microsoft has implemented a default feature called AutoRotation, which takes a document that is not oriented correctly and reorients it so that OCR can be performed. Turning documents is memory-intensive.

The OCR feature is language-aware. It works with English pretty well, but other languages result in more processing problems. For instance, the Slovenian language is problematic because the OCR feature in SPS recognizes only alphanumeric characters and ignores special characters in that language. This behavior is not uncommon for non-English languages. Best practice here is to test the OCR feature with your language and see whether the results are something you can work with (and live with).

To enable OCR, edit the following registry key:

```
HKLM\System\CurrentControlSet\Control\MSPaper
```

Change the value of 0 to 1 for the key `PerformOCR (REG_DWORD)`.

To enable OCR to scan and index single-page documents that are larger than 1MB, edit the following registry key:

```
HKLM\System\CurrentControlSet\Control\MSPaper\MaxImageSize
```

Enter the value in bytes, where 100,000 = 1MB.

If all your fax documents arrive right-side up or if existing documents are all oriented correctly, you can disable the AutoRotation feature in the registry. Doing so will improve performance. Edit the following registry key:

```
HKLM\System\CurrentControlSet\Control\MSPaper\AutoRotation
```

Enter the value of 0 to disable or 1 to enable.

TIP: The TIFF filter can be used with the Windows NT 4.0 Indexing Server.

Working with Protocol Handlers

Out of the gate, let's be clear about one thing: Don't confuse a protocol handler with a network protocol. There is no relationship between the two concepts.

In contrast to IFilters, which are document-type-specific, protocol handlers are URL-prefix-specific. In other words, protocol handlers are associated with URL prefixes. When the gatherer processes a URL before attempting to crawl a content source, it parses the URL prefix and then loads the associated DLL so that it is using the correct protocol handler to access the content source.

Recall (from the earlier discussion about how to create content sources) that when you type a path to a Web site, you type the full path, starting with `HTTP://`. By the same token, when you access an Exchange 5.5 public folder, you type `Exch://`. These URL prefixes indicate to the gatherer which protocol handler to load before attempting to crawl the data specified in the path. Hence, it makes sense that if SPS can crawl certain types of databases out of the box, it also ships with protocol handlers to access these databases.

Information about the SPS protocol handlers is stored in the registry, and a DLL for that handler must exist for the gatherer to use. The registry location can be found at

```
HKLM\Software\Microsoft\Search\1.0\ProtocolHandlers
```

Each handler is given its own ProgID and is registered in the `H_KEY_CLASSES_ROOT` portion of the registry. Table 9–1 outlines the URL prefixes, their associated DLLs, and their ProgIDs in the registry.

Because Web sites as well as remote WSS databases, such as SPS or Exchange 2000, use the `HTTP` prefix, the HTTP handler recognizes this and redirects the request to the WSS (PKM Exstore) protocol handler. This handler uses EXOLEDB to access a local WSS database, and uses Web DAV to access remote WSS databases. To access other database types, a protocol handler must be developed and then registered with the gatherer service. To learn more about developing a protocol handler for SPS, please consult the SDK for SPS.

Security for a protocol handler is implemented using the Windows 2000 security principles. In addition, the search service must exist in a domain that trusts the domain that holds the security principle that the search service will use to perform its functions. If no specific access account is specified for this

Table 9–1 Listing of URL prefixes, DLLs, and ProgIDs for default protocol handlers in SharePoint Portal Server

URL Prefix	DLL File	ProgID Registry Entry
File	Mssph.dll	Mssearch.filehandler.1
HTTP	Mssph.dll	Mssearch.httphandler.1
Exch	Mssexph.dll	Mssearch.mapihandler.1
HTTP (when accessing a remote Web store, or PKM Exstore)	Pkmexsph.dll	Pkm.exstorehandler.1
Lotus Notes	Notesph.dll	Mssearch.noteshandler.1
FTP (found in the resource kit)	FTPph.asp	Mssearch.ftphandler.1

service, the protocol handler will run in the security context of the local system account. This is the default configuration.

Working with Plug-ins

Plug-ins allow you to look at the data stream coming from a content source and either leave it alone or perform operations on the data or its metadata before the data is included in the full-text index. A plug-in works in the data pipeline from the source data that the IFilter is extracting from a content source to the SPS server. Plug-ins can either leave the data alone or perform actions either on the data or in response to what it learns from the data. There are four default plug-ins:

- Auto-categorization
- Persistent query service
- Indexing
- Gatherer

The auto-categorization plug-in looks at the data stream coming into the gatherer process and automatically associates the document with certain categories based on the words and data that it finds in the data stream. This is the plug-in that makes the Category Assistant run. To learn more about the Category Assistant, please consult Chapter 8.

The persistent query service (PQS) plug-in is used to create the subscriptions feature of SPS. The PQS checks the data stream against the current subscription rules to create notifications for end users.

The indexing plug-in does several things. First, it decides which properties should be indexed and stores this information when the data is streamed out of the content source to the gatherer service. Second, it governs how fast and how much data can be passed to the indexing engine at any given time. Third, the indexing plug-in ensures that metadata is saved to the property store first before the indexing engine saves its data to the full-text index.

The gatherer plug-in is an overall manager of the crawl process, as described earlier in this chapter in "The Gatherer Process."

Multiple plug-ins can look at the same data stream and then perform actions for which they are configured. For instance, while the auto-categorization plug-in is working with the data stream to suggest category associations for a document, the PQS plug-in can look at the same data stream and notice that there is an event that meets a subscription rule and thus generate a notification to the user. In addition, the indexing plug-in can ensure that the data stream of this document does not overload the indexing engine. All these functions are managed by the gatherer plug-in to ensure that they all function correctly. Hence, if you need another type of plug-in—such as one that looks for trademarks or copyrights to ensure that documents are being used correctly and with permission—that plug-in can be installed and used in concert with the native SPS plug-ins.

Crawling Metadata in External Documents

Crawling and indexing metadata is no small task, and it's crucial that you understand how to do it. This section outlines some ideas and tips on how to do this, especially when you're working with documents in Lotus Notes databases.

To map metadata from a file share or a Web site, you must write some customized code. There is no user interface in SPS to do this. To begin the mapping process, first create a document profile that includes the list of profile properties that you want to have available in SPS. This list can, of course, include custom properties.

After you've created a document profile that outlines the metadata you wish to have available in your workspace, create a content source that points to the external data you wish to index. However, when saving the content source, do not start the indexing process.

At this point, it's time to create the mappings of the external document's metadata to your document profile. A good approach is to use XML or Visual Basic. A Microsoft white paper, "Crawling Custom Metadata Using Microsoft SharePoint Portal Server 2001," [1] has two scripts that illustrate how to create this mapping: one in VB and the other in XML. The VBScript must have the PKMCDO (Publishing and Knowledge Management Collaboration Data Objects) type library as a reference. Notice that it is chock-full of instructions on what each section does and how you can modify it. I've included the Microsoft scripts here so that you can see it doesn't take reams of code to make this work. Here is the VB code taken directly from this paper:

```
Dim objCS As PKMCDO.KnowledgeStartAddress
    Dim objSPR As PKMCDO.IKnowledgeCatalogSitePathRule
```

---

[1] There are two executables that go along with this paper. You can find this paper at http://www.microsoft.com/sharepoint/techinfo/development/metadata.asp. This information is also available in Chapter 25 of the SharePoint Portal Server Resource Kit.

```
Dim colSitePathRules As IKnowledgeCatalogSitePathRules
Dim strUrlContentSource As String

' Change the following values to reflect the names of your server,
' workspace, content source, and target document profile.
Const MYSERVER = "SharePoint_Portal_Server_computer"
Const MYWORKSPACE = "SharePoint_Portal_Server_workspace"
Const MYSOURCE = "FileContentSource"
Const MYDOCPROFILE = "DocProfileName"

' Construct the URL to the Content Sources folder for your workspace.
strUrlContentSource = "http://" & MYSERVER & "/" & MYWORKSPACE _
    & "/Management/Content Sources/" & MYSOURCE

' Open the KnowledgeStartAddress (Content Source) item.
   Set objCS = New PKMCDO.KnowledgeStartAddress
objCS.DataSource.Open strUrlContentSource, , adModeReadWrite

' Indicate which content class (Document Profile)
' should be attributed to crawled files.
objCS.Fields(PKMCDO.cdostrURI_TargetContentClass) = _
    PKMCDO.cdostrNS_ContentClasses & MYDOCPROFILE

' All tags will have namespaces prepended to them.
' PKMCDO provides built-in constants for most of these. Change
' the array elements below to the property names you wish to use,
' adding or deleting lines as needed. NOTE: it is important that
' all three of the following arrays match up in terms of number of
' elements and the ordering of property names.

' If you are crawling HTML documents, all properties will have a
' standard HTML namespace prepended to them.  The source namespace
' may vary for other file types.  See below for details.
objCS.Fields(PKMCDO.cdostrURI_SourceProperties) = Array( _
    PKMCDO.cdostrNS_HtmlMetaInfo & "ExternalTag1", _
    PKMCDO.cdostrNS_HtmlMetaInfo & "AnotherTag2", _
    PKMCDO.cdostrNS_HtmlMetaInfo & "TheLastTag" )

' One data type entry is needed per source property.
objCS.Fields(PKMCDO.cdostrURI_SourceTypes) = Array( _
    "string", _
    "string", _
    "string")
```

```
' All SharePoint Portal Server properties are prepended with the
' standard Office namespace.  Ensure that they match up in order with
' their source properties.
objCS.Fields(PKMCDO.cdostrURI_TargetProperties) = Array( _
    PKMCDO.cdostrNS_Office & "SharePoint_Portal_Server_Property1", _
    PKMCDO.cdostrNS_Office & "SharePoint_Portal_Server_Property2", _
    PKMCDO.cdostrNS_Office & "SharePoint_Portal_Server_Property3 )

' Adding four properties to the content source definition item
' is not enough. You must also add a site path that corresponds to
' this content source.  You can see these by going to the Content
' Sources management folder and opening the "Additional Settings"
' item, then clicking the "Site Paths" button on the resulting dialog
' box.
Set colSitePathRules = objCS.Workspace.Catalog.SitePathRules

' NOTE:  this code does NOT check to see if a matching site path
' already exists.  Before you run this code, check to see if matching
' site paths are already present, and if so, delete them.
Set objSPR = colSitePathRules.Add(objCS.Address & "/*", True)
objSPR.ContentClass = objCS.Fields(PKMCDO.cdostrURI_TargetContentClass)
objSPR.PropertyMappingUrl = strUrlContentSource

' Clean up object references and save everything. The site path rule
' item does not need to be explicitly saved, but the content source
' does.
Set colSitePathRules = Nothing
Set objSPR = Nothing

objCS.Fields.Update
objCS.DataSource.Save
Set objCS = Nothing
```

This paper also presents the code for a fully functional XML application that you can tweak for your environment. This XML code is listed here for reference:

```xml
<?xml version="1.0"?>
<propertyMap>
<server>
<name>server1</name>
<workspace>
<name>test1</name>
<contentSource>
<name>dogbreeds</name>
```

```
<targetContentClass>DogBreed</targetContentClass>
<property>
<sourceName>breedOrigin</sourceName>
<sourceType>string</sourceType>
<targetName>breedOrigin</targetName>
</property>
<property>
<sourceName>breedName</sourceName>
<sourceType>string</sourceType>
<targetName>breedName</targetName>
</property>
<property>
<sourceName>breedFirstBred</sourceName>
<sourceType>dateTime</sourceType>
<targetName>breedFirstBred</targetName>
</property>
<property>
<sourceName>breedWeight</sourceName>
<sourceType>i4</sourceType>
<targetName>breedWeight</targetName>
</property>
<property>
<sourceName>Abstract</sourceName>
<sourceType>string</sourceType>
<targetName>Description</targetName>
</property>
<property>
<sourceName>ContentClass</sourceName>
<sourceType>string</sourceType>
<targetName>DAV:contentclass</targetName>
</property>
<property>
<sourceName>Categories</sourceName>
<sourceType>string</sourceType>
<targetName>urn:schemas-microsoft-com:publishing:Categories</targetName>
</property>
</contentSource>
</workspace>
</server>
</propertyMap>
```

Notice that this is only the input file for the `PropMap.swf` script provided by Microsoft. This file illustrates how to create an input file that includes the server name, workspace name, content source information, and property mapping information.

Overview of PKMCDO

The SharePoint Portal Server document management functions are exposed, from a developer's perspective, through PKMCDO. This object extends the functionality of the Web Storage System to support document management functions. You've probably read that SPS uses the same WSS as Exchange 2000 Server. Well, yes and no. It is the same architecturally, but SharePoint's implementation of the WSS (also known as the Extensible Storage Engine) includes the ability to check out, check in, publish, and approve documents. These capabilities are made possible though PKMCDO. Hence, SPS has a WSS that is enhanced in functionality over the WSS in Exchange 2000 Server.

After you have mapped the metadata properties, you must flush the schema cache by restarting the Microsoft Exchange Information Store, Microsoft Search, and SharePoint Portal Server services.

Then you should immediately start a full update on the content source, and your scripts should include the source document's metadata in the property store in SPS.

Troubleshooting Content Sources

A number of problems can arise that will give you fits if you don't know how to solve them.

One of the more common problems is an inability to connect to a content source because of incorrect permissions. As discussed earlier, you need a password when using Basic authentication, but the more common issue here is using a content access account that either does not have access to the content source or does not have the correct password installed. At the content source, ensure that the content access account has at least read permissions to all the content you want to index. Use site path rules to specify content that requires crawling under a security context that differs from the default server's security context.

You may still find that you are unable to access the content source. Unless there are network connectivity issues, such as a down link or incorrect IP configuration, the cause is probably that you have used an invalid path. Ensure that you have typed the correct path. If you know that the path is correct and you still cannot access the content source, then employ your connectivity troubleshooting methods. If you know that the path is correct and that there are no connectivity issues, you should make sure that your path is attempting to access a network file share, not a local file share or a mapped drive. Use of a mapped drive will return an error stating that you must use a valid path.

TIP: A content source is automatically created for the local workspace when the workspace is created. Although you can create new content sources for other workspaces on the same server, you *cannot* create additional content sources for the local workspace. If you try to create a new content source for the local workspace, you'll receive an error message indicating that the content location has already been added. Under normal circumstances, you'll not need to configure the properties of this default content source to the local workspace.

Finally, bear in mind that the security context in which the gatherer is able to connect to a content source is persistent and will not be changed for subsequent builds of the index. The first successful connection to the server is always used. If you need to change account credentials for a content source to which you currently are able to connect, you must first delete the current site path rule, then re-create it with the new account credentials, and then have the search service reconnect to the content source. If you need to change the credentials of the default content access account and have those new credentials take effect, you must stop and restart the MSSearch service.

You may encounter a number of protocol handler error messages, and you may have to look several places to find their meaning. First, some of these errors are recorded in the Windows 2000 application event logs. You use the Event Viewer to view these events and the errors they represent. Second, the gatherer logs, which are available through the Content Source Manager, record errors only. By default, a new log is created every day and only the most recent five days are saved. To change these options, open the SPS MMC and configure these values using the Logging tab of the workspace properties (Figure 9–8). You can also configure these values through the Content Source Manager in the workspace (Figures 9–9 and 9–10).

Table 9–2 lists the more common protocol handler error messages.

A smaller body of errors are specific to the IFilter registration process. Table 9–3 lists those error messages. You'll find these in the application log.

Figure 9–8 Logging tab in SPS MMC workspace properties

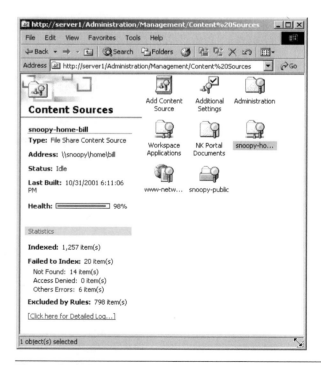

Figure 9–9 Content Source Manager using the Web folders view. When you click the Click Here for Detailed Log link, you get the screen in Figure 9–10.

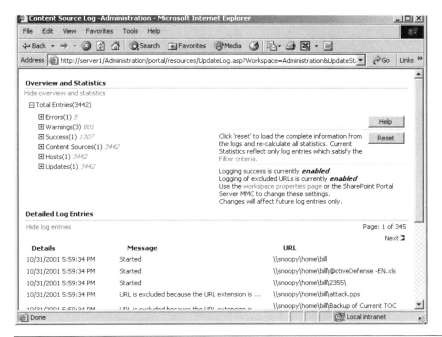

Figure 9–10 Detailed gatherer event log

Table 9–2 Protocol handler errors

Error Message	Meaning and Solution
URL is excluded because the URL protocol is not recognized or restricted.	Ensure that the protocol handler is registered correctly by looking at the `HKLM\Software\Microsoft\Search\ 1.0\ProtocolHandlers` registry key. Ensure that the ProgID is listed there. If it is, stop and restart the MSSearch process.
Error fetching URL (80040d1a): The protocol handler cannot be found.	The initialization of the protocol handler failed. Verify the protocol handler's registration, and then restart the MSSearch process. If you're testing a development environment, ensure that the `ISearchProtocol` method returns a successful `HRESULT`.
Error fetching URL (800700e9): No process is on the other end of the pipe.	Either there is an access violation of the content source by the protocol handler, or it is using too much memory, or the content source is experiencing some type of difficulty after the named pipe is created. Close other processes that might be using memory on the SPS server.

Table 9-2 Protocol handler errors *(continued)*

Error Message	Meaning and Solution
Error fetching URL (80040d7b): Document filtering could not be completed because the document server did not respond within the specified time-out. Try crawling the server later or increase the time-out values.	Well, the error message offers a couple of fixes. Follow them.
Error fetching URL 80041205L	Access was denied to the content source. Check your content access account and ensure that it has permissions to the content source and that you are using the correct user name and password.
Error fetching URL 80041211L	Item will not be indexed. The source's ACL does not allow the proper access to index the item.
Error fetching URL 80041212L	The ACL of the content source exceeds 64K. SPS cannot index an item with an ACL larger than 64K.
Error fetching URL 80041208L	Error with the URL path. The path is bad. Ensure that you've typed the correct path in the content source.
Error fetching URL 80041200L or 80041206L	Undetermined network connectivity issue to the content source or a communication error with the server.
Error fetching URL 80041207L	Redirected URL does not exist.
Error fetching URL 80041201L	The requested document does not exist.
Error fetching URL 80041210L	ACL on source document was changed so that everyone can read the document.
Error fetching URL 8004121BL	Parts of a document cannot be accessed. You may see this message if the document is larger than 16MB.

Table 9-3 IFilter registration errors

Error Value	Meaning and Solution
8007005L	Access has been denied to the user account on the SPS server for the IFilter DLL. Ensure that the user account under which the gatherer process is running has permissions to the IFilter DLL.
80004005L	May indicate a corrupt registry. This is an unspecified error.
800700EL	There is insufficient memory to load and run the IFilter. Close other processes on the SPS server.

Summary

This is a real nuts-and-bolts chapter that outlines how to create and manage content sources. Management of the content sources really depends on good configuration and a crawling schedule that you like. Beyond that, content sources pretty much run by themselves. This information is closely tied to the information in Chapter 7 on searching and indexing.

Chapter 15, the last one in Part IV, covers the resource kit utilities and some third-party software that may enhance your management of your SPS servers and increase their usability for your users.

Advanced Administration

CHAPTER 10

Advanced Management of SharePoint Portal Server 2001

This chapter discusses administrative tasks that you won't perform every day. Although not all of the tasks described here are difficult, they must be performed on occasion. These administrative actions, from moving databases to editing files, will have an immediate impact on your environment.

One of the things you'll find about SPS is that you need to understand *where* to perform an action. Some administrative acts are committed on a serverwide basis, whereas others are committed for an individual workspace. Most fall into the second category, but a few important tasks are performed on the server.

Let's start with a brief overview of the Microsoft Management Console. Then we'll focus on the individual tasks.

Understanding the SharePoint Portal Server Microsoft Management Console

The SPS Microsoft Management Console (MMC) is really not its own administrative program. Instead, the SPS server tool is a snap-in to the MMC, which provides a common environment for the management of all Microsoft products. Each product ships with one or more management tools, which, figuratively speaking, "snap in" to the MMC and are called snap-ins. Each tool has a common interface, and you can either use the default MMC or create a customized MMC.

The MMC itself does not provide functionality; that comes from the tools that are added to it. Administrators can create custom management interfaces using tools from different vendors. For instance, you can create a customized MMC that allows you to manage the SPS server plus several third-party vendor software products, all from the same interface.

When you first load the MMC, it looks and feels like Windows Explorer. But in reality, MMC provides an interface to administrative objects and tools. Here, I illustrate the MMC using the default SPS tool.

When you open the SPS MMC, you first see the root container called SharePoint Portal Server. If you expand this container, you'll find the name of your local SharePoint server. This object is also a container that has associated properties. When expanded, it lists all the workspaces that exist on the server. My example has two workspaces: Administration and Marketing (Figure 10–1).

If you highlight the server object, its contents will appear in the right-hand pane. This means that the server object is really a container, and the pane is listing its contents. The MMC works from the principle of having containers that can hold other containers or end points, also called *leaf* objects. In Figure 10–1, you can see that when the Administration workspace is highlighted, no contents are listed in the right pane, indicating that this is an end point or leaf object and not a container.

Containers can also have properties that, when configured, apply to all the other containers and leaf objects that they contain. It's important to remember this because permissions are applied to all objects, and if you change the permissions on a container, those permissions will flow down or be inherited by all the other containers and leaf objects inside the container.

When you right-click an object, you'll get a context menu that indicates the actions that can be performed on the object. Most often, you'll be interested in the properties item because this is where you make configuration changes. For instance, when you right-click the server object in the SPS

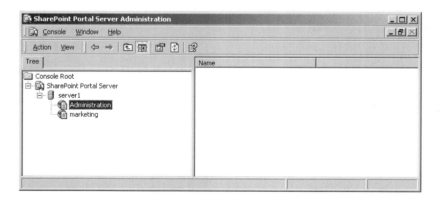

Figure 10–1 SPS MMC with expanded containers

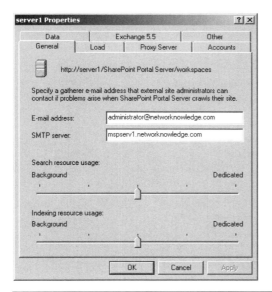

Figure 10–2 SharePoint server properties in the SPS MMC

MMC, you'll get serverwide configuration options that apply to all the workspaces located on the server (Figure 10–2). If you open the properties of a workspace, you'll find configuration choices that will apply to the workspace only. Hence, it is valuable to remember that when an author says that such-and-such option is "configured at the server level," it means that it is configured on the server object or that the configuration will apply to all workspaces created on the SPS server. There's a good chance that the option under discussion will exist in the server's properties or in the system registry.

Remember that an MMC has permissions applied to it and that they apply to all the tools installed inside the MMC. This tool can be given to other team members for their use. To learn more about how to create, customize, and share the MMC with other team members, please consult the Windows 2000 Resource Kit.

Moving Databases

Moving a database is one action that you perform at the server level. Open the server's properties in the SPS MMC, and navigate to the Data tab (Figure 10–3). Highlight the database or log file that you wish to move, and then click the

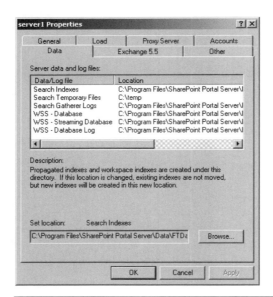

Figure 10–3 Data tab in server properties in SPS MMC

Browse button. Choose the target folder where you want to move the file, and click Apply. This will invoke the Move command, and the database will be moved automatically. Pretty slick, eh?

This may not seem like an advanced administrative function if you define *advanced* in terms of the degree of difficulty. As with most administration, configuring the object is the easy part. Knowing why you're doing it is more complicated.

In our example—moving log and database files—let's focus on moving the Web Storage System transaction logs; you'll want to do this to improve performance of your SPS server if you have a single disk (or mirrored pair of disks) that you can dedicate to hosting the WSS transaction logs. Because these log files write sequentially to the disk and because control is not returned to users until a transaction is committed in the transaction log, you can improve performance if you can get faster writes to the log. When you first install SPS, you should consider doing this and moving the WSS transaction log to its own disk or mirrored pair. For more information on the WSS, please consult Chapter 2.

A second reason to move logs and database files is that you are running out of disk space and need more space to hold these files. The database files can grow to be quite large, especially when you consider that a medium-sized organization could have 100,000 or more files (and Microsoft supports workspaces that hold as many as 1,000,000 documents).

You also might find other reasons to move databases or log files. But no matter why they are being moved, remember that while you're moving them, users will experience an interruption of service, especially if they are performing document management tasks such as check-in and check-out. When moving these files, be sure to use a window of time in which the users know that the workspace will be temporarily unavailable.

Editing Important Files

There are two files that you'll likely want to edit from time to time: the noise word file and the thesaurus. Both files will impact your indexing and search processes, although at different points in the architecture. For this reason, it's important to understand how to use these files to your advantage.

Editing the Thesaurus

The thesaurus is used to specify synonyms for words in a search query. In this way, if a user enters a specified word, the result set will include hits that match the word's configured synonyms. For instance, if a user searches on the word *book* and the phrase *collaborative applications*, you can configure the thesaurus to use *article* as a synonym for *book*, and this query result will include articles that discuss collaborative applications.

The thesaurus is held in XML files located in the `\program files\ sharepoint portal server\data\ftdata\sharepointportal- server\config` directory. These files have the format `TS<XXX>.XML`, where XXX is the standard three-letter code for a specific language.

The following languages are supported:

- Enu = English (United States)
- Eng = English (international)
- Chs = Chinese (simplified)
- Cht = Chinese (traditional)
- Deu = German
- Esn = Spanish
- Fra = French
- Ita = Italian
- Jpn = Japanese
- Kor = Korean
- Neu = neutral (explained in the next paragraph)

- Nld = Dutch
- Sve = Swedish
- Tha = Thai

The thesaurus always works with the language of the query, not the language of the operating system. Moreover, there is a neutral thesaurus file named `tsenu.xml` that is applied to every query along with the specific language thesaurus files. This allows cross-language associations and gives a hierarchical flavor to using the thesaurus files. It also allows documents that contain multiple languages to be queried against multiple thesauruses.

There is not much to the file, but editing it does require a bit of XML knowledge.[1] Here are the default contents of the file:

```
<XML ID="Microsoft Search Thesaurus">

    <thesaurus xmlns="x-schema:tsSchema.xml">
        <expansion>
            <sub weight="0.8">Internet Explorer</sub>
            <sub weight="0.2">IE</sub>
            <sub weight="0.9">IE5</sub>
        </expansion>
        <replacement>
            <pat>NT5</pat>
            <pat>W2K</pat>
            <sub weight="1.0">Windows 2000</sub>
        </replacement>
        <expansion>
            <sub weight="0.5">run**</sub>
            <sub weight="0.5">jog**</sub>
        </expansion>
    </thesaurus>
-->

</XML>
```

Notice that the code has two parts: an expansion set and a replacement set. The expansion set is used to specify a group of words that are synonyms. This means that search queries containing matches in one subgroup are expanded to include words in other subgroups that reside in the same expansion set.

---

[1] The Appendix presents a short tutorial on how to read XML. Please refer to this tutorial if you don't understand how to read basic XML.

For example, to return to the book illustration, you would create the code as follows:

```
<XML ID="Microsoft Search Thesaurus">

    <thesaurus xmlns="x-schema:tsSchema.xml">
        <expansion>
            <sub>book</sub>
            <sub>article</sub>
            <sub>chapter</sub>
        </expansion>
    </thesaurus>
```

This expansion set creates three synonyms: *book*, *article*, and *chapter*. If a query were to be performed against any one of these words in the expansion set, the search results would display documents containing any of the three words.

NOTE: When you make a change to a thesaurus file, the file is automatically reloaded to the search service without the need to restart the search service. This means that you can modify the thesaurus on the fly and get immediate results. In addition, the application log will display an event 4155 indicating that the file was loaded successfully. However, if the code is not well formed, the application event log will contain an error referencing the file and the line of code that is in error, and the file will not load to the search service.

Along with configuring the expansion set, you must configure weighting and stemming. The thesaurus that ships with SPS supports *weighting*, which allows you to indicate the relative importance of words in an expansion set by associating with each word a value between 0 and 1. The higher the weight value, the higher in the result set that documents containing that word will appear. Suppose that you want documents containing the word *book* to appear first, followed by those containing *chapter*, and then those containing *article*. You will give *book* the highest weight in the subgroup, and *article* the lowest weight. Hence, the code would look like this:

```
<XML ID="Microsoft Search Thesaurus">

    <thesaurus xmlns="x-schema:tsSchema.xml">
        <expansion>
            <sub>book</sub>
            <sub>article</sub>
            <sub>chapter</sub>
```

```
    </expansion>
    <expansion>
        <sub weight="0.7">book</sub>
        <sub weight="0.5">article</sub>
        <sub weight="0.6">chapter</sub>
    </expansion>
  </thesaurus>
```

The code order of the subgroup entries is not important because the entire file is loaded into memory after it is saved. And if you refer to the default XML file that ships with SPS, you'll find that you need not specify the synonyms first in the file to give them weight. In other words, you can specify the weight for a group of words so that if any combination of those words is selected for a search query, they will be ranked in the results based on their weight in the thesaurus. Also, there is no functional difference between using the weights 0.7, 0.6, and 0.5 versus, say, 0.9, 0.5, and 0.1. The relationship between the weights is absolute, not proportional. In other words, 1.0 is a higher weight than 0.1 and will affect the result set in the same manner as 1.0 and 0.9.

Another item that you can configure in the XML file is the ability to provide stemming information in the thesaurus. When you specify stemming, you can use the "pat" (pattern) or "sub" (substitution) entries by adding two asterisks (**) at the end of the word. When a search is performed on a word and there is a pat entry for the stem of that word in the thesaurus, the result set will include variants of the word and will include documents that contain these variants. Hence, in our ever-expanding example, if you want to ensure that when the word *book* is placed in a search query, the result set also includes documents that contain the word *books*, then you would create a pat entry in the XML file as follows:

```
<XML ID="Microsoft Search Thesaurus">

    <thesaurus xmlns="x-schema:tsSchema.xml">
        <expansion>
            <sub>book</sub>
            <sub>article</sub>
            <sub>chapter</sub>
        </expansion>
        <expansion>
            <sub weight="0.7">book**</sub>
            <sub weight="0.5">article</sub>
            <sub weight="0.6">chapter</sub>
        </expansion>
      </thesaurus>
```

Care must be taken to ensure that when you invoke stemming in a thesaurus, you don't create a large number of false positives. For instance, in this example, the word *books* would be returned, but so would other variants, such as *bookings*, *booked*, and *bookends*. There is no quick method in these XML files to say that you want *books* but not *bookends* using the stemming method. When you're faced with such a situation, it would be better to include the actual words and their variations in a subgroup rather than use stemming as the shortcut approach.

The thesaurus also lets you create a replacement set of words by specifying a pattern that will be replaced by a substitution set of one or more words. For example, you could create a replacement set that specifies the pattern *book writer* with the substitution *author* or *wordsmith*. In this example, when a user executes a query against the phrase *book writer*, the result set will include documents that have the words *author* and *wordsmith*. The code would look like this:

```
<XML ID="Microsoft Search Thesaurus">

    <thesaurus xmlns="x-schema:tsSchema.xml">
        <expansion>
            <sub>book</sub>
            <sub>article</sub>
            <sub>chapter</sub>
        </expansion>
        <expansion>
            <sub weight="0.7">book</sub>
            <sub weight="0.5">article</sub>
            <sub weight="0.6">chapter</sub>
        </expansion>
        <replacement>
            <pat>book writer</pat>
            <sub>author</sub>
            <sub>wordsmith</sub>
        </replacement>
    </thesaurus>
```

FOR MORE INFO: If you are unsure as to what kind of words you should place in a synonym subgroup, I suggest you use a book of synonyms, such as *The Synonym Finder*, by J. I. Rodale, 1978, Rodale Press. A companion book is *The Word Finder*, by the same author and publisher. Both are excellent works to have handy, especially if you write books! <g>

Editing the Noise Word File

Editing the noise word file is easy and important because this file tells the indexing engine which words to eliminate from the full-text index. Editing it is one way to help control the size of your indexes.

Noise words are those words that occur often in a language and don't add any value if they are included in an index. In English, words such as *a*, *and*, *the*, or *to* occur in nearly every document you place in a workspace, and they can (and will) be indexed if they are not included in the noise word file.

SharePoint ships with a default set of words configured in the noise word file. You can customize this file to include other words that are specific to your industry so that these noise words cannot be included in the full-text index. After you make changes to the noise word file, you must perform a full update of the index to incorporate the changes.

Like the thesaurus files, the noise word files are located in the `\program files\sharepoint portal server\data\ftdata\sharepoint-portalserver\config` folder and are named using `NOISEXXX.TXT`, where `XXX` is the standard three-letter language code (listed in the preceding section of this chapter).

You open the noise file using Notepad or another text editor, and modify it as needed. Numbers and symbols can also be included in the file, as illustrated in Figure 10–4. When you're finished, save the file to its original location and overwrite the old file if prompted to do so.

Figure 10–4 Default noise word file for the English (United States) language

Customizing the Portal Content

Part of the overall attractiveness of SPS for corporate customers is its ability to present new information to users quickly through the use of the portal. By default, when users go to their portal, it will display corporate announcements, news items, and even a list of links to Web sites that are worthy of note on a company-wide basis.

Under the hood, these items are documents that have been placed inside content folders and modified using the Web folders client of the workspace. Each folder's contents then appear in a separate Web part on the dashboard.

Configuring these items in each Web part is not intuitive, but once you learn how to do it, it's a piece of cake to create and post these items. Generally speaking, the documents that appear in these Web parts act as links to the hard information. Each folder type (announcements, quick links, and news) has its own document profile that displays the information in the proper format.

By default, the content folders are standard folders, but they can be configured as enhanced folders if necessary, something that is helpful if you need support for a development cycle or approval process for items posted in these folders. To learn more about document development and approval processes, please consult Chapter 8.

Announcements

The Announcements Web part displays content that the coordinator of the workspace wants all dashboard users to see. Announcement documents are usually in either HTML or Word format. A specific profile is used with announcement documents, including Title, Author, and Description.

To create a new announcement document, open Word and type the announcement. In the following example, you're going to tell users about an important salary raise that the board has approved (hey, you can dream, can't you?). You type the salary announcement in Word and then save it, using the Web folders client to the Announcements folder that is located inside the Portal folder. When you do so, the Announcements Document Profile dialog box appears asking you to type the necessary information (Figure 10–5). None of the profile parts is required, but without proper configuration, the document won't appear correctly in the dashboard.

Notice that the title of the document has become the link that appears in the Announcements Web part and takes the user to this document (Figure 10–6). Because this is a Word document, when the link is clicked, you'll get a message popup box asking whether you want to open the file or save it to your local

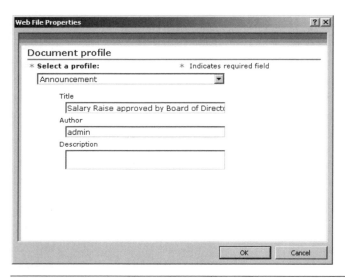

Figure 10–5 Document Profile dialog box for a new announcement document

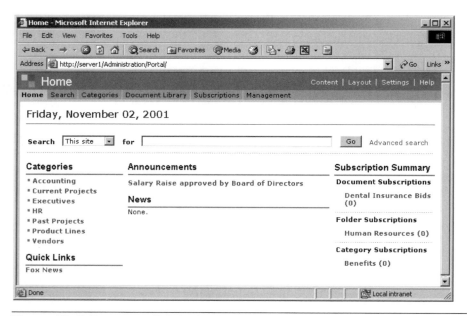

Figure 10–6 Document link in the Announcements Web part in the dashboard

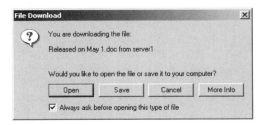

Figure 10–7 Message popup box asking whether the file should be opened or saved

hard drive (Figure 10–7). If you want to eliminate this popup box, save the Word document as a Web page with an `.htm` or `.html` extension; the document will appear in the browser when the link is clicked (Figure 10–8). The value of saving the document as a Web page is that you can include embedded links and graphics as a part of the announcement, instead of limiting the announcement to text, as it is in Figure 10–8.

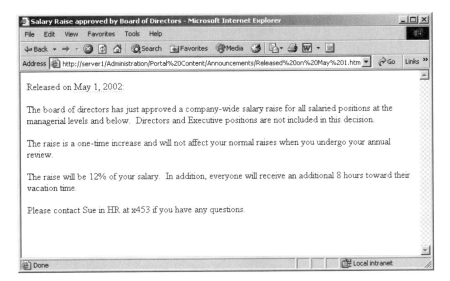

Figure 10–8 Announcement as a Web page in the browser after clicking the link in the dashboard

News

To create a new news item in the News Web part, you do exactly the same thing as you did to create a new Announcements Web part, except that you'll save it to the News content folder and not the Announcements content folder.

TIP: Even though it's not specifically intended to be used in this way, you can use the dashboard as a method of making documents available to users by saving them as either news or announcement items formatted as Office documents instead of Web pages. If you want users to have the option of storing certain important documents locally on their hard drives, this is one method of making them available.

Quick Links

Creating a quick link requires a different procedure from that of creating a news or announcement item. In a quick link document, it doesn't matter what content you place *in* the document because the content is not displayed. Instead, you can take an empty Word document and make all the configurations you need in the document's profile. Because you're saving this to the Quick Links content folder, you'll find that the profile is different (Figure 10–9).

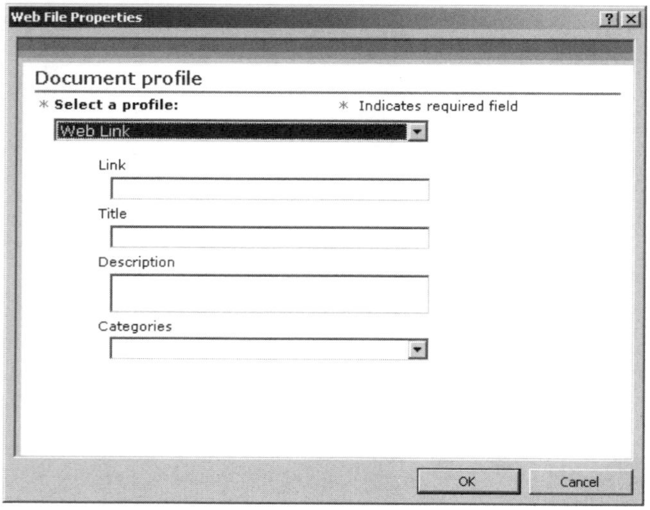

Figure 10–9 Quick Links document profile

Customizing the News, Announcements, and Quick Links Web Parts

If you want to customize one or more of these Web parts, it's not as difficult as you might think. Before calling a developer, see whether these instructions accomplish what you're after.

First, click the Content link of the dashboard where the Web part is located. For the Announcements, News, and Quick Links Web parts, this will be the Home dashboard. Then open the Web part's properties. Near the bottom of the Advanced Properties dialog box, there is a list box labeled Store the Following Data for This Web Part. The second line in this box defaults to `DAV:getlastmodified DESC`. This means that the contents of the Web part will appear in the order in which the items were created based on their last modified date, in descending order.

Suppose you want something different. Here are some of your choices:

- `DAV:href`: Sort the items by their URL.
- `DAV:displayname`: Sort the items by their filename.
- `Urn:schemas-microsoft-com:office:office#Description`: Sort the items by their description.
- `Urn:schemas-microsoft-com:office:office#Title`: Sort the items by their title.
- `ASC` (as opposed to `DESC`): Sort the items in ascending order instead of the default descending order.

Also, if you change the number at the end to something other than 5, which is the default, the desired number of items will be displayed in the Web part. If you change it to `empty`, there will be no limit on the number of items that can appear in the Web part.

Here, you'll see that you can type both a title and a link. The Link field hosts the URL to the Web site. The Title field displays what users will see. In the absence of a configured title, the document's name will be displayed. I've saved two files to the Quick Links content folder as an illustration, both pointing to the same Web site. You'll see that one has an informative description, whereas the base document name (`Doc2.doc`) is rather unhelpful and confusing (Figure 10–10).

Now let's suppose that you want to provide your users with regular, continuous data through a news item in the portal. This isn't streaming data per se, but rather regular, frequent updates to data that your users can use. For instance, it might be appropriate in your environment to create a spreadsheet listing current sales figures and inventories that is updated constantly. Here is how to do that easily.

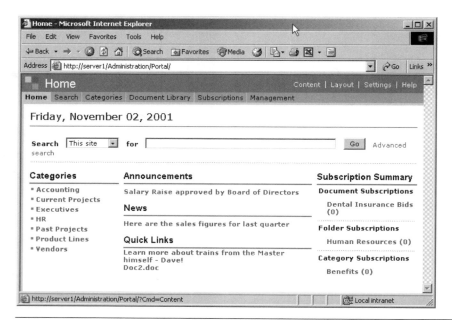

Figure 10–10 Two links to same Web site, one with an inviting title, the other with a document name

First, create a new spreadsheet using Excel. The sample spreadsheet (Figure 10–11) lists the current sales figures for three products: Widget1, Widget2, and Widget3. It also lists the inventory for each of these highly valuable products.

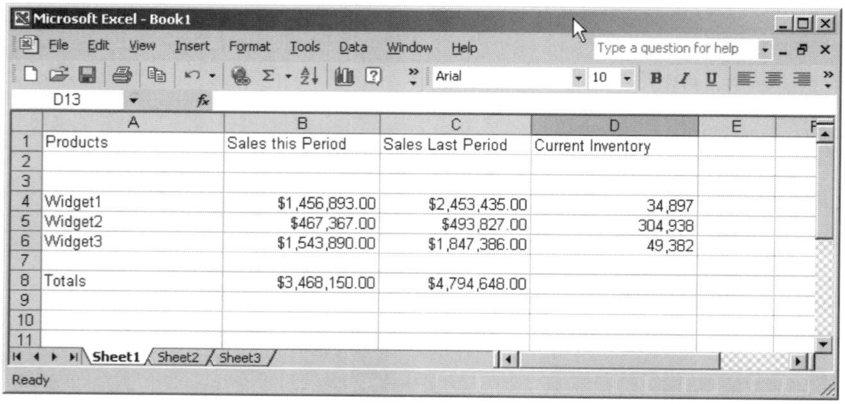

Figure 10–11 Sales spreadsheet with inventory adjustments

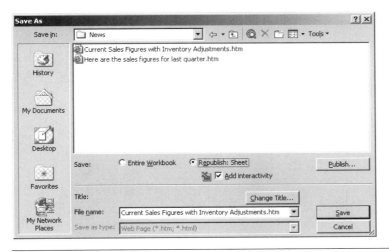

Figure 10–12 Save As dialog box

When you save this file, choose Save as Web Page from the Excel File menu. In the Save As dialog box, choose Republish: Sheet and Add Interactivity. Then give the file a name with an .htm extension, and click Publish, not Save (Figure 10–12).

After you click on Publish, the Publish as Web Page dialog box will appear, and this is where you make additional choices about how to publish this spreadsheet. In particular, note three configurations here. First, in the Choose drop-down list (Figure 10–13), if this is the first time you're publishing this

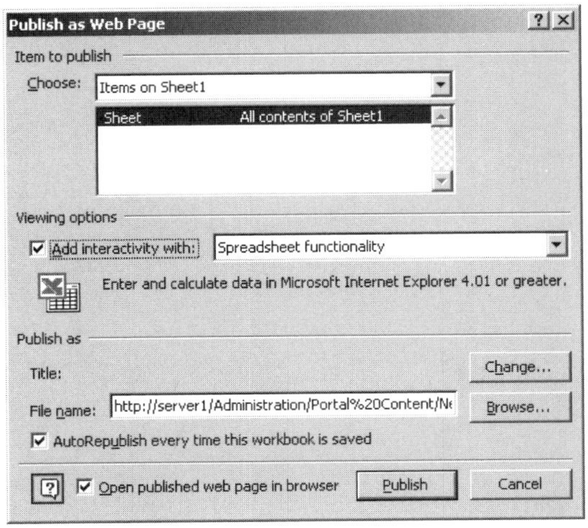

Figure 10–13 Publish as Web Page dialog box

spreadsheet, you'll choose either the correct range of cells, the entire workbook, or only the sheet in focus. Your choice will depend on what you want to accomplish. However, if this is not the first time you're publishing this spreadsheet, you'll see an additional option, Previously Published Items. This will be the default when you're republishing a spreadsheet. Unless you have specific reasons for making a different selection when republishing a spreadsheet, leave this as its default.

Second, you can add interactivity (or not add it) using the Add Interactivity With check box. If you make this selection, you will be able to make changes to the data in the spreadsheet *directly in the Web part where the spreadsheet is published*. Figure 10–14 illustrates what this spreadsheet looks like in the Web part. Notice that Excel functionality is available in the button bar above the data.

TIP: Before publishing this spreadsheet, secure the data with file permissions so that only certain people can make changes to the data using the portal interface.

If you choose to clear the Add Interactivity With check box, the data will be displayed statically as a spreadsheet. Changes made to the source spreadsheet will be reflected in the Web part the next time it is refreshed. If you choose not to add interactivity, be sure that the News Web part refreshes regularly so that updated information will be displayed quickly. The refresh intervals are configured in the Web part's properties, discussed in Chapter 3.

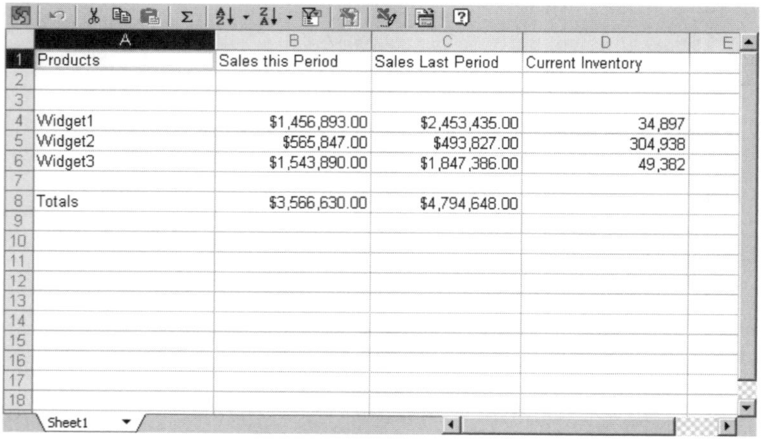

	A	B	C	D	E
1	Products	Sales this Period	Sales Last Period	Current Inventory	
2					
3					
4	Widget1	$1,456,893.00	$2,453,435.00	34,897	
5	Widget2	$565,847.00	$493,827.00	304,938	
6	Widget3	$1,543,890.00	$1,847,386.00	49,382	
7					
8	Totals	$3,566,630.00	$4,794,648.00		
9					
10					
11					
12					
13					
14					
15					
16					
17					
18					

Figure 10–14 Widgets spreadsheet published with interactivity

Finally (returning to Figure 10–13), if you want to ensure that the latest version of the spreadsheet is published automatically, select the AutoRepublish Every Time This Workbook Is Saved check box. This will force a republish event every time the document is saved.

NOTE: AutoRepublish works only with Office XP. This is also true for saving documents as Web parts. If you are running Office 2000, neither of these features will be available.

Figure 10–15 illustrates how the spreadsheet will appear if you have chosen not to publish with interactivity. It's pretty bland.

If you want to publish this spreadsheet as a Web part, click the Content link in the desired dashboard, and then click Import a Web Part File. From there, specify the path to the spreadsheet that was saved as an `.htm` file, and this file will be displayed as a Web part in the portal (Figure 10–16). For more information on how to build Web parts, please consult Chapter 3.

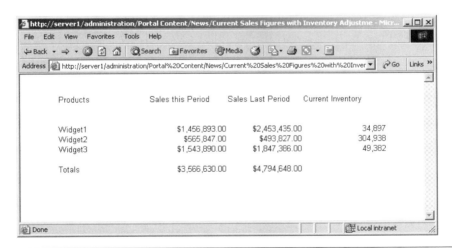

Figure 10–15 Widgets spreadsheet published without interactivity

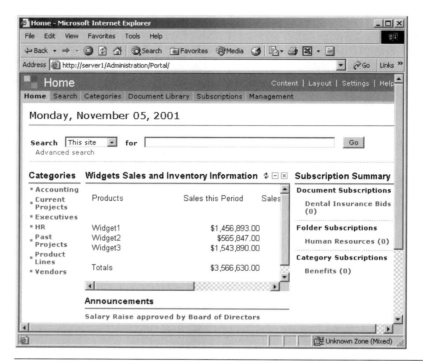

Figure 10–16 Spreadsheet as it appears in the portal in its own Web part

Summary

This chapter looks at some advanced administrative functions that you might be involved with from time to time. These are not day-to-day functions, but it is important to know about them and understand how they work. Chapter 11 focuses on the backup and recovery of SharePoint Portal Server, which is a daily administrative function that is worthy of special consideration.

Backup and Recovery of SharePoint Portal Server 2001

There are some feelings in life you simply don't want to experience. One of them is realizing that all the data you thought you had backed up is not backed up, and it's now totally lost. Forever. I've never felt this, but I've come close because of unforeseen hardware problems. That feeling was awful, and I don't want you to ever experience it. That's why this chapter spends considerable time on a little, itty-bitty backup utility whose day-to-day functions can be explained in about 90 seconds. That utility, msdmback.vbs, is the backup program for SharePoint Portal Server.

Backing up your SPS data is as important as the recoverability of any of your other information. This chapter outlines how use the SharePoint backup utility, along with four other SPS tools, to ensure that your workspace data is recoverable in the event of a disaster. It also discusses some limitations of these utilities and the SharePoint program in general and explains how that impacts planning issues for this product. Let's start with the backup program.

The msdmback.vbs Utility

The backup and restore solution that ships with SharePoint Portal Server is intended to solve the problem of an entire server recovery. It is not intended to be a recovery mechanism for an individual workspace or document. (Later in this chapter I discuss workspace export tools that can be used to back up an individual workspace.) The msdmback.vbs script can be scheduled using the Windows 2000 scheduler service.

When you stop to think about it, SPS is the first server platform that uses a script to back up its data. Previously, Microsoft products were written to use the Windows Backup API in the underlying operating system. But SPS does not include any integration with the Windows 2000 Backup API. So the SPS team had to create a script to back up its data. This script is the only method native to SPS of backing up workspace data.

This script creates only an image on disk. It does not work with or recognize a backup tape system. Hence, to back up SPS to tape, you must do it in two steps: First, run the `msdmback` utility and create the server image on disk, and then back up the image to tape. There are no other options here.

The `msdmback.vbs` script installs in the \bin directory when SPS is installed. When the backup is complete, you'll have an image in a single file that is an identical copy of the server at the time the backup operation was performed. The script is run from a command line and backs up the following:

- Store schema
- All workspaces, including documents
- Content indexes
- Propagated indexes
- All Web Storage System files
- Server and system configuration

The backup image does not include the following:

- Content source indexes that are built using the Windows 2000 Task Scheduler. These indexes must be re-created after a restore process.
- Subscription processing schedules that have been modified.
- Search gatherer logs.

Before you run a backup, you must ensure that you have an existing folder path in which to create the backup image as well as enough disk space to hold the image. In addition, you must make sure that the SharePoint Portal Server service is started and that you're using the NTFS file system.

To calculate the size of the backup file, add up the sizes of your full-text indexes, the `.mdb` database, and the `.stm` database. This total will be about 95 percent of the size of the backup image that will be created.

You can back up SPS to a file share on a remote server. When doing so, however, you must ensure that the security account that will be used to perform the backup has write permissions to the share on the remote server and is a member of the Local Administrators group on the target server.

Partial backups of SharePoint data are not possible using `msdmback.vbs` (although some third-party products may offer this feature). For instance, you cannot back up only the documents in the workspace. You must back up everything associated with SharePoint at the same time. While the backup process is running, a lock is placed on the document management infrastructure. Because changes made to any part of SPS during a backup process may not be saved, it is recommended that access to the SharePoint server be restricted during the backup process.

SPS can be backed up only to a local hard disk or to a share on a remote hard disk. Backup directly to tape is not supported, although after the backup image is created, it can be backed up to tape. If you do back up the image to tape, you cannot restore it directly from tape. You must first restore the image to a hard disk and then use the `msdmback.vbs` utility to restore the data from the hard disk back to the WSS.

Even though, in theory, you can back up all the files using a backup program that works with the Windows 2000 Backup API, any restore efforts for the SPS WSS will fail using this method. Therefore, you are advised to use only the `msdmback.vbs` utility for both backup and restore operations for SPS data in the SPS WSS.

During the backup process, index builds are suspended. Users can add new documents to the workspace during a backup, but any newly published documents will not be part of the backup image, nor will these documents be available for searching until after the backup operation is completed.

If you use a password in the backup command, you should know that the password is stored in an encrypted form inside the backup image. However, the contents in the backup image are not encrypted using this password. If the password is lost or forgotten, a restore of the image will not be possible.

As mentioned, you can back up the image to a remote server's hard disk. To do this, you first need to run the following command:

```
Msdmback /a {domainname\username} password
```

This command makes a configuration in the SharePoint workspace to run the `msdmback` command inside this user name security context. If you don't run this command first, the backup operation will fail even if you are logged on as the default administrator for the forest and are a member of the Enterprise Admins security group. The error message is illustrated in Figure 11–1. You can see how unhelpful this error message is in diagnosing the real problem.

NOTE: When you run this command, the password will be displayed in plain text on your screen. If you are running this command as a member of the Administrators security group, ensure that your monitor is visually secure. Otherwise, it is possible for your password to be compromised.

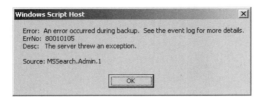

Figure 11–1 Error message when you try to run `msdmback` without first configuring the security context for the backup script on your SPS server

If you type `msdmback /?` at the command prompt, you'll get a listing of the various parameters available, as illustrated in Figure 11–2. If you get stuck and can't find this book anywhere (of course, you'd never lose this book, right? <g>), use the `/?` switch to help you understand the `msdmback` syntax.

A common backup scenario is to back up the SPS data to a file location on the local server. Here's the command-line syntax for this situation:

```
Msdmback /b backup_folder_path
```

NOTE: You can specify the backup folder path by typing either the directory path in a local file system or a Universal Naming Convention (UNC) path. To password-protect the backup image file, you can also supply a password following the folder path name. If you use a password, be sure to write it down and save it because you'll be required to supply the same password to use the image in a restore operation. Losing the password will mean losing the data because the backup image will not be recoverable.

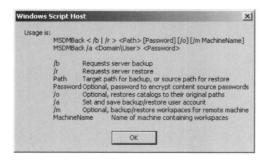

Figure 11–2 The Help screen for `msdmback`

As an illustration, let's assume that your backup folder is named `d:\spsfullbackup` and you want to name your backup image file `Marketing`. Here is the command that you would use:

```
Msdmback /b d:\spsfullbackup\marketing
```

TIP: Use the `cscript` command to ensure that the popup dialog boxes do not appear while this command is running.

You need to remember a couple of things. First, the target folder—in this example, the `spsfullbackup` folder—must exist before you run the utility. Second, the target filename `marketing` cannot exist. If it does exist, the backup process will stop (see "Troubleshooting" at the end of this chapter). In the example in Figure 11–3, I'm backing up my SPS server to the `c:\backup` folder, and I'm using the day name, `Monday`, as the name of my backup image.

Once the backup process is started, a small box (Figure 11–4) displays the number of bytes that have been backed up. There is no status or progress bar to indicate how large the image will be or how much longer the process will run. You can estimate the image's size and then guesstimate the length of the backup process, but the utility itself won't give you the information.

When the backup is completed, you'll see four entries in the application log. Figure 11–5 illustrates the first entry. The first pair of entries records that the information store backup has started and then was successful. The second pair of entries records that MSSearch is starting a full backup and then was

Figure 11–3 Command line for running `msdmback`

Figure 11–4 Status bar indicating the number of bytes that have been processed

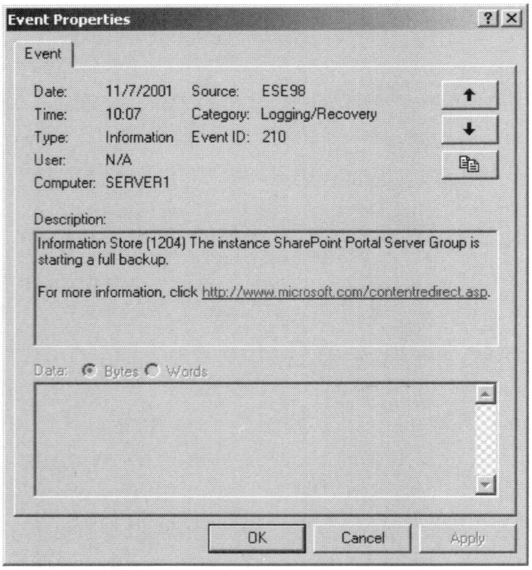

Event Properties

Date:	11/7/2001	Source:	ESE98
Time:	10:07	Category:	Logging/Recovery
Type:	Information	Event ID:	210
User:	N/A		
Computer:	SERVER1		

Description:

Information Store (1204) The instance SharePoint Portal Server Group is starting a full backup.

For more information, click http://www.microsoft.com/contentredirect.asp.

Data: ⦿ Bytes ○ Words

OK   Cancel   Apply

Figure 11–5 Event 210 from ESE98 starting the backup process

successful. If the backup fails for some reason, be sure to check the application log for indications as to why it failed. See also "Troubleshooting" at the end of this chapter.

Because SPS, like Exchange 2000 Server, is built on the WSS, some people may attempt to mount the M: drive and then perform backups using that drive. This method of backup is not only discouraged but also not supported by Microsoft. Moreover, performing a backup using the M: drive will not flush the transaction logs to the database and will likely result in information loss. The moral of the story is, don't use the M: drive for your backups.

If you want to create a batch file to run this command using the scheduler service, here is a simple set of commands that you can use:

```
@echo off
Setlocal
Cd program files\sharepoint portal server\bin
```

```
Cscript msdmback.vbs /b "c\spsbackupfolder = fullbackup.bfk"
Endlocal
```

Be sure to place this batch file in the root of drive `C:`, and change `c:\spsbackupfolder` to the true path for the location where you want the backup script to save the images.

Restoring a Server

Before a restore operation, you should ensure the following:

- SPS is installed.
- The restore server is running NTFS.
- There is sufficient disk space.
- You are using the same WSS platform as the backup server.

A restore operation will destroy all existing data on the restore SPS server. You can overwrite the files with a restore operation, but you should realize that existing data will be lost forever. Best practice here is to ensure that if you need the current data on the restore server, you back up that server first before restoring the image from another server.

The backup image will contain all the user role security settings from the backup server that existed at the time the server was backed up. If some of these users have been deleted or if a security identifier is no longer resolvable to a user or group, you must manually configure the folder or resource in the SPS workspace accordingly. There is no method of automatic failover to a default user or group account.

Hence, best practice is to use domain user and group accounts, rather than local user and group accounts, for security assignments in the workspace. If the restore server is in a different domain from the source server, you must ensure that all the security roles are reset to include users from the local domain. You will know that a user account is not resolvable when you look at the Security tab and see a security identifier number instead of a user or group name.

Restoring a backup file is not difficult. Here's the correct command-line syntax to perform a restore operation:

```
Msdmback /r <backup path to image>
```

Hence, if I wanted to restore the image I've just created (see Figure 11–3, presented earlier), I would run the following command:

```
Msdmback /r c:\backup\Monday
```

The image has the information necessary to restore all the files, including the store files, the search files, and the registry keys. Like nearly all restore processes, this one takes longer than the backup process. Moreover, as with the backup process, no status bar or time estimates are shown. Once the files have been restored, they will be ready for use by the workspace users. You need not reboot the server in order to register or jump-start SPS into using the files.

A restore operation will result in more than 40 events logged in the application log. You'll see logged events for the start and ending of a database restore; catalogs are rebuilt, and all the content sources are recrawled automatically.

Integrity Checker for an SPS Workspace

To verify the integrity of the SPS workspaces, you can use `spsinteg.vbs`, a resource kit utility that ships with SPS (and is also available for download at `http://www.microsoft.com/sharepoint/techinfo/reskit/spsinteg.asp`). This tool is not a database tool but rather is focused on verifying the integrity of the following:

- Category dictionary
- Categories associated with documents
- Document profile associations with documents
- Metadata for documents in the document library
- Publishing and approval routing

When you run the `spsinteg.vbs` script, the verification steps will appear, along with warnings and failures. If you enable verbose logging, you can check a log file for detailed information about these warnings and failures. Be careful with verbose logging, however, because each document in the workspace will mean about 5K of logged information.

Microsoft estimates that it takes about one second to verify each document. Moreover, as you might suspect, this is a memory- and processor-intensive activity, so don't do this when your indexing and gatherer engines are firing. Doing so will add unnecessary stress to your system.

The syntax to run this utility is as follows:

```
Spsinteg.vbs <server|workspace> [logfile] [level]
```

If you specify the server name, all the workspaces will be verified. If you specify an individual workspace, only that workspace will be verified. You should not use both the server name and the workspace name. Only one or the other is needed to make this utility fire.

If you run the `spsinteg.vbs` script with the `/?` switch, you'll get a series of popup boxes (some of which have no information and only an OK button) that will inform you as to how the command should be typed into the command line. Here are the examples given in the utility:

```
Spsinteg.vbs servername \\servername\sharename\spsinteg.log verbose
Spsinteg.vbs http://servername/workspacename verbose
Spsinteg.vbs http://servername/workspacename
```

When you run this script, it goes through and verifies the items listed earlier in this chapter. The output will be in the form of popup boxes displaying the successes and failures. Figure 11–6 illustrates a successful message.

Because this is a Visual Basic script, it is an event-driven utility. This means that if you don't click OK in each popup box, the script will not continue to run in the background.

Running the script in the verbose mode will mean that each event is recorded in the log file you specify. This log file does not need to exist before you run the script; it will be created with the name in the location that you specify. It is a simple text file. Figure 11–7 illustrates entries in the log file.

Because this script requires user actions to continue to run, you'll have to baby-sit it until it finishes. Running this script in verbose mode will drive you to a therapist for long-term therapy. Take another look at Figure 11–7, which was produced using the verbose mode. Each entry in that log file resulted in a popup dialog box that required me to click OK! If you have more than 100 files in your workspace, it will take you at least 20 minutes (in verbose mode) to read and click through all the message popup boxes. Coordinators who manage workspaces that contain thousands of documents will find the verbose mode laughable and not an option. Don't run `spsinteg` in verbose mode if you have lots of documents. Just don't do it.

Frankly, as this script is written, you should use it only when absolutely necessary because of the administrative time it will take to click all those OK

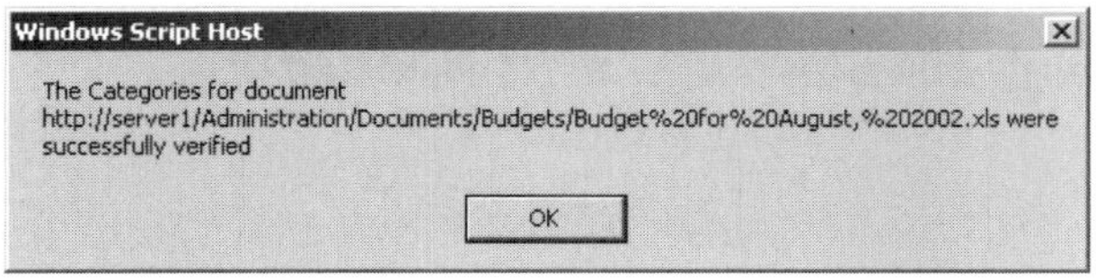

Figure 11–6 Successful verification message

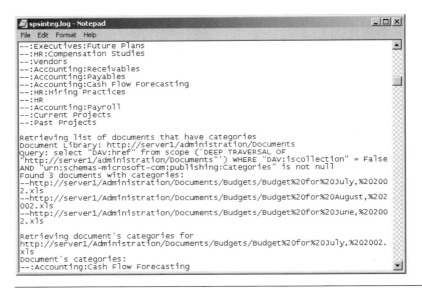

Figure 11–7 `spsinteg.log` file created by the `spsinteg` script

buttons, even when you're not running it in verbose mode. My advice is to have a developer recode the script to get rid of the message popup boxes and have those messages output to a simple text file on the fly. Why Microsoft didn't do this is beyond me. This is way below their normal standard of excellence.

This script has two other glaring irritants. First is the lack of status information on how much longer the script will run or how many more documents need to be processed. Couple that with the lack of an overall user interface to let you dump out of the script, and you have an elementary utility that is much less than administrator-friendly. If you need to end the script before it is finished running, you must kill the Windows Scripting Host thread in Task Manager. There is no other way to end the script during its operation—other than rebooting the server, I suppose. We can only hope that Microsoft will improve on the administrative interface for this script by building an MMC tool that will allow you to check a workspace's integrity without wearing out your mouse.

Workspace Exporting, Importing, and Archiving

Two other resource kit utilities allow you to export workspace information to an XML file and then use that file to reimport the information. Another utility allows you to archive the workspace. Let's discuss each one.

The Workspace Archive Tool

This archiving utility stores the workspace data to a file directory and its meta-data to an XML stub file. You can call this utility from a COM-aware application or run it from the command line.

To install the Workspace Archive Tool, first create a subdirectory to hold its files. In my example, I'll create a directory called `spsutil` in the `C:\` drive. Second, I copy the `spsutil.dll` file to this newly created directory. After copying the DLL, I register it using the following syntax from the Start|Run option:

```
Regsvr32 c:\spsutil\spsutil.dll
```

Of course, your path may be different from mine. If you ever want to unregister the DLL, type the following command:

```
Regsvr32 c:\spsutil\spsutil.dll /u
```

Once registered, the utility can be used from a command prompt or scheduled to run by using the `AT` command or the Windows 2000 scheduler service. In addition, the accompanying Help file explains how to modify the code in the script to have it run on a scheduled basis.

This utility is not ready to go out of the chute. You must modify its code to run in your environment. If you don't know how to do this, call your friendly neighborhood developer and have him or her do it.

Exporting a Workspace

You can use SPSIMEX Export, a workspace export tool, to copy a workspace to an XML file. You must register its DLL (`spsexport.dll`) in the same manner as described for the `spsutil.dll` file. After you register it, there will be a VB application (`spsimexexport.exe`) that will run another small VB application. Happily, SPSIMEX Export has an administrative interface (Figure 11–8) that allows you to specify which workspace you wish to export and the directory location of the XML file. Only coordinators and local administrators can run this utility.

The XML file is created automatically and runs pretty quickly. Of course, workspaces with tens of thousands of documents will find it to run much slower than those with only hundreds of documents. Figure 11–9 illustrates the part of the export file that holds the default e-mail message for approvers configured for one of my enhanced workspace folders. This indicates that not only documents but also other workspace information are exported.

Figure 11–8 Workspace export utility administration interface

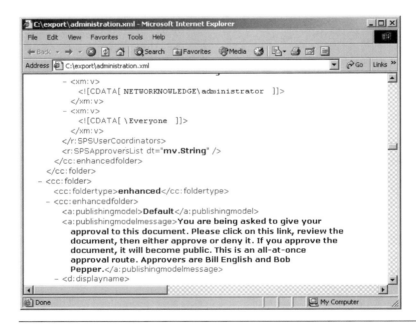

Figure 11–9 Export XML file showing approver default e-mail message

The XML file does not hold the actual documents and their content. Instead, these items are copied separately to a directory structure that is a mirror of the Document Library folder structure. The XML file is merely stub information on the metadata for the documents and folders in the document library.

However, lest you think that this is a great way to ensure you've got a complete copy of your workspace, please note that this utility does not reference or include discussion items nor any new dashboards that you have created. You really should think of it as a document export tool that will export the document folder structure and metadata.

Importing a Workspace

The SPS Resource Kit includes SPSIMEX Import, a workspace import utility that you can use to import contents and schemas into a new or existing workspace. The content and schema information must exist in a directory structure, and the schema information must exist in XML format.

SPSIMEX Import can be used for several important functions:

- Distributing a set of standardized document profiles to all your SPS servers
- Migrating content from file- and Web-based servers
- Migrating content from Exchange public folders, both 5.5 and 2000
- Creating a workspace template from an existing workspace to create a new workspace on another SPS server
- Rebalancing document locations across multiple SPS servers

When you run this utility, if the target workspace does not exist, the workspace will be created automatically. This feature is especially helpful when you are trying to deploy another read-only SPS server in your organization. For more information on how to deploy SPS in the enterprise, please see Chapter 14.

SPSIMEX Import does not import any discussion threads into a workspace. But it does import the version history of a workspace's documents, with a couple of limitations. First, it does not allow you to specify individual users or a modified time on documents that exist in the version history. Second, it does not rebuild the approval history of a document.

This utility has a `setup.exe` program to install it on your SharePoint server. When run, the setup app takes you through a quick installation wizard and places menu shortcuts under your Programs menu list. From there, you can run SPSIMEX Import, whose initial interface is illustrated in Figure 11–10. A companion document explains this tool. You might want to reference this document for detailed information on the XML syntax for this tool.

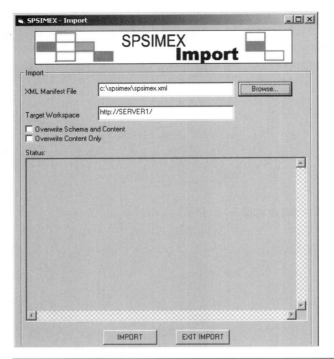

Figure 11–10 Initial administrative interface for the SPSIMEX Import tool

Troubleshooting

Although it is not possible to cover every conceivable error that might occur during a backup process for SPS, here are a few I've encountered.

First, be sure that the folder names and paths do not include any spaces. If they do, the backup utility will read the first space in the path as the end of the path name, and the backup file will be incomplete. For instance, let's assume you want to back up your data to the D: drive and you create a backup folder named SharePoint Portal Backup. Then you run the backup command as follows:

```
Msdmback /b d:\sharepoint portal backup\dailybackup.bak
```

When you run the backup program, it will create a backup image named SharePoint in the root of drive D: because it will read only d:\sharepoint and not the full path name.

In addition, if the path name matches an existing folder or filename, you'll get a very unhelpful error message saying that the backup program "cannot create a file when that file already exists." It will also tell you to see the event log for more details, but no messages will be recorded in the log.

The solution here is to use a unique folder name and to name the directory path without spaces.

Second, if you get an "access denied" error message when you run the `msdmback.vbs` utility, be sure that the System account has at least write privileges to the backup folder and that you have configured SPS to use the Administrator account.

Third, if you get an 80070050 error and the message "The file exists," be sure to give your backup file a unique name.

Summary

This chapter discusses how to perform a backup and restore of SharePoint Portal Server. You've learned about four resource kit utilities that provide additional functionality. As you can see, these utilities are really in a developmental stage—not robust and not ready for prime time. But they are what you have to work with, and work with them you must. In Chapter 12, we'll dive into the important topic of monitoring SharePoint Portal Server.

CHAPTER 12

Monitoring SharePoint Portal Server 2001

Like architecture, monitoring is viewed by many people as both boring and optional. Although I can see the first assessment, I can't agree with the second. Monitoring your servers should not be optional. Instead, it should be one of the main focuses of your administrative function matrix. Monitoring is an important part of delivering a high-quality knowledge management solution to your organization and for achieving the commitments of Service Level Agreements.

Why monitor SPS? The answer is simple: to avoid service outages by detecting problems before they become critical. Monitoring can help you quickly make adjustments when user demand significantly changes or your server resources become overstressed. Monitoring your SPS server can yield information in the following areas:

- Overseeing overall system health
- Detecting and predicting trends
- Detecting errors
- Ensuring good backups of your server's data

This chapter provides information on how to monitor SPS on a Windows 2000 server.

Developing Monitoring Policies

You've probably heard variations of the worn-out phrase used by financial planners in the last few decades: "If you fail to plan, you're planning to fail." As cheesy as this phrase might be, there is a truckload of truth in it, especially when it comes to monitoring. No matter which tools you use to monitor SPS—Windows 2000, NetIQ, Microsoft Operations Manager (MOM)—if you don't use them properly or regularly, they become meaningless. What is required, when it comes to monitoring, is discipline. And you can establish such discipline by creating monitoring policies that are a result of discussions between you, your server team, and the managers in your company.

Monitoring policies should define the following:

- Objects to be monitored
- Servers to be monitored
- Polling frequency
- Actions to be taken given certain events
- A 24/7 plan for notifications and resolutions

Problems will occur with SharePoint Portal Server. This doesn't mean that it's a shoddy product; problems occur with all software packages. How quickly these problems are solved depends largely on how early they are detected and diagnosed. For example, if you don't monitor the available disk space on the physical disks that hold your Web Storage System databases, you could be surprised one day to learn that you've run out of disk space. On the other hand, monitoring could tell you when you have 100MB of disk space left and give you time to move the databases to a larger disk or install a larger disk and move them in a planned, thoughtful manner. Reacting to problems after they occur is called putting out a fire. Preventing a problem from occurring is called good administration. Monitoring will help you with good administration.

Be sure that you spend time with your manager and other team members mapping out monitoring policies. Then implement them after they have been approved. Often, such policies will result in better management of your system and will help you avoid having to put out fires.

Microsoft Operations Manager

New to the suite of server products from Microsoft is Microsoft Operations Manager. MOM offers capabilities not previously found in the base operating systems:

- Support for monitoring of your Windows 2000 systems enterprise-wide from a single console
- Centralized collection of event data
- Event-driven alerts
- Modeling and trends development based on past experience
- Generation of management reports based on a criteria mix you select

MOM supports both Windows NT 4.0 and Windows 2000 servers. Microsoft is committed to ensuring that as new server products ship, there will be a corresponding management pack or set of counters that will integrate the MOM capabilities with each new product. The ability to monitor and manage an enterprise-wide set of servers from a single console is one of the key selling features of this new product.

MOM also contains built-in timescales, allowing you to meet any Service Level Agreements (SLAs) you might have with the departments you support. When problems are detected and reported, MOM contains numerous links to Knowledge Base articles on Microsoft's Web site to help you troubleshoot and solve the problem.

MOM can be installed on more than one server to provide fault tolerance and redundancy in the event one MOM server becomes disabled. When you're tracking events and trends, this is a business imperative.

There is no management pack for SPS at the time of this writing. However, I want to mention MOM so that you'll know to keep an eye out for the SPS management pack and use it to help monitor all the SharePoint servers in your organization.

Overseeing Overall Server Health

This section doesn't go over how the System Monitor tool works. (If you need help with this, please read the relevant sections in the Windows 2000 Resource Kit.) Instead, this section outlines various mixes of counters that will give you a starting point in getting to know about your server's health. A good understanding of SharePoint's architecture will aid in your understanding of how to monitor this system. If you haven't read Chapter 2, it's a good idea to go back and read it first.

It seems to me that one big reason most administrators don't do much monitoring is that they don't understand what each counter means and how it relates to the larger operating system. This betrays a lack of understanding of how the pieces of the OS architecture work together to produce the functionality of a program.

If you can understand a program's architecture, you're more likely to use monitoring tools to learn about the current functioning of each part of the program. Hence, this chapter is structured around the SPS architecture described in Chapter 2. Figure 12–1 gives you another look at the SPS architecture.

Before we discuss monitoring each part of SPS, let me make some general comments about overall monitoring. Which counters can give you an overall

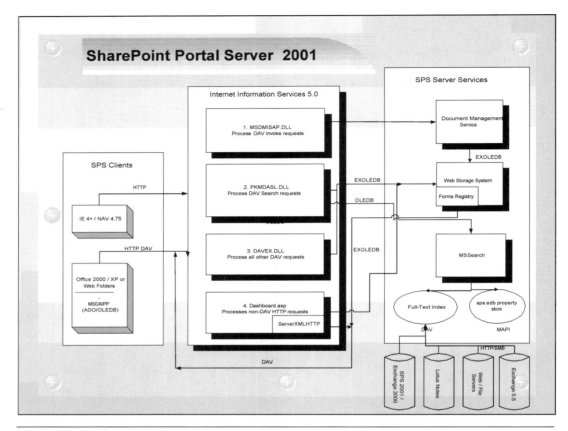

Figure 12–1 SharePoint Portal Server architecture

sense about how SPS is functioning? To get a "big picture" view of your server's overall health, consider these counters to be an excellent method of gaining baseline data:

- Processor—% Processor Time
- Memory—% Committed Bytes in Use
- Active Server Pages—ASP Request Execution Time
- Active Server Pages—ASP Request Wait Time
- Active Server Pages—ASP Requests Queued
- Microsoft Gatherer—Documents Filtered
- Microsoft Gatherer—Documents Successfully Filtered (if there is a large difference between this counter and the Documents Filtered counter, use the gatherer logs to discern why so many documents are attempting to be filtered but are failing)

- Microsoft Gatherer—Documents Delayed Retry
- Microsoft Gatherer—Reasons to Back Off
- Microsoft Gatherer—Server Objects
- Microsoft Gatherer—Time-outs
- Microsoft Gatherer—Adaptive Crawl Accepts
- Microsoft Gatherer—Adaptive Crawl Errors
- Microsoft Gatherer—Adaptive Crawl Error Samples
- Microsoft Gatherer—Adaptive Crawl Excludes
- Microsoft Gatherer—Adaptive Crawl False Positives
- Microsoft Gatherer—Adaptive Crawl Total
- Microsoft Gatherer Projects—Crawls in Progress
- Microsoft Gatherer Projects—Status Success
- Microsoft Gatherer Projects—Status Error
- Microsoft Gatherer Projects—URLs in History (remember that every URL that is crawled is recorded in the gatherer log and is referenced again when the next crawl begins)
- Microsoft Gatherer Projects—Waiting Documents
- Microsoft Search—Failed Queries
- Microsoft Search—Successful Queries
- Microsoft Search Indexer Catalogs—Merge Process 0–100%
- Microsoft Search Indexer Catalogs—Number of Documents
- Microsoft Search Indexer Catalogs—Index Size

The Processor—% Processor Time counter measures how much time, expressed as a percentage, your processor is busy executing non-idle threads. When not busy, the system will give your processor a thread to loop through that is considered an idle thread. When a thread of code needs to be executed, this idle thread is replaced with an active (non-idle) thread and is executed. Figure 12–2 shows how busy one processor was on a server that was accepting documents into a workspace. Over a period of 40 hours in which text files were being continually added to the workspace (less than half the total time it took), the average use of the processor was only 14.8%. Incidentally, the test machine has a Pentium III processor, 733MHz, with 512MB of RAM.

The Memory—% Committed Bytes is a ratio of two other counters: Memory—Committed Bytes and Memory—Commit Limit. *Committed* memory is the physical memory in use for which space has been reserved in the paging file should that memory ever need to be written to disk. The *commit limit* is determined by the size of the paging file and can be increased only by increasing the size of the paging file. Hence, a value of 50 for the Memory—% Committed Bytes counter would mean that of the amount of memory in the paging file that is reserved for data held in RAM, 50% has been used relative to the total

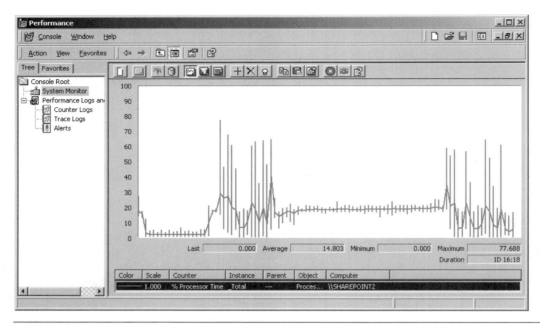

Figure 12–2 Processor activity while copying files to a workspace

amount that is allowed in the page file, as defined by the commit limit. You can see in Figure 12–3 that while files were being copied to the test server, an average of 41.1% of the space allocated to the paging file for data held in RAM was in use.

The Active Server Pages—ASP Request Execution Time counter measures, in milliseconds, how long it took to service the most recent request. This is not an average, but only a measure of the execution time of the last request. Similarly, the Request Wait Time and the Requests Queued counters measure only the most recent transaction, not an overall average. The Request Wait Time counter measures, in milliseconds, how long the most recent request had to sit in the queue before being processed. The Requests Queued counter reports how many requests at any given time are sitting in the queue, waiting to be processed.

When monitored in real time, these three counters can be used in the Alert mode to help you understand when your processor is beginning to be overloaded. If these counters become high (when measured against your baseline), you should see whether a faster or second processor is in order.

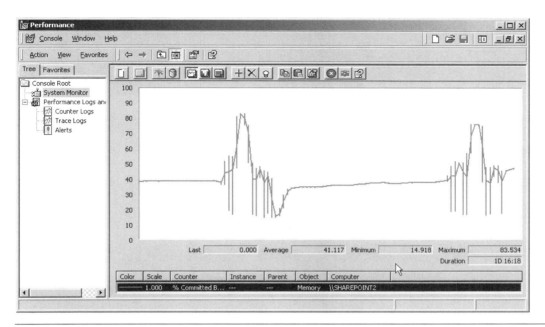

Figure 12–3 Committed bytes in use in the `pagefile.sys` file

Monitoring the Major Processes of SharePoint Portal Server

This section uses the architecture of SPS to discuss the various objects and counters. I've divided this section into two parts: SPS server services and Internet Information Services (IIS). Each section outlines the counters that are available for monitoring. Let's start by looking at the portal services, then the client services, and then IIS services.

From an overall perspective, here are the objects and the parts of the architecture that they monitor:

- SharePoint Portal Server Document Management Server, `msdmserv.exe`: provides counters for all document management functions, such as check-in, check-out, publishing, and approving
- SharePoint Portal Server Subscriptions: works with `mssearch.exe` to provide counters on all subscription activities through the persistent query service (PQS) plug-in

- Microsoft Gatherer: provides counters that monitor the activities of the gatherer process when crawling local documents and can report IFilter and protocol handler errors
- Microsoft Gatherer Projects: provides counters that monitor the activities of the gatherer process when crawling external documents and can report IFilter and protocol handler errors
- Microsoft Search: provides counters for search activities
- Microsoft Search Catalogs: provides counters for the search catalogs
- Microsoft Search Indexer Catalogs: provides counters for the indexer catalogs
- MSExchange OLEDB Resource: Provides counters for measuring interactions of other processes with the Web Storage System; does not provide an exhaustive range of counters that tell you how the Web store is functioning
- MSExchange OLEDB Events: provides counters of OLEDB-specific events
- MSExchange Web Mail: installs with the WSS but is not relevant to SPS

SharePoint Portal Server Services

This section describes three main services that you might want to monitor: the document management (DM) services, the Web Storage System (WSS), and the Search service (MSSearch).

Monitoring Document Management Functions

When you monitor DM functions, there are a few counters that you may want to pay attention to. For every counter, there is also a latency counter that measures the time required to perform the operation. Hence, you should be sure to monitor the latency counters: Successful Checkins Latency, Successful Checkouts Latency, and so forth. These counters give you, in milliseconds, how long it is taking to perform a function.

For instance, in my system I checked in 1,200 documents and marked them to be published at the same time. I found that it took, on average, only 85 milliseconds to check in and another 126 milliseconds to publish each document. These numbers came from the latency counters. Another latency counter told me I'd been waiting a bit longer to enumerate the document folder hierarchy using the Web folders client. As you can see in Figure 12–4, during this little test, it took, on average, more than 64,000 milliseconds to bring up the document folder list. That list has more than 5,000 folders, and it really did take longer than usual to bring up the folder list.

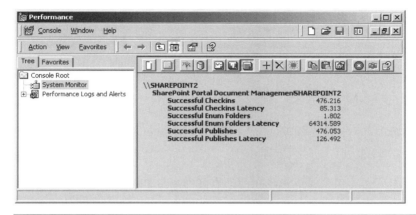

Figure 12–4 Document management counters in Report view

When you compare these numbers against a baseline, they can be very helpful in determining whether your SPS server can handle an increase in the number of users (and stress). Building a baseline of numbers when your server is functioning well gives you a standard against which to track trends and make predictions.

Also pay attention to the number of failed DM actions. These numbers are reported on an average basis. A marked increase in numbers after you add new users to a workspace might indicate the need for additional training for those who use the DM functions. A steadily increasing set of numbers without a corresponding increase in the number of users accessing the server might indicate that other processes are becoming bottlenecks and are not allowing DM functions to finish. Be sure to monitor the processor, disk, memory, and network subsystems to ensure that your server can handle the load being placed on it by users.

Table 12–1 shows all the DM counters, as taken from System Monitor.

Table 12–1 Document management counters

Counter	Description
Failed Approves	Total number of failed approve requests
Failed Approves Latency	Average latency at which failed approve requests are processed
Failed Checkins	Total number of failed check-in requests
Failed Checkins Latency	Average latency at which failed check-in requests are processed
Failed Checkouts	Total number of failed check-out requests
Failed Checkouts Latency	Average latency at which failed check-out requests are processed

Table 12–1 Document management counters *(continued)*

Counter	Description
Failed Copies	Total number of failed copy requests
Failed Copies Latency	Average latency at which failed copy requests are processed
Failed Deletes	Total number of failed delete requests
Failed Deletes Latency	Average latency at which failed delete requests are processed
Failed Enum Folders	Total number of failed enumerate folders requests
Failed Enum Folders Latency	Average latency at which failed enumerate folders requests are processed
Failed Moves	Total number of failed move requests
Failed Moves Latency	Average latency at which failed move requests are processed
Failed Publishes	Total number of failed publish requests
Failed Publishes Latency	Average latency at which failed publish requests are processed
Failed Rejects	Total number of failed reject requests
Failed Rejects Latency	Average latency at which failed reject requests are processed
Failed Undo Checkouts	Total number of failed undo check-out requests
Failed Undo Checkouts Latency	Average latency at which failed undo check-out requests are processed
Failed Version Histories	Total number of failed version history requests
Failed Version Histories Latency	Average latency at which failed version history requests are processed
Successful Approves	Total number of successful approve requests
Successful Approves Latency	Average latency at which successful approve requests are processed
Successful Checkins	Total number of successful check-in requests
Successful Checkins Latency	Average latency at which successful check-in requests are processed
Successful Checkouts	Total number of successful check-out requests
Successful Checkouts Latency	Average latency at which successful check-out requests are processed
Successful Copies	Total number of successful copy requests
Successful Copies Latency	Average latency at which successful copy requests are processed
Successful Deletes	Total number of successful delete requests
Successful Deletes Latency	Average latency at which successful delete requests are processed
Successful Enum Folders	Total number of successful enumerate folders requests
Successful Enum Folders Latency	Average latency at which successful enumerate folders requests are processed
Successful Moves	Total number of successful move requests
Successful Moves Latency	Average latency at which successful move requests are processed
Successful Publishes	Total number of successful publish requests

Table 12–1 Document management counters *(continued)*

Counter	Description
Successful Publishes Latency	Average latency at which successful publish requests are processed
Successful Rejects	Total number of successful reject requests
Successful Rejects Latency	Average latency at which successful reject requests are processed
Successful Undo Checkouts	Total number of successful undo check-out requests
Successful Undo Checkouts Latency	Average latency at which successful undo check-out requests are processed
Successful Version Histories	Total number of successful version history requests
Successful Version Histories Latency	Average latency at which successful version history requests are processed

Monitoring Search: The Gatherer and Indexing Processes

Several objects relate to the indexing and search processes: SharePoint Portal Server Subscriptions, Microsoft Search, Microsoft Search Catalogs, Microsoft Search Indexer Catalogs, Microsoft Gatherer, and Microsoft Gatherer Projects. The Microsoft Search Indexer Catalogs object can be measured on each workspace that has been created on the SharePoint server, or it can be measured on all the workspaces as a unit. If you're interested in learning about the indexer catalogs for a specific workspace, be sure to measure only that workspace by selecting the Select Instances from List radio button and highlighting the desired workspace.

When monitoring the gatherer and indexing processes, you may want to know about specific items, such as the following:

- If you need to know how many documents the gatherer crawled but did not include in the index, use the Microsoft Gatherer Projects—Status Error counter.
- To see how fast notifications are being generated, use the Microsoft Gatherer—Notifications Rate counter.
- To see how many crawls are in progress simultaneously, use the Microsoft Gatherer Projects—Crawls in Progress counter.
- To find out how many documents are in the index, use the Microsoft Search Indexer Catalogs—Number of Documents counter.

A couple of counters deserve a quick mention here. You might want to place these counters in an Alert view in case you find yourself needing to know immediately when a crawl process is not working.

Robots.txt

Whenever the gatherer attempts to crawl a Web site, it first looks for a file on the site called robots.txt. An example is found at www.archive.org, a Web site dedicated to archiving the Internet. In some searches on that site, you'll find references to further crawling being blocked by the site's robots.txt file. Other examples are the major search engines, such as www.altavista.com, www.yahoo.com, and www.google.com. You can monitor how many robot.txt files have been accessed by the gatherer process by monitoring the Microsoft Gatherer—Access robots.txt File counter.

The robots.txt file lists the portions of the Web site that are restricted and specifies whether there are any restricted crawlers. The robots.txt file should be found in the directory that is considered the home directory of the site. By default, Internet Information Services does not install this file, nor does SPS. However, you can create your own file if needed by using Notepad. After the file is created, SPS will refer to it once each 24-hour period, based on the last time the Search service was started. If you make changes to the file and want those changes effective immediately, you must restart the Search services.

If you like, you can have a robot.txt file generated for you automatically at various Web sites, such as http://www.rietta.com/robogen/index.shtml.

Sample text entered into a robot.txt file might look like this:

```
User-agent: InfoSeek Sidewinder/1.0
Disallow: /directory1/
Nofollow: /directory2/subdirectory
```

If you like, you can use FOLLOW/NOFOLLOW and INDEX/NOINDEX in the HTML meta tags of an HTML document. For example, you can mark a document with the following:

```
<META name="robotname" content="NOINDEX/NOFOLLOW">
```

This type of meta tag instructs the robot not to index the document and not to follow any of the links on the page.

For more information, see Q217103 in the Microsoft Knowledge Base.

First, the Delayed Documents counter indicates the number of documents that are waiting to be crawled based on the site hit frequency rules. If you have a plethora of rules and this number is steadily increasing over time, consider relaxing or simplifying your site hit frequency rules. A very high number may indicate a conflict in the rules that the gatherer cannot resolve or follow with efficiency.

Second, the Documents Filtered Rate counter indicates the number of documents that were filtered on a per-second basis and is expressed as an average (Figure 12–5). If this rate is decreasing over time, you should perform some troubleshooting to find out why your server is not filtering documents as quickly as it did in the past. Look for memory issues, processor issues, network issues, or site hit frequency rules that slow the gatherer process.

The Documents Delayed Retry counter indicates whether the target server's Web Storage System is shut down. If the value for this counter is greater than 0, you can assume that the WSS is shut down and that the crawl should be performed later.

The Filter Process Created counter indicates the number of times a filter process was either created or started. A very high number can indicate a problem in crawling one or more content sources. If this number is high, troubleshoot your IFilters and perhaps your protocol handlers.

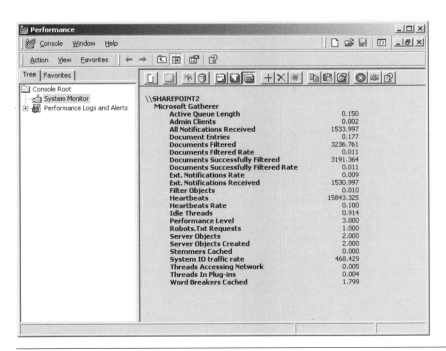

Figure 12–5 Gatherer counters displayed in the Report view

Sometimes, the gatherer process will *back off*, and the reasons for this action are expressed in a numeric value. The values correspond to the following meanings:

- 0: The gatherer service is up and running.
- 1: There is high system I/O traffic on the target server.
- 2: There is a high notifications rate.
- 3: Delayed recovery is in progress.
- 4: Back-off is due to a user-initiated command.
- 5: There exists a low-battery situation.
- 6: Memory is low.
- 99: Undefined reason generated by the search process.

During a back-off period, indexing is suspended. To manually back off the gatherer service, pause the search service. If the search service itself generates the back-off, an event will be recorded and the search service will be paused automatically. There is no automatic restart, so you must manually start the search service in order to end a back-off state. Note that there is little reason to start the search service until you've solved the problem that caused the back-off in the first place.

The counters beneath the Microsoft Gatherer Projects object focus on crawling documents that exist in a file system or Web site. Be sure to pay close attention to one or more of these counters. I discuss some of the more important ones here.

The Adaptive Crawl False Positives counter indicates the number of times the adaptive update has predicted that a document has changed when it has not.

The Retries counter indicates the number of times that access to a document has been retried. A high number means that the gatherer is attempting to access a document numerous times, without success. You should check the gatherer logs and identify the problem document. Then ensure that it has the correct extension and that you have the correct IFilter for it.

The Threads Accessing Network counter measures the number of threads that are waiting for a response from the filter process. If you don't see any activity, this counter equals the number of filtering threads; this number may indicate a network problem or unavailability of the server being crawled.

These are only some of the counters associated with the search and indexing functions. I focus on the gatherer counters because I believe that if you experience a problem indexing a document, most likely it will fail during the gatherer phase. Best practice, when monitoring your server, is to monitor all the counters for a given object so that you can perform a complete analysis of the server after the data is gathered. Remember that with Performance Monitor, you don't need to store the log file locally; it can be created and built on a remote server. Please consult the Windows 2000 Resource Kit for more information about this.

When you're working with the SharePoint Portal Server subscriptions counters, there are two that you might want to monitor if users are complaining that they are not being notified in a timely manner of document changes. The Total Hits Received and Total Notifications Sent counters will help you to understand how many notifications are being generated and how many should have been generated. For instance, if you have a high number of hits but a low number of notifications sent, it means that you have a problem with one or more of your plug-ins. However, if the number of hits and the number of notifications sent are close to the same, you can be assured that your SharePoint server is sending notifications for the hits that it has received.

Another possibility is that your Exchange 2000 Server (I'm making an assumption here) cannot handle all the notification e-mails. In other words, SPS is generating the notifications, but there is a bottleneck in your mail delivery system that is either stopping or hindering e-mails to users. Be sure to look at this part of the e-mail delivery system, too.

Table 12–2 shows all the subscriptions counters.

Table 12–2 SPS subscriptions counters

Counter	Description
Errors Access Denied	Total number of access-denied errors received during access check
Total Access Checks	Total number of access checks that the subscriptions engine does
Total Discarded Hits	Total number of hits that the subscriptions engine discards
Total Documents Processed	Total number of documents that the subscriptions engine processes
Total Documents Processed/sec.	Rate at which the subscriptions engine processes documents
Total Duplicate Hits	Total number of duplicate hits that the subscriptions engine processes
Total Full Access Checks	Total number of access checks done by contacting the domain controller
Total Hits Received	Total number of hits that the subscriptions engine processes
Total Hits Received/sec.	Rate at which the subscriptions engine receives hits
Total Notifications Sent	Total number of e-mail subscription notifications that the system sends
Total Notifications Sent/sec.	Rate at which the subscriptions engine sends e-mail notifications
Total Subscriptions	Total number of subscriptions defined in the system

Now let's look at the search counters. You may want to monitor three counters in tandem: Current Connections, Failed Query Rate, and Succeeded Query Rate. Why? One reason is to see whether your user training has done any good. For instance, you can monitor these counters before training commences and after it has terminated. In theory, you should see a rise in the Current Connections counter because after training, people will be more likely to use this service. In addition, you should see a drop in the Failed Query Rate because training should teach them how to use the Search Web part more effectively. And finally, you should see a rise in the Succeeded Query Rate for the same reason: After training, people should understand how to use the Web part and should be more successful at finding documents.

If your training was effective, the Failed Query Rate should decline *even though the Current Connections rate is on the rise*.

A second way to use these counters is to monitor the Query Rate counter. If this counter is increasing over time, you may need to set a benchmark that you and your manager agree on that will indicate when it's time to dedicate a server to search queries. Also take into account other measurements—on the disk, processor, and memory subsystems—but be sure to include this rate when considering this question.

Table 12–3 shows the search counters.

Table 12–4 shows the search catalogs counters. One counter to watch here is the Catalog Size counter. Be sure you've placed your catalogs on a disk that

Table 12–3 SPS search counters

Counter	Description
Active Threads	Total number of threads currently servicing queries
Current Connections	Number of currently established connections between MSSearch and all clients
Failed Queries	Number of queries that fail
Failed Query Rate	Number of failed queries per second
Queries	Cumulative number of queries posted to the server
Query Rate	Number of queries posted to the server per second
Result Rate	Number of results returned to the client per second
Results	Cumulative number of results returned to clients
Succeeded Queries	Number of queries that produce successful searches
Succeeded Query Rate	Number of queries per second that produce successful searches
Threads	Total number of threads available for servicing queries

Table 12–4 SPS search catalogs counters

Counter	Description
Catalog Size (MB)	Size of catalog data in megabytes
Failed Queries	Number of queries that fail
Failed Queries Rate	Number of failed queries per second
Number Of Documents	Total number of documents in the catalog
Persistent Indexes	Number of persistent indexes
Queries	Cumulative number of queries posted to the catalog
Queries Rate	Number of queries posted to the catalog per second
Results	Cumulative number of results returned to clients
Results Rate	Number of results returned to the client per second
Successful Queries	Number of queries that produce successful searches
Successful Queries Rate	Number of queries per second that produce successful searches
Unique Keys	Number of unique words and properties in the catalog

can hold them going forward. Also, if you monitor this counter over time, you can get a sense of how long you have before the disk will run out of free disk space.

Use the search indexer catalogs counters shown in Table 12–5 to help you set benchmarks as to when you should initiate a full indexing procedure to clear out shadow indexes and any newly created word lists. You might also use

Table 12–5 SPS search indexer catalogs counters

Counter	Description
Active Documents	Number of documents currently active in content index
Build In Progress	Indicator that an index build is in progress
Documents Filtered	Number of documents filtered since the catalog was mounted
Documents In Progress	Number of documents for which data is being added
Files To Be Filtered	Number of files waiting to be filtered and added to the catalog
Index Size (MB)	Current size of index data in megabytes
Merge Progress	Percentage of merge complete for the current merge
Number Of Documents	Number of documents in the catalog
Number Of Propagations	Number of propagations in progress
Persistent Indexes	Number of persistent indexes
Unique Keys	Number of unique words and properties in the catalog
Wordlists	Total number of word lists

the Files To Be Filtered counter to track trends over time to see whether your content sources are growing to the point where a dedicated indexing server is necessary. Most likely, this would be indicated by the indexing process taking more and more time. If this is the case, you should see a commensurate rise in the Active Documents, Index Size, Number Of Documents, and Unique Keys counters. If all these numbers are steadily increasing, you may reach the point where a dedicated indexing server would be a good idea. Discuss this with your manager, and set benchmarks where appropriate.

In the gatherer counters (Table 12–6), you might want to pay attention to the Documents Delayed Retry counter. If this counter is substantially higher than your baseline and you've just added a content source, you should check the gatherer logs on the content source to identify the errors. This number, if anything, should not be rising if each content source is configured correctly.

Table 12–6 SPS gatherer counters

Counter	Description
Accessing Robots.txt File	Number of current requests for robots.txt, which is requested by the system implicitly, for every host, through HTTP
Active Queue Length	Number of documents waiting for robot threads; if not 0, all threads should be filtering
Admin Clients	Number of currently connected administrative clients
All Notifications Received	Total number of notifications received from all notification sources, including file system
Delayed Documents	Number of documents delayed due to site hit frequency rules
Document Entries	Number of document entries currently in memory
Documents Delayed Retry	Number of documents that are retried after time-out
Documents Filtered	Number of times a filter object was created; corresponds to the total number of documents filtered in the system since startup
Documents Filtered Rate	Number of documents filtered per second
Documents Successfully Filtered	Number of documents successfully filtered
Documents Successfully Filtered Rate	Number of documents successfully filtered per second
Ext. Notifications Rate	External notifications received per second
Ext. Notifications Received	Total number of notifications received from all notification sources, excluding file system
Filter Objects	Number of filter objects (each corresponding to a URL) currently being filtered in the system

Table 12–6 SPS gatherer counters *(continued)*

Counter	Description
Filter Process Created	Total number of times a filter process was created or restarted
Filter Processes	Number of filtering processes in the system
Filter Processes Max	Maximum number of filtering processes that have existed in the system since startup
Filtering Threads	Total number of filtering threads in the system
Heartbeats	Total number of heartbeats counted since startup; a heartbeat occurs once every 10 seconds while the service is running; if the service is not running, there is no heartbeat and the number of ticks is not incremented
Heartbeats Rate	One heartbeat displayed every 10 seconds
Idle Threads	Number of threads waiting for documents
Notification Sources	Currently connected external notification sources
Notifications Rate	Notifications received per second
Performance Level	Level of the amount of system resources that the gatherer service is allowed to use
Reason to back off	Code describing why the gatherer service went into back-off state
Robots.Txt Requests	Total number of requests for `robots.txt`
Server Objects	Number of servers that the system recently accessed
Server Objects Created	Number of times a new server object needed to be created
Servers Currently Unavailable	The servers unavailable because a number of requests to that server are timed out
Servers Unavailable	The servers unavailable because a number of requests to that server are timed out
Stemmers Cached	Number of available cached stemmer instances
System I/O Traffic Rate	System I/O (disk) traffic rate in kilobytes per second (KBps) detected by back-off logic
Threads Accessing Network	Number of threads waiting for a response from the filter process
Threads blocked due to back off	Number of threads blocked due to back-off event
Threads In Plug-ins	Number of threads waiting for plug-ins to complete an operation
Time-Outs	Total number of time-outs that the system has detected since startup
Wordbreakers Cached	Number of available cached instances of wordbreakers

One way to know when the crawling has stopped is to use the "in progress" counters outlined in Table 12–7. When their numbers return to 0, you can be assured that the crawling process has ended. If you need to know when the crawling process has ended in real time, consider using the alert monitoring method to generate a notification about this. To learn how to create and use alerts in System Monitor, please consult the Windows 2000 Server Resource Kit.

Table 12–7 SPS gatherer projects counters

Counter	Description
Accessed File Rate	Number of documents accessed through the file system per second
Accessed Files	Number of documents accessed through the file system
Accessed HTTP	Number of documents accessed through HTTP
Accessed HTTP Rate	Number of documents accessed through HTTP per second
Adaptive Crawl Accepts	Documents accepted by adaptive crawl
Adaptive Crawl Error Samples	Documents accessed for error sampling
Adaptive Crawl Errors	Documents incorrectly rejected by adaptive crawl
Adaptive Crawl Excludes	Documents excluded by adaptive crawl
Adaptive Crawl False Positives	Documents incorrectly accepted by adaptive crawl
Adaptive Crawl Total	Documents to which adaptive update logic was applied
Changed Documents	Documents that have changed since the last crawl
Crawls In Progress	Number of crawls in progress
Delayed Documents	Number of documents delayed due to site hit frequency rules
Document Add Rate	Number of document additions per second
Document Additions	Number of add notifications
Document Delete Rate	Number of document deletions per second
Document Deletes	Number of delete notifications
Document Modifies	Number of modify notifications
Document Modifies Rate	Number of modify notifications per second
Document Move and Rename Rate	Number of document moves and renames per second
Document Moves/Renames	Number of notifications of document moves and renames
Documents In Progress	Number of documents in progress
Documents On Hold	Number of documents on hold because a document with the same URL is currently being processed
Error Rate	Number of filtered documents that returned an error per second
File Errors	Number of file protocol errors received while getting documents
File Errors Rate	Number of file protocol errors received per second

Table 12–7 SPS gatherer projects counters *(continued)*

Counter	Description
Filtered HTML	Number of HTML documents filtered
Filtered HTML Rate	Number of HTML documents filtered per second
Filtered Office	Number of Office documents filtered
Filtered Office Rate	Number of Office documents filtered per second
Filtered Text	Number of text documents filtered
Filtered Text Rate	Number of text documents filtered per second
Filtering Documents	Number of documents currently being filtered
Gatherer Paused Flag	Indicator that the gatherer has been paused
History Recovery Process	Percentage of the history recovery completed
HTTP Errors	Number of HTTP errors received
HTTP Errors Rate	Number of HTTP errors received per second
Incremental Crawls	Number of incremental crawls in progress
Iterating History In Progress Flag	Indicator of whether the gatherer is currently iterating over the URL history
Not Modified	Number of documents that were not filtered because no modification was detected since the last crawl
Processed Documents	Number of documents processed since the history was reset
Processed Documents Rate	Number of documents processed per second
Recovery In Progress Flag	Indicator that recovery is currently in progress; indexing is not resumed until this flag is off
Retries	Total number of times access to a document has been retried; high number may indicate a problem with accessing the data
Retries Rate	Number of retries per second
Started Documents	Number of documents initiated into the gatherer service, including the number of documents on hold, in the active queue, and currently filtered; when this number goes to 0 during a crawl, the crawl will be completed soon
Status Error	Number of filtered documents that returned an error
Status Success	Number of successfully filtered documents
Success Rate	Number of successfully filtered documents per second
Unique Documents	Number of unique documents in the system; documents are considered not unique if their content is the same
URLs in History	Number of files (URLs) in the history list, indicating the total number of URLs covered by the crawl, either successfully indexed or failed
Waiting Documents	Number of documents waiting to be processed; when this number goes to 0, the catalog is idle; indicates the total queue size of unprocessed documents in the gatherer

Monitoring the Web Storage System

You may want to monitor the Web Storage System. Because the WSS is the foundation database for SPS, it stands to reason that you'll want to pay attention to this database. The object that you'll want to monitor—the MSExchange OLEDB resource object—contains counters for monitoring the number and rate of transactions that are committed to the WSS.

Because control is returned to the user only when a transaction has been committed, you should pay attention to two counters: Transactions Started Rate and Transactions Committed Rate. Both measurements occur once per second. Hence, if 40 transactions were starting their commitment during a given second, most if not all should be committed during the ensuing few seconds. Make sure that the started rate and the committed rate are roughly equal. If the transactions started rate greatly exceeds the transactions committed rate, it means that you are having problems with the creation of your transaction logs or the commitment of data to the logs after they are written. Any of the following causes, or a combination, may be to blame:

- Slow hard drive
- Not enough memory
- System can't create log files fast enough
- Slow processor
- Poorly configured Web server (see Chapter 4 on optimizing IIS services)

Table 12–8 shows the MSExchange OLEDB resource counters, and Table 12–9 shows the MSExchange OLEDB events counters.

Table 12–8 MSExchange OLEDB resource counters

Counter	Description
Active Commands	Number of Command objects that are currently active
Active DataSources	Number of DataSource objects that are currently active
Active Rows	Number of Row objects that are currently active
Active Rowsets	Number of Rowset objects that are currently active
Active Sessions	Number of Session objects that are currently active
Active Streams	Number of Stream objects that are currently active
Resource Bindings Rate	Number of successful resource bindings per second
Resource Bindings Total	Total number of successful resource bindings
Rowsets Opened Rate	Number of times that rowsets are opened per second

Table 12–8 MSExchange OLEDB resource counters *(continued)*

Counter	Description
Rowsets Opened Total	Total number of times that rowsets have been opened
Transactions Aborted Rate	Number of transactions aborted successfully per second
Transactions Aborted Total	Total number of transactions that have been successfully aborted
Transactions Committed Rate	Number of transactions committed successfully per second
Transactions Committed Total	Total number of transactions that have been successfully committed
Transactions Started Rate	Number of transactions started per second
Transactions Started Total	Total number of transactions that have been started

Table 12–9 MSExchange OLEDB events counters

Counter	Description
Events Completion Rate	Number of events completed per second
Events Completion Total	Total number of events that have been completed
Events Submission Rate	Number of events submitted per second
Events Submission Total	Total number of events that have been submitted

Internet Information Services

There are three main counters to use when monitoring IIS. First is the Internet Information Services Global object. This object contains the counters that report on bandwidth throttling and the *object cache*, a cache in memory shared by the IIS services. *Bandwidth throttling* is a technique used to keep IIS from using more bandwidth than is specified by the IIS administrator. If the bandwidth used by the IIS services approaches or exceeds this limit, bandwidth throttling delays or rejects IIS service requests until more bandwidth becomes available.

NOTE: The object cache retains in memory frequently used objects. Repeated retrieval of the same objects could slow IIS considerably, so these objects are cached after they are retrieved for the first time. The object cache counters provide insight into the size and content of the IIS object cache as well as its effectiveness, such as cache hits and misses.

The Web service object counters show data about the anonymous and authenticated connections to IIS. This object focuses on the HTTP protocol. It also monitors calls to Common Gateway Interface (CGI) applications and Internet Server Application Programming Interface (ISAPI) extensions. The Active Server Pages object provides counters for monitoring applications running on your Web server that use Active Server Pages.

Tables 12–10, 12–11, and 12–12 show the counters and their explanations for these three objects.

Table 12–10 Active Server Pages counters

Counter	Description
Debugging Requests	Number of debugging document requests
Errors During Script Runtime	Number of requests failed due to runtime errors
Errors from ASP Preprocessor	Number of requests failed due to preprocessor errors
Errors from Script Compilers	Number of requests failed due to script compilation errors
Errors/sec	The number of errors per second
Request Bytes In Total	The total size, in bytes, of all requests
Request Bytes Out Total	The total size, in bytes, of responses sent to clients, not including standard HTTP response headers
Request Execution Time	The number of milliseconds that it took to execute the most recent request
Request Wait Time	The number of milliseconds the most recent request was waiting in the queue
Requests Disconnected	The number of requests that were disconnected due to communication failure
Requests Executing	The number of requests currently executing
Requests Failed Total	The total number of requests failed due to errors, authorization failure, and rejections
Requests Not Authorized	Number of requests failed due to insufficient access rights
Requests Not Found	The number of requests for files that were not found
Requests Queued	The number of requests waiting for service from the queue
Requests Rejected	The total number of requests not executed because there were insufficient resources to process them
Requests Succeeded	The number of requests that executed successfully
Requests Timed Out	The number of requests that timed out
Requests Total	The total number of requests since the service was started
Requests/sec	The number of requests executed per second

Table 12–10 Active Server Pages counters *(continued)*

Counter	Description
Script Engines Cached	The number of script engines in cache
Session Duration	The number of milliseconds that the most recent sessions persisted
Sessions Current	The current number of sessions being serviced
Sessions Timed Out	The number of sessions timed out
Sessions Total	The total number of sessions since the service was started
Template Cache Hit Rate	Percent of requests found in template cache
Template Notifications	The number of templates invalidated in the cache due to change notification
Templates Cached	The number of templates currently cached
Transactions Aborted	The number of transactions aborted
Transactions Committed	The number of transactions committed
Transactions Pending	The number of transactions in progress
Transactions Total	The number of transactions since the service was started
Transactions/sec	Transactions started per second

Table 12–11 Internet Information Services global object

Counter	Description
Active Flushed Entries	Cached file handles that will be closed when all current transfers complete
BLOB Cache Flushes	Binary large object (BLOB) cache flushes since server startup
BLOB Cache Hits	Total number of successful lookups in the BLOB cache
BLOB Cache Hits %	The ratio of BLOB cache hits to total cache requests
BLOB Cache Misses	Total number of unsuccessful lookups in the BLOB cache
Current BLOBs Cached	BLOB information blocks currently in the cache for WWW and FTP services
Current Blocked Async I/O Requests	Current requests temporarily blocked due to bandwidth throttling settings
Current File Cache Memory Usage	Current number of bytes used for file cache
Current Files Cached	Current number of files whose content is in the cache for WWW and FTP services
Current URLs Cached	URL information blocks currently in the cache for WWW and FTP services
File Cache Flushes	File cache flushes since server startup
File Cache Hits	Total number of successful lookups in the file cache
File Cache Hits %	The ratio of file cache hits to total cache requests

Table 12–11 Internet Information Services global object *(continued)*

Counter	Description
File Cache Misses	Total number of unsuccessful lookups in the file cache
Maximum File Cache Memory Usage	Maximum number of bytes used for file cache
Measured Async I/O Bandwidth Usage	Measured bandwidth of asynchronous I/O averaged over one minute
Total Allowed Async I/O Requests	Total requests allowed by bandwidth throttling settings (counted since service startup)
Total BLOBs Cached	Total number of BLOB information blocks ever added to the cache for WWW and FTP services
Total Blocked Async I/O Requests	Total requests temporarily blocked due to bandwidth throttling settings (counted since server startup)
Total Files Cached	Total number of files whose content was ever added to the cache for WWW and FTP services
Total Flushed BLOBs	The number of BLOB information blocks that have been removed from the cache since service startup
Total Flushed Files	The number of file handles that have been removed from the cache since service startup
Total Flushed URLs	The number of URL information blocks that have been removed from the cache since service startup
Total Rejected Async I/O Requests	Total requests rejected due to bandwidth throttling settings (counted since service startup)
Total URLs Cached	Total number of URL information blocks ever added to the cache for WWW and FTP services
URL Cache Flushes	URL cache flushes since service startup
URL Cache Hits	Total number of successful lookups in the URL cache
URL Cache Hits %	The ratio of URL cache hits to total cache requests
URL Cache Misses	Total number of unsuccessful lookups in the URL cache

Table 12–12 Web service counters

Counter	Description
Anonymous Users/sec	The rate users are making anonymous connections using the Web service
Bytes Received/sec	The rate that data bytes are received by the Web service
Bytes Sent/sec	The rate that data bytes are sent by the Web service
Bytes Total/sec	The sum of Bytes Sent/Sec and Bytes Received/Sec; the total rate of bytes transferred by the Web service

Table 12–12 Web service counters *(continued)*

Counter	Description
CGI Requests/sec	The rate at which CGI requests are simultaneously being processed by the Web service
Connection Attempts/sec	The rate at which connections using the Web service are being attempted
Copy Requests/sec	The rate at which HTTP requests using the `COPY` method (used for copying files and directories) are being made
Current Anonymous Users	The number of users who currently have an anonymous connection to the Web service
Current Blocked Async I/O Requests	Current requests temporarily blocked due to bandwidth throttling settings
Current CAL Count for Authentication	The current count of licenses used simultaneously by the Web service for authenticated users
Current CAL Count of SSL Connection	The current count of licenses used simultaneously by the Web service for SSL connections
Current CGI Requests	The current number of CGI requests that are simultaneously being processed by the Web service
Current Connections	The current number of connections established with the Web service
Current ISAPI Extension Requests	The current number of extension requests that are simultaneously being processed by the Web service
Current NonAnonymous Users	The number of users who currently have a non-anonymous connection using the Web service
Delete Requests/sec	The rate at which HTTP requests using the `DELETE` method (generally used for file removals) are made
Files Received/sec	Rate at which files are received by the Web service
Files Sent/sec	Rate at which files are sent by the Web service
Files/sec	Rate at which files are transferred, both sending and receiving, by the Web service
Get Requests/sec	The rate at which HTTP requests using the `GET` method (generally used for basic file retrievals or image maps, although can be used with forms) are made
Head Requests/sec	The rate at which HTTP requests using the `HEAD` method (generally indicates that a client is querying the state of an in-use document to see whether it needs to be refreshed) are made
ISAPI Extension Requests/sec	Rate at which ISAPI extension requests are simultaneously being processed by the Web service
Lock Requests/sec	The rate at which HTTP requests using the `LOCK` method are made
Locked Errors/sec	The rate of errors due to requests that couldn't be satisfied by the server because the requested document was locked; generally reported as an HTTP 423 error code to the client

Table 12–12 Web service counters *(continued)*

Counter	Description
Logon Attempts/sec	The rate at which logons using the Web service are being attempted
Maximum Anonymous Users	The number of users who established concurrent anonymous connections using the Web service since service startup
Maximum CAL Count for Authenticated Users	The maximum count of licenses used simultaneously by the Web service for authenticated connections
Maximum CAL Count for SSL Connections	The maximum count of licenses used simultaneously by the Web service for SSL connections
Maximum CGI Requests	The maximum number of CGI requests simultaneously processed by the Web service
Maximum Connections	The maximum number of simultaneous connections established with the Web service
Maximum ISAPI Extension Requests	Maximum number of extension requests simultaneously processed by the Web service
Maximum NonAnonymous Users	Maximum number of users who established concurrent non-anonymous connections using the Web service since service startup
Measured Async I/O Bandwidth Usage	Measured bandwidth of asynchronous I/O averaged over one minute
Mkcol Requests/sec	The rate at which HTTP requests using the MKCOL method (used to create directories on the server) are made
Move Requests/sec	The rate at which HTTP requests using the MOVE method (used for moving files and directories) are made
NonAnonymous Users/sec	The rate at which users are making non-anonymous connections using the Web service
Not Found Errors/sec	The rate of errors due to requests that couldn't be satisfied by the server because the requested document could not be found; generally reported as an HTTP 404 error code to the client
Options Requests/sec	The rate at which HTTP requests using the OPTIONS method are made
Other Requests Methods/sec	The rate at which HTTP requests are made that do not use the OPTIONS, GET, HEAD, POST, PUT, DELETE, TRACE, MOVE, COPY, MKCOL, PROPFIND, PROPPATCH, MS-SEARCH, LOCK, or UNLOCK method
Post Requests/sec	The rate at which HTTP requests using the POST method (used for forms and gateway requests) are made
Propfind Requests/sec	The rate at which HTTP requests using the PROPFIND method (used to retrieve property values on files and directories) are made
Proppatch Requests/sec	The rate at which HTTP requests using the PROPPATCH method (used to set property values on files and directories) are made
Put Requests/sec	The rate at which HTTP requests using the PUT method are made

Table 12–12 Web service counters *(continued)*

Counter	Description
Search Requests/sec	The rate at which HTTP requests using the `MS-SEARCH` method (used to query the server to find resources that match a set of conditions provided by the client) are made
Service Uptime	Uptime for W3CSVC Service or W3 sites
Total Allows Async I/O Requests	Total requests allowed by bandwidth throttling settings since service startup
Total Anonymous Users	Number of users who established an anonymous connection with the Web service since startup
Total Blocked Async I/O Requests	Total requests temporarily blocked due to bandwidth throttling settings since service startup
Total CGI Requests	Requests (since service startup) for custom gateway executables (`.exe`) that the administrator can install to add forms processing or other dynamic data sources; CGI requests spawn a process on the server, which can be a large drain on server resources
Total Connection Attempts (All Instances)	Number of connections that have been attempted using the Web service since startup; this counter is for all instances
Total Copy Requests	Number of HTTP requests using the `COPY` method (used for copying files and directories) since service startup
Total Count of Failed CAL Requests	Number of HTTP requests (total since startup) that failed due to a license being unavailable for an authenticated user
Total Count of Failed CAL Requests SSL	Number of HTTP requests (total since startup) that failed due to a license being unavailable for an authenticated users over SSL
Total Delete Requests	Number of HTTP requests using the `DELETE` method (generally used for file removals) since service startup
Total Files Received	Total number of files received by the Web service since service startup
Total Files Sent	Total number of files sent by the Web service since startup
Total Files Transferred	Total number of files sent and received by the Web service since service startup
Total Get Requests	The rate at which HTTP requests using the `GET` method (generally used for basic file retrievals or image maps, although they can be used with forms) are made since service startup
Total Head Requests	Total number of HTTP requests using the `HEAD` method since service startup
Total ISAPI Extension Requests	Total number of ISAPI extension requests since service startup
Total Lock Requests	Total number of `LOCK` requests since service startup
Total Locked Errors	Total number of requests for resources that were locked at the time of the request since service startup

Table 12-12 Web service counters *(continued)*

Counter	Description
Total Logon Attempts	Total number of logon attempts using the Web service since startup
Total Method Requests	Total number of all HTTP requests since service startup
Total Method Requests/sec	The rate at which all HTTP requests are made
Total Mkcol Requests	Total number of all MKCOL requests since service startup
Total Move Requests	Total number of all MOVE requests since service startup
Total NonAnonymous Users	Total number of all users who established a non-anonymous connection with the Web service since service startup
Total Not Found Errors	Total number of all requests (since service startup) that couldn't be satisfied because the server couldn't find the requested document; generally results in an HTTP 404 error code to the client
Total Options Requested	Total number of HTTP requests using the OPTIONS method since startup
Total Other Request Methods	Total number of HTTP requests that are not OPTIONS, GET, HEAD, POST, PUT, DELETE, TRACE, MOVE, COPY, MKCOL, PROPFIND, PROPPATCH, MS-SEARCH, LOCK, or UNLOCK methods since startup
Total Post Requests	Total number of HTTP requests using the POST method since startup
Total Propfind Requests	Total number of HTTP requests using the PROPFIND method since startup
Total Proppatch Requests	Total number of HTTP requests using the PROPPATCH method since startup
Total Put Requests	Total number of HTTP requests using the PUT method since startup
Total Rejected Async I/O Requests	Total requests rejected due to bandwidth throttling settings since service startup
Total Search Requests	Total number of HTTP requests using the SEARCH method since startup
Total Trace Requests	Total number of HTTP requests using the TRACE method since startup
Total Unlock Requests	Total number of HTTP requests using the UNLOCK method since startup
Trace Requests/sec	Rate of HTTP requests using the TRACE method (allows the client to see what is being received at the end of the request chain and use the information for diagnostic purposes)
Unlock Requests/sec	Rate of HTTP requests using the UNLOCK method (used to remove locks from files)

In Table 12–12, you should be using the Current CAL Count for Authentication counter to ensure that you have sufficient licenses purchased for your SPS server. Because this counter measures current, *simultaneous* connections—and not the total number of connections since service startup—it stands to reason that you need to purchase only the number of client CALs that is reflected in the highest number from this counter. Notice also that there is no counter that measures all the connections, since startup, that require a CAL, because the same user might connect many times and drive up this number artificially high. I highly recommend that you monitor this counter regularly to ensure that you have purchased enough licenses to be considered in compliance. Compare this number with the Current NonAnonymous Users counter, which measures the total number of non-anonymous users simultaneously using the Web service, a number that includes both WAN and LAN authenticated users. These two counters should be close.

Getting All Stressed Out with SharePoint Portal Server

The Microsoft Web Application Stress (WAS) tool, a free application available at `webtool.rte.microsoft.com`, lets you create or record a script that can be used to put stress on a SharePoint Portal Server by reproducing multiple Web requests to a single Web server. By realistically simulating multiple browser connections, you can gather performance and stability information about your SharePoint server. This information is invaluable in planning.

FOR MORE INFO: To learn more about capacity planning issues for SharePoint Portal Server, please see Chapter 4.

When you download the WAS tool from Microsoft's Web site, it is a single file named `setup.exe`. Copy this file to each client machine from which you want to run the test, and then double-click it to start the installation. Take the defaults in the setup wizard. Because you are stress-testing your SPS server, do not install WAS on your SharePoint server. Running this application on your SharePoint server against its own Web pages would skew the results because your SharePoint server would be busy executing the application as well as answering calls from the other client machines.

A sample script, creatively named `sample script`, is installed with WAS. You can use this script to acquaint yourself with the features of WAS.

To start WAS, click the menu selection under the Programs menu. The WAS program will start. In the left-hand window is a display of all the scripts stored in the current version of WAS. Out of the gate, you'll find the sample script and nothing else.

If you highlight the sample script, in the right pane you'll see a place to type the server's name, a description, and then the commands to be run along with the exact pages against which to run them. The WAS utility has a set of sample pages that you can copy to your default root location on the Web server. As a start, you can run this utility against the sample pages to get a sense of how it runs.

Each script item is built from an HTTP or HTTP DAV command. If you double-click a particular command, you'll be able to edit the query string name-value pairs, change POST data, modify the header, and enable Secure Sockets Layer.

This script also allows you to create the desired number of users and the number of concurrent threads your workstation will use to execute the threads. You also select the Performance Monitor counters to monitor. These can be monitored on any client running WAS, but you should monitor only on one because multiple monitoring places unnecessary stress on your SharePoint server. If you are going to run this script from one workstation, you must understand that the total number of users being simulated equals the number of threads multiplied by the stress multiplier. So if you put in 75 threads and use a multiplier of 3, you're simulating 225 concurrent connections to your Web server.

In the report, you'll see the Time To First Byte (TTFB), which calculates the time from the request for the page until WAS receives the first byte of data, in milliseconds. The Time To Last Byte (TTLB) calculates the total time from the request until the last byte of data has been received on the client, in milliseconds. The results are then divided into percentiles for further evaluation. The average should be around 50 percent.

When using WAS, remember the following:

- Try to keep your thread usage between 10 and 100 threads. Also, be sure to monitor the processor utilization on the clients. Ensure that it is sustained at less than 80 percent; otherwise, the test will be invalid.
- Use only one socket (stress multiplier) unless you are performing a special type of test. If you want to learn more, see the online Help topic "Stress level vs. stress multiplier."
- The greater the number of users in the test, the more time it will take to initialize the test. Keeping this number less than 1,000 will help the test run faster. This number, however, is limited only by the RAM in the workstation.

- Keep the number of scripts items to less than 1,000. RAM is an issue here, too.

Used correctly, WAS is a very cool tool. When you first run it, try to apply stress to the Web site and measure the maximum number of requests per second that the Web server can handle. Then increase the stress and begin to determine which resource prevents the Web server from handling more requests. Once you've figured out where this breaking point is on your server, you will have an idea as to the server's real capacity.

In some situations, you'll find that the processor is the bottleneck. To verify this, watch three counters: System—% Total Processor Time, Web Service: Connection Attempts/sec, and Active Server Pages—Requests Queued. If the processor is running at greater than 80 percent sustained, it is likely the bottleneck. If the Requests Queued increases after the processor hits a certain percentage, and memory is relatively low, this is the point at which the processor is entering into a bottleneck state and represents the best functioning of the server given its stress. If the Requests Queued counter fluctuates considerably during the test and if the processor utilization remains relatively low, it indicates that the script is calling a server COM component that is receiving more calls than it can handle. In this case, the server COM component is the bottleneck.

When you conduct this test and use bandwidth throttling, be sure to look at the Internet Information Services Global Object—Current Blocked Async I/O Requests counter. This counter indicates the number of current requests that are blocked due to bandwidth throttling. In a production environment, it would be a very good idea to set an alert on this counter so that you can know when your SPS server is being overworked for a sustained period of time.

WAS and SPS

So far, I've explained how to use this tool to test your Web site. But how do you test the unique functions of SPS in the site? You could hire a developer to write all the paths for you, or you could simply record a session, something that is much easier. When you record a session, you actually create a script that you can then run against the SPS virtual directory in IIS. The first step is to clean out the browser cache on your workstation. You must be using Internet Explorer 3.0 or later to make the recording work properly.

The second step is to set your browser's proxy settings to `localhost` with a port number of 8000. There's nothing magic about the 8000 port; it's just that it's easy to add two zeros to the port number 80 that already exists in your browser. If you don't use a proxy server, you can skip this step.

Third, in WAS, click the Scripts menu, point to Record, and then choose Create. This will invoke a two-screen wizard, which will ask you what you want to record. Make your selections, and then click Next and then Finish. When you click Finish, the browser will start, and you can type the SPS URL. Then perform the actions you wish to stress.

NOTE: Because the SPS Web sites are automatically secured using Windows Integrated Authentication (WIA), you must change the directory security settings to accept Anonymous only. The WAS will not work with the WIA methods when recording or running a script. Therefore, if you don't make this change, when recording the script, you'll be presented with an HTTP 402.1 "You are not authorized to view this page" error message. Changing the directory security settings on the SPS virtual directory and workspaces will allow you access to the Web pages during both the recording and the stress phases.

Figure 12–6 shows the output of a sample script I created using WAS. The important thing to remember when you use this tool is that if you want to stress a certain function in SPS, you must actually *perform* that function during the recording. For instance, if you want to stress the check-in of a document, you must actually check in a document during the recording phase. If you merely open a document in the browser, the counters in the Document Management object won't do you any good because you haven't actually performed a document check-in. Hence, before recording a script, be sure to understand exactly which actions you wish to stress on your SPS server.

There's no sense in stressing a server if you don't use the data to make decisions. As a test, I decided to stress the document check-out, check-in, and publishing features of my SPS server. After performing these tasks to create my script, I then used the counters shown in Figure 12–7 to measure performance on my SPS server. As you can see, I used a combination of Active Server Pages counters, a memory and processor counter, and the appropriate counters from the SharePoint Portal Server document management object. When I ran my script, these counters measured how well the DM features were performing on my SharePoint server. I won't show you all my numbers because this test server is only a P/233 with 512MB of RAM. It's a fine test server for writing books, but it's underpowered for any production environment, and hence it's not useful to present these skewed numbers.

After a test is run, the performance results are given in the Perf Counters section using the Report view. Figure 12–8 shows these numbers. Again, remember that these numbers are for illustration only.

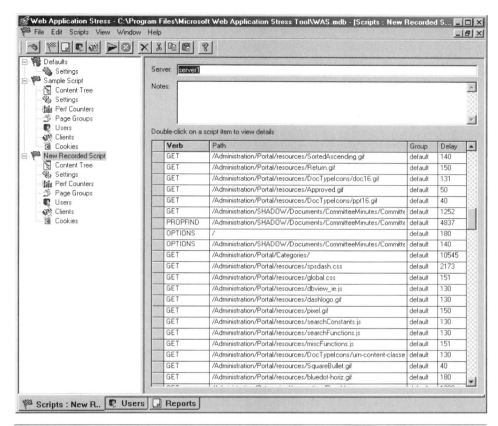

Figure 12–6 Sample script generated by WAS

If you run your own test and look at your results, you'll notice that there are 25th, 50th, and 75th percentile ratings as well as a Max number (Figure 12–8). Microsoft uses percentiles as a way of summarizing the data in usable chunks. A percentile number is the value of the data relative to the other data. For example, assume that WAS has 100,000 response time measurements. The minimum measurement is the 0th percentile, and the maximum measurement is the 100th percentile (or Max). Now let's assume that the minimum number is 100 milliseconds and the maximum number is 40,000 milliseconds. Suppose you're looking at one particular measurement of 2,000 milliseconds. What you need to know is how this number relates to the other measurements in the test. Were most measurements near this 2,000 mark, or were most of them higher or lower? The percentiles give you a way to evaluate the hard numbers.

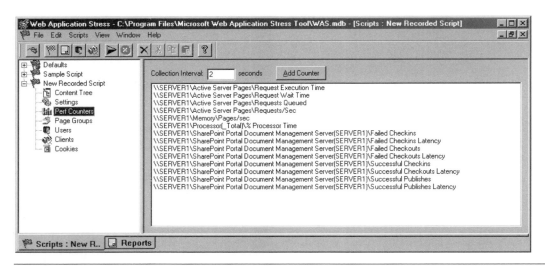

Figure 12-7 Performance Monitor counters in WAS

The 50th percentile gives you the midway point and helps you identify the middle of these numbers. If 18,000 is the 50th percentile in my running example, then 2,000 would be a very fast response. However, if 1,500 milliseconds were the 50th percentile, then 2,000 milliseconds would be considered a bit slow.

For a typical test, the 25th percentile represents the mark at which 25 percent of the measurements were less than the number indicated and 75 percent of the measurements were more. In Figure 12-8, for the Active Server Pages—Request Execution Time counter, the 25th percentile is 511.53 milliseconds. This means that of all the measurements taken, 511.53 is a pretty fast response. Also, the 50th percentile is 640.15 milliseconds, and the average is 680.33 milliseconds. By looking at these two numbers, we can see that of all the measurements taken, the midpoint (or *medium* in statistics-speak) is 640.15 but the average is 680.33. This tells us that the average is slightly skewed toward the high end, meaning that there were individual, large measurements that pulled the average higher. This means that, at points, the server was much slower than usual, as shown by the Max number, which was 3,455 milliseconds.

With these numbers in my example, we could predict that 50 percent of users will see response times between 411 and 640.15 milliseconds, and another 25 percent of users will see response times as slow as 729.89–3,455 milliseconds.

I encourage you to use the Web Application Stress tool as part of an ongoing method of monitoring your SPS server. When management informs you that another 150 users will be added to your SharePoint server, you now have the tools and knowledge to run tests on the server, stress it, and then give accurate numbers that reflect how your SharePoint server will react to the new

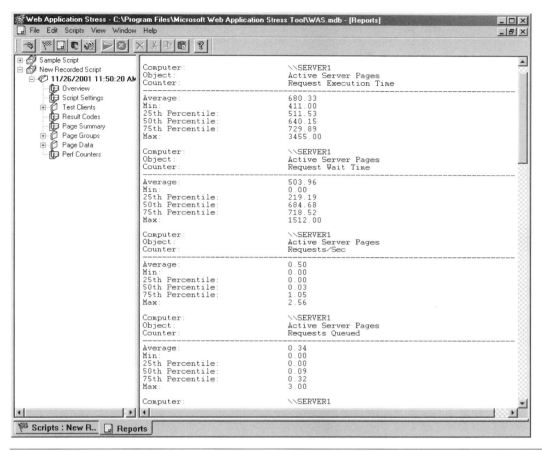

Figure 12-8 Report view of completed test on Performance Monitor counters

stress. Such information could be invaluable and nip potentially large problems in the bud.

Summary

This chapter discusses some of the key monitoring counters for SPS and outlines a matrix of counters to measure your server's health. Monitoring can provide you with crucial evidence and data from which to track trends and make predictive evaluations of specific scenarios.

Chapter 13 focuses on security measures and describes how you can secure your SharePoint Portal Server.

Securing SharePoint Portal Server 2001

This chapter is probably the most important one in the book because more people will read it first than any other. When I make presentations at conferences, I get more questions about security than about any other topic. When I'm consulting, security is almost always at the top of my clients' list of problems. Some variation of "How do I secure this resource?" is the most often asked question.

Security is huge, and companies are waking up to the fact that they are responsible for their own security. Networks are not secured by default, especially with Microsoft products. For all their excellence, Microsoft's products are thought to be some of the most insecure platforms you can run on your network. (At a recent conference, I listened to a speaker introduce Microsoft's Internet Security and Acceleration Server. This speaker mentioned that ISA was designed to compete with Cisco and CheckPoint for firewall protection. Predictably, the audience laughed.) Unfortunately for Microsoft, it doesn't have a good reputation for having operating systems that can be hardened as well as some versions of UNIX—and there is reason for this reputation. Microsoft's focus has not been on security; instead, it has focused on building operating systems and applications that meet business needs.

This chapter covers a number of items, some of which are specific to SharePoint Portal Server, and others that are good practices to consider for your network in general.

General Network Security Principles

As a general statement, network security has three parts: prevention, detection, and response. By far, prevention is the most cost-effective.

One excellent method of prevention is to ensure that there is only one, and I mean *one*, way in and out of your network, physically speaking. Independent dial-up modems are one of the best ways to expose your network to intruders if you don't have a firewall—or even if you have one. Consider the example of a network that has a dedicated T1 line to the Internet and a robust firewall. The firewall is doing its job. Now add to that scenario a user in the accounting department who must connect via a dial-up line to a paycheck vendor to perform payroll data transfers. A hacker with energy, interest, and time can figure out approximately when that user is dialing the vendor, scan the company's phone lines for your user's connection, and, armed with that information, upload files to the user's computer that will reveal your network layout, passwords, and other critical information. And in the absence of attention from you, it is likely that the modem or the operating system will be set to automatically receive calls, so the hacker could simply call the computer, get an answer, and begin the process of compromising your network. Even though you have a great firewall, the game's over. To prevent this kind of attack, do not allow any independent dial-up modems on your network.

Another major type of prevention is to conduct security training for your end users. Train them on what, you ask? Your network security policy. If you don't have such a policy, you are really behind the game here. Lack of a well-written policy, coupled with a lack of training, often creates vulnerabilities, but administrators and managers routinely fail to recognize these matters as worthy of attention. As humans, employees tend to want to be helpful, and most companies do not train their users about basic security measures. For instance, most Help desk people would positively respond to the following question without hesitation: "Hi, this is <name of VP>, and I'm trying to access my e-mail account. I keep getting a message that tells me my password is wrong. I must have forgotten it. Could you reset my password to 'newyork,' and I'll change it once I'm in? Thanks."

Get my point?

You need to ensure that you have created good network security plans and policies and that you have taken the time to invest energy in prevention. Enforced policies are often one of the best ways to minimize vulnerabilities that we humans create on our network.

In addition, by checking security Web sites nearly every day, you'll find new worms, viruses, and Trojans being released and discovered. How does this impact SharePoint Portal Server? Most of these little bugs are aimed at either Internet Explorer or Internet Information Services. Because these two programs are central to SPS, you'll need to remove the server's vulnerability by installing the latest patches and fixes on your SharePoint server.

However, in the case of Microsoft and SPS, this presents a huge dilemma. Allow me to quote from the Microsoft Official Curriculum course 2095, "Implementing Microsoft SharePoint Portal Server 2001," module 2, page 3:

> Warning: IIS hot fixes are known to affect SharePoint Portal Server and may cause it to stop running. Always check the Microsoft Support Knowledge Base before installing an IIS hot fix to verify that there are no known issues.

If you go to Microsoft's security site at `www.microsoft.com/security`, you'll find that in 2001, more than 55 security bulletins were issued for all Microsoft products, most of them reporting vulnerabilities within IIS. In a white paper, "Manage Security of Your Windows IIS Web Services," Microsoft recommends that you "ensure that all the latest hot fixes are applied to all managed systems in the environment."

The problem is that a patch is developed quickly for a vulnerability, and it is not fully regression-tested against all Microsoft systems. The Knowledge Base articles that describe the patch usually lag behind the patch's release. If the patch creates a problem for your SharePoint server, there is a good chance that a Knowledge Base article describing this problem may not appear for some time. I don't think you can depend on a quick search of TechNet to see whether the latest patch has any known issues with SPS.

Best practice, then, is to do one of two things. Either don't allow Internet access to your SPS server, or else have a full, up-to-date test server that is an exact image of your production server and install the IIS hot fix patch first on that server. Then run some tests against your lab server and ensure that the patch is not creating any problems before you install it on your production SharePoint server.

Microsoft and Security

Microsoft is finally getting onboard with security and is becoming proactive in helping companies more closely secure the Microsoft operating systems. Ever since the Gartner group (`www.gartner.com`) recommended that businesses use a Web service platform other than Microsoft's IIS because of all the holes in the platform, recent estimates (at the time of this writing) have put the number of companies that have moved away from using IIS as their Web services platform at approximately 150,000. It's an understatement to say that this has not gone unnoticed at Microsoft, even though Microsoft doesn't lose any money by such a move (remember, the company gives away the IIS server as part of the Windows 2000 operating system).

Microsoft has created the Strategic Technology Protection Program, which includes a toolkit and an 800 number to call in case you've been hit with a worm or virus and you want to repair your IIS servers.

Microsoft's security site contains a Windows 2000 Server Baseline Security Checklist, which recommends that you do the following:

- Verify that all disk partitions are formatted with NTFS.
- Verify that the Administrator account has a strong password.
- Disable unnecessary services.
- Disable or delete unnecessary accounts.
- Disable the Schema Administrator account except when using it to extend the schema.
- Protect files and directories with the minimum NTFS permissions needed.
- Ensure that the Guest account is disabled.
- Protect the registry from Anonymous access.
- Apply appropriate registry ACLs.
- Restrict access to public Local Security Authority information.
- Set strong password policies.
- Set an account lockout policy.
- Remove unnecessary file shares.
- Install antivirus software and keep it updated.
- Install the latest service pack.
- Install the latest hot fixes and security fixes.

Knowing that you can't make any network totally invulnerable, here are some tips to keep in mind when you're thinking about securing your SPS server and the base Windows 2000 operating system. I know that these are more general to your network, but your success at ensuring network security will directly relate to the success of keeping your SharePoint server up and running when the next worm is released.

The list I present here is adapted from a number of articles I've read on ensuring that your IIS or Windows 2000 server is secure. Here then are some basic, no-brainer suggestions on hardening your Windows 2000 and IIS servers:

- Open only the needed ports on your firewall. Opening ports that aren't actively used gives hackers another hole through which they can exploit potential vulnerabilities.
- Move the `cmd.exe` file from the default location to a different location. Many known IIS vulnerabilities allow a URL to be constructed

that causes `cmd.exe` to be invoked on the server. If `cmd.exe` resides in a location not expected by the hacker's tools, you've made it harder for the hacker to exploit the vulnerability.

■ Perform a trial backup and restore of your data once a month. This will ensure that your backup hardware is working properly.

■ Filter outgoing packets as well as incoming packets. Most firewalls don't do this. If you are filtering for outbound traffic, you give yourself a chance to stop unwanted outbound connections from programs that hackers have planted on your systems to their own systems or Web sites.

■ Ensure that you are running the latest antivirus software and definitions from your antivirus manufacturer. Most Trojan horses and viruses are caught by such software based on their signature. Not running such software, on every machine in your organization, exposes you to significant risk.

■ Perform logging of your Web site and then *read the logs*.

■ Do not allow users to have their own phone line to the Internet. Just don't allow it. Figure out a way to meet their business need without the addition of a phone line.

■ Give your users plenty of security training on which information not to release to anyone. Appoint someone to answer security questions, and make sure your users know whom to call.

FOR MORE INFO: For a list of ten actions you can take to better secure your network, go to `http://www.sans.org/topten.htm`. This list comes from SANS, a premier security organization. Another great article on this topic can be found at *Information Security Magazine* at `http://www.infosecuritymag.com/articles/september01/features_IIS_security.shtml`.

I hope this section has been helpful. If nothing else, it should stir your thinking in regard to security and should help you see how important it is. The rest of this chapter focuses on security issues specific to SharePoint Portal Server.

Understanding Role-Based Security: The Architecture of Security in SPS

Let's look first at the architecture of the security model employed by SPS. Understanding a system's architecture is fundamental to diagnosis and resolution of problems.

In the SPS security model, all items in the workspace are secured using roles, not file permissions. This includes document folders and documents. The important distinction is that any file that resides in a workspace is secured with a role that represents a configured set of permissions or actions that can be performed on that file.

Who can hold a role? Anyone with an account in the security accounts database for the domain can hold a role, and this goes for both Windows NT and Windows 2000. In other words, SPS can pull user accounts (also called *security principles*) from either a Windows NT domain controller or a Windows 2000 domain controller. Note that because SPS can pull accounts from a Windows NT domain controller, it does not require that Active Directory be present.

The configured permissions for a role in a workspace cannot be modified. I suspect that future releases of SPS will allow this, but for now, you can't modify the permission set.

Each item in the workspace has two sets of access control lists. An ACL is simply a listing of the user and group account *security identifiers* (SIDs) that are allowed access to the resource along with the level of access that the SID (think "user" or "group") enjoys. There is a Web Storage System ACL and an SPS ACL. Analogous to traditional file-level NTFS security, the WSS ACL controls read/write access to a document. The SPS ACL controls the publishing security, including the check-in, check-out, publishing, and approving functions. The WSS ACL holds the role to user mapping.

Each entry on an ACL is called an *access control entry* (ACE). The WSS ACL does not support the DENY ACE.

When SPS is deployed on a server that is a member of the domain, it uses the domain's security services for authentication of a user to the workspace. If SPS is deployed on a stand-alone server, the user accounts are authenticated against the server's local security database. Users connect with their own security context, and authentication is performed in this context.

Unlike items in the workspace, the portal is secured by configurations you set in IIS. Because each item in the WSS has its own URL, IIS security is enforced for each item in the workspace. By default, the portal is configured to use Windows Integrated Authentication (WIA) for the SPS virtual root. If you want to use either Basic or Anonymous (IUSR_CompterName) authentication, you must create a new Web site and modify its security setting accordingly. Those who connect to an SPS workspace anonymously cannot create subscriptions from the dashboard.

You can apply a DENY permission to items in a folder, but not to the folder itself. When you configure a DENY permission on a document, that permission applies to all versions of the document, not just the version that you are working with to input this permission.

Members of the Local Administrators security group have a nonconfigurable, irrevocable right to view and access all documents in the workspace. Because coordinators can restrict access to a document, it is possible for them to configure security so that no one can see or access a document, including themselves. Because you are working with role-based security, there is no concept of "ownership" as there is in NTFS. Hence, to ensure that no document is ever completely locked out, Microsoft gave the local administrators the right to read and browse all documents in the workspace, including those that have the DENY permission set.

The one gotcha with this Administrators backdoor is this: If you install SPS on a domain controller, there is no Local Administrators group. Therefore, if a coordinator makes an error and locks out all users to a resource, there is no local administrator to resolve the issue. This means that you should seriously think about installing SPS only on member or stand-alone servers, not domain controllers.

Working with Access Accounts

When you work with user accounts in the workspace, note that only coordinators and members of the Local Administrators security group can configure role memberships in the workspace. Users can be assigned one or multiple roles, but nesting of roles is not allowed. Security groups can also be assigned roles in the workspace. Security roles for the workspace are assigned in the SharePoint Portal Server Administrators Microsoft Management Console (MMC) snap-in. Permissions granted at this level control who can access the workspace. To configure these permissions, open the SharePoint Administration snap-in, right-click the workspace you wish to set permissions on, and then choose Properties. Configure as needed on the Security tab (Figure 13–1).

The default permissions for any workspace are to give the Everyone security group the Reader role and to give the local Administrator account the Coordinator role.

Although anyone with access to the SPS Administration snap-in can configure security for an entire workspace, only those who have the SPS client installed on a Windows 2000 machine can configure the folder- and item-level permissions. This is because these permissions are configured using the Web folders client; you open the folder's or item's properties and then configure permissions on the Security tab.

Notice that this tab (Figure 13–2) is similar to the workspace Security tab, with two important options that affect permissions inheritance. First is the Use

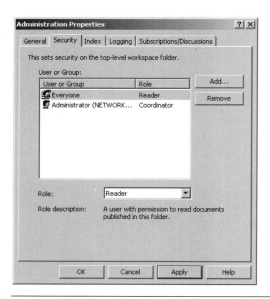

Figure 13–1 Security tab in Administration snap-in

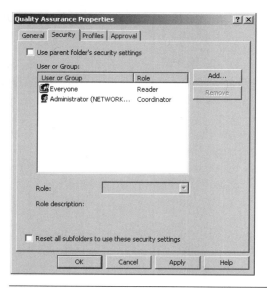

Figure 13–2 Security tab in folder properties

Permissions Inheritance

Most coordinators use permissions inheritance to apply permissions to large numbers of documents and folders. *Permissions inheritance* allows you to create a small number of security policies in the workspace and apply them to large directory structures in the Web Storage System. By default, every folder is configured to inherit its permissions settings from its parent folder.

Once a permission has been set on a folder, it can be changed at any time in the manner described in this chapter. However, such changes can be configured to apply only to the folder and its items or to all subfolders and all their items. Changes in security on a folder do not affect its parent's security settings.

One role that is not so flexible is the Approval role. Like other permissions, this role is inherited from its parent folder when the folder is created. However, once this folder is configured, any changes will not propagate to any child folders. This means that if you want to change the Approval role for a set of folders in a hierarchy, you must manually configure the new Approval roles and routing policy individually on each folder.

Parent Folder's Security Settings check box. When selected, this dims out the User or Group box because you'll configure the folder to inherit its permissions settings from its parent's folder. If you clear this box (as illustrated), the User or Group box colors in, meaning that you can set permissions on the folder directly. At the bottom of the tab is a Reset All Subfolders to Use These Security Settings check box. Selecting this box forces all subfolders (and documents) to inherit the security roles you are creating on the current folder. This action overwrites all security settings, including those subfolders that have cleared the Use Parent Folder's Security Settings check box.

The actual roles that are created for a folder and its items vary a bit between enhanced and standard folders. Six roles can be created in the workspace:

- Reader: People holding this role can read documents that have been published, browse folder contents, and conduct searches in the workspace. Its specific permissions are Read Items and Browse Folders.
- Author: People holding this role can perform all the functions of those with the Reader role, and in addition can add items to folders, edit items owned by the Author role, and create and delete subfolders. People with this permission can read and modify files that have been checked in. They can also perform the document management functions check-out, check-in, and publish. This permission does not

include the ability to act as an approver for published documents. Its specific permissions are Read Items, Browse Folders, Create Items, Edit Items, Delete Items, Create Folders, and Delete Folders.

■ Approver: This is a role given to those who are charged with the responsibility of approving documents before they are published. Technically speaking, the approval process is part of the publishing process, which you can read about in Chapter 8. The Approver role does not include any other role in the workspace. For instance, if an approver does not have the Reader role for a given document but is the approver on that document, the approver can read the document during the approval process but cannot read it after it has been approved and published. Hence, approvers have read-only access to a document during the approval routing process.

■ Lock Holder: This is a hidden role assigned to the user account that last checked out a document. For more information, see Chapter 8 in the SharePoint Portal Server 2001 Resource Kit.

■ Submitter: This is a hidden role assigned to the user account that submitted the document for approval by publishing a document housed in a folder configured with an approval routing process. For more information, see Chapter 8 in the SharePoint Portal Server 2001 Resource Kit.

■ Coordinator: This is the "big kahuna" role. Top dog. Big cheese. People holding this role can do everything, including all the functions of a reader and author. Coordinators can also set metadata and security roles and can configure document profiles and category hierarchies. Coordinators also create and delete Web parts in dashboards and even create new dashboards. They can force the expiration of out-of-date permissions and can configure the approval process. The account that is used to create a new workspace is automatically configured as the first Coordinator account in the workspace.

Standard folders do not support the document management permissions because all documents are automatically published in standard folders.

NOTE: Do not use the M: drive (Installable File System) to configure security on folders and documents in the workspace. Security roles are not exposed on items in the workspace when accessed through the IFS, so you can't configure security through the IFS anyway. By default, the M: drive is not mounted, so don't mount it and then try to use it for permissions configurations. You're just asking for trouble if you do.

Because security roles are tied to the security principles, it's good to remember that when you restore a workspace to a server, it will contain exactly the same security configurations as when it was backed up. If the security principles no longer exist, you must manually reconfigure the resources in the workspace to reflect the new security principles that are available to the SPS server. This is most often the case when the restored server uses local groups and the image is restored to a different server. Another example is the restoration of an SPS server to a domain other than the source server from which the image was created.

Configuring Portal Security

You must also think about security at the portal level. So far, we have discussed documents and folders, but another area of security focuses on the Web parts and dashboards in the portal. Permissions inheritance plays a role (no pun intended <g>) here, too. Let's briefly look at how permissions inheritance works with dashboards.

When you set permissions at the workspace level (described earlier in this chapter), you are also setting permissions on the default Home dashboard. All the other dashboards, except the Management dashboard, inherit these permissions settings. By default, the Everyone security group has the Reader role, and the local Administrator account has the Coordinator role. Hence, every dashboard created—including the Search, Category, Document Library, Document Inspection, and Subscriptions dashboards—inherits these settings.

By default, the Management dashboard is visible only to the coordinator of the workspace. Authors and readers will not see this dashboard because they do not have permissions to see it. This brings up an interesting point: A user must have at least the Reader role on any given dashboard or Web part in order to *see* the part in the portal. If a user does not have the Reader role on a dashboard or Web part, that user will not be able to see it.

To configure security on a dashboard, use the Web folders client to access the workspace, and then double-click the Portal folder. Inside this folder, you'll see the dashboards that make up the portal. They will be dimmed a bit, but you should be able to right-click one anyway and configure security for it using the Security tab. This tab appears the same as that in Figure 13–2.

For the default Web parts in the dashboard—such as News, Announcements, and Quick Links—you set security by using the Web folders client to access the workspace, then double-clicking the Portal Content folder, and then opening the Web part's properties and making the security changes on the Security tab.

For other Web parts, such as the MSNBC Weather Web part that can be downloaded from Microsoft's Web Part Gallery, you must open the file's properties inside the Portal folder. On the Security tab, you can set only those who are denied access (Figure 13–3). The other permissions are inherited from the dashboard itself.

Along with your ability to deny a user or group access to (and visibility of) a Web part, you may be tempted to work with the three settings illustrated in Figure 13–4. As discussed in Chapter 3, these three settings do not do what they say they do. At best, they apply only to coordinators and not to authors or readers. You can make these configuration settings, but understand that they won't make any difference to your readers and authors.

Beyond setting roles for users in the workspace and working with the security of the dashboards and Web parts, there is little direct action you can take to secure the workspace. However, you should consider one other area when securing a workspace: securing the site itself in IIS. The next section discusses this task.

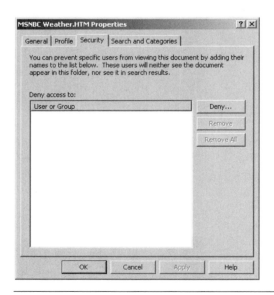

Figure 13–3 Security tab in the MSNBC Weather Web part

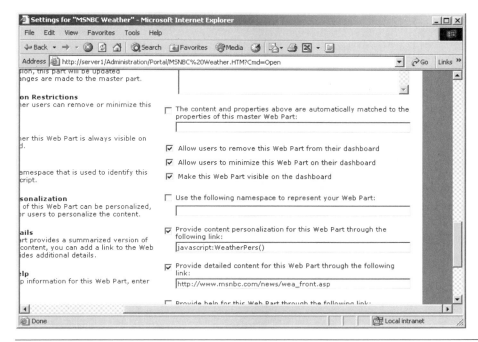

Figure 13–4 Advanced Web part settings

Securing Internet Information Services

Because SPS is fully accessed through IIS, it is important to understand how to secure your IIS server. This section doesn't address the various authentication methods and discuss which ones you should use in certain situations. You can read about all that in the *Microsoft Internet Information Services 5.0 Resource Guide*.

What I am concerned about here is using Secure Sockets Layer (SSL) for your extranet users. Using SSL is one of the best ways to encrypt data that flows between your SharePoint server and the extranet users. So let's look at how to use SSL with SPS to ensure that your data is encrypted when traveling over the Internet.

Enabling SSL in IIS for SPS

For SSL to work, you need some type of *certificate authority* (CA). You can set up a *certificate server* (CS) on a Windows 2000 server, or you can work with an external certificate vendor. My illustrations use the Certificate Services utility in Windows 2000. This server does not need to be a domain controller. The role of a CS is to act as the CA for users when they connect to your SPS server. The CA receives certificate requests from clients and servers, verifies the information in the request, and issues a corresponding X.509 certificate. When you install Certificate Services, a Certificate Services Manager snap-in is also created on the CS. To learn how to install and configure Certificate Services, please consult the Windows 2000 Resource Kit.

There are several gotchas when you create a Web site for SPS that will use SSL. In most instances, you can create a CS, configure the Web site or virtual directory to use SSL, and that's it. However, with SPS, it isn't this simple. Fortunately, Microsoft has given you a tool to make part of this configuration a bit easier.

This tool, the SPS Site Configuration Tool, ships with the SPS Resource Kit. You can also download it at `http://www.microsoft.com/sharepoint/techinfo/reskit/spsextranet.asp`. This tool will help you create the new Web site that is necessary to enable SSL in SPS. It is a Visual Basic script that you run by double-clicking the `spsconfig.wsf` file. The first screen is an instructional screen, as illustrated in Figure 13–5.

Figure 13–5 Instructions that appear when the SPS Site Configuration Tool is run

At the bottom of the screen is a Continue button, which you click to continue the script. The next screen, Enter Site Configuration (Figure 13–6), asks for configuration information for the new Web site. Notice that you can specify a current workspace to be enabled on the new site, and this means that you can tie a current, populated workspace to a new Web site. Very cool.

In Figure 13–6, notice that I've typed the name `SSLServer1.networknowledge.com`. This will become both the Web site name and the host header name when this tool creates the new Web site. You're not required to enter a fully qualified domain name (FQDN) here, but it helps. Second, unless you are permanently changing the host name of the machine, be sure that you've entered a canonical name (CNAME) for this alias name (in my example, `SSLServer1`) in DNS.

Why use a CNAME instead of a second host name? It's because in the best of worlds (or worst, depending on your viewpoint), you'll be using DHCP (Dynamic Host Configuration Protocol) to both dynamically assign IP addresses to all your servers and have them register their host names to IP mapping in DNS. Because a DHCP client can register only one host name

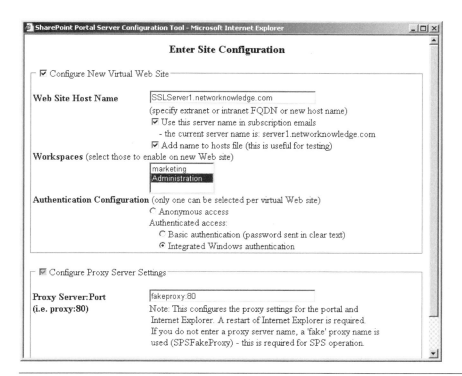

Figure 13–6 Enter Site Configuration screen in the SPS Site Configuration Tool

dynamically with the DNS server, you must either create a CNAME for the server's host name or change the host name directly. If you simply type a second host name in DNS, you'll be forever checking to ensure that the server obtained the same IP address each time after reboot to ensure that the second host name entry in DNS is still valid. That's too much administrative work, if you ask me.

Also, the reason that I mention the DNS entry is that this tool, by default, adds an entry for the new host name into the local hosts file. This means that when you test the configuration (described later), you'll find that it will work because of the host name entry. However, if you haven't made an entry into DNS for this new Web site, name resolution won't work from any other server or workstation because there is no DNS entry for the host name of the new Web site.

After making your configuration choices, click the Perform Configuration button. It won't take long. Soon you'll be presented with a colorful screen indicating that the configuration is complete (Figure 13–7). It outlines the changes that were made. At the bottom of the screen, you can click Validate Configuration to run through some simple ways to ensure that your configuration is working properly.

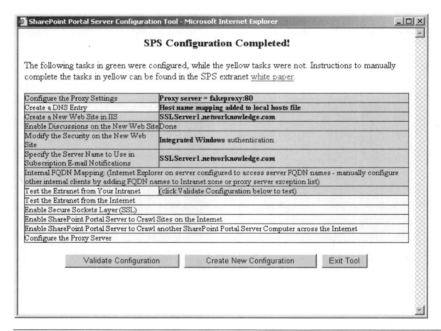

Figure 13–7 SPS Configuration Completed screen in the Site Configuration Tool

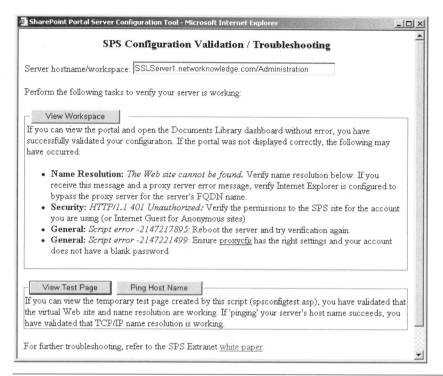

Figure 13-8 Validation/Troubleshooting screen in the Site Configuration Tool

The Validation/Troubleshooting screen (Figure 13–8) shows three methods of validation. First, you can view the workspace. Click the View Workspace button to start the browser and view the workspace Home dashboard. If it doesn't appear, the tool lists some common error messages that you can use as a starting point for diagnosis.

Click the View Test Page button to see a text-only page (Figure 13–9) that is created by the script. This page validates that the Web site and name resolution are working. You can also click Ping Host Name to validate that the reverse DNS resolution is working. You're then referred to the SPS extranet white paper for further troubleshooting tips.

Once the process is completed, you can either create a new configuration by clicking the Create New Configuration button or exit this tool by clicking the Exit Tool button.

Chapter 12 in the SharePoint Portal Server 2001 Resource Kit outlines a step-by-step approach to creating a new Web site, Web discussions, and security settings, and it reviews the functions of the Site Configuration Tool. I

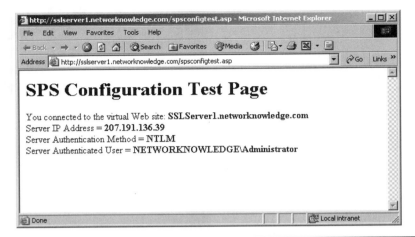

Figure 13–9 SPS Configuration Test Page

strongly recommend using this tool to create the initial Web site from which you'll run SSL services.

After the Web site is created, it will be listed in the Internet Services Manager (ISM), with the host header configured over port 80. This is illustrated in Figure 13–10.

After you've created the new Web site, you enable SSL on the site. Follow these steps:

1. Navigate to the new Web site in the ISM and open its properties.
2. On the Directory Security tab, click Server Certificate. This will invoke the Welcome screen of the Web Server Certificate wizard. Click Next.

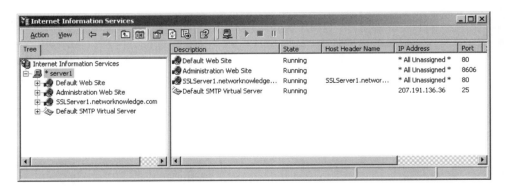

Figure 13–10 New Web site in the ISM

3. Choose the Create a New Certificate radio button, and then click Next.
4. Choose the radio button labeled Prepare the Request Now, but Send It Later, and then click Next.
5. In the Name input box, ensure that the exact name of the new Web site is entered. Select the desired bit length, either 512 or 1024. Although the 1024 key is harder to break, server performance is improved if you use the 512 bit length. Click Next.
6. Enter your organization information. For organizational unit, choose any word. If this SSL connection is for your entire organization, use your organization's name. If it's for one of your departments, use the department name. Click Next.
7. In the Common Name input box, type the FQDN of your server. Click Next.
8. Enter your geographical information, and click Next.
9. Specify a filename for the certificate. The default is `c:\certreq.txt`. Click Next.
10. On the Request File Summary page, click Next.
11. Click Finish.

This action produces a text file that is placed, by default, in the root of drive `C:` on your server. At this point, the SPS Resource Kit is not very helpful because it tells you to submit the text file to your certificate vendor to generate a new certificate for the Web site. Let's look at how to do this using Certificate Services in Windows 2000.

Point your browser to `http://<servername>/certsvr`, where `servername` represents the host name of the CA on your network. On the Welcome screen, choose the Request a Certificate radio button. Then click Next. On the Choose Request Type screen, click on the Advanced Request radio button, and then click Next. On the Advanced Certificate Requests screen, make the selection illustrated in Figure 13–11. This tells Certificate Services to use the information in the certificate file you generated earlier to create a certificate for your server.

Copy the entire contents of the certificate text file into the Base64 Encoded Certificate Request input box, and choose the Web Server certificate template (Figure 13–12).

When you click Submit, a new certificate is generated for you. On the next Web page, choose to download the CA certificate, and select the Base64 encoding. You can rename the certificate if you like, and then save it to a secure location. I chose to name my certificate `sslserver1.cer`.

Next, you install the certificate into your newly created Web site. To do this, open the properties of your new Web site, click the Directory Security

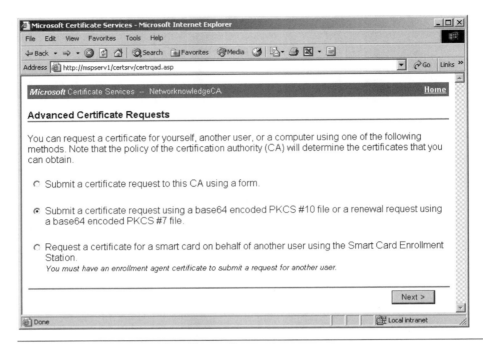

Figure 13–11 Advanced Certificate Requests screen

tab, and then click Server Certificate. As before, this starts the Web Server Certificate wizard. Click Next on the Welcome screen. Then choose the radio button labeled Process the Pending Request and Install the Certificate, and then click Next.

Specify the path and filename you've chosen for the certificate you just downloaded from the CA, and click Next. On the Certificate Summary page, click Next. Then click on Finish and then OK to close the properties page.

At this point, you might think you're ready to enable SSL and get going, but you would be wrong. You must take care of some other things before walking down that path. One of them is to remove the port 443 default assignment from the default Web site. If you do not remove this port assignment, SPS will have problems because competing Web sites will vie for port 443.

To remove this port assignment, you must assign a certificate to the default Web site. Navigate to the Server Certificate button in the default Web site properties, and then start the Web Server Certificate wizard. Run the wizard, and choose to assign an existing certificate to the Web site. Click Next and on Finish to complete the wizard, and then click OK to close the default Web site's properties. After you've assigned the existing certificate to the default Web site, you must first run a script before removing port 443 from the default

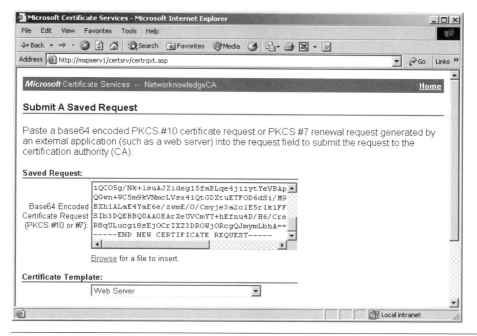

Figure 13–12 Submit a Saved Request Web page, where the text file contents are used to create a new Web server certificate

Web site assignment. This script ensures that the host header for the new site is made part of the secure bindings in IIS. (Note that you can also accomplish the same thing by navigating to the default Web site and opening the advanced properties for the IP address, choosing SSL, and then clicking Remove.)

The script that you want to run is `adsutil.vbs`, which is located, by default, in the `inetpub\adminscripts` directory. Here is the syntax from a command prompt inside the `adminscripts` directory (Figure 13–13):

```
Cscript adsutil.vbs set W3SVC/number/securebindings
 "x.x.x.x:443:FQDN_of_web_site "
```

Where:

- `x.x.x.x` = IP address of the server.
- Number = instance of the W3SVC you are referring to. Each Web site gets its own W3SVC number. The default Web site is number 1, and the Administration Web site is number 2; so more than likely, your new site

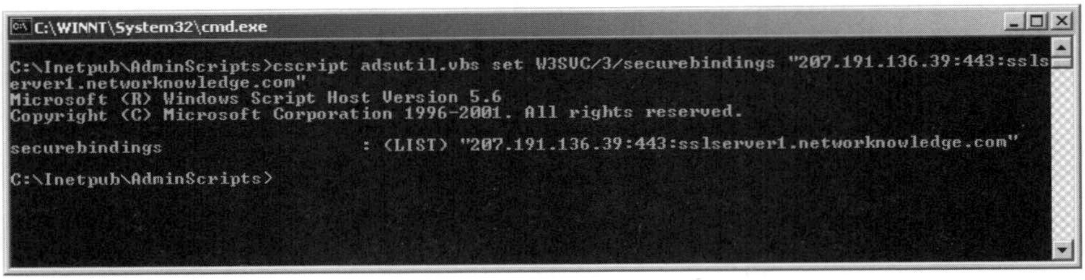

Figure 13–13 Cscript command to configure secure bindings with the host header name

is number 3. If you don't know the number, run this command at the command prompt from inside the adminscripts directory (see Figure 13–14):

```
cscript adsutil.vbs enum W3SVC/number
```

- FQDN_of_web_site = the FQDN that you used to name the Web site when you created it.

After you've run these scripts, you can remove port 443 from the Multiple SSL Identities area of the default Web site. To do this, open the advanced properties from the Web site tab in the default Web site properties, highlight the 443 port number, and click Remove (Figure 13–15).

After you make these configuration changes, it is a good idea to stop and start both the default Web site and your newly created SSL Web site.

You're still not finished. Now you need to configure your SSL Web site to require SSL. Open your new Web site's properties, and click Edit under Secure Communications. On the Secure Communications dialog box, choose the Require Secure Channel (SSL) check box. Do not click Require 128-bit Encryption unless all your extranet users are in the United States.

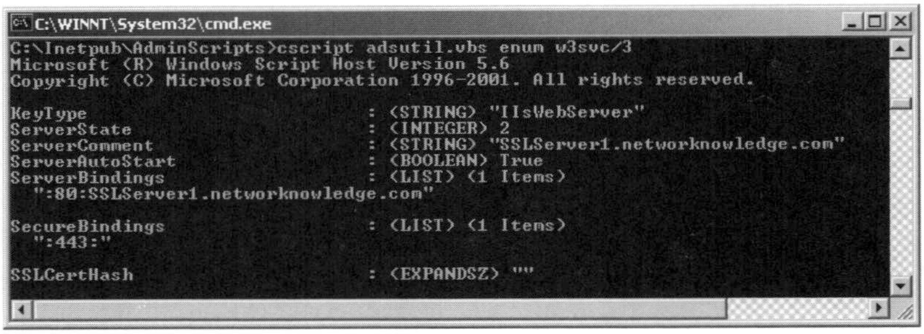

Figure 13–14 Cscript command to enumerate the Web site W3SVC number

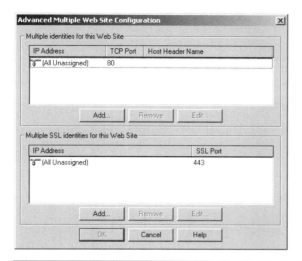

Figure 13–15 Removing port 443 from default Web site properties

Also, at this point, you can choose to ignore, accept, or require client certificates. The default is to ignore client certificates; this means that users can access the site without being prompted to present a client certificate. If you plan to map client certificates to specific user accounts, you can choose either to accept or to require client certificates. Accepting client certificates means that the SSL Web site will allow users with client certificates to access the Web site, but it does not require the certificates. Users who don't have a certificate will use other authentication methods. If you choose to require client certificates, only those users with a valid client certificate will be able to access the site. When coupled with a one-to-one client-to-certificate mapping, this is the most secure option. Essentially, it requires that each extranet user obtain a client certificate that is mapped directly to the user account in Active Directory and that users must present this certificate when attempting to access the SPS extranet site. Failure to do so means that they are not allowed in, even if they type a correct user name and password.

Finally, at this point, you should be able to access your new Web site using SSL.

Securing External Content

SPS recognizes security policies configured on external resources, such as NTFS permissions. When SPS crawls an external content source, it brings in the security on that source and then enforces the security restrictions at the time the user performs a search query. Restricted documents do not appear in the result set. However, SPS recognizes only file-level security structures that exist on an NTFS partition or in a Lotus Notes database. It does not understand the security descriptors on remote file systems, such as NFS (Network File System) or Novell file systems. When SPS crawls these content sources, per-file security descriptors are lost, but the per-share security descriptors are retained and enforced.

Summary

In this chapter, you have learned about the various roles that are used to secure content in SPS and have seen how to configure IIS to use SSL for SPS services. You have also seen that security on the SPS server is pretty straightforward and that you also need to pay attention to the larger issues of overall network security.

Security is an endless topic, one that could consume several chapters. This chapter presents an overview of security in SPS. Chapter 14 takes a look at how to use SharePoint Portal Server in the enterprise and how to make the same portal and documents available across a large installation.

Deploying SharePoint Portal Server 2001 in the Enterprise

More than a few corporations are looking at SharePoint Portal Server from an enterprise-level viewpoint and wondering how well it works for large groups of users. So far, this book has focused on administering SPS from a single-server perspective. If you've been looking in each chapter for lots of information on enterprise-wide planning and deployment tips, you're probably a bit disappointed.

You haven't found this information because SPS is not ready for prime-time, big-time, enterprise deployment. That's my honest assessment. Admittedly, my opinion is based on what I think an enterprise capability requires. For instance, if you define an enterprise-wide deployment as ensuring that the same information is readily available to a wide range of users across multiple servers, then I'm wrong—SPS does have that capability. But if you define an enterprise-wide deployment as ensuring that the same information is readily *and quickly* available *with little administrative effort*, then no, SPS does not have this capability. I say this because SPS lacks any type of replication mechanism between servers.

This chapter discusses how to plan for an enterprise-wide deployment and how to get information from a single master SharePoint server to one or more read-only SharePoint servers.

This chapter depends on information presented in Chapter 11. If you haven't read that chapter or if you aren't familiar with how backup and restores are done in SPS, I suggest that you read that chapter before continuing.

Planning an Enterprise-Wide Deployment

Before you purchase numerous servers, you should first evaluate your environment. Applying what you learned in Chapter 4 about capacity planning and in Chapter 12 about monitoring, you need to discern whether you really need two or more SharePoint servers. Given that each workspace can hold as many as 1,000,000 document versions and 3,500,000 documents in the full-text index, even a large company can use one SharePoint server effectively. Yet in some cases it will make sense to have more than one SharePoint server. Let's discuss some of these scenarios.

First, if you will have more than 1,000,000 document versions or more than 3,500,000 documents in a given database, you'll definitely need more than one server. Where I would draw the line, however, is not based on the number of document versions in a workspace; instead, the consideration is the size of the databases and the time it would take to restore them. This concept is covered better in the discussions in Chapter 4 on capacity planning and in Chapter 11 on backup and restore procedures, but suffice it to say that any internal Service Level Agreements that you have with management on a maximum time that users can be without SharePoint services will probably dictate how many documents your workspace can hold and thus how many servers you'll need.

Second, you need to estimate how much growth is expected in the number of SharePoint users and the number of documents. Based on current usage and anticipated future growth, you could be looking at quite a number of new SharePoint servers.

Third, take a serious look at how SharePoint is to be used. Do your users use it primarily for searching? Document management? Portal access of Web parts? Answering this question is of great importance. If your users are using SPS primarily for portal services, such as a weather Web part, there is a good chance that a single server can service many more users than can a SharePoint server that is crawling hundreds of content sources daily. If users are executing a large number of search requests, it will place considerable load on the server compared with portal access. The document management functions also place additional stress on a server, so looking at these three areas is critical in determining how to configure services across several SharePoint servers.

Deployment Scenarios

You can deploy SPS in several ways in your environment. Most smaller companies deploy a single server. Larger companies may want to provide SharePoint services across a range of physical servers.

The first deployment scenario is what I call the *workgroup-DM* scenario. This deployment is the easiest because it is a single server that stores a large number of documents that are developed and managed by a large number of authors. This server is installed primarily for its DM functions, as opposed to its search, indexing, and portal functions. This server might host several workspaces, but it is usually sufficient to deliver timely services to a workgroup of people accessing its resources.

The second deployment scenario is what I call the *workgroup-search* scenario. Like the workgroup-DM, this deployment employs a single server that is used primarily for crawling external content sources so that users can find needed documents outside the workspace. This deployment scenario also has DM activities, but the number of authors is small and the number of readers executing searches is large. In a sense, this deployment scenario is the flip side of the workgroup-DM scenario.

The third deployment scenario is what I call the *workgroup-cluster* scenario. In this scenario, you're doing both the workgroup-DM and workgroup-search deployments on two servers, but the number of users is relatively small. Don't take the word *cluster* to mean that I'm referring to Windows 2000 Cluster services or a hardware-based cluster service. Instead, take the word *cluster* to mean that there are multiple SharePoint servers offering a unified set of SharePoint functions to a group of users.

The fourth deployment scenario is what I call the *enterprise-search* deployment. This scenario is designed for a large number of readers who need to search a large amount of data that is crawled by a dedicated SharePoint server. There is limited use of the DM functionality. In this scenario, one server is dedicated to indexing and the other to searching. This scenario deploys at least two servers. DM functions are handled by other SharePoint servers. The search and indexing servers do only their own specific functions.

The fifth deployment scenario is what I call the *enterprise-search and DM* deployment. In this scenario, you add aggregated DM services across multiple SharePoint servers to the enterprise-search deployment method. In this scenario, the DM functions of check-out, check-in, publish, and approval are implemented on a single DM server. The other DM servers host a read-only copy of the documents from which readers access necessary information.

The sixth deployment scenario is what I call the *enterprise-wide* scenario. Here, you add to the fifth deployment scenario robust portal services, complete with customized Web parts, aggregated data flow, and launch points from which users access Web sites, applications, and information necessary to their job functions. In this scenario, customized portal services are offered on dedicated Web servers but do not include the search and DM functions. In such a scenario, the search and DM functions are redirected from the enterprise portal to the appropriate dedicated search and DM servers.

Why run through all these deployment scenarios? It's because they represent the various ways that SPS can be used in small, medium, and large deployment situations. But I don't want you to think that these scenarios are based solely on the number of users in an environment. Instead, the main thing you need to look at is the demand, stress, or load placed on the SharePoint servers relative to their primary functions. Such an evaluation is less sensitive to the number of users but more sensitive to the overall use and stress on the SharePoint installation. Use these scenarios as a springboard from which to design your own SharePoint deployment.

Duplicating a Master SharePoint Portal Server across the Enterprise

In some cases, you may need to duplicate a Master SPS (MSPS) across an enterprise environment. Duplicating a server allows you to create one master server exactly the way you want it and then create clones or duplicates of that server on other SharePoint servers. In the most common scenario, you want to make a large number of documents available to a large number of readers. Because SPS has no replication method between servers, the best practice is to support all the document development on a single SPS server and then to use the duplication methods to push out read-only copies of the document library to other servers so that reader access to documents is load-balanced across servers.

To duplicate a server, you use the backup and restore scripts that ship with SPS. Use them exactly as described in Chapter 11. Remember that this copies the entire server and not just an individual workspace, so when you restore an image using the `msdmback` script, you create an exact copy of the MSPS.

Once restored, the Duplicated SPS (DSPS) is a fully functioning server that is no different from the MSPS. Hence, after you've pushed out an image to a DSPS, you must manually (or by using a custom script) perform some administrative steps to ensure that you don't end up with version conflicts on documents.

Although content source configurations on the MSPS are copied to the DSPS during the restore process, no Windows 2000 scheduled tasks are copied to the DSPS. Thus, content source crawls that are executed using the Windows 2000 Task Scheduler will not execute on a DSPS. Similarly, subscriptions do not operate normally on the DSPS. Changes or additions to the subscriptions on the DSPS are lost after the MSPS is duplicated. These must be configured manually or by a script after each duplication process on each DSPS.

Here are the steps to configuring duplication. First, create and configure your MSPS as you like. Second, ensure that each DSPS has SharePoint installed before the restore process begins. Third, back up the MSPS using the `msdmback.vbs` utility (discussed in depth in Chapter 11). Fourth, make the backup image available to the other servers via either a network share or a burned copy of a CD-ROM. Fifth, restore the image to the DSPS servers. Remember that during the restore process, the servers will not be available to your users, so plan accordingly. Finally, make the following configuration changes on each DSPS (this can be done manually or by script):

- Change permissions on the root Document folder to Everyone–Reader. Force all subfolders to inherit this change.
- Remove all scheduled tasks, if any, from the Windows 2000 Task Scheduler.

For this duplication to work properly, make sure that the DSPS has network connectivity to the MSPS backup image. In many cases, this access will be through a mapped drive to the image's location on an image distribution server.

Also, ensure that the DSPS is in the same or a trusted domain of the MSPS server. This is critical; if your MSPS and DSPS are stand-alone servers, the DSPS won't function properly even if the account names used in the workspace are the same. That's because the SIDs for those accounts will be different. Stand-alone servers use their own security database, and not a domain security database, for user reference. Remember, too, that role-based security is not based on the account name but on the account SID. Therefore, server duplication works only with servers that are members of the same domain or members of different domains that have proper trust relationships between them. In Windows 2000, all domains are installed automatically with transitive trust relationships between parent and child domains, so this isn't as much an issue as in Windows NT 4.0.

One more thing: The Local Administrators account on the DSPS must have at least read access to the MSPS backup image. Otherwise, the `msdmback.vbs` script will fail because of a permissions-based error.

Developers can initiate the server duplication process using the `IKnowledgeServer::Backup` and `IKnowledgeServer::Restore` methods. For information on how to call this method from a script, see the SharePoint Portal Server Software Development Kit.

If duplication fails, it is probably because of insufficient disk space on the DSPS, or the drive is not formatted with NTFS. Other reasons include having different versions of SPS (called *platform incompatibility*), insufficient permissions to read the image file or perform a restore operation, lack of a trust relationship between domains or a wrongly configured trust relationship, lack of network connectivity, firewalls not properly set for connections between the two servers, or perhaps the restore operation is already running.

Rapid Portal Deployment

It's one thing to duplicate all your information to DSPS servers. But what if you want to duplicate a portal's configuration *without* the same information? In other words, what if you want to take the categories and dashboard structures of one workspace and duplicate them for a different workspace? Server duplication doesn't help you here, but the Rapid Portal Deployment (RapPort) tool does.

This utility is well outlined in the SharePoint Portal Server Resource Kit, so I won't go into detail here. However, I want to mention some of its features.

To get RapPort going, you create a new SharePoint Portal Server and configure it with all the basic workspaces you think your organization will need. These workspaces become *templates* for the RapPort utility. Then you install the RapPort software on this SharePoint Portal Server.

The RapPort software installs a number of ASP pages, ActiveX DLLs, and XML files in the server's default Web site, which acts as the location from which the templates can be downloaded to another SPS. Hence, to install templates on another SharePoint server, the administrator connects to the Web site hosting the RapPort Web pages, types the information required in the Web pages, and then lets RapPort do its thing.

When all the information has been collected from the administrator in RapPort's Web pages, RapPort initiates the creation of a new workspace. After the workspace on the target SharePoint server has been created, RapPort assigns user security roles, creates a new virtual server in IIS, and ensures that proper WINS or DNS (or both) entries are registered for the new virtual server.

Using RapPort, a large organization can gain economies of scale on portal development costs by focusing those efforts on the RapPort server instead of duplicating efforts on multiple servers across the network. For instance, if an organization estimates that it will need 50 new departmental workspaces, each with the same basic configuration, the workspace can be created once on the RapPort server and installed as a template when the departments need it.

Without RapPort, a large organization would be faced with having to perform some functions 50 times to deploy those workspaces. Microsoft estimates that RapPort can save an organization as much as 80 percent of its original intended development and deployment costs. Obviously, that figure is optimistic, but in many organizations even a 40 percent savings would cause the CFO to sit up and take notice.

The resource kit does a good job of discussing RapPort's architecture, installation, and deployment methods. If you need to deploy the same workspace multiple times, I suggest you take a hard look at using RapPort.

Summary

This chapter explores how to make SPS work in the enterprise. You have learned that this takes little more than backing up a master server and restoring that image to one or more duplicate servers. You have also learned about the various deployment scenarios that you might use as templates from which to deploy your own SharePoint environment. Chapter 15 focuses on the tools in the resource kit and outlines some third-party software that integrates with and enhances SPS.

Extending the Functionality of SharePoint Portal Server 2001

Earlier chapters have focused on how to administer SharePoint Portal Server and have explained how the program works. This chapter presents the SharePoint Portal Server Resource Kit (also known as the *resource kit* or simply the *kit*) as well as third-party software that extends and enhances the SPS functionality.

Resource Kit Tools

This section outlines how to use the resource kit tools that are not illustrated in other parts of the book. You can purchase the resource kit from several book stores or view it online at `http://www.microsoft.com/sharepoint/techinfo/reskit/default.asp`.[1]

Here are the current resource kit tools:

- Category Smart Tags Component
- Document Usage Tracking Tool
- Edit File Tool
- Extranet Configuration Tool
- FTP Protocol Handler
- Index Active Directory Tool

---

[1] The number of resource kit tools will continue to grow, and new ones are regularly being released by Microsoft, so I assume that by the time this book gets into your hands, Microsoft's Web site will have tools not mentioned in this book. If they are not mentioned, you can assume that they were released after this book was written.

- Integrity Checker (discussed in Chapter 11)
- RTF Filter Tool
- Server Latency Tool
- Workspace Archive Tool
- Workspace Export Utility (discussed in Chapter 11)
- Workspace Import Utility (discussed in Chapter 11)
- XML IFilter Tool

Let's take a brief look at each one.

Category Smart Tags Component

This tool lets users of Office XP find information based on your category structure while working on a document. Each time a smart-tag-enabled Office XP application starts, it connects to all the workspaces listed in the user's My Network Places and retrieves the names of the categories in each workspace.

This might present a problem if your users have moved (not copied) the Web folders client to their desktop from the My Network Places location. If the Web folders client isn't represented in My Network Places, this smart tag component won't know to look at the categories in that workspace. When the smart tag appears, users can click it and then look at the contents of that category.

A readme file explains how to install and uninstall this component. Essentially, you must register a DLL (`spscategories.dll`) and create registry entries on each client workstation that needs this functionality. Both tasks can be pushed out to the desktop using Windows 2000 Group Policies. Figure 15–1 illustrates this smart tag. `SharePoint` is a category in my portal, so by holding the cursor over the target word, I make the smart tag appear. Very cool.

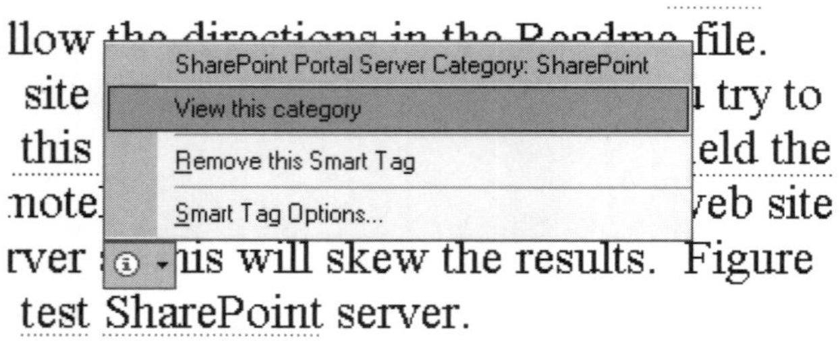

llow the directions in the Readme file.

	SharePoint Portal Server Category: SharePoint	
site	View this category	try to
this		eld the
note	Remove this Smart Tag	
	Smart Tag Options...	eb site
rver	this will skew the results.	Figure

test SharePoint server.

Figure 15–1 Smart tag for the word `SharePoint` in a Word 2002 document

Document Usage Tracking Tool

This simple tool lists the number of times users access a particular document. The value of this tool is that it can be used to determine which documents are accessed most frequently. The Internet Information Services (IIS) logs are used to make this determination. Hence, this tool will do you no good unless you've first enabled logging on your Web site. To do that, open the properties of your Web site in the Internet Services Manager snap-in and select Enable Logging (Figure 15–2) on the Web Site tab. Then let the logging begin. Thereafter, run the document usage script as follows:

```
Cscript.exe doc_usage.vbs <IIS log file path>
```

The script reads each log file and then generates a report. Note that running this tool will peg your processor between 95 percent and 100 percent usage by the `cscript` process. If you have a large number of IIS log files or very large log files, you can anticipate that this script will take some time to run and that performance for other services will be degraded. Plan accordingly, my friend.

One other thing about this tool: It must be extracted under the security context of the user account you plan on running it with. Moreover, it must be run locally on the server you wish to query. I found that this tool readily

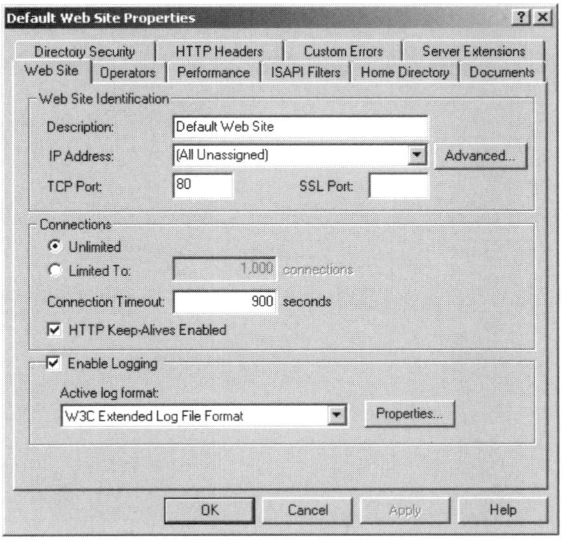

Figure 15–2 Enabling logging on default Web site in ISM snap-in

returned permission error messages even though both the script and the log files were given the Full Control permission for the user account under which I was attempting to run the script. After I extracted the script locally, instead of copying it from another server, it ran fine without any security configuration. So a word to the wise: If you keep getting permission error messages, extract it again locally on the server and then run it.

Edit File Tool

This handy tool adds a style sheet to allow the Edit action to be displayed (Figure 15–3) for each document in the document library. Users running Office XP or later can click the Edit link to open the document automatically in the appropriate Office application.

You'll need to add a new style sheet (`FolderItemsPart.xsl`) to the Portal folder and then flush the application-level cache. The readme file explains how to do this.

If the document you are trying to open is already checked out, you can open only a read-only copy. However, if the document is checked in, you are presented with a dialog box asking whether you want to check out the document or open a read-only copy. Checked-out versions are then opened in the native application and work just as if you used the Document Inspection screen to check out the document.

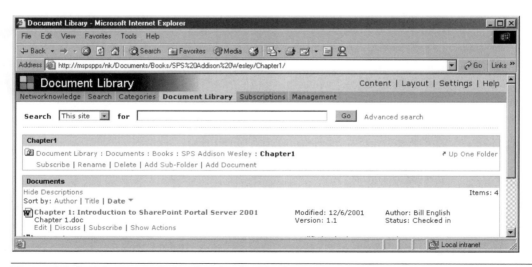

Figure 15–3 Edit menu choice for checked-in document

FTP Protocol Handler

This resource kit tool installs an ftp protocol handler so that documents hosted on an ftp site can be crawled during an indexing process. It is a DLL (`ftpph.dll`) file that must be registered using the `regsvr32` command. It also automatically registers itself (like most other DLL files) when the system boots up.

Index Active Directory Tool

This tool enables the workspace user to execute a search in the portal against user accounts in Active Directory. The value of this tool is that you can use the portal to find basic user information instead of using the Outlook client. This is another small indication that our focus for the desktop will be toward the portal and away from individual applications on a desktop.

The installation is fairly involved. You must make manual edits to the `ad_generator.asp` file, change permissions on individual files in the root directory, make a registry change, and add a content source. The readme file explains how to do all this.

One gotcha is that Microsoft recommends you have at least 512MB of RAM on the server that will perform the crawling function of Active Directory. If you don't have this much RAM, ensure that you've bumped up your RAM to meet this recommendation.

RTF Filter Tool

This tool lets you crawl rich-text file documents. You must register this DLL file (`rtffilt.dll`) with the operating system either by using the `regsvr32` command or by restarting the MSSearch process.

Server Latency Tool

This tool tells you how fast your users are able to access a document stored in the WSS. Using this tool is simple—just follow the directions in the readme file. Make your edits to the file, and then copy it to a Web site in which it should run. If you try to run it outside a Web site, it will fail. However, running it from within a Web site will yield the average access time of the Web store. It should be run remotely—that is, from one Web site to your workspace. Don't run it on your SharePoint server because this will skew the results. Figure 15–4 illustrates the results that were generated when I ran this tool against my test SharePoint server.

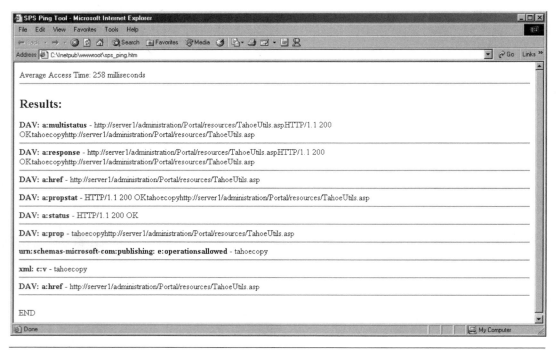

Figure 15–4 Server Latency Tool results in a Web browser

Third-Party Software to Extend SharePoint's Functionality

Nifty software packages are available that extend SharePoint's functionality in very cool ways. Each package has something to offer. This section briefly discusses some of the more popular packages and describes what they can realistically do for you.[1]

---

[1] Let me put in a disclaimer here. You'll find that some products received more page space than others. This is and is not by design. Several of the products mentioned were still in early development when I wrote this chapter, so some manufacturers had a difficult time getting me either written information or code that I could test on my SharePoint test servers. Their information simply wasn't ready for release. So do not consider the amount of page space dedicated to a certain vendor to be an indication that I prefer one product over another. Instead, consider it an accurate reflection of what the manufacturer was able to provide when I was writing this chapter. Also, I chose only those products that were focused mainly on SharePoint Portal Server. Also, new products are constantly being introduced that integrate with SharePoint Portal Server. If you use or are considering a product not listed here, that doesn't mean anything negative about that product. It simply means either that the vendor wasn't ready with documentation or code, that it was introduced after this book was completed, or that I did not know about the product at the time I wrote this chapter.

Max Retriever

The Max Retriever system is unique. The program's main function is to provide capabilities to create extremely long reports in the Max Retriever database on nearly any type of data. Its hook with SharePoint is that it breaks the reports into individual items, which are indexed by SharePoint Portal Server and made available in the Search Web part for users to query. For large reports, this is a good tool.

For instance, if you have a telephone call report of 2,500 pages—a document that may be too large for SharePoint to handle individually—you can have each entry in the report made available as an individual piece of information that can be indexed by SPS. Each item can appear as an independent data item in a search result set that is executed from within SPS. This program works with invoices, purchase orders, and other types of documents, too.

Max Retriever works especially well for making accounting records available in the portal. For instance, if you are developing a set of documents for a customer, with the Max Retriever system you can find invoices, payments, and other accounting information along with the customer's documents in the same search request.

To learn more about this product's integration with SharePoint Portal Server, go to `www.maximal.com`.

Webridge Extranet! for SharePoint Portal Server

Webridge Extranet! for SharePoint Portal Server (`www.webridge.com`) solves several thorny problems for those wishing to use the extranet feature in SPS. First, as you might suspect, SPS has no way of creating a portal with Web parts that host sensitive information *and* allow access to each Web part on a part-by-part basis for individual extranet users. Windows 2000 and SPS are simply not set up to do that. Webridge provides this enhancement by controlling access to information through the use of a SQL Server database to store the security profiles of the users who visit your extranet. Webridge automatically creates and manages the Windows NT/2000 user accounts and groups that are necessary for SPS to secure your data. This enables you to protect your data without having to redesign your Windows NT/2000 domain architecture or create multiple portals for each unique security context matrix that you might encounter.

Securing your information on an extranet means that all those who visit the extranet site see only the information that they are allowed to see. Access to extranet content is based on a matrix of each user's attributes. The information that people are allowed to see depends on who they are, the company they work for, what they do for that company, and their relationship to you.

Interestingly, Webridge enables you to specify a matrix of security attributes for each folder in SPS. Security is based not only on the user's identity and group membership but also on a combination of attributes specified by you. These attributes include each person's identity, role, and company, and the company type. Together, these attributes create the user's *profile*. The user profiles are stored in a SQL Server database. Very cool.

Webridge uses a cookie-based authentication mechanism. This means that user names and passwords are not sent with every request from the browser to the Web server; instead, an encrypted cookie is sent. These cookies are session-based, so they are different for each session the extranet user creates to the portal.

Webridge also allows you to specify that certain dashboards be secure. This specification means that users are required to log in before they can view any secure dashboards. When a user tries to browse one of these secure dashboards, Webridge will present a logon page in which the user must enter a user name and password.

Packaged in the Webridge software is XSL Studio, a visual portal page design tool. With XSL Studio, you get a WYSIWYB (what you see is what you browse) visual design tool for creating your own look and feel for your dashboard sites. You first create an HTML prototype of the page using an HTML editor, such as Dreamweaver or FrontPage. Then you are ready to use XSL Studio.

You import into XSL Studio your HTML prototype page and a sample of the XML data generated by your SPS dashboard. You then use XSL Studio to connect the XML data elements with the HTML design elements to produce the desired look and feel. XSL Studio produces an XSL style sheet for SPS to use when it renders the dashboard.

Webridge also lets you redirect visitors to pages that are specially branded for them. As business managers create branded dashboards with a tool called Site Studio, they can specify that certain users should be redirected to these pages after login.

Webridge, unlike SPS, enables usage data to be stored in a SQL Server database, which is then available for analysis. Webridge includes a Web part that uses the Microsoft Office Web component. In the Internet Explorer browser, this Web part can display an Excel pivot table, which can show usage data such as the following:

- Visits to the site
- Document requests
- Dashboard hits

These can be evaluated in the pivot table against data such as the user's identity, company, the date of the visit, geography, and so on.

eManage

eManage lets you manage documents in SPS custody as corporate records and gives you additional records management functionality. The product makes your SPS workspace fully compliant with the U.S. Department of Defense 5015.2 certified records management functionality. eManage leaves your documents in the SPS WSS instead of copying them to another database. When coupled with the eManage e-mail system, this product can provide a complete and seamless solution for the management of records, including e-mail, within a unified file classification system.

At the time of this writing, eManage is in its early stages. You can find out more about it at www.emanagecorp.com.

Encompass

This solution has tight integration with SharePoint Portal Server. The focus of Encompass is to improve the document management features of SPS. It has both a server and client software, and you must install both to realize its full potential. Encompass allows you to extend a document's metadata by entering new document properties and then having those exact properties appear in the Advanced Search Web part on the SPS dashboard. This integration gives you the flexibility of designating customized data properties as being important enough to be directly searchable.

The client piece places Encompass hooks in the Office suite of applications so that you can search on the Encompass-specific properties from within the application. It also allows you to save documents directly to the workspace and then have the customized properties appear in the document's profile.

Other features offered by Encompass include the following:

- You can number your documents.
- Encompass document profile fields are held in an SQL database.
- Administrator-controlled folders can be used to define and direct document storage for users.
- Lookup buttons can be used to refine the search criteria by profile type and any document property.
- It provides offline support for users who wish to read a document while allowing others to check out the document in the portal.
- A directory structure is created automatically on the user's local hard drive for DM functions.
- Network connectivity loss is detected automatically, leading the user to save a document locally.

An extranet "deal room" can also be created to allow documents to be shared with those outside the organization without sacrificing functionality or security of your intranet-based portal. You can learn more about this product at www.eliteis.com.

Summary

In this chapter, you have learned about some of the tools that exist in the resource kit and on the open market that improve and extend the functionality of SharePoint Portal Server. As SharePoint matures, the number of vendors offering integrative software products will increase. This is a good thing. Also, you'll find that the resource kit tools will mature and become more numerous. New Web parts will be created, and the functionality of the existing ones will be expanded.

I hope you enjoy your SharePoint Portal Server. This is a great product that will be a part of your overall platform strategy for the foreseeable future.

Brief XML Tutorial

It's not uncommon for network administrators to know very little about programming or programming languages. However, to customize the thesaurus in SharePoint Portal Server 2001, you need some elementary knowledge of XML (Extensible Markup Language). So let's get started learning some basic XML.

The first thing you need to understand about XML is that its main focus is on how to present, or describe, data. Let's go over an example. Here is a number: 2. Does it mean anything to you? Probably not—unless you put it into some type of context. Perhaps that's the number of new cars you purchased this year, or the number of apples on your kitchen table. You could even be referring to the number of dogs you own. The point is that raw data, out of context, can be meaningless. XML provides a context or description in which data becomes meaningful.

Here's another comparison. Even though XML is an extension of HTML, its focus is very different from that of HTML. For the most part, HTML is a *presentation* language whose function is to *display* data on a Web page. By contrast, XML is a *description* language whose function is to *describe* data on the Web page. XSL is used to in conjunction with XML to display XML-described data.

Yet XML is still considered a markup language because you can use it to define data by using markup tags. You can define your own tags to describe the data in any way you find useful. In addition, XML documents contain text rather than binary data. XML-aware applications can parse an XML document, looking for specific tags of interest to those applications. Unknown tags and their associated data can be freely ignored.

XML documents primarily contain tags and text. The text is the data, and the tags define the data. The basic syntax of an XML statement is as follows:

```
<description_of_data>DATA</description_of_data>
```

Note the / character in the second tag; it denotes that this is the end of the description for this data. The following line holds data (a person's name) as well as a description of the data (<name>, </name>) in an XML document:

```
<name>Bill English</name>
```

XML elements can be nested within each other to form a hierarchy of related information. Each nesting of data must have a start tag (< >) and an end tag (</ >) around the data, but the data can be on multiple lines. For example, the following XML code shows how to group the name and address for an employee inside the <employee> element:

```
<employee>
  <name>Bill English</name>
  <street>12345 Oak Street</street>
  <city>Anywhere</city>
</employee>
```

If the document needed to list a number of employees, this cycle would be repeated:

```
<employee>
  <name>Bill English</name>
  <street>12345 Oak Street</street>
  <city>Anywhere</city>
</employee>
<employee>
  <name>Sally Summer</name>
  <street>123 Maple Street</street>
  <city>Anywhere</city>
</employee>
<employee>
  <name>Wally Winter</name>
  <street>123 Snow Street</street>
  <city>Anywhere</city>
</employee>
<employee>
  <name>Frank Fall</name>
  <street>123 Leaf Street</street>
  <city>Anywhere</city>
</employee>
```

At the beginning of each XML document is a processing instruction to tell the XML processor how to interpret the data. This processing concept is an interesting one. Just as a computer ships with a processor to process data bits, the Windows 2000 operating system ships with program processors that will process various kinds of programming languages. To see this, open Notepad. Go ahead—don't just read this, but really open Notepad. Then type the following sentence:

```
Msgbox "Hello, World!"
```

Save the file as `hello.vbs`. Then double-click the file. You should get a message box that says "Hello, World!" This box is produced by the VBScript processor, which recognizes VBScript code in a file with a `.vbs` extension. That's built into the operating system. Cool, eh?

Now back to XML. As I was saying, each XML document has at least one processing instruction at the beginning. For instance, you must tell the XML processor which version of XML you're working with, so your instruction would look like this:

```
<?xml version="1.0"?>
```

If you want to place a comment in the file to help other developers understand what you're trying to do with your code, the comment line is entered as follows (note that comments can be placed anywhere in the file):

```
<! Comment Text !>
```

If you want to create a placeholder for data that will be entered later, you create an empty element. These elements can be expressed in one of two ways:

```
<salary></salary>
```

or

```
<salary/>
```

Attributes that further describe the data are enclosed in quotation marks. For instance, if you wanted to further describe `<salary>` by specifying the currency, you would enter the following code:

```
<salary currency="US$">50000</salary>
```

Each XML document must be *well formed*. This means that it must have the following:

- A single, unique *root element*: There can be only one root element in each XML document. All other elements must be defined within the root element.
- Matching *start* and *end* tags (also called *open* and *close* tags): You can't have a start tag <name> without a corresponding end tag </name>.
- Consistent capitalization: XML is case-sensitive. Hence, the open tag <name> cannot be closed with the tag </Name>. The tags are both case-preserving and case-sensitive, and the cases must match.
- Correctly nested elements: Each element must open and close before another element is introduced. For instance, the following syntax is illegal:

```
<A>
    <B>
    <C>
    </B>
    </C>
</A>
```

The correct way to nest B and C inside A is to code the following:

```
<A>
    <B>
    </B>
    <C>
    </C>
</A>
```

Repeating data must be represented in elements, not attributes, and attributes must be enclosed within either single or double quotation marks.

To learn more about XML and how to create and read XML documents, please pick up a copy of *XML: The Microsoft Way* by Peter G. Aitken, *The XML Companion, Third Edition* by Neil Bradley, or *Essential XML Quick Reference: A Programmer's Reference to XML, XPath, XSLT, XML Schema, SOAP, and More* by Aaron Skonnard and Martin Gudgin.

Index

<u>Also from Addison-Wesley</u>

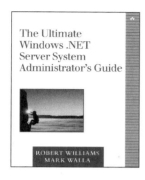

The Ultimate Windows .NET Server System Administrator's Guide
By Robert Williams and Mark Walla

0-201-79106-4
Paperback
960 pages
©2003

Experienced system administrator's comprehensive, authoritative guide to both the new Windows .NET Server and Windows 2000.

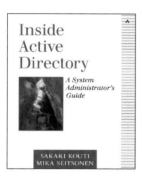

Inside Active Directory
A System Administrator's Guide
By Sakari Kouti and Mika Seitsonen

0-201-61621-1
Paperback
960 pages
©2002

Detailed, thorough, and based on practical experience, this guide is indispensable to anyone working with Active Directory.

Managing Enterprise Active Directory Services
By Robbie Allen and Richard Puckett

0-672-32125-4
Paperback
600 pages
©2002

Expert advice on how to manage and monitor Active Directory in a large-scale environment. The authors led Cisco's AD deployment and management initiative.

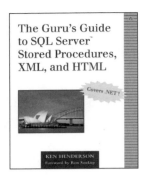

The Guru's Guide to SQL Server™ Stored Procedures, XML, and HTML

By Ken Henderson

0-201-70046-8
Paperback
800 pages with CD-ROM
©2002

Comprehensive, well-written, and full of practical information and guidance, this book is an indispensable reference for anyone working with SQL Server.

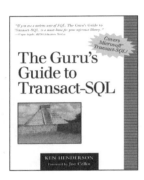

The Guru's Guide to Transact-SQL

By Ken Henderson

0-201-61576-2
Paperback
592 pages with CD-ROM
©2000

More than just a catalog of coding tricks and syntax subtleties, this book explores the philosophy of Transact-SQL programming and teaches you how to apply it to develop coding techniques and discover solutions to real-world programming problems.

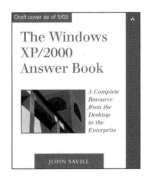

The Windows XP/2000 Answer Book

A Complete Resource from the Desktop to the Enterprise
By John Savill

0-321-11357-8
Paperback
820 pages
©2003

Using this book, administrators, developers, and users will be able to quickly and effectively find answers, solve problems, and get the best performance possible from Windows 2000 and XP.

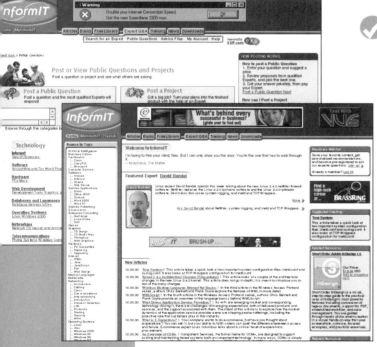

Register
Your Book
at www.awprofessional.com/register

You may be eligible to receive:
- Advance notice of forthcoming editions of the book
- Related book recommendations
- Chapter excerpts and supplements of forthcoming titles
- Information about special contests and promotions throughout the year
- Notices and reminders about author appearances, tradeshows, and online chats with special guests

Contact us

If you are interested in writing a book or reviewing manuscripts prior to publication, please write to us at:

Editorial Department
Addison-Wesley Professional
75 Arlington Street, Suite 300
Boston, MA 02116 USA
Email: AWPro@aw.com

Addison-Wesley

Visit us on the Web: http://www.awprofessional.com